CW01390264

Ethnomusicology and Modern Music History

Ethnomusicology and Modern Music History

Edited by

Stephen Blum
Philip V. Bohlman
Daniel M. Neuman

University of Illinois Press
Urbana and Chicago

Publication of this book was made possible in part by a subvention from the University of Illinois Research Board.

Illini Books edition, 1993
© 1991 by the Board of Trustees of the University of Illinois
Manufactured in the United States of America
P 5 4 3 2 1

This book is printed on acid-free paper.

Library of Congress Cataloging-in-Publication Data

Ethnomusicology and modern music history / edited by Stephen Blum, Philip V. Bohlman, Daniel M. Neuman.
p. cm.
Includes bibliographical references.
ISBN 0-252-06343-0 (alk. paper)
1. Ethnomusicology. I. Blum, Stephen. II. Bohlman, Philip Vilas. III. Neuman, Daniel M., 1944–
ML3799.E83 1990
780′.89—dc20 90-10741
CIP
MN

Digitally reprinted from the first paperback printing

To Bruno Nettl

wise teacher,

generous friend,

pioneer in the study of modern music history

Contents

Acknowledgments

Prologue: Ethnomusicologists and Modern Music History — *Stephen Blum* 1

PART ONE: Music and the Experience of History

1. When Music Makes History — *Anthony Seeger* 23
2. Ethnomusicology and the Meaning of Tradition — *David B. Coplan* 35
3. *Jùjú* History: Toward a Theory of Sociomusical Practice — *Christopher A. Waterman* 49
4. Historical Worldviews of Early Ethnomusicologists: An East-West Encounter in Cairo, 1932 — *Ali Jihad Racy* 68

PART TWO: Authority and Interpretation

5. The Interpretation of History and the Foundations of Authority in the Visnupur *Gharānā* of Bengal — *Charles Capwell* 95
6. Sufi Music and the Historicity of Oral Tradition — *Regula Burckhardt Qureshi* 103
7. The History of a Peruvian Panpipe Style and the Politics of Interpretation — *Thomas Turino* 121
8. Music Institutions and National Consciousness among Polish and Ukrainian Peasants — *William Noll* 139

PART THREE: Brokers and Mediators

9. Ravi Shankar as Mediator between a Traditional Music and Modernity — *Stephen M. Slawek* 161

10. An Eighteenth-Century Critic of Taste and Good Taste — *Amnon Shiloah* 181

11. Arzelie Langley and a Lost Pantribal Tradition — *Victoria Lindsay Levine* 190

12. Music and the History of Tribe-Caste Interaction in Choṭanāgpur — *Carol Babiracki* 207

PART FOUR: Musical Reproduction and Renewal

13. Indian, East Indian, and West Indian Music in Felicity, Trinidad — *Helen Myers* 231

14. Stability in Blackfoot Songs, 1909–1968 — *Robert Witmer* 242

15. Of *Yekkes* and Chamber Music in Israel: Ethnomusicological Meaning in Western Music History — *Philip V. Bohlman* 254

Epilogue: Paradigms and Stories — *Daniel M. Neuman* 268

List of References 278

Contributors 306

Index 309

Acknowledgments

The editors acknowledge their deep gratitude to the University of Illinois Research Board for a generous subvention toward the costs of publication.

The book was planned by all three editors, and the responsibilities for editing the papers and corresponding with the authors were shared by Stephen Blum and Philip Bohlman. Stephen Blum is grateful for the typing and word-processing help he received from three doctoral students at the CUNY Graduate School: Christian T. Asplund, Michael Laderman, and, especially, Ehrick V. Long. Philip Bohlman thanks Carolyn Schiller Johnson for her editorial assistance.

The editors wish to express special gratitude to Judith McCulloh for her support of this project to honor Bruno Nettl.

Prologue: Ethnomusicologists and Modern Music History

Stephen Blum

As a discipline involving close contact among scholars working in all parts of the world, ethnomusicology benefits from a rich inheritance: the knowledge that is continually reproduced by musicians and other participants in musical life. Reproduction of musical knowledge is one of the many human activities that foster and are sustained by various types of historical consciousness. Hence, even within small communities (and within ourselves), ethnomusicologists are continually faced with conflicting "attitudes toward history." The essays in this volume examine some of the "typical ways in which these attitudes are both subtly and grandly symbolized" (Burke 1961:Introduction) or *realized* through musical performance and discourse about music. We are concerned with musical interpretations of history and with historical interpretations of music and musical life.

Seeking to encourage and assist in the preservation and renewal of musical knowledge, many ethnomusicologists have feared that certain practices and even whole communities of musicians might not survive. The fears proved to have been well founded in too many cases (see, e.g., Chapman 1972, 1978 on Lola Kiepja, d. 1966; Slobin 1982, 1986 on Moshe Beregovski, d. 1962). Even more significantly, however, ethnomusicological research has shed new light on human creativity and resilience, on the breadth and depth of our capacities to adapt, and on the fundamental importance of musical skills in human adaptive responses. Music often serves to reconcile opposing attitudes and modes of life (including different attitudes toward time and history): "Through experiencing music, people can attain a perspective which allows validly opposite opinions to coexist without damage to either" (Ellis 1985:2).

Modern music history became a subject of scholarly inquiry as musicians and scholars in several parts of the world raised questions about the causes and consequences of differences between "newer" and "older" practices and styles. These studies ran up against a massive barrier: the inhibitions and certainties that prevented many researchers from hearing and attempting to understand the thoughts, desires, and actions of their "informants" (see Nettl 1984b:174). The study of modern music history only begins in earnest when scholars move to overcome such inhibitions by joining some of the conversations that take place with or without our participation. We take part in, report on, and interpret these conversations, recognizing that each report is an interpretation and that "listeners [and performers] define for themselves a historical stance a particular music may take" (Neuman 1976:2).

Arguments over names and their interpretations—treated in several of these essays—are one of the most common manifestations of cultural, class, and ethnic contact. The term "ethnomusicology" is itself misleading, to the extent that it implies the possibility of a musicology unaffected by differences of culture, class, and sex. It is not the presence or absence of such differences that distinguishes one musicology from another but the ways in which these differences are acknowledged or concealed.

The prospect that ethnomusicology may give way to a general musicology has increased, inasmuch as dialogue among musicians and musicologists in all parts of the world now provides frequent opportunities for comparison of terms and stories, theories and methods. The best setting for these conversations would be "a network of intercultural scholarship consisting of individuals from many societies who [would study] each other's music from many perspectives" (Nettl 1983:260). Current practice falls far short of this ideal. There is too little critical analysis of the myths attached to musical performance in the West and elsewhere (see, however, Clément 1979; Kingsbury 1988; Leisiö 1983; Leppert and McClary 1987; Robertson 1987; Treitler 1989:1–18). For the most part, ethnomusicologists are "members of affluent societies who study the music of the poor" (Nettl 1983:260).

Of necessity, students of modern music history have sought to name and understand powerful destructive forces. At the points of greatest danger to the student's own community or people, research is urgently needed but barely possible. For three decades, the Armenian musician Komitas (1869–1935) was deeply engaged in public performance, teaching, and composition, as well as in basic research on the music of Armenians, Kurds, and Turks (see Poladian 1972). During the massacres that accompanied the dissolution of the Ottoman Empire, his mind collapsed and his spirit was broken; the greater portion of the four thousand or so songs he had notated was lost. After the catastrophe, most aspects of Komitas's work on Armenian music were taken up by his followers, who recognized his central role in the creation of a modern Armenian musical culture. A "modern Armenia" would be impossible without a "modern Armenian music."

More than six decades after the end of the Ottoman Empire, Komitas's vision of a broadly conceived program of research on the music of Armenians and neighboring peoples remains a utopian project. One major obstacle comes from policies of the modern state of Turkey, which make it almost impossible to carry out field research on the music and culture of the approximately ten million Kurds who live in eastern Turkey. The case is not atypical; numerous governments prohibit or actively discourage studies of the cultures they prefer not to recognize, and institutions dominated by men tend to neglect the musical and cultural activities of women. The variable political and economic constraints within which scholars, like everyone else, pursue their daily activities and define their long-term projects have hindered more than they have fostered the study of modern music history.

A history of the ways in which scholars and musicians have resisted or succumbed to pressures channeled through various state institutions would offer valuable guidance to contemporary ethnomusicologists. It is crucial that the institutional basis of ethnomusicological research provide for unrestricted exchange of ideas (and for sharing of resources) among all interested parties. The real growth of ethnomusicology as a discipline remains dependent upon such progress as we have made and can make toward meeting this challenge. Less-beneficial types of growth are those in which the system of research "has detached itself from the object of study, the native peoples" (Maceda 1979:161), or those in which the increasing power of centralized institutions has reduced the options available to "peripheral" musicians and scholars (see Noll 1986:635–94 on Poland since 1945). Music has often been named by Africans and Asians as one of the "raw materials taken from our part of the world" (Āl-e Ahmad 1962:5–6) and processed by a system in which scholars adopt roles that resemble those of other manufacturers and distributors (Maceda 1979).

It is now widely acknowledged that scholars must not "push others into the position of objects in order to look upon themselves as subjects" (Miłosz 1968:80). We must judge institutions by the extent to which their policies enhance or diminish the freedom of all whose lives they affect. The unity of modern music history comes from the universality of claims to fundamental human rights, which can be realized only through continual dialogue and argument.

2

According to the conceptions that inhabitants of each region have formed of their own histories, modern music history extends over different periods of time in various parts of the world. The singular form of the term "modern music history" designates this very large set of regional and supraregional histories. Each of them has been affected by "the major forces driving the interaction of cultures since 1492—the forces propelling Europe into commercial expansion and industrial capitalism" (Wolf 1982:ix). As experienced in different regions, these forces have assumed many guises, and they are not the only, or even the principal, factors in every interpretation of a region's music history.

European views of the world as a whole have sustained various attempts at "world history," including the "general histories of music" first undertaken by European scholars in the mid-eighteenth century. Until quite recently, most European writers on music have treated "non-Europeans" as "people without history" (Wolf 1982), as representatives of early stages in "general history," or as subjects of local histories but not of modern world history. The comparative musicologists of the early twentieth century criticized the first of these attitudes (Hornbostel 1905:96 repr. 1975:269) but carried the second to unfortunate extremes. Part of the reasoning behind the third attitude is made explicit in a parenthetical question posed by Carl Dahlhaus:

> . . . the most cursory historical reflection reveals that the subject of history is ethnically as well as socially variable. And although in the past there was no world history including non-European cultures, with all of humanity as its subject, it can scarcely be denied that at present [a world history] is gradually taking on firmer outlines. (Whether contemporary humanity can become the subject of world history depends on whether humanity as subject of history is constituted immediately upon enduring the entanglements of world history, or only through conscious action with world-historical intent.) In place of "histories" (in the plural), the countless local and regional chains of events, "history" (in the singular)—which was formerly only a notion or a presumption—begins to assume a real shape. (1977:145)

The terms of the question ("enduring the entanglements" vs. "conscious action with world-historical intent") refer to "contemporary humanity" as the "subject" of world history. However, all "conscious action" is taken by specific parties, who often refuse to acknowledge the numerous ways in which other humans construct their histories before, during, and after whatever series of "entanglements."

Human groups make themselves subjects of histories as they find reasons and means for doing so. As Anthony Seeger shows in the first essay in this collection, the Suyá Indians of central Brazil construct and reproduce history in song. The acquisition and domestication of "foreign" songs and other desirable goods form the very substance of Suyá history, made available to the community as singers reproduce songs obtained from outside the community. Strategies that have enabled the Suyá to acquire songs through encounters with many peoples have also proven to be applicable in their relations with the Brazilian state. Seeger shows how structures of Suyá myth have been reproduced in the events of Suyá history during the migrations of the past two hundred years.

The difficult situations of Amazonian Indians, Kurds, Armenians, Tibetans, and many others—as they sing of "countless local and regional chains of events"—may spur ethnomusicologists to ask who will write the world history of which Dahlhaus speaks. One point is clear: attempts at world history that do not merely reproduce the prejudices of powerful elites will respect (rather than explain away) the voices that are raised wherever history is sung, danced, enacted, or narrated. We cannot expect these voices always to agree, and we must acknowledge, in Bruno Nettl's eloquent words, that "whether what has happened is good or not must be judged by the people to whom it has happened" (1983:350)—and not merely by self-appointed speakers for "the people" or by "majority opinion." Among the results of such judgments are the "countless local histories" that complement, oppose, and engage one another at every point imaginable. Song remains an indispensable medium for many local and supralocal histories, not least because some humans "must of necessity sing their difference" (C. Seeger 1939b:149). As Robertson observes, "the dissenting opinion is crucial to understanding the dynamics of control and access to authority among all peoples" (1987:243).

The uses of music in human experience and the comprehension of history warrant greater attention than they usually receive from historians and anthropologists. The importance of the topic is made clear in several recent studies of North and South American populations. The singing of highland shamans in the Putumayo Intendency of Colombia, invoking the magical power of lowland shamans, brings into play "mnemonic images of distinct historical modes of memory production and reproduction" (Taussig 1987:392). In the course of the girls' puberty ceremony of the Mescalero Apache of New Mexico, "the singers sing women into their adult roles, sing tribal history, and sing the people into their concerted existence" (Farrer 1980:126). Performance of the vocal genre *tayil* by Mapuche women of central Andean Argentina is "the 'material' or explicit manifestation of the patrilineally inherited and shared soul," and the itineraries conceptualized by performers are "outlines of or directions to Social Order as devised in cosmological time" (Robertson 1979:395–96, 412). Participants in the Ecuadorian ritual dance-drama of killing the *yumbo* move within "the space between two cultures which have long been spotlighted by folk consciousness as the polar extreme of primally 'savage' and primally 'civilized' identity: the jungle 'tribes,' on the one hand, and the highland's sacred and secular power center, on the other" (Salomon 1981:164). It is conceivable that, in a great many circumstances, music and dance have provided the most effective means for reproducing and, on occasion, for challenging conceptions of "savage" and "civilized" identities. By playing with musical resources, performers often manage to transcend some of the more confining aspects of stereotyped identities.

In all cultures, anthropological investigation of "genres in which mythic and historical modes of consciousness are brought together" (Hill 1988:10) remains woefully inadequate, if the musical dimensions of each genre are not examined. The second and third essays in this volume, by David Coplan and Christopher Waterman, are studies of two modern African genres, Sotho *lifela* and Yoruba *jùjú*. Performers of both genres draw upon the rich funds of "deep Sesotho" and "deep Yoruba" metaphors and meanings, in this manner reproducing mythic structures as they interpret historical events.

Coplan shows how migrant mineworkers of Lesotho become *likheleke* ("eloquent ones," "poetic masters") by creating extemporaneous songs (*lifela;* sing. *sefela*) that use traditional poetic and musical resources to articulate and express the realities of their experience. In acting as likheleke, the migrants can deny the common charges that they have become *likoata* ("rude, uncivilized ruffians") and have lost touch with Sotho *mekoa le maele* ("custom and wisdom"). The rapid development of the new genre *sefela* by Sotho migrant workers and their female companions over the past century affords a particularly compelling example of musical action that enables a group to identify itself by discovering links between past and present. Coplan draws the appropriate conclusions: traditions live as they are realized in performance. The so-called invention of tradition (Hobsbawm and Ranger 1983) is but one of the strategies followed in this century by social groups with conflicting interests. The term "traditional music" is a pleonasm; and, as Coplan argues, it is an error for scholars "to confuse historical continuity with 'timelessness.' " This point of view is wholly compatible with the recognition that performance may function as "a present-time exhibition of a never-ending creative source" (Ellis 1984:154; cf. Robertson 1976, 1979).

Waterman continues the attack on the misconception that "change inherently requires more explanation [and more work] than continuity." This point was beautifully articulated by Charles Seeger in the 1950s, with reference to the "unexpected" vitality of oral traditions in the United States: replacement of an older repertory by a newer one will not inevitably weaken the underlying musical idiom. In Waterman's view, musical structures are "learned configurations of habit, knowledge, and value predicating a range of performance strategies"; and performers are thus equipped to respond to numerous contingencies as structures are realized in performance.

Waterman is surely correct in maintaining that a general theory must enable us to investigate any and all ways that "historically situated human subjects . . . perceive, learn, interpret, evaluate, produce, and respond to music." His study of jùjú is framed by the argument that ethnomusicologists have erred in separating the "musical" from the "social" and in constructing questions about relations between "text" and "context," or "musical" and "social" processes. These and several other dichotomies—including "tradition" and "change," "systematic" and "historical" orientations, "theory" and "practice," "art" and "folklore"—belong to, in Waterman's words, the "learned configurations of habit, knowledge, and value" that are commonly reproduced in writings and other performances by ethnomusicologists. Waterman's essay may serve as a reminder that illegitimate great-grandchildren of Hegel's ghost continue to wander unchecked through too many of our pages. The lamentable result is a loss of contact with "historically situated human subjects," ourselves among them.

A severe criticism of most musical scholarship, voiced by Charles Seeger, has been articulated in various forms by many others: "The lack of adequate systematic study of our own musical life and of our own personal parts in it stares us in the face—a great gap between the creative musical life of our day and the creative linguistic approach to music we call musicology. We have no well-organized idea of what the relationship of a knowledge of history or of comparative musicology is to the person who lives in a musical life in our own culture" (C. Seeger 1939a:124). Yet the numerous dichotomies by means of which Seeger defined a program for musical research—notably his "systematic" and "historical," or "synchronic" and "diachronic," orientations—have served more to reproduce misconceptions than to dispel them.

One such misconception is illustrated by Seeger's repeated insistence that the historical orientation provides only "indirect experience" of "secondary" data, while the systematic allows "direct" access to "primary" data (1951:246; 1977:12). The theme of "direct access" is a common one in the mythology of the United States, elaborated in religion, politics, and marketing, as well as in music and literature. In practice, musical "traditions" are reproduced by performers who engage themselves and others in sequences of actions, experiencing relations among sounds, gestures, and values with direct as well as indirect links to earlier and contemporary actions of spirits, ancestors, kinfolk, enemies, friends, oppressors, providers, animals, birds, and other participants. All of us are like the Suyá, inasmuch as we produce and reproduce names, attributes, narratives, and designs for the future through musical performance.

Some of the most telling criticism of academic dichotomies between "text" and "context," between the "musical" and the "social," has come from African musicologists (e.g., Ekwueme 1975; Nketia 1981; Agawu 1991), who have correctly identified the bad faith with which too many Western ethnomusicologists have emphasized "social function" over "artistic value." It is superfluous as well as condescending for scholars to find "redeeming sociological significance" in musical practices they treat as undeveloped or as products of "restricted" rather than "elaborated" codes. Who performs in what manner, at what times, and with what restrictions and elaborations is a sociomusical question. The meanings of one performance and its timings are conveyed first and foremost through the sociomusical action of those who respond during and after the performance.

Waterman's approach to the study of musical practice begins with the question "How does the reproduction of a structure become its transformation?" (Sahlins 1981:8). When the same question is applied to scholarly practice in ethnomusicology, many of the answers describe the reproduction and transformation of terms and stories by scholars with diverging interests. Stories attached to the concept of "non-Western music" (fundamental to some conceptions of ethnomusicology) have been reworked in a variety of ways by Asians and Africans who rejected certain implications of these tales (particularly the implications that their music ought to remain "non-Western").

An illuminating instance of conversation and misunderstanding between Western and "non-Western" musical scholars is the 1932 Congress of Arab Music, held in Cairo. Two incompatible attitudes toward history, and the terms in which they were expressed by participants in this "East-West encounter," are carefully examined in Ali Jihad Racy's essay. Racy traces some of the consequences of the Western myths that made "Occidental" a synonym for "new," "Oriental" a synonym for "old." As reproduced by residents of "the Orient," these myths were reshaped into scenarios for planning and implementing policies of "modernization." With great sensitivity, Racy analyzes the different implications of the dualisms "new versus old" and "West versus East" in the arguments of European and of Near Eastern scholars at the congress. He helps us to understand the reasons underlying the sharply dualistic worldviews of the latter and the less-pronounced, more-concealed versions of these dualisms in the "pluralistic" outlooks of the European "Orientalists" and comparative musicologists. Racy's account brings out the continuing relevance of Mohammad Fathi's plea to the congress: "Before you pronounce the verdict that our music should be confined to its distinctive style, let us appeal to your own conscience." A lively exchange between Chinese and Western participants in the 1979 Durham (England) Oriental Music Festival (see Fang 1981) indicates that this set of issues remains very much alive.

The engagement of ethnomusicologists in the conflicts of their own times and places raises issues that are critical to any reading of their work. What Bartók described in 1931 as "the concept of ideal simplicity devoid of trashiness" (Suchoff 1976:8) informed his work as a composer and a student of peasant music in ways that were closely attuned to the desires of many Eastern and Central European artists and scholars. But, as Racy points out, most Egyptian participants in the Cairo Congress remained unmoved as Bartók urged them to recognize the greater "animation and originality" of Arab peasant music in comparison to "city-Arab music" (Suchoff 1976 [Bartók 1933]:38).

3

The ideas, attitudes, and actions of the powerful are seen, in most of these essays through analysis of responses made by the less powerful. One of the principal contributions of ethnomusicology to the study of modern history is the recognition that musical power remains a vital source of nourishment for many of the world's peoples. Without the empowerment gained through music, it is impossible to keep the past alive in the present, or to recognize and respond to the realities that are transforming the present into the future.

One of the principal subjects treated here is the variety of ways in which reproduction of names, stories, songs, dances, and instrumental music may enhance, support, or undermine the power and authority of particular groups. In many cases, the power of a name, a song, or a style is unquestioned, and the legitimacy of an individual's or a group's claims to the name, song, or style may or may not be questioned (and defended) by telling stories.

Among the Aranda, the Pitjantjatjara, and other Aboriginal peoples of central Australia, the most important acts of singing are also acts of naming (Ellis 1984:150–51). By reproducing acts of singing/naming from the cosmic time of the Dreaming, singers can "actuate the power of the Dreaming through the acoustic process of present-day naming of objects and persons from that time long ago" (ibid.:153). The Suyá practice of appropriating songs from "powerful strangers," as described by Anthony Seeger, is rather different, but the community's dependence on musical power from outside its immediate boundaries is an important similarity, as is the "unimpeachable authority" of the song texts. For the Suyá, "only beings and individuals outside the group have the power to effect transformations." The belief that knowledge is power and must originate outside rather than within the community may be more the norm than the exception among human societies.

Nowhere are stories and disputes concerning the transmission of musical knowledge more prominent than in North India; nowhere do musicians have a greater need for "the authority of a tradition as well as a tradition of authenticity" (Neuman 1978:187). In their respective essays, Charles Capwell and Stephen Slawek discuss controversies over the names and origins of particular *gharānās*, discipular successions of musicians. Regula Qureshi outlines a general approach to "the orally shared knowledge of hereditary specialist groups" by analyzing the relationship between several types of authority in the Sufi community of India and Pakistan.

Examining the origin myth of the Visnupur gharānā, Capwell suggests that stories of a particular type have served to confirm the legitimacy of several Bengali institutions, including the Visnupur gharānā, by recounting the transfer of specialized knowledge from *Aryavarta* (the "Aryan heartland") to Bengal. In Capwell's interpretation, the stories have two essential components: agents credited with transmitting cultural knowledge to Bengal must have come from "upcountry" to the north and west, and they must have acquired their knowledge from fully "authoritative" sources. In music, the latter requirement could be met only through an association with the Mughal courts of the fifteenth and sixteenth centuries; hence the origin myth of the Visnupur gharānā necessarily referred to this court tradition as its "ultimate authority."

Capwell briefly mentions a second professional lineage, sometimes called the "Allauddin gharānā" after Allauddin Khan (teacher of the prominent Bengali musicians Ali Akbar Khan and Ravi Shankar). Slawek's essay on Ravi Shankar provides a very different perspective on the same group of musicians under a different name, the Maihar gharānā. The existence of two names for one discipular succession illustrates Daniel Neuman's point that gharānās "exist at a number of different conceptual levels" (1978:188). The only gharānās that are "universally accepted as genuine" consist primarily of vocalists; most are named after cities (ibid.:189, 187). According to Neuman (personal communication), it is one thing for a group of instrumentalists to attach the name of their master (e.g., Allauddin Khan or Imdad Khan) to the new gharānā they wish to establish; it is a bolder move (likely to arouse more intense controversy) to name an instrumental gharānā after a city (e.g., Maihar). Slawek's long experience as a disciple of Ravi Shankar informs his account of the importance that Shankar and his associates attach to the "Maihar gharānā."

The needs of Sufi religious observance, as detailed by Qureshi, place strong constraints upon the hereditary musicians (known as *qawwāls*) whose services are indispensable to the Sufi institution of *samā*ᶜ ("listening" to sung poetry in order to attain spiritual ecstasy). Qureshi interprets Sufi oral traditions as "a kind of spiritual currency," validated by religious leaders according to their degree of spiritual authority. The spiritual lineages of sheikhs are thus the most important manifestation of Sufi historical consciousness, affecting the reproduction of every type of knowledge.

Qureshi describes the figure of Amir Khusrau (ca. 1253–1325) as a metaphor representing the Muslims who presumably introduced many characteristic features of Sufi musical practice. As performed at the Nizamuddin Auliya shrine in Delhi, ritual songs attributed to Amir Khusrau carry meanings that depend, in part, upon stories of his acts as a disciple of Nizamuddin Auliya. The members of three intermarrying lineages who hold the exclusive right to perform these songs at the shrine have had good reason to control the transmission of the repertory so as to preserve its aura of authenticity. Qureshi's analysis of the function of the repertory—legitimizing local shrine authority by comparing Nizamuddin Auliya and his disciple Amir Khusrau to their modern representatives—provides a specific justification for her adaptation of the familiar point that ritual repertories offer the greatest resistance to change. Each use of the repertory in the annual *basant* ritual allows for a mythic structure to be reproduced as a historical event.

Thomas Turino analyzes three very different interpretations of one Peruvian panpipe style, finding that the style "became an emblem of three different identities." His own interpretation of the political process through which disparate meanings were constructed for one style emphasizes the asymmetrical power relations among the groups involved and the social consensus that members of subordinate groups have internalized.

It is common for a group to give a name to that class of outsiders whose social and aesthetic norms it is determined to resist. Peruvian mestizos are called *q'ara* ("outsiders") by the Aymara of the southern highlands. The Muṇḍas of east central India are "human beings" (*hoṛo*), as opposed to the Indo-Aryan *dikus* ("outsiders"; "aliens"; "exploiters"). The reactions of the Muṇḍa to the culture as well as the political and economic power of *dikus* are treated in Carol Babiracki's essay. In their very different ways, the histories of interaction between Aymara and *q'ara,* Muṇḍa and *diku,* recall the Suyá history of appropriating something from the music of "powerful strangers." In all three cases, music is essential to communal life.

Turino describes the fundamental sociomusical value of the Peruvian Aymara as collective action in which each member of a social unit can play any role. What he terms "Aymara sociomusical priorities" proved to be incompatible with mestizo claims that "sound quality" might be improved by restricting participation to those who could demonstrate "competence" when challenged to do so. Turino shows how accounts of conflict between "sound quality" and equality among group members resulted from mestizo attempts to alter Aymara practice. A broader lesson for contemporary musical scholarship is implicit in his analysis: the terms of scholarship must not be exclusively those of the parties (here, the mestizos) who have posited conflicts between the "artistic" and the "functional"—even though many such conflicts have arisen in the modern history of various peoples. Turino does not underestimate the power of urban-Western aesthetics in circumstances of acute political conflict. He observes that certain values of mestizo musical culture—harmonies in parallel thirds, timbres that are soft and smooth rather than loud and shrill—have been retained in recent interpretations of "indigenous panpipe style," so that the "indigenous style" might be more effectively used in political action at the national level.

The reinterpretation of rural musical practices is also the subject of William Noll's essay. Noll describes the establishment of new sources of authority in several national institutions, and he compares the effects of different urban-based institutions on Polish and Ukrainian villagers in one part of Galicia. The creation of musical symbols for Polish and Ukrainian national identities was not marked by vigorous resistance to urban social and aesthetic norms; rather, Noll describes the institutional basis of what Turino would call an internalized social consensus that originated among urban intellectuals and was transmitted to villagers. For most of the twentieth century, of course, the military power of the Soviet Union has restricted the autonomy of the Polish nation and has blocked the creation of an autonomous Ukrainian state; such circumstances usually strengthen the need for musical symbols of national identity.

4

Influential interpretations of the new in relation to the old are produced by individuals "who serve as 'brokers' between community-oriented and nation-oriented groups" (Wolf 1956:1075), or between the claims of local and supralocal interests and values. Turino's essay relates the successes and failures of one such broker, Natalio Calderón of Conima District, Huancanè Province, Puno Department, Peru. Calderón's effort to impose a mestizo standard of "excellence" upon a communal panpipe ensemble was ultimately overcome by the community's rejection of mestizo leadership and mestizo rehearsal techniques. Divorced from his unacceptable model of ensemble organization, Calderón's innovations in harmony and voicing proved far more lasting. An aural image of "Conimeño tradition" had been created and placed in circulation, to be adopted or modified by many participants in the cultural and political struggles of the 1980s.

Noll, Capwell, and Racy describe musicologists who acted as brokers between various local, national, and international interests. Noll summarizes the proposals made by the great Ukrainian ethnomusicologist Filaret Kolessa (1871–1947) at the 1909 Congress of Tovarystvo Prosvita ("The Society for Enlightenment") in L'viv. Kolessa advocated a wide-ranging program of collection, transcription, arrangement, and publication through which village choirs might learn songs from many regions of the Ukraine—arranged in a "national," that is to say urban, style. The program called for brokerage on several levels: musically literate directors of village choirs would promote urban musical values as they rehearsed their choirs, and they would transcribe regional melodies; experts in L'viv would arrange some of these melodies, collect more, and provide training for prospective choir directors and collectors. Noll mentions an important respect in which Kolessa served as an advocate for regional music at the Prosvita congress: he argued that the new national practice should supplement, but not replace, existing village practices. Other congress participants found some regional practices to be incompatible with national values.

Capwell notes that members of the Visnupur gharānā were well equipped to act as brokers in the modernization of Bengali culture, given the importance they assigned to scholarship and general education. The activities of Ksetromohan Goswami in the 1850s and 1860s—devising a system of musical notation, helping to organize a music conference, and publishing a fundamental treatise on music—are representative of the types of work undertaken in many parts of the world during the first half of the twentieth century. Racy stresses the key role played by Maḥmūd Aḥmad al-Ḥifnī (1896–1973) in organizing the 1932 Congress of Arab Music, shortly after he completed a doctoral dissertation in musicology at the University of Berlin; al-Ḥifnī also edited the two works in which the decisions of the congress were published—the book of proceedings and the journal *al-Mūsīqá.*

Specific actions of many other brokers and mediators are discussed in several of these essays. Waterman, for example, lists the steps taken after World War II by Akanbi Ege, Ayinde Bakare, and other bandleaders to make *jùjú* music at once "more Yoruba" and "more modern," transforming the relation of jùjú to ethnic and class identities. The task of the bandleaders as cultural brokers—"to enact and exploit emergent patterns of modern Yoruba identity"—can be compared with that of the urban activists who promoted "national music" in Polish and Ukrainian villages early in this century. In each case, the identity presented as Yoruba, Polish, or Ukrainian was shaped far more by the interests of a broad-based elite than by those of the urban working class or the peasantry.

Four essays examine mediators of very different types. Stephen Slawek assesses the achievements of one musician who has excelled as both a traditional performer of Hindustani music and an innovative artist with an international career. Amnon Shiloah looks at one of the earliest European efforts to arrive at a sympathetic understanding of Turkish music. Victoria Lindsay Levine reconstructs the history of a pantribal musical practice to which many brokers and mediators contributed. Carol Babiracki outlines several stages in the long history of interaction between the Muṇḍas and other tribes and castes in Choṭanāgpur, where members of marginalized groups have often served as cultural brokers.

Slawek views Ravi Shankar as an exemplary mediator between the demands of very different milieus and ways of life. He quotes Shankar's remark that "when the gurus are living this jet set life, it is hard to preserve the old ways." Shankar's solution to the problem is illustrated by his belief that the inner self may remain intact as a musician explores multiple facets of his or her creativity.

The ideology that is implicit in stories about gharānās attributes the formation of a musician's inner self to a rigorous process of instruction. Recent efforts to present Shankar's teacher, Allauddin Khan, as the founder of a gharānā serve several purposes, one of which is to present Allauddin Khan as a model for his eclectic, innovative, and versatile disciples. The history of a gharānā can be constructed so as to emphasize both profound knowledge of the old ways and openness to experimentation. In presenting themselves as members of the Maihar gharānā, disciples of Allauddin Khan interpret their history along these lines. Slawek describes several of Shankar's strategies for responding to his numerous critics, particularly to those who complain of the "damage he has done to our classical music." Appealing to the Maihar gharānā as a source of legitimacy and authenticity is an important part of his response, as are performances that demonstrate his mastery of archaic forms and techniques.

Slawek suggests that Shankar's childhood experiences strengthened both his desire and his capacity to convince Western audiences of the value of North Indian classical music. According to Slawek, Shankar has chosen to appear on Western concert stages, as soloist in his own concertos for sitar and orchestra, in order to dramatize the equality of the Hindustani classical tradition with that of the West.

We move from the late twentieth to the mid-eighteenth century as Amnon Shiloah summarizes the arguments of Charles Fonton that Turkish classical music is worthy of respect. Reading Fonton's little-known treatise, Shiloah hears the author attempting to convince his contemporaries that musical "taste" is not utterly lacking among the "barbarous" nations. Fonton's insistence that taste "is as particular to each [nation] as it is general to all" states a theme that was taken up by many other Europeans in the next two centuries. As happened at the Cairo congress and the Durham festival, any restatement of the theme may rekindle the long-standing disputes that accompany it.

Examining the fragmentary evidence of pantribal musical practices in Louisiana, Victoria Lindsay Levine finds signs of optimism on the part of the Choctaw, Coushatta, and Alabama, and of other tribal specialists who believed that intertribal gatherings might enable a reinterpreted "Indian culture" to survive. This optimism may have motivated the many brokers who succeeded in creating a pantribal style from elements of distinct tribal cultures (perhaps the activists who created "national musics" to link Polish and Ukrainian villagers with cities were likewise optimistic). Levine notes that a number of intertribal communities have retained their languages and crafts but not the intertribal gatherings or the songs associated with these. She raises the possibility that local white residents may have been hostile to the gatherings.

In her study of tribe-caste interaction in Choṭanāgpur, Carol Babiracki identifies some of the cultural brokers who have acted as intermediaries between communities that would otherwise have kept themselves apart: the mendicants whose devotional songs have found greater acceptance among Muṇḍas than has their religious message; the caste musicians who have served tribal as well as caste patrons; the rajas who have imported musicians with knowledge of North Indian classical music. The significance attached to music and dance by the

Muṇḍas has made the *akhaṛa* dancing ground one of the principal arenas where Muṇḍāri identities are negotiated. Babiracki shows that the communal dance event has retained its central importance in Muṇḍāri life, despite the breakdown of the Muṇḍāri system of communal land tenure in the nineteenth century.

The songs that Muṇḍas have borrowed from others are confined to one seasonal repertory—that of the *karam* village festival, a distinctively Muṇḍāri transformation of a Hindu household festival. For Muṇḍas, as for the Suyá, singing the songs of others contributes to the social reproduction of the community. The ordering of songs in Suyá ceremonies may combine items that were acquired at any point in Suyá history; what remains constant are the social identity of the performers and the locations of performance. The karam repertory of the Muṇḍas, however, is a relatively recent acquisition. By performing in their own version of the regional musical dialect at the fairs and festivals of the postmonsoon season, Muṇḍas can demonstrate to themselves and their neighbors that they have mastered a new repertory without for a moment abandoning the central Muṇḍāri values of communal performance in the dancing ground.

5

The individuals whose actions are discussed in these essays have adopted various roles, not the least of which is the role of cultural broker—but also those of innovator (Shankar), witness (Fonton), and healer (Langley). Like Natalio Calderón, Ayinde Bakare, Ravi Shankar, and Arzelie Langley, ethnomusicologists and our precursors have also faced conflicting demands, articulated by members of various communities and by representatives of regional, national, and international (or transnational) institutions. In countless situations, the interests of scholars have overlapped but also clashed with those of performers who were obliged to evaluate the possibilities for retaining, renewing, or altering specific practices.

The final three essays take different approaches to the study of musical reproduction. With Coplan, Waterman, and many others, Helen Myers insists that musical traditions are often reinterpreted and renewed by performers who recognize what they are doing and make intelligent choices. Drawing upon a long series of conversations with the villagers of Felicity, Trinidad, Myers finds that two classes of songs—the "local-composed" and those "from away"—allow for conscious and deliberate modifications of traditional styles. "Indian music" thrives in Felicity as a rich assortment of styles and repertories. Music that is new and unfamiliar can be quickly incorporated into village life when it appeals to (or extends) some of the multiple meanings of "Indian culture." The residents of Felicity have resisted Afro-Caribbean musical values, and there seems to have been rather little exchange between East Indian and other populations in Trinidad. The agents of musical change in Felicity have acted more as importers of new practices from the homeland than as brokers between the different West Indian communities.

An old (1909) and a new (1968) recording of what sounds like one song provided the stimulus for Robert Witmer's speculation on possible reasons for the close similarity of the two performances. Witmer questioned the recordings and his transcriptions as sharply as Myers questioned the residents of Felicity. His essay concludes with a list of further questions, to be asked of other Blackfoot recordings.

Philip Bohlman studies the *Hauskonzerte* of Central European Israelis in the Reḥavia neighborhood of Jerusalem as "ritual" observances that obtain some of their meanings from reference to the group's history. He observes that the repertory of chamber music performed at these concerts is a product of the economic and political liberalism from which Central European Jewish communities benefited in the period between the late eighteenth and late nineteenth centuries.

Bohlman invites us to compare the *Hauskonzerte* of the German-speaking Israelis with the ceremonies of other peoples—such as the rites of passage that initiate Suyá men and women to adulthood, and the Sufi ritual of *samāʿ*. Through the social ritual of Hauskonzerte, residents of Reḥavia reproduce a situation in which the values of their community have long been shared with others. They are not "incorporating the music of powerful strangers" but cultivating ties of friendship: by joining performers and listeners in what Goethe termed a "conversation among intelligent people," chamber music is above all a music of friends. In suggesting that a group is in large part "the product of its musical activities," Bohlman recapitulates one of the main themes of Anthony Seeger's essay.

6

The diversity of modern music history makes it all but impossible for scholars to agree on any proposed division of musicological labor. We cannot restrict ethnomusicology, in principle, to studies of non-Western societies, conducted by Western scholars, for use within the West. Attempts to limit the scope of ethnomusicology (whether to "orally transmitted," "traditional," "non-Western," or "ethnic" music) have run up against the realities of musical practices that move across these categories.

Few topics are as central to the history of ethnomusicology as are the strategies by which scholars and musicians have dealt with differences and conflicts between "old" and "new." Several fields of study—including comparative musicology, musical folklore, and musical ethnography—were defined, in large part, as scholars articulated conceptions of history with reference to ideal types. Thus, *ethnologie musicale*—as cultivated by André Schaeffner and several of his colleagues and pupils—has been concerned with orally transmitted musics; according to Schaeffner and many others, these retain capacities no longer possessed by musics that depend to some extent upon written transmission (Schaeffner 1936:342). Similarly, an influential view of musical folklore made the folklorist "a close observer of an as yet homogeneous, but unfortunately rapidly disappearing social structure, expressing itself in music" (Bartók 1943, repr. Suchoff 1976:34). Here, ignorance of writing was but one aspect of the presumably unified way of life that enabled all members of a community to share common property, including musical folklore (Brăiloiu 1949:329–30). The continuing power of oral transmission in contemporary societies was more apparent to Schaeffner (1936) than to many of his contemporaries.

Development of the concept of "musical culture" by Russian and Soviet musical ethnographers involved close attention to the social history of various crafts and professions (Kvitka 1924; see also Slobin 1982:6, 543–47) as well as schematic overviews of the "evolution" of professional musical arts (e.g., Belyayev 1962, 1965). Identification of types or degrees of systematization and "rationalization" (e.g., Weber 1921; Lachmann 1935) resulted from the interest of comparative musicologists and sociologists of music in reconstructing the history of tone-systems (see Blum 1985). Working with these and other fundamental concepts of ethnomusicology, musical scholars have addressed (but also evaded) some of the leading questions of sociology, including: "What accounted for the special dynamism of Europe compared to other civilizations, of some parts of Europe compared to others?" and "How would changes proceed in the rest of the world under the impact of European expansion?" (Skocpol 1984:1).

Ethnomusicological work is necessarily bound up with reflection on these and other sociological questions. Ivo Supičić maintains that ethnomusicologists and music historians "study concrete musical facts in depth on factual ground, taking them in their singularity" and that "sociological typification . . . is the task of the sociology of music" (1987:35). Yet many ethnomusicologists and music historians have found that recognition and interpretation of "concrete musical facts" are dependent upon theoretical and methodological inquiry, which may well include sociological typification. Accounts of typical learning processes in oral traditions, for example, have been formulated by scholars concerned with consequences of the increasing use of musical notation in Java (Becker 1980:11–25) and Iran (During 1984:29–36, 124–31). As Becker notes, we can only hope that musicians will free themselves from the tyranny of the notion that oral transmission is not "modern" (1980:25, 104).

Such successes as ethnomusicologists have achieved in studying modern music history have been won through willingness to question the terms in which problems are defined. Descriptions of ideal types have been recast as lists of diagnostic questions (e.g., Powers 1979:11–12 on "traditional art music"), and other sets of questions have been designed to allow "broad meaningful comparisons . . . to be based on accurately detailed, careful local ethnographic models" (Feld 1984:385–88; see also Robertson 1987:242–43). Models for describing the production and distribution of popular music have been developed by Wallis and Malm (1984) after an intensive study of the music industry in several small countries. In many circumstances, the greatest stimulus to reworking our questions has come from conversations with interested parties.

However powerful they may appear from particular vantage points, the long-term effects of European expansion are not the only subject to be considered in the formulation of ethnomusicological theory. Barbara Hampton has warned of the temptation "to control a complex situation statistically by narrowing the variables to a manipulable and deceptively simple number," resulting in excessive concern with the Western impact on African music and insufficient attention to the interaction of numerous musical and other institutions within Africa (1983:212–13). Margaret Kartomi has analyzed the underlying assumptions of the terminology used in discussions of musical culture contact, concluding that "musicologists have hardly given themselves the opportunity to begin to understand the forces at work in culture contact situations" (1981:228–29). One of her major points bears upon the "strong likelihood that all musics are syntheses of more than one culture (and, in some cases, class) influence" (1981:230). From Kartomi's perspective, an intercultural or interclass musical "synthesis" is at once a partial resolution of earlier tensions and a new set of possibilities for further conflict and change. In contemporary African popular music, for example, the creators of new genres have drawn on many earlier cultural syntheses carried out in the Americas and in Europe, as well as in Africa.

Our experiences and analysis of recent situations of contact may eventually extend our ability to recognize signs of musical exchange in the more distant past. This prospect has been emphasized by Bruno

Nettl (1983:172–86), developing his view that "the value and contribution of ethnomusicology seem to me to be essentially and very broadly historical" (1983:11). With Kartomi, he considers musical change to be more the norm than the exception (1983:178). He has consistently encouraged studies of modern music history in all parts of the world, pointing out the necessity of such studies if ethnomusicology is to realize its potential contribution to a general musicology.

The authors of the following essays deeply appreciate Bruno Nettl's scholarship and friendly counsel. We hope that this volume, dedicated to him on the occasion of his sixtieth birthday, reflects some of the lessons he has taught us.

PART ONE

Music and the Experience of History

When Music Makes History

1

Anthony Seeger

The literature on Native American song indicates that many groups in both North and South America sing songs of other communities, often maintaining the texts in a language they themselves do not understand. Bruno Nettl (1954) speaks of this in passing and mentions the Ghost Dance, the Native American Church, and the propensity of the Plains Indians to sing one another's songs. In his discussion of the origin of Flathead songs, Alan Merriam (1967) reports that songs have been learned from supernatural beings, by individual dreamers, and by the introduction of new songs from other groups. Beverley Cavanagh, in a paper on Algonkian hymnody (1985), shows that the Algonkians went out of their way to obtain hymnals from missionaries long before the missionaries arrived in their communities. In Brazil, too, many groups have learned songs from strangers, and Brazilian Indian mythology is filled with accounts of the introduction of songs from outside sources. Many native Brazilian communities are monolingual but polymusical: they know songs, and often entire ceremonies, from three, five, or even more different groups. This essay investigates why one Native American group learned so many songs from other societies. After delving into the ethnographic detail of a single case, I propose an answer that may suggest explanations for similar polymusicality in other regions.

Although this essay dwells on the Suyá Indians of Brazil, its subject matter is really history itself. History is the subjective understanding of the past from the perspective of the present. Events do not simply happen; they are interpreted and created. I argue that members of some social groups create their past(s), their present(s), and their vision(s) of the future partly through musical performances. Musical structures, values, and performance practices are themselves informed by concepts of history, and their realization in the present is a demonstration of certain attitudes about the past and the future. The performing arts, including narratives and music, may occupy a special place in small-scale, nonliterate societies where history can only be created and interpreted through repeated performances. In each repetition lies the possibility for reaffirmation, reinterpretation, repression, rebellion, or some combination of these. From the Suyá, we learn that music can make history in more ways than one.

Historical Contacts of the Suyá of Central Brazil

The Suyá are a good example to discuss because they sing songs from at least ten different societies with whom they have interacted in the past two hundred years. These contacts occurred over a long period during which the Suyá migrated hundreds of miles (see Figure 1). The Gê-speaking Suyá say they used to live far to the east of their present village, in the State of Maranhão—a region now occupied by Timbira groups who speak closely related languages. The Suyá exodus took the form of a large arc—they crossed the Tocantins and Xingu rivers and nearly reached the Tapajos; then a part of the group returned to the headwaters of the Xingu, and the rest continued south to the Arinos River. The Xingu group continued to the mouth of the Suiamissu River where they were encountered in 1884 by the German scientist-explorer Karl von den Steinen. They had fought enemies and learned songs the whole way. In the period from 1970 to 1982, when I left the field, the 120 survivors of the migrations sang songs they had learned from the "White Indians" (whom the Brazilians call the Munduruku), the Manitsauá and the Iarumá (now both extinct), the Kamayurá, Waurá, Trumai, Juruna, Kayabi, and Txukahamae, as well as from Brazilians and Americans they had met since their peaceful settlement on a reservation in the Xingu National Park in 1959.

When the Brazilian "pacification" expedition, headed by the Villas Boas brothers, reached the Suyá village in 1959 to establish permanent, peaceful contact, each group sang songs for the other. Both parties described to me how the others had sung. During my field research in the 1970s, when non-Suyá men visited the village and spent the night, they were usually invited to recount news, tell stories, and sing, both in family houses and in the center of the village where the men gathered at night. In the 1980s, visitors began to bring cassette tapes recorded in their villages, which were often traded for Suyá recordings of their own ceremonies.

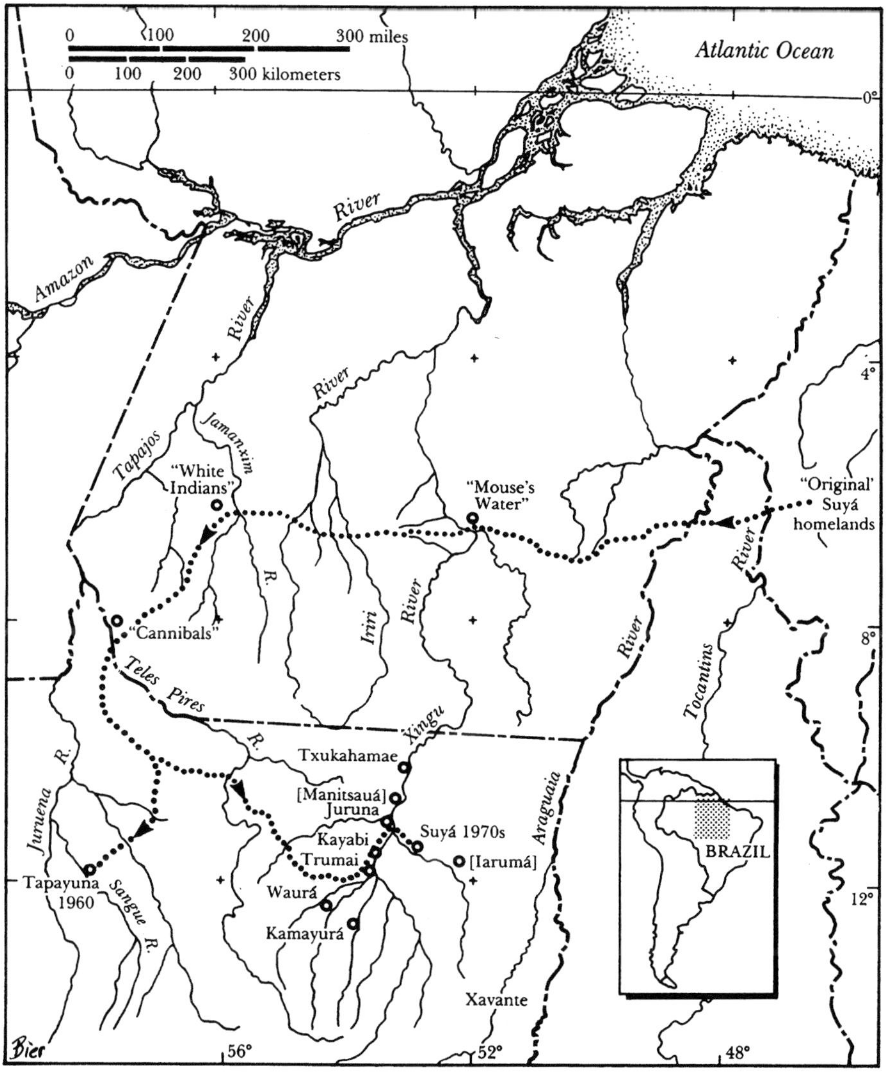

Figure 1. Map showing Suyá migration and approximate location of groups from whom they learned songs (after Malcher 1961). Extinct groups in square brackets.

The Specificity of Music

Although they are polymusical, most Suyá speak only one language. When Suyá meet individuals from other groups they usually each speak their own language and try to come to an understanding. Yet they often sing songs, in the original language, of groups whose languages they have not learned, sometimes with a vague idea as to their general content. In order to understand this, we need to distinguish between speech and song. For the Suyá, songs are different from other verbal genres—they are at one extreme of a continuum ranging from everyday speech to song (A. Seeger 1987:25–51). Song is characterized by (1) the priority of melody over text, (2) the higher redundancy of its parallel forms (repetition), (3) the more fixed length of its phrases, (4) the more fixed relations among pitches, and (5) the unimpeachable authority of what the Suyá maintain are entirely fixed texts. Here I am most concerned with the authority and origin of the texts (and their associated melodies).

Song texts deal with a limited number of topics and are performed almost exclusively in ritual-related activities. There are no protest songs or lullabies. Singing is one of the means through which time, space, and social processes are created and recreated. All societies constantly re-create themselves, but the importance of repeated performance for the perpetuation of social life is particularly great in the small-scale societies of Amazonia, which have neither writing nor full-time specialists of any kind.

Songs are distinct from other verbal forms in that they alone are said to have extrasocietal origins. Everyday speech, oratory, most recitative, and even invocations for curing have their origins with individual Suyá men and women; songs, however, come from outside the society. The Suyá say that they have learned new songs throughout their history. These have been introduced in three ways. Some songs were introduced in the distant past, when entire ceremonies were learned from enemies or from humans being transformed into animals. The second method, which continues today, is the introduction of songs by certain men and women ("people without spirits"), who learn them from bees, birds, fish, trees, and other nonhuman species that nevertheless all sing and perform ceremonies. Finally, for the past two hundred years, other native communities have provided a major source of new songs and ceremonies. The Suyá learned songs and ceremonies from captives, from visits to other villages, from peaceful visitors, and from records and tape recordings. The newly introduced songs are usually performed in the village plaza by men, women, or children, often as segments of larger rites of passage learned originally from animals, monsters, or mixed beings.

The three mechanisms for introducing songs share a common feature: all songs have their origins outside the community but are used as part of the social reproduction of the community, that is in the rites of passage that initiate men and women to adulthood. Because songs that come from the distant past are often combined with newly introduced songs and foreign songs into a single series of major calendrical rites of passage, Suyá musical tastes result in a kind of musical montage. This mixture (and occasional separation) effectively creates a continuity between the new, powerful outsiders and those who came before them; between the present, tense, intergroup relations and those that established society in the past; and between the role of the Suyá as victors in the past and their hopes for similar success in the present and future.

Regardless of their origins, all Suyá songs are sung in basically the same social space. Although they constantly introduce new songs, the social groups that perform the new songs are the same ones that performed the old ones. Suyá society is based on the fundamental and enduring distinctions of gender, age, and name-based ceremonial groups. While text and tune may change over the years, the location of the performances and identity of the performers have remained much the same and continue to reflect and produce the values of collective social and ceremonial life, as opposed to those of the kin-based economic units of everyday life. The structure of the long ceremonies facilitates the inclusion of new kinds of musical events while preserving a traditional, or established, structure. Further, there is a continuity in the emotions expressed in all musical forms. The Suyá say they perform songs in order to create (and express) a kind of "collective euphoria" (*kin*). Night after night, for months on end, year after year, Suyá sing and dance and eat and are "euphoric" and "beautiful." New ceremonies are inserted into longer ritual events on the calendar, and all music serves similar social and emotional ends.

Songs come from outside partly because only beings and individuals outside the group have the power to effect transformations. Living Suyá adopt the songs and take on some of the power of those outside while reinforcing their own stability by the groups that perform the new songs.

Why would the members of one community want to perform the songs of so many different groups? What is the significance of learning songs from outsiders? One could argue that the Suyá's interest in foreign songs is the natural result of a historical set of encounters between different societies. But why should wars and captives involve musical exchange? How many Vietnamese songs entered the American repertory during the Vietnam War? Is "Hinky-Dinky Parlez-Vous" really a French song from World War I?

The Suyá's enthusiasm for others' songs is cultural and is not the natural result of migration. Physical contact need not include musical interaction, and here even the concept of "history" requires careful investigation. Before the Suyá met the White Indians early in their migrations, they had learned songs from a man being transformed into a deer, from another man in the final stages of transformation into a wild pig, and from a woman who had a penis growing on her right thigh. Before that, they had learned songs from cannibals who lived in a huge underground cave, from the jaguar, and from other animals. Learning songs from nonhumans continues today. New songs are still introduced and taught to the community by specialists who learn them from animals, bees, and fish. Clearly we are not dealing with "objective" history, but with a history of learning from *outside the community* that includes the historical past but extends beyond the simple contact of identifiable historical groups to individuals and communities whose attributes are apparently more mythical than historical.

Songs and History

The clue to understanding the introduction of outsiders' songs by the Suyá lies in their own understanding of history. History is not a simple sequence of events but the creation of patterns of events that make sense not only of the past but also of the present and that implicitly make a statement about the future. This point has been made repeatedly, and elegantly, by historians and anthropologists, and its salience is demonstrated by the bitter arguments over history textbooks in U.S. school systems. (The groups involved in the latter are concerned about the presentation of American history, and its effects on the present and future of this country.)

In an extremely interesting book, Marshall Sahlins writes: "In speech is History made. Here signs are set in various and contingent relationships according to people's instrumental purposes—purposes of course that are socially constituted even as they may be individually variable. Signs thus take on functional and implicational values in a project of action, not merely the mutual determinations of a synchronic state" (1981:5). In other words, people construct their own history, and their construction of history is itself a social action that can be used to influence the future. Karl Marx recognized, and condemned, this process in the poetic opening passage of *The Eighteenth Brumaire of Louis Bonaparte:*

> Men make their own history, but they do not make it just as they please; they do not make it under circumstances chosen by themselves, but under circumstances directly encountered, given, and transmitted from the past. The tradition of all the dead generations weighs like a nightmare on the brain of the living. And just when they seem engaged in revolutionizing themselves and things, in creating something that has never yet existed, precisely in such periods of revolutionary crisis they anxiously conjure up the spirits of the past to their service (1963[1869]:15).

Paraphrasing Marx's famous aphorism about history repeating itself as farce (ibid.), Sahlins writes, "Hawaiian history often repeats itself, since only the second time is it an event. The first time it is myth" (1981:9). He elaborates further that "mythical incidents constitute archetypal situations. The experiences of celebrated mythical protagonists are reexperienced by the living in analogous circumstances. More, the living *become* mythical heroes" (ibid.:14).

This is all central to an understanding of Suyá musical borrowing. But first, we must analyze the patterns with which the Suyá construct their past.

According to Suyá accounts, they and the world always existed; they give no description of the creation of the physical world or of primal chaos. Instead, their myths describe a distant past when the Suyá had no fire, no knowledge of what to eat, no horticulture, no names, no lip discs, and no ceremonies. They lived in circular villages and ate rotten wood instead of garden crops. Because they had no fire, they ate meat warmed in the sun. Over time, cultural items were acquired in a series of relatively separate episodes, described in myths (see Suyá myths in Wilbert and Simoneau 1984). The Suyá represent their history as the gradual incorporation of items taken from monstrous outsiders and used for the benefit of the entire community. These myths follow a general pattern: (1) an individual Suyá (or group of young men) encounters a stranger (animal, human, or mixture), resulting in (2) a collective male expedition that (3) takes every example of the desired item, leaving nothing, and (4) distributes it to the entire community.

Myths recount how the Suyá obtained fire from the jaguar, corn and garden crops from the mouse, names from underground enemies, body ornaments from cannibals, and many songs and ceremonies from animals, enemies, or humans in the process of becoming animals. In almost every case the Suyá not only took the items but completely deprived the original owners of their use. They took every cinder of the jaguar's fire and every ear of the mouse's corn, wiped out the enemy Indians, killed the cannibals, and often killed the transforming human, so that humans (Suyá) were subsequently the sole possessors of the item. As Lévi-Strauss has demonstrated, for many South American societies cooking fire separates humans from animals (1969). Body ornaments, songs, and the ceremonies of which they are a part also separate humans from animals. Among the Suyá, the biological family is contrasted to a social identity, instilled in men and women through a series of rites of passage (this process is fully described in A. Seeger 1981).

Similar narratives of the origins of fire, horticulture, and other cultural items have been recorded among most of the Gê-speaking societies in Brazil (Wilbert and Simoneau 1978, 1984), and certain similarities have been demonstrated for much of South America (Lévi-Strauss 1969). Since many of the Gê-speaking groups did not interact with one another afterward, it is probable that the narratives predate division into separate communities and that the pattern of the stories has its origin in the distant past. The general structure of Suyá myths is therefore not the result of their recent historical experience.

The Suyá do not limit the pattern of obtaining items for the collective good to events that occurred in the distant, mythical past, before their migrations. Suyá descriptions of what we would consider historical encounters follow a pattern nearly identical to that of their myths. When they arrived in the Upper Xingu in the mid-nineteenth century, they encountered a number of Indian societies whose existence was also documented by subsequent explorers. The Suyá relations with the Waurá, specialists in the construction of large pots for manioc processing in the Upper Xingu trading system (Gregor 1977), followed the pattern of their myths of the origins of fire and maize. After some trading, the Suyá attended a Waurá ceremony and surprised the Waurá, killing some men. Instead of taking pots, they took the women who produced the pots. They did this on at least two separate occasions, and the surviving captives, now old women with grandchildren, were still making pots for the entire village in the 1970s. From the same women the Suyá also learned, and incorporated into their repertory, the Upper Xingu women's ceremony, *Yamuricumã,* which eventually replaced the earlier Suyá women's songs. Some other encounters also reproduced their myths: the Suyá captured most of the surviving Manitsauá and Iarumá and incorporated all of them into their population, learning from them items of both material and musical culture that survive to the present.

While Suyá historical encounters with Upper Xingu and other groups resulted in the incorporation of many new songs, rarely did they obtain *only* songs. In almost every case they incorporated women and material items, as well as songs, into their lives. Material culture is part of production; as women are essential for biological reproduction, so are songs part of social reproduction (the Suyá separate biological from social reproduction by distinguishing biological parents and kinship-based groups from name-givers and name-based groups). Suyá history shows the steady acquisition of both means of production and reproduction, first from animals and monsters, then from historical Indian groups, and now from non-Indians.

Even recent activities, such as raiding encroaching cattle ranches and hijacking a National Indian Foundation airplane, can be interpreted as reproducing the Suyá mythical pattern of the way collective good can be served by dramatic (sometimes sly) confrontation with powerful outsiders and by the appropriation of items for communal use. Although infused with political consciousness, the raids on ranches and the airplane hijacking repeated the pattern found in the myth of the origin of fire. The goods obtained (fire in the one case, and land concessions, in the other) were shared by the entire community. All the songs the Suyá have learned are also performed by or for the entire community in their circular village by members of the enduring social groups. I believe there is a strong continuity in Suyá reactions to strangers, from the mythical mouse, to the 1884 encounter with Karl von den Steinen (A. Seeger, ms.), to the tumultuous events of recent years. While the form changes, the social groups and cultural incorporation endure, and it is these that provide the continuity in both Suyá music and Suyá political action.

I do not wish to make the integration of different musical forms appear to be without strategy and conflict. One result of learning many songs from many different powerful strangers is that the Suyá have to choose what to sing at any given time. They do not sing other people's songs with equal intensity. They appear to sing with greater frequency and fullness the songs of groups from whom they have recently obtained women and material culture, as opposed to songs from groups with whom they have little intermarriage. Thus they sing more songs from the Upper Xingu and Juruna than from the Panara, the Kayabi, the Txukahamae, Brazilians, or Americans. In the past they appeared to sing more songs of the Manitsauá and the Iarumá than they do now, perhaps because the captives they incorporated from these groups are long since dead.

Learning songs is part of material production and social reproduction on a number of levels. It appeared to me that Suyá sang more frequently and more seriously songs from groups (1) with whom they have intermarried or stolen many captives, (2) from whom they have obtained a fairly large amount of material culture, and (3) from whom this occurred more recently.

Today, the decision of which ceremony to perform during any given season involves many factors. The Xingu National Park, in which the Suyá reside, is a complex social arena, and ceremonies are markers of an ethnic identification, as Stephen Schwartzman (1988) has described in considerable detail. Singing different songs, the Suyá have indicated their alliance with different Indian communities during the past twenty years (A. Seeger 1987:132–35). One of my students, who visited the area after my last visit, was informed that in 1984 the single Suyá community had fissioned into two groups. She was told that the motive for the village fission was a disagreement over the kinds of songs that the community members wanted to sing. Although there doubtless were other contributing socioeconomic factors, the conflict specifically revolved around whether the community would sing mostly women's songs learned from the Upper Xingu groups or mostly traditional Gê-style Suyá ceremonies. The musical preferences of each of the factions in the dispute were related to its alliances and intentions. Deemed unresolvable, the disagreement led a large part of what had been a single village to secede and form a separate community, at least for a while. Each community continued to attend the other's ceremonies, but each stressed different features of their multifaceted potential identities. That a disagreement over which music to perform could be cited as the motive for a major political upheaval is an indication of the importance the Suyá attribute to musical performances.

Summary and Conclusion

To summarize, the evidence suggests that the Suyá adopt songs from powerful strangers for four reasons:

1. They consider songs to be quite distinct from language. While the Suyá do not consistently try to learn other languages, they do learn songs in other languages. The power of song to mobilize a group lies partly in the fixity of its texts, its phrases, and its melodic form. The exact referential meaning of a song is not central to Suyá concerns. Song comes imbued with legitimacy from outside the group. It is an ideal collective expression, above the opinions of individuals or factions.

2. Knowledge is power in much of lowland South America. By taking and performing the songs of other groups, the Suyá incorporate some of the power and knowledge of those groups for the benefit of their own community.

3. Musical development in the course of Suyá ceremonies, as among

many other Brazilian Indian groups, consists of the steady addition of separate musical elements to form a kind of multilayered sound and conglomerate structure. This enables the Suyá to introduce new musical elements from other places with ease and makes innovation particularly attractive.

4. The strategy of incorporating the songs of outsiders parallels the Suyá conceptualization of their own history, which recounts the ways in which the Suyá processes of economic production, social reproduction, and musical performance all took on their present (perfected) form. Singing their songs creates both the past and the present, and shows the parallels between the two.

When the Suyá sing a song, they are making a statement about who they are, as well as establishing the otherness of the original performers and reaffirming their own sense of community. When they learn new songs today, whether it be from animals, from other Indians, or from a tape recording, they are reproducing an old pattern and are re-creating the patterns of their history in the present while proposing them as a future destiny. Every collective musical performance associated with a rite of passage is a re-creation of a historical pattern, and every performance makes history, just as every telling of a myth contributes to the formation of the present. By singing the songs of strangers, the Suyá incorporate the power and material resources of the outsider into the reproduction of their own society and simultaneously establish the otherness of the others and the changing, growing, selfness of themselves.

Every Suyá musical performance makes history, not in the sense that it is an outstanding event that will go into a chronological list of events (as the first performance of Stravinsky's *Rite of Spring* made history), but in the sense that it reproduces the pattern of history: the incorporation into the life of the collectivity of the otherness of the others, and the reproduction of human beings and society through the incorporation of new melodies and texts.

While comparison is beyond the scope of this essay, it is striking that Nettl singles out the Plains Indians as learners of songs. The social organization of many Plains Indian groups resembles that of the Gê-speakers. The fact that both seem to establish social groups through differentiation and complementary opposition may be related to the search for songs outside the community. Alan Merriam, in *Ethnomusicology of the Flathead Indians* (1967), describes a threefold division of song origins that resembles that of the Suyá. Songs are categorized as sacred songs of the past, individually introduced songs resulting from contact with spirits, and songs introduced from outside. He does not propose that all three may essentially be part of the same process. On the basis of the Suyá data, however, I suggest that the three may well be the result of a single process of bringing in songs from outside the society.

In the interest of stimulating discussion, I will hazard a few suggestions for further research. First, in considering the origin of songs in Native American communities, I suggest that we can expect groups to adopt songs from outsiders especially when all the other songs of that group come from outside the society in one form or another. Second, I suggest that there will be a greater adoption of songs from outside the group in cases where material and social interaction between groups is strong, since music is often part of social and cultural reproduction. Third, I suggest that the adoption of songs will occur more frequently where rituals may combine different forms in the course of their performance, linking new songs with old ones in a single performance practice.

The performance of songs from other groups should not necessarily be treated as a recent phenomenon or an aberration but rather as a fairly common occurrence even in relatively isolated small-scale societies. Music is part of a larger set of processes and concepts of which it is simply a single expression. When groups sing, they are doing more than creating sounds in the present; they are creating both the past and the present and projecting themselves into a future of their own construction, even in situations of domination and apparent powerlessness. In these cases music not only makes history but constructs the future, helping to unite the present with both past and future in an intelligible way.

NOTE

Some of these ideas were presented at the 1986 annual meeting of the Midwest Chapter of the Society for Ethnomusicology, in Urbana, Illinois. I am grateful to participants for their comments. This manuscript was completed before the appearance of an excellent collection of essays on history and myth in South America (Hill 1988).

Ethnomusicology and the Meaning of Tradition

2

David B. Coplan

On the surface, the discussion in ethnomusicology of the Western impact on the world's traditional musics seems troubled by an inherent self-contradiction. On the one hand, we proudly, and correctly, proclaim our unique dedication to the study of all forms of music making. On the other, we are by tradition dedicated to the appreciation and study of musical currents from other-than-Western wellsprings. Should we not protest the crushing of those traditions of artistic diversity that are our professional raison d'être by the juggernaut of Western popular culture, traditions that their inheritors are casting voluntarily beneath the wheels? Many of us, resigned to the restricted milieu of institutionally subsidized Western classical music, may see no irony in the artificial preservation of other traditional musics in universities, cultural centers, concert halls, folk festivals, and other extensions of the modern state. But all of us, surely, are to some degree concerned by the retreat of genuinely non-Western music and musicians into dwindling, ever more remote areas, and by traditional music's loss of currency and involvement in the actual daily life of so many of the world's peoples.

As the material and social conditions under which traditional musical genres or styles arose and crystallized change, so of course must this music and its meaning change for its creators. The twentieth century is not the first time that this has happened. We cannot doubt that some sensitive and aesthetically adventurous Greek or Roman rulers of remote provinces bewailed the smothering of local entertainments by imperial Hellenistic or Latin fashions. Cultural authorities among the colonized certainly protested, as the accounts of resistance by the Hebrew priesthood to theological Hellenization during the Alexandrian period attest. Nor must the impact of the dominated upon the dominant be ignored. Classical Roman culture was first challenged by Judaism, then overcome by Roman Christianity, whose musical liturgy is much in debt to its Hebraic predecessor. Turning back to the imperial culture at hand, the popular music of the Americas is in large part a creation of the descendants of enslaved Africans who used sub-Saharan musical principles to create a new, syncretic musical culture in the lands of Babylonian oppression and exile.

The realization that traditional music inevitably changes in response to encompassing social and cultural movements is hardly a comforting one, and some of us have not been deterred by Alan Merriam's dismissal of musical preservationists as self-appointed "White Knights," saving folk music from the carelessness of the folk (1963). My research in southern Africa, however, has given me substantial comfort indeed, albeit of a different kind from that taken by the intrepid collector who at last records a few songs played on an obscure mouth-bow somewhere in eastern Swaziland. Explaining what I mean requires a reexamination of the concept of musical tradition, a term it is now just short of impossible to use without quarantine between quotation marks.

Tradition is a core concept common to ethnology, folklore, and ethnomusicology, and its use has remained current and indispensable despite its inherent contradictions, doubtful empirical status, and ideological entanglements. The central contradiction revolves around the necessarily social and historical origins of tradition, in opposition to its status in both native and scholarly discourse as something immutable, a structure of historical culture fundamentally immune to history. Harold Scheub expressed this paradox most clearly in discussing the largely ahistorical nature of African folklore studies. Tradition, he proposes, is "the timeless in time," composed of "cultural precipitates" that obviate history while depending on history for their images (1984:4–19). Scheub's mistake, of course, is to confuse historical continuity with "timelessness," but he is correct in observing that oral traditions, including song, are essential to the symbolic construction of history and social experience. Empirically, the notion of immemorial tradition so popular with native informants and folklorists alike all too often evaporates under the scrutiny of historical research. Thus "national traditional dances" often turn out to have had conscious origins at a specific place and time. Further, performance traditions as reified forms of identity are rarely unitary, and their status is often a matter of who claims them, under which conditions, and for what purposes within the dynamics of internal and external relations of social power.

Thus one of the most sophisticated current approaches to tradition deals with its invention: the reification of cultural patterns as invariant group identifiers for political purposes. This process is not confined to any specific region of the world, but nowhere is it more pronounced than in black Africa, as Ranger (1983) has shown. In his polemical but salutary essay, Ranger argues that many "tribal" identities as well as ethnic traditions were in reality invented by colonial officials, who sought to codify African oral law and fix ethnic boundaries and territories in order to facilitate their administration. The result was often the creation of a new category in the minds of the colonized, the category of "tradition." As John Comaroff and Jean Comaroff observe of the Batswana: "Tswana 'tradition' (setswana) was to be fashioned during the course of the 19th century. If not wholly invented [Hobsbawm and Ranger 1983], it was at least to be objectified; to be made into a heritage with imagined reference to the past but with its signs oriented toward the present" (1987:194–95). In their sometimes sincere attempts to respect "age-old native law and custom," colonial codifications such as Basutoland's Laws of Lerotholi (1903) turned resilient, adaptable oral custom into brittle, invariant tradition. In response to "repugnancy clauses" in colonial law, which nullified customs that Europeans found distasteful, Africans themselves changed their accounts of custom, so that in the native courts "those whose traditions lost a case came back a year or two later with better traditions" (Wyatt McGaffey, quoted in Ranger 1983:251). This process has not been confined to the legal sphere, nor has it slowed with independence. Thomas Blakeley (personal communication, 1986) noted the discovery during ethnomusicological research in Zaïre that groups whose performance styles were judged insufficiently spectacular to merit attention or resources from Western-trained government officials often developed new "traditional" dance displays more in line with the aesthetic standards of the Tourist Bureau and the Ministry of Culture.

The difference between reified, hegemonic "tradition" and organic, accommodative "custom," according to Hobsbawm and Ranger (1983:8), depends upon the degree of consciousness with which they are elaborated. This distinction, however, breaks down in Ranger's brief attempt to identify something called "authentic culture," where he echoes the Kenyan writer Ngugi wa Thiong'O in referring to the exploited groups within post-colonial society, who "have sometimes been able to tap the continued vitality of the mingled continuity and innovation which resides within indigenous cultures as they have continued to develop underneath the rigidities of codified colonial custom" (Ranger 1983:262). The distinction between ideology and culture is not, after all, coextensive with dominant and subordinate classes in society, and Ranger's own discussion reveals that "exploited" groups also invent traditions. Some of the most fascinating and ambiguous examples come from South Africa, where African cultural traditions have been debased by the dismantling of African institutions, which were then reinvented by Europeans as part of the theoretical justification for apartheid. For Africans, the use of their cultural heritage as an instrument of their oppression has led to the emergence of forms of accommodation and resistance that throw the outlines of the problem of tradition into extreme relief.

In many respects the heart of apartheid is the homelands-migratory labor system, designed to provide white South Africa with cheap African labor while avoiding responsibility for the social welfare and human and political rights of Africans. For nearly a century, one of the justifications for imposing and maintaining this system has been the preservation of the timeless, changeless values of African traditional life in the so-called reserves or homelands, free from the corrupting influences of urban industrial society. How African tradition is to survive in communities where at any time over half the adult men under sixty are absent and their families live in poverty on overcrowded, unproductive lands is not a question the white government cares to address. Since the homelands are now nominally independent or autonomous, this, like physical survival, is an African problem. Anthropologists such as A. R. Radcliffe-Brown are partly to blame for this situation since, like colonial officials, they searched for the sources of stability in society and consequently invented and codified African traditions as models of hierarchical social equilibrium. By representing African polities as rigidly bounded, stationary sociocultural units, British social anthropology created an artificial universe of "tribes" that would serve as an ethnographic basis for apartheid (Ranger 1983:252). The sprawling African ghetto of Soweto, southwest of Johannesburg, for example, is not inhabited by a mass of undifferentiated black humanity, but is divided up into twenty-two townships along linguistic lines, with separate housing, schools, and other amenities for Zulu, Xhosa, Tswana, Northern Sotho, Southern Sotho, Swazi, Tsonga, Venda, and Shangaan speakers.

Having thus seen where the "timeless" amd "uncorrupted" concept of tradition leads us, we should not be surprised to learn that the early generation of African graduates of mission schools often rejected their heritage as a detour into heathen darkness; a tradition whose inferiority was confirmed by its retreat before the terrible swift swords (and field cannons) of Queen Victoria's Christian soldiers. In seeking to distance themselves from African tradition, African Christians expected to escape the severe disabilities suffered by their rural nonliterate brethren in colonial society. To their dismay, they discovered that once they were militarily and politically emasculated, pre-colonial African savages had somehow become ennobled in the minds of the whites, whose culture black Christians were making such strenuous efforts to acquire. By this logic, salaried chiefs sporting leopard skins were the true self-respecting African leaders, while the Christians and city dwellers—"mission boys" and "town boys"—with their starched collars and vested suits were the "cheeky kaffirs" ("uppity niggers") of South Africa. Worse still, white officials and industrial managers undermined urban black security, wages, and political unity by creating the migrant labor system, under which Africans were expected to be both industrial workers and permanent members of "traditional" rural communities. Having destroyed the economic viability of rural African peasant farming, the white authorities justified the denial of stable urban residence and the separation of African household heads from their families with claims of the need to preserve "autonomous" African social and cultural traditions.

Within this ideological context, African intellectuals were understandably ambivalent on the subject of tradition. This from an African contributor to the *Bantu World* newspaper (April 16, 1932) commenting on the staging of traditional dances by the Johannesburg Non-European Affairs Department: "There is no objection to war dances, provided they are staged by the enlightened Bantu. When they are staged by the uncivilized, it is a sign of retrogression, because finding his performance so patronized, he has no inducement to progress." By the 1970s, however, the Black Consciousness Movement was proclaiming that the alienation of urban Africans from the concept of cultural tradition must be consciously reversed. Cultural activists recognized the importance of a sense of tradition to a positive and autonomous definition of African identity and social being. More important, they came to understand the dynamism of tradition as both a social and a historical process, requiring active appropriation, perpetuation, and transformation by members of the community among whom it is shared. This recognition helped to inspire an explosion of musical drama in the black townships, a diverse and vital new medium of expression that draws heavily upon the historically rooted aesthetic principles and values of African performance traditions (Coplan 1986).

Among scholars, the analytical value of the concept of tradition is limited by uncertainty as to whether there are universal symbolic representations that can be regarded as coextensive with a culture or society conceived as an integrated whole. Statements in the classic ethnographic style beginning with such phrases as "The Basotho believe . . ." or "Among the Basotho, men's choral dance songs enjoy the highest prestige," have been undermined by the recognition that ethnography can make no claim as a comprehensive account. It is at best a dialogue and a discovery process among particular subjects and particular observers, and any statement can only apply to social actors with specific perspectives in given interactional contexts. As Marcus and Fischer (1986:95) have ruefully observed, today the ethnographic method must be adapted to "cultures in fragments increasingly held together by their resistance and accommodation to penetrating impersonal systems of political economy." Interpretive analysis can no longer rely upon "societal metaphors" with unified meanings, or even assume a coherent social system as its social referent. "Rather the social context of the cultural construction of meaning—the production of culture—becomes an integral part of interpretive analysis itself" (ibid.:185).

Tradition, despite such circumstances, does not cease to exist, but functions as the historically emergent framework of culturally grounded perception, in which "both the identity and meaning of a specific action or event as well as its possible interpretations, are dependent upon a symbolically constituted past whose horizons extend into the present" (E. P. Thompson, cited in Ulin 1984:150). Among the most important and continuous repositories of such symbolism are oral genres, including song forms. Tradition, conceived as the "established structures of creativity" (Joyner 1975:262), provides images, expressive principles, and aesthetic values by means of which performances are both fashioned and made sensible. In performance, tradition provides authority to representations of the present by a "seamless connection with the remote past" (Beisele 1986:165). Such authority is essentially moral, and tradition thus substantiates what Thomas Beidelman calls the "moral imagination: the art by which individuals struggle to transform their social baggage into gear that suits urgent situational needs in terms of meanings and moral judgments" (1986:203). In reproducing tradition in performance, oral genres represent both a "mnemonic code," elaborating the complex symbolism of a historical culture, and a critical reapplication of autonomous social values (Vail and White 1978:19).

Returning to South Africa, one finds urban intellectuals and artists looking to the performing arts to reverse "the loss of cultural memory" among black South Africans (Larlham 1985:86). But where to find African traditions, not as animated museum pieces, tourist displays, commoditized diversions, instruments of state policy, nor even as conscious reinventions for the creation of a new identity or political ideology, but as organic, living expressions of collective experience in aesthetic form? One such place, it turns out, is among the migrant workers, those often-derided transients and victims of "rural urbanization," neither acculturated nor traditional, forced into homelessness to save their homes. In Lesotho, an independent country entirely surrounded by South Africa, the earnings of migrants account for 70 percent of the Gross Domestic Product. Yet at home male migrant workers are often called *likoata,* "rude, uncivilized ruffians," who have exchanged Sotho propriety and custom for the class cussedness and hard-drinking camaraderie of the mines (see Coplan 1985:19ff).

A closer acquaintance with the migrants and their female companions exposes the falseness of this "uncultured" image. Some degree of toughness and irascibility is no doubt a useful quality for black workers in the South African mines, and no one could accuse miners home on leave of an inability to enjoy their respite, often with wine (beer), women, and of course, song. The songs turn out to be lengthy poetic extemporizations called *lifela tsa litsamaea-naha* ("songs of the inveterate travelers"), imagistic autobiographies in which migrants and their women represent their common experience through the eloquent display of cultural knowledge in performance (see Coplan 1987). Whether performed to the accompaniment of the accordion and drum in a *sopoto* ("spot"), *bara* ("bar"), or *shebeen* ("little shop" in Gaelic)—unlicensed taverns where female singers dominate—or in the intense, quiet, unaccompanied competitions between male *likheleke* ("eloquent ones," "poetic masters"), these songs make use of the full range of expressive resources available in Sotho verbal and aural art.

To locate *lifela* (sing. *sefela*) in Sesotho oral literary tradition, we must heed Landeg White's call to understand the association of expressive forms with the periods of history and structures of society that gave rise to them (White 1982:10). These "travelers' songs" emerged from the early experiences of migrants as they walked the hostile byways of the Orange Free State to the diamond mines of Kimberley in the late nineteenth century. Thus the popular lifela singer's formula, apostrophizing in biblical terms the moral atmosphere of the diamond rush:

. . . ke buoa ka Gemele;	I speak of Kimberley;
Ke buoa ka Sotoma. . . .	I speak of Sodom. . . .
	(Majara Majara)

The creation of a new genre seems to have been required, both to express the particular social experience of migrant laborers and to signify their partial alienation from pastoralist clientage to the aristocrats of the royal Bakoena clan. Predictably, however, sefela drew freely upon the established verbal genres, including chiefs' and commoners' praise poetry, initiates' songs and praises, war anthems, proverbs, and folk narratives. The incorporative fluidity of an emerging genre thus facilitated "intertextuality": the interpenetration of genres and texts such that one context of experience is represented in the symbols and literary codes associated with another (Sherzer 1977:143). The incorporation of prestigious genres was far more than a convenient or unreflective compositional strategy of extemporaneous performers groping for their next phrase. The essence of *bokheleke* ("eloquence") is to connect the present and the past, creating continuity between familiar and alien realms of experience (home and the mines) through the display of cultural knowledge. Such knowledge includes familiarity with *mekoa le maele,* Sotho "custom and wisdom," and with traditional performance genres; and the ability to embody them in poetic images drawn from "deep Sesotho." When a singer borrows metaphors, symbols, proverbial usages, characters, or incidents from another genre, he at once revitalizes and transforms tradition and clothes himself in its authority. This ability to manipulate as well as display cultural knowledge establishes his right to his audience's attention, and sustains his moral imagination. Bringing past and present into the same rhetorical frame, the experience of the latter can be assessed in terms of the idealized cultural values of the former:

> I say to you, inveterate travelers,
> (our) Fathers they died in peace;
> The old ones of long ago,
> They were wearing shoes home-made of oxhide,
> They wore lambskin loincloths;
> When they fornicated,
> They said they were inlaws.
> Young men you have gone astray;
> When you love people's wives,
> You call for her rudely here at the shebeen.
> At the beer house canteen here,
> You pull-pull her about among people.
> Once again you wink at her (boldly),
> When you don't even know if her husband's around. . . .
> (Makeka Likhojane)

While some poets explained that praise poetry is "spoken" while lifela are "sung," others insisted that you could perform praises (*lithoko*) in the midst of a sefela. In one case, a performer reached such a level of excitement in his sefela that he "broke through into performance" (Hymes 1981) of a traditional war anthem (*mokorotlo*) of recent vintage, and then into praises of the late chief of his district, Lerotholi Mojela (1895–1961).

Lifela composition also thrives upon images drawn from Sesotho folklore, and one of the most popular is the *thokolosi,* a demon sent by a witch in the form of a hairy dwarf. It infests a village, doing every kind of mischief until the *ngaka,* a powerful diviner and herbalist, performs appropriate magic to drive it out. The ngaka is a key figure in Basotho village life, and his cultural knowledge is applied equally to physical, psychological, and social disorders. The concept of *bongaka* ("medicine") involves the application of all forms of socially constructive knowledge. For example, veteran sefela performers who instruct less proficient singers in compositional techniques are called *lingaka tsa lifela,* "doctors of lifela." The metaphoric equivalence between herbalist diviner and poet is based in part upon the value assigned to cultural communication in Sotho society. In lifela, the ngaka symbolizes the role of cultural knowledge, both magical and poetic, in the reharmonization of social relationships. In the following passage, Makeka Likhojane pictures himself as a ngaka, sent to drive a cunning thokolosi from a village, pursuing it even to the courts of a civil magistrate and the current King Moshoeshoe II at Matsieng:

My precious (divining) bones, you children,
I scattered them and examined them. . .
. . . Cattle bones, the revealers of people,
I skinned a brown dog,
I took a male ant,
Monkey fat and rabbit brain,
A mouthful of marigold.
The thokolosi ran from the fields,
It even went to the kraal:
Boys told me, there is an evil spirit in the kraal.
When I came to the kraal, it ran to the stable,
It ran to the fields,
It chased the bird-scarers.
When I came to the fields,
The bird-scarers ran away from the fields.
They said, when they came home,
"There is evil in the fields,
It breaks pumpkins,
Leaving wild watermelons,
It cuts the flowering maize,
It pulled out the cornsilk,
It pulled out potatoes by the roots.
When I came to the lands,
It went under a rock:
I spat in my hand,
Then rubbed it continuously:
Bees came flying out of my hand.
Now bees it's afraid of,
They chased it out from under the rock,
It ran away to the shop, at Fako's at Masupha's place,

> It bought bread and coffee.
> I came following it,
> When I came to the shop,
> It ran away, leaving the change,
> It ran away to Matsieng [the court of the king].
> . . . At Ramokoatsi's place,
> It reports to the magistrate:
> The summons was issued, calling me;
> (but) Men, you should know my name
> [you know my reputation]:
> When I came to court,
> It ran away to Mojela's . . .

Asked to explain, the poet replied in effect that just as the ngaka must expel the thokolosi, the poet uses his expressive powers to expose social misconduct and to expel misunderstanding, conflict, and poor self-expression wherever they are found, even (not surprisingly) amidst the councils of the powerful. Poetic song thus becomes a form of ritual action in which the moral imagination is brought to bear upon the contemporary structure of social relations through aesthetic representations of tradition.

In regard to form as well as content, lifela illustrate Lestrade's highly perceptive observation a half century ago that "new traditional literature in Southern Bantu languages is being composed all the time" (1937:299). The idea that something new can also be traditional is fundamental to my argument, even, or especially, when a distinct genre and not just additional items are created. In Southern Bantu oral genres, narrative sequence is subordinated to the delineation of character against the background of normative cultural values. Praises and poetic songs advance more through the concatenation of imagery than through narrative. Images are ordered according to an emotional and aesthetic logic of incremental effect, and the spirit of the story is more important than the plot. Oral prose narratives also reflect this principle, stringing together independent episodes around a central character (Guma 1967:160) and using "parallel sets of images to embody a theme" (Scheub 1975:3). As Scheub (1984:4) remarks, "patterning of imagery is the most visible artistic activity, involving the blending of the contemporary world and the fanciful fabrications of the tradition."

Lifela singers, of course, would never describe their efforts at composition (really recomposition) in performance in terms of an emotional and aesthetic logic of incremental effect. But they do often speak of a flow of feeling between themselves and their listeners, channeled and intensified by the rhythmic demands of Sesotho song. The word *sefela* in Sesotho also applies to Christian hymns, though it seems originally to have been borrowed by the missionaries from a term for the solo declamations performed by young male initiates over choruses of *mangae* initiation songs. When asked to comment on the possible relationship between Christian hymns and migrants' songs, informants explained that both song forms constituted "cries from the heart." As one female singer commented, referring to her initial interest in sefela performance: "When I was deeply depressed and worried, in order to express myself and feel contented, like a Christian would open a page in a bible, with me I went to the shebeen to sing these things. I had gone (to town) to visit my husband and I found him but we separated. I suffered a lot because of that. So I had to go to these places and get some joy out of life and unburden myself. Others came for similar reasons, and to share their feelings with others. . . ." (Coplan 1985:101).

Music itself, therefore, is crucial to the reapplication of memory and the creation and re-creation of the emotional qualities of experience in the maintenance of a living tradition. Interpretive analysis of oral genres most often focuses on formal structuring and the exegesis of symbolic images. Yet the ability of oral genres to reverberate between past and present is greatly dependent on their capacity for emotional expression. Ethnomusicologists can make a crucial contribution by demonstrating how music establishes the cultural ground of emotional communication that guides the realization of tradition in performance. In sefela, emotional communication through "sounding" (*ho luma*), the marriage of music and speech, is the key to creating an environment of feeling within which personal experience articulates with larger social forces and the moral imagination of tradition.

What, then, has ethnomusicology to offer history, and history, musical and otherwise, to offer ethnomusicology? Ethnomusicologists working in Africa and Asia, and with the Aboriginal populations of Australia and the Americas are in many cases students of the performance cultures of peoples who have moved from nonliteracy to illiteracy and, along with ourselves, to postliteracy. Historians of these peoples must perpetually seek ways of overcoming the paucity of written documents relating to "pre-colonial" periods, as well as the scarcity of indigenous voices and the overabundant misrepresentations of foreign voices in the written record. Hence Vail and White in their discussion of plantation workers' songs in colonial Mozambique cite the need for historians to look at "the creations of the people themselves, the forms in which their own major concerns are expressed. Of these, the most accessible are songs and oral narratives, which often . . . make symbolic statements about common experiences and concerns," giving us a sense of "popular consciousness [and] social history 'from below' " (1983:887). Similarly, historian Robert Harms (1983:812) has recognized that the aesthetic and symbolic formulations of social ideology found in oral traditions, including musical sound and texts, are often rooted in historical processes and events.

As in the case of the *lifela tsa litsamaea-naha* of the Basotho, it may be proposed that in musical representations the people being questioned speak more clearly for themselves. In dealing with the more remote past, performance traditions and texts may be among the only, or perhaps the richest, sources available. The problem comes in the process of interpretation: knowing what to make of such aesthetic and symbolic forms of expression without a detailed knowledge of the cultural concepts, values, and institutions of their creators. It is here that the ethnomusicologist, in the dual guise of cultural anthropologist and structural analyst of performance traditions, can be of invaluable assistance to the historian. What the latter must realize most fundamentally in this instance is that

> it is as crucial to explore the forms in which a people chose to speak and act as it is to examine the content of their messages. . . . History lies in its representation; for representation is as much the making of history as it is consciousness speaking out. Moreover, realism and rhetoric do not stand opposed. The poetry of representation, in short, is not an aesthetic embellishment of a "truth" that lies elsewhere. . . . [It is] the stuff of everyday thought and action, of the human consciousness through which culture and history construct each other. (Comaroff and Comaroff 1987:207)

Historians unfamiliar with the analytical techniques of folklorists and ethnomusicologists may doubt, mistakenly, that one can "translate" the logic of an alien cultural production (Ulin 1984:103). It is here, then, that the bridge between history and ethnomusicology must be most firmly constructed. As the social theorist Anthony Giddens observes (1984:284), analysis must be in terms of a "double hermeneutic," involving translation and interpretation between different cultural milieus and between practical (organic) and analytical frames of meaning.

From this it follows that history can contribute to ethnomusicology the recognition that in the elaboration of musical traditions in performance, "the constitution of symbols and their meaning . . . always reflects the character of power relations in a historically specific social formation and cultural tradition" (Ulin 1984:123). In this vein, Waterman's discussion of Yoruba *jùjú* music in this volume clearly supports Landeg White's insistence on the "need to understand the association of expressive forms with periods and structures of society that gave rise to them" (White 1982:18). This, the study of the context of context in the analysis of musical structures, processes, and events, enables us to understand more fully how performances achieve their particular location, intention, and form. Conversely, the production of meaning in music is undeniably part of the transformative energy of history. Above all, the study of performance gives us a full sense of the texture of life, which is what social history is all about (Vail and White 1983:919).

Tradition, that old red herring, also represents the immanence of the past in the present, linking modes of musical communication to the forces that have shaped them, and revealing the intervention of expressive culture in popular consciousness.

Conclusion

It was Franz Boas (1916:393) who first observed that oral genres are a people's autobiographical ethnography. The concept of tradition, at that time simply identified with culture, has since been reified, manipulated, and stretched entirely out of analytical shape. Yet ethnomusicologists persist, for lack of an alternative, in opposing the notion "traditional music," like some ever-receding ethnographic horizon, to whatever it is that the folk are (alas!) actually performing, hearing, and dancing to now. A closer examination of contemporary forms, however, reveals the survival and even the progressive development of the distinctive principles, values, and structures of cultural tradition. Ultimately, the concept of tradition may be indispensable as a focus for exchange among anthropologists, ethnomusicologists, and historians of Third World societies.

For all its perniciousness, apartheid cannot destroy the traditions of black South Africans, for tradition lives in their new genres of self-expression, rooted in the historicity of their very being in the world, in the very ground of their conscious existence. Among Basotho migrants and their women, the right to construct the present in public performance is based on the capacity for emotional and social self-recognition through the reapplication of the cultural knowledge of tradition. The vitality of Sotho tradition in lifela songs supports the migrants' contention that the Basotho were there before the white man arrived, survive as a nation now, and will be there when the present system is gone. In the words of the poet Makeka Likhojane:

> . . . I'm not impatient, I'm not incensed,
> I'm not in a hurry, I'm not in a rush . . .

. . . At Tsekelo's, Phutiatsana River,
Goats there give birth to twins,
Kids in threes and fours,
In fives now and in sixes;
The wombs of the goats are up to the task,
Even in sevens they still arrive. . . .

Jùjú History: Toward a Theory of Sociomusical Practice

3

Christopher A. Waterman

Jùjú is a syncretic popular music performed and patronized by the Yoruba of southwestern Nigeria. The development of jùjú music, the substantive focus of this essay, may be divided into two major periods. Each of these is characterized by the dominance of a stylistic paradigm, a configuration of knowledge and values guiding musical performance. The first paradigm—early jùjú—was dominant from 1932 through World War II. The second—modern jùjú—began to emerge in 1948 and had attained dominance by the early 1950s. This periodization is supported by many veteran jùjú musicians, who recount a burst of innovation, followed by a series of minor variations, and a period of relatively rapid change after the World War II.

Bruno Nettl has suggested that we might define ethnomusicology as a "science of music history" (1983:11). It is, of course, one thing to describe the historical trajectory of a style on the basis of available source materials, and quite another to account for it. Several alternative levels of explanation, each associated with an intellectual stereotype, immediately present themselves. The hypothetical vulgar Marxist might ground jùjú history in the economic infrastructures that condition the production, commodification, and consumption of music. From this perspective, the relative stability of jùjú style before the war might be viewed as a cultural epiphenomenon of a stagnant Depression-era colonial economy, while the expansion and diversification of modern jùjú would reflect a relatively vigorous postwar economy and the formation of a Yoruba bourgeoisie. The social anthropologist might, on the other hand, suggest that jùjú style exists because it serves a range of functions, including the reinforcement of relationships between musicians and significant others (e.g., patrons, A and R people, deities). The interpretivist anthropologist would spurn functionalist behaviorism and seek instead to portray the gossamer webs of urban Yoruba musical experience through a reflexive "reading" of affecting stylistic metaphors (reading music over other people's shoulders, even if they don't). The musicologist might adopt a hermeneutic approach, focusing on the internal order of musical style as revealed in a corpus of transcriptions of recorded performances. From this viewpoint, modern jùjú could be explained as a transmutation of the structural principles of early jùjú. The term "music in context" would be deployed here as a means of keeping detailed cultural and social analysis safely at bay.

These caricatures are not meant to offend, but to suggest that various levels of explanation are available. Each method is important as a way of "putting the jigsaw puzzle together" (Bateson 1958:281), but no single one accounts exhaustively for what is known about continuity and change in jùjú style. Ethnomusicology's uncomfortable perch between the social sciences and the humanities, in regard to which much ink has been spilt, provides unique opportunities for theoretical creativity and brokerage. I believe that adequate accounts of musical continuity and change must deal, to the extent that sources and scholarly competence allow, with relationships among patterns of musical sound and performance behavior, cultural symbolism and value, social transaction and ideology, and the material forces that encourage or constrain particular forms of expression.

> Whether the researcher's ultimate aim is to approach social reality through the arts, or to approach the arts through their social context, the procedure must be the same. In either case, the arts cannot be 'read' without *both* comprehending their nature as aesthetic constructs with their own principles and conventions, *and* locating them in the specific social universe which is the grounds of their existence. . . . The point at which the two dimensions meet is in the *production* of the arts: not just in its material but also in its ideational aspects. We need to ask by whom and by what means, in what circumstances, under what constraints, in whose interests and in accordance with what conventions, these arts are produced. (Barber 1987:5)

The Relevance of Practice Theory to the Study of Music History in Urban Africa

Jùjú history provides a venue for evaluating the utility of aspects of contemporary social theory for the study of musical continuity and change. Many ethnomusicologists would, I think, accept Nisbet's assertion that "between the study of change—in stark contrast to the mere motions, movements, actions and interactions which are so commonly confused with change—and history there is quite evidently an unbreakable relationship, when we come down from the empyrean heights of abstractions, wholes, and universals" (1969:303). However, the unhelpful notions that the relationship between continuity and change is paradoxical, and that change inherently requires more explanation than continuity, have proved tenacious in ethnomusicology. Although no generalized framework for the study of society can account for the specific features of a musical style, *practice theory*, influenced by Marx's dialectical approach to social history, poses an interesting question for ethnomusicologists: "How does the reproduction of a structure become its transformation?" (Sahlins 1981:8).

Structures, from this perspective, are learned configurations of knowledge and value, stabilized in memory and guiding human practical activity in the world. Though quotidian behavior is largely guided by enculturated psychomotor habits and unexamined assumptions concerning the nature of social and material reality (*habitus*), humans engaged in practical activity characteristically "know what their actions are, under some description, and why it is they carry them out" (Giddens 1987:3). No one, however, can accurately predict all ramifications of his or her purposive actions; unexpected consequences are thus an inescapable aspect of practice. Social behavior—for example, musical performance—is always more than "the mere *execution* of the model" that guides it (Bourdieu 1977:29).

For practice theorists, cultural continuity is not best thought of as stasis, but as a recursive process. The reproduction of individual representations of culture patterns is grounded in a flow of activity continually shaped by actors' interpretations of and reactions to constraints and incentives encountered in the world. Practice feeds back onto structure, opening the possibility of transformation when actors are confronted with contradictions grounded in circumstances not of their own choosing, and are thus forced to rethink normally tacit assumptions and values. "[A]ction and structure stand in a relation of logical entailment: the concept of action presumes that of structure and vice-versa. I use the term 'duality of structure' to mean that structure is both the medium and the outcome of the social practice it recursively organizes" (Giddens 1981:171).

Some historical implications of this approach have been explored by Sahlins, who has been concerned "not merely to know how events are ordered by culture, but how, in that process, the culture is reordered" (1981:8). Defining structure as "the symbolic relations of cultural order," he argues that:

> on the one hand, people organize their projects and give significance to their objects from the existing understandings of the social order. . . . On the other hand . . . as the contingent circumstances of action need not conform to the significance some group might assign them, people are known to creatively reconsider their conventional schemes. And to that extent, the culture is historically altered in action. We can speak even of a "structural transformation," since the alteration of some meanings changes the positional relations among the cultural categories, thus a "system-change." (1985:vii)

Practice theory provides an alternative to functionalist approaches that presume cultural equilibrium and view change as exceptional, alternatively adaptive or dysfunctional. Blacking's (1977) analytical distinction between musical change and social change, and Herndon's (1974:246) suggestion that "in discussing the structure, or patterning, of music, we cannot turn to the social sciences," raise an interesting question: if ethnomusicologists were to adopt aspects of practice theory in rethinking tenacious conceptual dichotomies—continuity and change, norm and variation, structure and history, and so on—what form might the more specific notion of *musical practice* take?

It is immediately clear that the broad outlines of practice theory are compatible with certain ethnomusicological formulations concerning continuity and change. In the schematic model of musical process presented by Merriam (1964), the concepts and values of actors—that is to say, performers and interpreters of music—are reproduced or transformed through musical practice. This dynamic is rooted in the flow of perception, learning, and social interaction (1964:145). The notion that systemic continuity depends upon the reproduction of patterns of perception, motor behavior, and value is not unlike Herskovits's psychocultural concept of "cultural tenacity" *via* reinterpretation and syncretism, applied by R. Waterman (1952), Merriam (1955), Roberts (1972), Hampton (1980), and Thompson (1983) to the stylistic trajectories of performance traditions of the African diaspora. In addition, practice theory provides a processual grounding for comparative typologies of the musical correlates of culture contact (Nettl 1978a; Kartomi 1981).

Stephen Blum, drawing upon the work of Walter Benjamin, has characterized "the *practice* of a performing musician as a mode of human labor. A performer works within the constraints imposed by a particular set of social relations. He learns, elaborates, exercises, and refines the *techniques* which make it possible for him to act as a performer within one or more (changing or stable) contexts" (1975:217). The implicit theories guiding performance are thus encoded and represented in musical forms, and not necessarily in discourse about such forms. Such techniques or "conceptual tools" guide the selection and deployment of alternative resources in performance. The emergent musical "product" thus "carries traces of the processes through which the performer has effected and realized his choices, has established his personal (and social) 'stance' or position" (1975:217). This formulation links the dialectics of performance practice to patterns of social interaction and the enactment and negotiation of identity.

Musical structures—defined as learned configurations of habit, knowledge, and value predicating a range of performance strategies—and musical performance—the contingent, dialectical realization of musical structure in social action—are interdependent aspects of a more inclusive system, animated by the flow of perception and memory. Put simply, musical styles perdure when performers and other competent listeners reproduce through practice the understandings that guide their conventional expressive behavior. When confronted with contradictions generated by the unintended consequences of their actions or changes beyond their control in the material and social world, people may come to reinterpret traditional musical values, symbols, and methods.

In the cities of sub-Saharan Africa, as elsewhere in the so-called Third World, such contradictions have been precipitated by the pervasive political and economic transformations attendant upon colonial conquest and the formation of modern nation-states. Under these conditions, the very notion of tradition has often taken on a powerful ideological valence; styles have been reinterpreted and reconstructed; and genre categories repositioned.

A growing body of historical scholarship on African popular music (e.g., Ranger 1975; Collins and Richards 1982; Low 1982; Coplan 1985; Bemba 1985; Erlmann 1987) broadly supports a view of performance practice as the dynamic point of articulation between musical structures and the social and material exigencies of urban life. Some recent studies of African popular music have traced interconnections among musical processes, the symbolic portrayal of identity, and colonial political economies. Coplan, for example, links musical reproduction and transformation to the strategic role of performance: "Cultural forms are produced and reproduced through systems of rules and resources employed by individuals with definite intentions and interests. Every attempt to reproduce forms such as musical or theatrical styles in performance is mediated by the experience and circumstances of the participants. The potential for change is therefore present in any act which contributes to the reproduction of structures of performance" (1985:240). Collins and Richards (1982:132–33) suggest a broad distinction between the development of popular music in

South Africa, an industrialized economy dependent upon African wage labor, and anglophone West Africa, in which merchant capital has been dominant and Africans have had more leeway to develop brokerage positions. Although the comparative study of urban African music is still in its infancy, it is clear that the most convincing accounts of the historical development of particular styles are concerned with musical practice as it is conditioned by, and in turn helps to shape, emergent patterns of social interaction and cultural order.

Early Jùjú Music (1932–48)

Jùjú originated in Lagos, Nigeria during the early 1930s, a localized variant of the pan-anglophone West African urban palm-wine music style cluster (Collins 1976). The typical early jùjú group was a trio consisting of a leader who sang and played banjo, a *ṣẹ̀kẹ̀rẹ̀* (netted bottle gourd rattle) player, and a jùjú (tambourine) drummer. Some groups operated as quartets, adding a second vocalist. The imported banjo and tambourine symbolized the cosmopolitan orientation of the new style, and distinguished it from the generic sociomusical category of "palm-wine" or "native blues," while the ṣẹ̀kẹ̀rẹ̀ rattle bespoke jùjú's roots in Yoruba tradition.

Early jùjú musicians performed in two contexts: the parlors of homes owned by members of a black bourgeoisie dominated by Yoruba-speaking repatriates from Sierra Leone (*Saro*) and from Cuba and Brazil (*Amaro*), including civil servants, lawyers, doctors, merchants, and teachers; and urban palm-wine bars, frequented by a heterogeneous audience of proletarian African migrants. Although most jùjú musicians were part-time wage workers, a handful were able to become fully professional musical specialists.

Abdulrafiu Babatunde (Tunde) King, born in the Saro quarter of Olowogbowo on August 24, 1910, was the first jùjú musician to construct patronage links with a segment of the African bourgeoisie in Lagos. His father was a chief Native Court clerk, and had lived for some time at Fourah Bay in Sierra Leone. A member of the small Muslim segment of the Saro community, Tunde received his primary and secondary education at Christian schools in Lagos. He learned to play the guitar as a member of an informal neighborhood-based association of young men, "area boys"or "rascals" who gathered at the mechanic's shop of Akamo Davies, son of the Saro leader of a syncretic Christian church movement (Alaja-Browne 1985:23). In 1929 King was a clerk at the United Africa Company and a part-time professional guitarist and singer. His band started as an informal trio, with King on guitar, Lamidi George on the square *sámbà* frame drum, and Isola

Caxton-Martins on maracas, with a fourth member, "Snake" Johnson, added later as a supporting vocalist. In the early 1930s the tambourine, six-stringed guitar-banjo, and ṣẹ̀kẹ̀rẹ̀ were introduced, the latter two instruments given to King by "area boy" and patron Esumbo Jibowu (Aig-Imoukhuede 1975:226; Alaja-Browne 1985:37).

By the mid-1930s, King's patronage network had expanded to include a number of wealthy residents of the Olowogbowo quarter. A public performance at the wake for Dr. Oguntola Sapara in 1935, another at the Yoruba Tennis Club in 1936, a series of recordings for Parlophone, and broadcasts on the colonial shortwave radio service helped to bolster his reputation and generate more elite contacts. As Alaja-Browne describes it, King's success was grounded in a " 'salon culture,' which meant quiet entertainment during the late evenings in family compounds and drawing rooms, but never in the streets of Lagos, and with 'T.K.,' as Tunde King was affectionately known, supplying the desired music . . . while they [the hosts] enjoyed themselves with their women friends over the game of cards or billiards" (1985:31). As Tunde King describes it: "Going around with these friends, I started to sing, to enjoy all these things. Then it started to spread, spread, spread, and people told me, 'Well, this thing is no more a joke! You must try and realize something as fees. If they want to call you, they should give you fees, say five shillings or ten.' . . . I said, 'All right!' " (personal communication, 1982).

Tunde's major competitor, Ayinde Bakare, was born in Lagos, the son of Ilorin and Ijebu Yoruba migrants. Just as King was supported by his Olowogbowo "mates," Bakare played for the "area boys" of Lafiaji, a Yoruba settler neighborhood. Although Bakare was very popular before the war, partially as a result of recordings released in 1937 on the His Master's Voice label, King was widely regarded as the paradigmatic jùjú singer. The status distinction between the two musicians paralleled that between their communities of origin—Olowogbowo, home of the Sierra Leonean repatriates who dominated the Lagosian black elite, versus Lafiaji, home of working-class migrants from the Yoruba hinterland. Other groups, including those led by Alabi Labelu of the Brazilian quarter, Ladipo Esugbayi of the indigenous Lagosian Yoruba quarter of Isale Eko, Tunji Banjo of Ebute Metta on the mainland adjacent to Lagos Island (Alaja-Browne 1985:62), and Ojo Babajide of Ibadan, a Yoruba city ninety miles north of Lagos, were also ranked in relation to their communities of origin and primary support. A broad distinction was drawn between bands that performed at urban working-class bars and those patronized by elites who "could afford to drink 'schnapps' and 'cased beer,' not 'palmwine' " (ibid.:43). A syncretic resolution of this fluid antithesis was developed around the time of the Second World War: *kakaji,* a mixture of palm-wine and Guinness stout.

Jùjú song texts were through-composed, drawn from a pool of traditional Yoruba verbal formulas and urban slang phrases. "Deep" (*ìjìnlẹ̀ẹ̀*) Yoruba metaphors were a crucial aspect of jùjú's role as a medium of social communication, a means of condensing and symbolically portraying patterns of urban African experience within a traditional rhetorical framework. Thus, in singing the praises of an urban voluntary association of African entrepreneurs, King deployed the following textual sequence:

agbe ló l'áró, kìí ráhùn áró
àlùkò ló l'ósùn, kìí ráhùn ósùn
lékéléké, kìí ráhùn ẹfun
ìyàwó àkọ̀fé, kìí ráhùn ajé
òkèlè ẹ̀bà. kìí ráhùn ọbẹ̀
k'árìrà máà mà jẹ́ ẹ ráhùn owó
k'árìrà máà mà jẹ́ ẹ ráhùn ọmọ

The blue Touraco parrot is the owner of indigo dye, it doesn't usually complain for want of indigo dye.
The red Aluko bird is the owner of rosewood [used to make red dye], it doesn't usually complain for want of rosewood.
Cattle egret [a white bird], it doesn't usually complain for want of chalk.
The first wife one marries, she doesn't usually complain for want of money.
The first morsel of cassava porridge, it doesn't usually complain for want of soup.
Good fortune, don't let us complain for want of money.
Good fortune, don't let us complain for want of children.
(Tunde King and his Juju Group; Parlophone P0.500, recorded in Lagos, 1936)

The efficacy of jùjú texts was grounded in the immediacy of sung language, and the predication of identity through metaphor. In the above sequence the singer uses traditional Yoruba images to forge a correspondence between the natural relationship of birds and bright colors, on the one hand, and the cultural relationship between beginnings and richness of experience, on the other. He then uses this evocative metaphoric bundle to plead with Good Fortune, personified, on behalf of his patrons. In another text, composed at a Christian wake-keeping for a prominent African doctor in Lagos, King linked three deaths in the elite African community—the doctor, a prominent politician's child, and a lawyer—in order to make a general philosophical observation concerning Death.

papa Vaughn yé, má ronú
mama tó bí Vaughn yé, má ronú
jẹ́ kí á rántí Aronke
ọmọ Macaulay mi
ikan ṣoṣo náà lọ̀wọ́ dọ́kítà ni
tí ówá di olóògbé o, l'ékó o
kò mà sí ẹni tí ikú ò lèpa
ká rántí Káyọ̀dé, Káyọ̀de o
onídàjọ́ tó tún d'olóògbé sose, l'ékó o
ikú tó nfọ́lé aládùn
òhun ló pa Aronke, ọmọ Macaulay

Dr. Vaughn, please do not brood
Mrs. Vaughn, please do not brood
Let us remember Ronke Macaulay
The only child of Dr. and Mrs. Macaulay
Who died in Lagos, oh
There is no one that Death can't kill
Let us also remember Kayode, Kayode, oh
The magistrate who died unexpectedly not too long ago in Lagos.
Death, that shatters/steals all the sweetness in a house,
Is the one who killed Aronke, child of Macaulay
(Alaja-Browne 1985:148–49; this song was also released on Parlophone P0.502, 1936)

In discussing the above song, King described the circumstances of its composition:

> I remember when this fellow died, I was in a party, and I just sing. I remember late Dr. Vaughn, and Ronke Macaulay was a small kid. See, Dr. Vaughn is an old man, but when he dies, it pains a lot of people. So [I sang that] Dr. Macaulay has to take it easy. The only son he got, and he has finished all his education, taken his father's post [in the colonial civil service]. He died unexpectedly, and the father was alive. So I said he must remember this man, this man, this man, as a sort of condolence. (personal communication, 1982)

Early jùjú performances were necessarily adapted to the temporal flow of particular social events, alternating praises for patrons with general observations on life in the city. Non-Yoruba textual materials available for deployment in particular situations included hymn texts, phrases in languages spoken by African migrants (e.g., Kru, Krio, Twi), and sections of Qur'anic chant.

The vocal melodies of early jùjú, initiated by the bandleader, were predominantly diatonic and descending in contour, with an ambitus between an octave and a tenth. Conjunct movement alternated with melodic leaps, often outlining leading-tone resolutions at cadential points, a feature stereotypically associated with Christian hymns. Vocal harmonies, usually parallel thirds, were provided by the second singer. Most traditional Yoruba group singing is in octaves or in unison, and the use of parallel thirds was associated with Christianity and, at a more general level, Western influence. Melodies and lyrics often followed an AABA or ABA pattern, akin to the rhetorical structure of Yoruba proverbs, in which the first pattern is repeated, followed by a contrasting pattern that responds to and comments upon the first, and concluding with a repetition of the opening phrase. Such sections alternated with longer sections composed of short verbal formulae and more limited in melodic compass.

The vocal style of early jùjú is cited by informants as a highly distinctive feature, using the upper range of the male full-voice tessitura (the octave above middle C), and being moderately tense with little or no vibrato. This voice quality, while within the wide range employed in specialized traditional heightened-speech genres, appears to have been influenced by "precentors" in the syncretic African churches that flourished in Lagos between the wars, who characteristically chanted in "a high and rapid voice" (Turner 1967:113).

The banjo—including such varieties as the guitar-banjo and mandolin-banjo—was used to produce melodic lines introducing or bridging between vocal segments, intermittent tonic or dominant pedal patterns, and heterophonic accompaniment for the vocal line. Introductory banjo sequences also followed a general AABA or ABA pattern, and were based upon a set of paradigms, including "*Tal'o Ri?*" ("Who [i.e., what patrons] did you see?"), "*Yabonsa*" (based on the archetypal Akan highlife pattern *Yaa Amponsah*), and "Johnny Walker" (associated with African railway workers). The basic harmonic ground was a schematic version of the tonic/dominant relationships in church music. Banjo techniques were derived from a generalized thumb and forefinger guitar style spread along the West African coast by sailors and other wage-earning migrants, and referred to by Lagosian musicians as "Krusbass."

Jùjú rhythms were derived from the syncretic social dance music *aṣíkò*, performed on a set of square frame drums (*sámbà*) and a scraped carpenter's saw, and patronized after World War I by the Sierra Leonean and Brazilian repatriate communities. The rhythmic infrastructure of jùjú was supplied by the *ṣẹ̀kẹ̀rẹ̀* and tambourine, with the leader occasionally striking the front of his banjo for percussive effects. The ṣẹ̀kẹ̀rẹ̀ player generally produced a density-referent pattern, while the tambourinist alternated between complementary interlocking patterns and short rhythmic improvisations, the latter during breaks in the singing. Some jùjú drummers developed a technique for flinging the drum high into the air and catching it at an appropriate rhythmic moment; one popular Yoruba etymology for the term jùjú thus derives it from the verb *jù*, "to throw something."

Tempo distinguished jùjú from most traditional Yoruba social dance music. Recordings from the mid-1930s suggest tempos ranging from 120 to 134 beats per minute, regarded as relatively fast and "sharp" (intense) and likened to the ballroom "one-step" by older Lagosian informants. Early jùjú was regarded primarily as a music for listening rather than dancing. As "Speedy" Araba, a Lagosian guitarist who heard Tunde King's group during the 1930s, describes it:

> In those days, Tunde played like a preacher. He'd philosophize, you know, tell you about life. People who try to do more than themselves and ended their life by committing suicide. Or wives that are ferocious to the extent that they kill their husband. . . . And it is not meant for just every Dick and Harry to dance. Because, by sitting and listening like that, we used to call it *wáàsí*. *Wáàsí* means to go to church to listen to a sermon, as if to say we are going to church. From his songs you will get some understanding of life, you know. (Julius O. Araba, personal communication, 1982)

The new style and its practitioners were viewed with distaste by more conservative members of the black bourgeoisie who attended the mainstream Anglican and Baptist churches, and by the *ọmọ èkó*, traditionalist Lagosian Yoruba residing in a community headed by several lines of chiefs and a sacred king (*ọba*). According to Ayinde Bakare the term *jùjú*, derisively applied by Europeans to traditional African religion and magical/medical practices, was satirically deployed by Yoruba to refer to elements of the genre derived from Christian musical practice (vocal harmonies, hymn melodies, the tambourine). Yoruba wits inverted and subverted the insulting term: "It was '*jùjú*'; their [the Christians'] '*jùjú*'!" (Keil 1966–67).

Most jùjú musicians in Lagos and large hinterland towns such as Ibadan used musical performance to supplement their wages as laborers, drivers, sailors, railway workers, or lower-level clerks. As we have seen, the ability of the most successful practitioners, such as King and Bakare, to shift from wage-work to full-time musical specialization was rooted in the patronage of a segment of the literate African elite. This social category was still dominated by descendants of the repatriate black elite of late nineteenth-century Lagos, whose position as brokers between the English and traditional Yoruba had been weakened by racist colonial policies formulated after 1900. Elite contacts provided access to lucrative parlor engagements and contact with the European oligopolies that produced and sold gramophone records (e.g., United

Africa Company/His Master's Voice, Compagnie Française d'Afrique Occidental/Parlophone, Busch and Witt/Odeon). Although profits realized by Lagosian musicians from sales of recordings were minimal—King was paid five shillings by Parlophone in 1936 for each 3-minute side, plus a theoretical 1 1/2 penny royalty per disk—the distribution of disks among Africans who could afford to purchase gramophones resulted in greater demand and remuneration for their services. Those musicians without elite contacts were caught in a negative cycle: no recordings, no elite engagements, and vice versa.

The reproduction of early jùjú style was grounded in the efforts of musicians in Lagos to consolidate stable patronage networks within a stagnating Depression-era urban economy, and in the role of musical performance in enacting patterns of identity and experience, nascent structures of feeling (Williams 1977:128–35). The patronage of a segment of the black bourgeoisie was a crucial resource for urban musicians seeking to augment and eventually supplant their non-musical wages with earnings from performance. It is nonetheless important to note that early jùjú musicians created an audience, a community of taste, that extended over the social and economic boundaries that subdivided the African population of Lagos. Demographically centered in an expanding urban wage-work force that was predominantly Yoruba, semiliterate, and Christian, jùjú's total patronage network also included wealthy African merchants, members of a progressive Muslim community, and a variety of non-Yoruba and non-Nigerian migrants.

If we regard classes and class consciousness not as things that exist, but as relationships that develop, it is clear that this intermediate sector of the Lagosian population, sandwiched between the European colonists and a traditionalist Yoruba community, was an emergent African working class, united by racist policies excluding blacks from the upper reaches of colonial society. Jùjú music, a syncretic style transcending preexistent boundaries of class and culture, was a musico-symbolic (Peña 1985) correlate of the political interdependence "between bourgeoisie and proletariat in a colonial society born of a common subordination to alien rule and perceived injustice" (Hughes and Cohen 1979:48).

The Emergence of Modern Jùjú Style (1948–1950s)

Early jùjú style was reproduced in performance practice through the late 1940s, when changes in social and material factors impinging on performance practice catalyzed shifts in the range of expressive resources and techniques deployed by musicians. Sociohistorical processes influencing the creative choices of jùjú practitioners in the postwar period included rapid, though uneven, growth in the agricultural export market; increased rural-urban migration; "Nigerianization" of the colonial civil service and expansion of primary education; the concomitant emergence of a broad-based Yoruba elite; the negotiation of Yoruba identity and tradition in the political struggles preceding Independence (1960); and the growth of electronic media linking the hinterland to cities such as Ibadan and Lagos, centers of the popular music economy of southwestern Nigeria. Although the most lucrative context for jùjú performance continued to be elite parties, the identities, interests, and aesthetic values of upwardly mobile Yoruba celebrants, many of them raised in hinterland towns and villages, differed from those of the interwar Lagosian elite. Modern jùjú was a labile expressive structure simultaneously rooted in Yoruba tradition and oriented toward the world socioeconomic system into which Nigerians were ineluctably drawn.

The first major change in jùjú performance practice was the introduction in 1948 of variants of the Yoruba hourglass-shaped pressure drum or "talking drum" (e.g., *dùndún, gángan, àdàmọ̀n*). Bandleader Akanbi Ege, who as an early jùjú bandleader had worked under the Creole surname, Wright, is reputed to have pioneered in this regard. Other jùjú groups operating in Lagos and hinterland Yoruba towns followed his lead quickly; Ayinde Bakare, for example, brought the drum into his group later that same year. The talking drum was for various reasons an ideal resource for jùjú musicians seeking to enact and exploit emergent patterns of modern Yoruba identity during a period of intensive economic growth and political competition. Traditionally distributed over a wide area of the Yoruba hinterland and used in diverse sacred and secular contexts, talking drums effectively symbolized pan-Yoruba identity and were used at political rallies to mobilize the newly enfranchised masses.

The dùndún, gángan, and àdàmọ̀n were also introduced into syncretist Christian movements as a means of attracting Yoruba converts. Whereas drums such as the *bàtá,* unambiguously associated with *òrìṣà* (traditional deity) worship, were interpreted as antithetical to Christian piety, the pressure drum was regarded by clergy in the more strongly indigenized churches as sufficiently generic in its customary uses to be appropriate for accompanying hymns. The incorporation of talking drums into jùjú had important consequences for performance practice, including the introduction of lineage-trained musicians into many bands, expansion of the available corpus of surrogate speech idioms, and, most important, co-optation of a traditional surrogate speech medium for praise, abuse, and social commentary.

Another major factor in the transformation of jùjú style was the availability of electronic amplifiers, microphones, and pick-ups. Portable public address systems had been introduced during the war and were in regular use by Yoruba musicians by the late 1940s. The first jùjú musician to adopt the amplified guitar appears to have been Ayinde Bakare. He experimented with a contact microphone in 1949, switching from ukelele-banjo to "box" (acoustic) guitar, because, he has said, there was no place to attach the device to the body of the former. There is also evidence to suggest that the banjo was regarded as anachronistic, given the dominance of the guitar in imported popular musics. Electronic amplification of voices and guitar catalyzed an expansion and restructuring of jùjú ensembles during the 1950s. In particular, it enabled jùjú musicians to incorporate a greater number of percussion instruments without upsetting the aural balance between singing and instrumental accompaniment. The band of Ayinde Bakare, whose recordings and live performances were influential, serves as an example of the expansion of jùjú groups during the postwar period (Keil 1966–67):

1939: ukelele-banjo, jùjú, ṣẹ̀kẹ̀rẹ̀, supporting vocalist (four members).
1946: ukelele-banjo, jùjú, ṣẹ̀kẹ̀rẹ̀, maracas (derived from Afro-Cuban music), supporting vocalist (five members).
1948: ukelele-banjo, jùjú, ṣẹ̀kẹ̀rẹ̀, maracas, gángan ("talking drum"), supporting vocalist (six members).
1949: amplified guitar, jùjú, ṣẹ̀kẹ̀rẹ̀, maracas, gángan, àgídìgbo (large five-key lamellaphone), supporting vocalist (seven members).
1954: amplified guitar, jùjú, ṣẹ̀kẹ̀rẹ̀, maracas, gángan, àgídìgbo, akúbà (a conga-type drum, based on Afro-Cuban prototypes), supporting vocalist (eight members).

The introduction of the large *àgídìgbo* lamellaphone in 1949 is one indication of the continual interchange between jùjú and other popular styles, in this case *mambo* or *àgídìgbo* music. Àgídìgbo was a descendant of earlier pan-West African neo-traditional percussion musics such as *aṣíkò, gòmbé,* and *kónkómbà,* and was first played by boys' groups in Lagos and recorded in the late 1940s and 1950s by Adeolu Akinsanya's Rio Lindo Orchestra.

The instrumental balance in Bakare's paradigmatic jùjú group shifted from one stringed instrument and two percussion instruments before the war, to one stringed instrument and five percussion instruments in 1954. Further expansion took place during the early 1960s, and by 1966, on the eve of the Nigerian Civil War, the ratio of instrument types in Bakare's still popular group stood at one chordophone to eight percussion instruments. These changes were accompanied by an increase in the size of the responsorial vocal chorus, including both specialized singers and other members of the group.

The strategic innovations of Bakare and other jùjú musicians during the 1950s defy classification as straightforward examples of Westernization, modernization, and revitalization. Seeking to construct patron-client linkages that would ensure their own upward mobility, they created substyles based on the jùjú paradigm, drawing variously upon pan-Yoruba dance rhythms and verbal traditions spread via radio and primary schools: localized melodies, rhythms, and texts, evoking the sacred kingdoms that were the main referent of cultural identity before the "invention" of Yoruba identity in the nineteenth century; Afro-Latin instruments, rhythms, and forms (e.g., *montuno* structure); syncretic church hymns and Islamic vocal qualities; country-western songs; and Indian film themes.

The expansion of jùjú ensembles was closely interrelated with other shifts in performance practice. The expanded percussion section was modeled on the hierarchical structure of traditional drum ensembles. Various imported drum types—the European tambourine, the Afro-Brazilian sámbà frame drum, and locally produced drums modeled on Afro-Cuban prototypes—were used to produce a layered rhythmic infrastructure. Various Yoruba social dance rhythms (*alùjó,* "dance drumming") were incorporated, most notably a cluster of 12/8 patterns called *wọ́rọ̀,* performed at political rallies. The large àgídìgbo lamellaphone, ṣẹ̀kẹ̀rẹ̀ rattle, agogo iron gong, and Afro-Cuban claves and maracas also played interlocking patterns. The talking drum occupied the traditional role of "mother drum" (*iyá'lù*), improvising patterns during breaks in the singing, foregrounding and focusing particular aspects of the supporting rhythmic framework, and, via its function as a surrogate speech medium, reinforcing or commenting on the praise lyrics sung by the bandleader/guitarist.

Reorganization of the jùjú ensemble was accompanied by a slowing of tempos. For example, recordings made by Ayinde Bakare and his quartet before the World War II center around 132 pulses per minute, while recordings made with the larger group in the early 1950s range from around M.M. 98 to 106. This was regarded by participants as a convergence with Yoruba secular dance drumming styles. The slowing of tempos in the postwar period, incorporation of the talking drum, and development of a standardized ensemble structure based on traditional Yoruba norms were also linked with changes in the aural texture and timbre of jùjú. The Yoruba, like many West African peoples, express an aesthetic preference for complex "buzzing" sounds, adding noise-producing attachments to all sorts of instruments. The new jùjú ensembles of the early 1950s not only produced satisfying dance rhythms, but also dense, continuous aural textures, generated by the complexly layered interplay of percussion, guitar, and voices. Western technology was put in the service of Yoruba aesthetic norms, as the channeling of singing and guitar through cheap and infrequently serviced tube amplifiers and speakers augmented the sizzling timbre and aural flow of the music.

New melodic models were introduced, based on songs in Standard Yoruba dialect sung in church and primary school, imported popular songs, and localized Yoruba styles. While the practice of singing in diatonic thirds continued to dominate, there were notable exceptions. Bandleader C. A. Balogun, for example, developed a style that utilized parallel major second intervals, a characteristic of vocal styles in his home area of Ekiti. In addition, the generalized mode of vocal production shifted, from the high, tense style of the 1930s and 1940s, to a lower, more relaxed style compatible with most traditional Yoruba singing and with the imported model of the "crooner." In this as in other regards there was considerable room for variety; the high tessitura style of Tunde King was, for instance, continued by Tunde Nightengale, a popular Lagosian bandleader of the 1950s who was known as "the bird that sings at night." The increased heterogeneity of jùjú style, variation around the stabilizing paradigm established by Bakare, was a direct outcome of the diverse origins and cultural values of the new Yoruba elite, jùjú's primary patrons.

The sensually satisfying soundscapes (Schafer 1980) produced by the enlarged, restructured jùjú groups became a crucial feature of elite naming, wedding, and funeral ceremonies. Increasingly flamboyant presentations of cash to musicians during such events provided a public, meta-communicatively framed idiom for the consolidation of symbolic capital. Jùjú performance temporally patterned and experientially focused social action at urban rites of passage, events crucial to the status advancement of upwardly mobile Yoruba merchants, bureaucrats, and politicians. The ability to generate appropriate aural environments in celebratory contexts was a crucial resource for jùjú practitioners seeking to broaden their patronage networks during a period of economic expansion and increased social mobility. Proxemics also played a role in the social economy of jùjú performance: the bandleader, dressed distinctively from his *ègbè* (supporting chorus, literally "supporters" or "protectors"), was generally surrounded by them in a semicircle. This visual image is a traditional Yoruba idiom for leadership, reflected in sculptures where the king (*ọba*) is protected by his entourage.

Another crucial aspect of jùjú performance practice after World War II was the increased activity of European recording companies

(His Master's Voice, Decca, Philips), who also licensed local Yoruba-owned labels. The first Nigerian to establish such an enterprise was E. O. Badejo, an Ijebu Yoruba record dealer based in Lagos who began recording local musicians in a small studio in 1947. The autonomy of local labels vis-à-vis the international companies was limited, since they did not own the means of production of disks, but they were an important factor in the dissemination of jùjú and the establishment of stylistic paradigms. Broadcasts on the colonial "wired-wireless" rediffusion service were also an increasingly important source of publicity for bands. Performances by Yoruba musicians were taped during the 1950s at the Nigerian Broadcasting Service studios at Tugwell House (formerly a sailors' boarding house). The music sessions featured taped and live performances by Nigerian bands and artists, and Nigerian musicians made regular appearances. There was scant interest in Western classical music, and the trend was toward "highlife" [a term used generically by Europeans to refer to African popular music] and disk jockeys, some with strong personal followings (Mackay 1964:36). The stylistic decisions of musicians were strongly influenced by economic considerations. Many bandleaders produced records with a song in Standard Yoruba dialect and mainstream jùjú style on the A side, and a local Yoruba dialect and style on the B side.

> I want to be identified with my area, You see? I'm not from Lagos, I'm not from Ibadan, I'm from Ekiti, where all this music originates. So, why not? A lot of my people cannot dance to the jùjú, real jùjú music, and they can dance to their native songs. If I want to be popular with my people and the Yorubas, all I have to do is record in Yoruba and record in my Ekiti dialect, and then the record will sell over there and sell in Yorubaland generally. It's a sort of market strategy. (personal communication, Dele Ojo, 1982)

Bandleaders sought to expand and focus their patronage networks by juxtaposing the dominant standard jùjú style and localized or idiosyncratic variations around the norm. Although patronage expanded during the 1950s, the number of bands also skyrocketed. The matrix of competition among bandleaders, as among their patrons, involved not only the manipulation of musical style and symbolism, but gossip, impression management (Goffman 1959), and traditional magical attacks and defenses. Changes in jùjú style after the war may in fact have been influenced by the absence of the pioneering Tunde King, who missed the period of transformation and expansion. He left Lagos in 1939 as a Merchant Mariner and was kept away from home for fifteen years by an *oògùn* (magical object) nailed by a jealous competitor to the pier from which he embarked.

Conclusion

The study of "music in context," which implicitly reifies musical sound and fragments the dynamic wholeness of performance as social practice, cannot produce an adequate explanation of the development of a style. If we define style not as "a collection of tunes" but rather as a constellation of values that "form the bases of discrimination between what is music and what is not music, between what is proper music and what is improper music, between what is our music and what is someone else's music, between what is good and meaningful music, and what is bad and inept music" (R. Waterman 1963:85–86), then it becomes clear that the irreducible object of ethnomusicological interest is not *the music itself*, a somewhat animistic notion, but the historically situated human subjects who perceive, learn, interpret, evaluate, produce, and respond to music.

Early jùjú, a syncretic style configuration linking a segment of the Lagosian repatriate black bourgeoisie with an expanding population of Yoruba migrant workers, was reproduced in the practical action of cosmopolitan musicians. These quintessential culture brokers, situated at interstices in the transforming colonial urban social structure, were able to create a broad audience, negotiating perceived cultural differences through the manipulation of musical symbolism. Postwar jùjú pioneers Akanbi Ege and Ayinde Bakare reproduced and expanded this multivocal symbolism by applying "deep" Yoruba socioaesthetic rules and resources, breathing new life into the style and repositioning it as the emblem of an emergent elite. Jùjú music, like the Standard Yoruba dialect disseminated in schools, media, and popular theater, played a crucial role in the invention of modern pan-Yoruba tradition (Hobsbawm and Ranger 1983); the construction of the past with an eye toward an uncertain future. "Popular arts penetrate and are penetrated by political, economic and religious institutions in ways that may not always be predictable from our own experience. . . . But popular arts are, of course, much more than constellations of social, political and economic relationships—they are expressive acts. Their most important attribute is their power to communicate" (Barber 1987:1–2).

Jùjú history suggests that the role of musical style in the enactment of identity (Feld 1984:405; Nettl 1985:19; Keil 1985) makes it not merely a reflexive but also a potentially *constitutive* factor in the patterning of cultural values and social interaction. Yoruba musicians, responding creatively to changes in the Nigerian political economy, fashioned a mode of expression that enacted, in music, language, and behavior, a syncretic metaphoric image of an ideal social order, cosmopolitan yet firmly rooted in autochthonous tradition. This dynamic style configuration, consonant with Yoruba ideologies of the "open hierarchy" as an ideal pattern of aesthetic and social organization (Lloyd 1974; Thompson 1974), allowed jùjú performance to play a role in the stereotypic reproduction (Peel 1984) of "deep" Yoruba values during a period of pervasive economic and political change.

Our understanding of modern music history can only be impeded by the a priori imposition of a schism between the musical and the social, a conceptual disjunction that reproduces, as it reflects, the institutional structure of professional academia. "Musical facts are," as Shepherd asserts, "socially located, and musical analysis, like social and cultural analysis, must be grounded in categories immanent to the object of enquiry" (1982:146–47). Sentient human actors, the creators and bearers of culture patterns, are the agents of musical continuity and change. Thus, the aesthetic and economic valuation of performance, the rhetorical and ideological functions of style, and dominant modes of musical technology and dissemination are not "contextual" factors, but fundamental aspects of musical practice taken as a whole. Was the postwar transformation of jùjú a musical or a social process? If we regard socioeconomic transaction and the production of meaning as aspects of musical practice, it was precisely and essentially both.

Historical Worldviews of Early Ethnomusicologists: An East-West Encounter in Cairo, 1932

4

Ali Jihad Racy

This article examines early ethnomusicologists' views of world music history from a comparative perspective. The Congress of Arab Music, held in Cairo in 1932, became a significant landmark in world music history. It hosted musicians and researchers from Europe and the Near East, and provided a forum for expressing various philosophical and musicological opinions. Published in a large volume titled *Kitāb Muʾtamar al-Mūsīqá al-ʿArabiyyah* (Book of the Congress of Arab Music, or *KMMʿA*),[1] the proceedings present us with a unique vantage point from which to observe two worldviews in juxtaposition. One of these was expressed primarily by the Egyptians, the other by the European participants, especially the "comparative musicologists" of the Berlin school. Here I use the term "worldview" to encompass "the collection of notions a people has of how reality is at base put together" (Geertz 1968:97), or the diachronic conceptual constructs according to which styles and traditions are fitted together in a broad scheme of world music history. I approach the topic with an interest in both the history of ethnomusicology and the history of musical attitudes in the Arab world. My aim is to observe ideologies as they are expressed and applied.

Aims and Procedures of the Congress

The congress was of prime concern to the government of Egypt, including King Fuʾād himself, and was linked to reforms intended to bring Egypt up to par with the modern "civilized" world. An introduction to the proceedings by Maḥmūd Aḥmad al-Ḥifnī (1896–1973) presents the congress as a high point in a long cultural and musical history that began with Islam, grew to a golden age in medieval times, became decadent and regressive during the Mamluk era (mid-thirteenth through late eighteenth centuries), and began to flower again with a sequence of reforms by the ruling Khedives, from Muḥammad ʿAlī (reigned 1805–1849) to King Fuʾād. The congress was ideologically and administratively connected with the Academy of Oriental Music, which was inaugurated by King Fuʾād on December 26, 1929. According to al-Ḥifnī's introduction, the king, while officially inaugurating the academy, had voiced his desire to hold an Arab music conference in Egypt. The conference would be attended by Western scholars involved in various ways with Egyptian music, "in order to discuss all that was required to make the music civilized, and to teach it and rebuild it on acknowledged scientific principles" (KMMʿA 1933:19).

The congress also owed its inception to Dr. al-Ḥifnī. Educated at the University of Berlin, where he remained for about ten years and where he met his German wife, al-Ḥifnī has been recognized as the first musicologist to return from Europe after being sent abroad by the Egyptian Ministry of Education (Bin Dhurayl 1969:15; Elsner 1973:37). Al-Ḥifnī must have known some of the major German musicologists who, reportedly due to his influence, were later invited to attend the congress (Wolf 1932:122; al-Khūlī 1974:3). Having worked with Robert Lachmann on translating al-Kindī's treatise (the topic of his doctoral dissertation, Lachmann and el-Hefny 1931), al-Ḥifnī stood at the forefront of Egyptian musical scholarship in 1932 and served as inspector of music at the Ministry of Education. He was appointed general secretary of the congress and subsequently undertook the monumental task of compiling the Book of the Congress.

The conception and preliminary planning of the congress also involved a few Western scholars, among them Curt Sachs and Baron Rodolphe d'Erlanger. In the spring of 1930 the Academy of Oriental Music, with the approval of Egypt's Ministry of Public Education, invited Sachs to come from Berlin to examine various aspects of Egyptian music. After spending several months in Egypt and meeting with officials and with the king, Sachs prepared a report that supported the king's idea of a large-scale conference (Sachs 1932:448). D'Erlanger, known for his translations of medieval Arabic treatises, visited Egypt in January of 1931 to confer with members of the Academy. Subsequently, al-Ḥifnī and d'Erlanger prepared a plan for the issues to be discussed, the scholars to be invited, and the procedures to be followed (KMMʿA 1933:20).

The government of Egypt was visibly represented throughout these early stages. When all preliminary work had been completed, the academy asked Muḥammad Ḥilmī ʿĪsá, minister of public education, to request the king to order the convening of the congress. Consequently, a royal decree of January 20, 1932, authorized the appointment of an arrangements committee, with ʿĪsá as chairman of the congress and with the entire event placed under the king's sponsorship. The committee included local administrators; the musicians Muṣṭafá Riḍā, director of the Academy of Oriental Music, and F. Cantoni, director of the Royal Opera in Cairo; and the scholars al-Ḥifnī and d'Erlanger, who was also appointed technical vice-chairman of the Arrangements Committee.

The specific aims of the congress were outlined by the organizers. In a letter presented to the ministry on January 18, 1932, Muṣṭafá Riḍā stated that, since its inception in 1913, the Oriental Music Club had pursued the goal of "reviving and systematizing Arab music so that it will rise upon an artistic foundation, as did Western music earlier," adding that the king's cultural endeavors "will bring the country to a zenith of cultural refinement and lead it to compete in the arena of civilized nations" (ibid.:23). According to the academy director, there were high hopes that through cooperation among Western and local participants, the congress would lead to the attainment of Arab music's highest goals. He emphasized the need to organize the music upon solid scientific and artistic foundations accepted by all Arab nations. The academy director specified the main issues that the congress should address: a) enhancing the "evolution" of Arab music, b) establishing a fixed musical scale, c) adopting specific symbols for transcribing Arab tunes, d) systematically organizing Arab compositions, e) investigating musical instruments and assessing their appropriateness, f) organizing music education, g) recording indigenous songs from various localities,[2] and h) discussing relevant musical and scholarly works in both printed and manuscript forms. These aims were reiterated by other Egyptian participants and administrators. Addressing the European and Near Eastern scholars at the opening of the congress, the minister of public education echoed the views of Riḍā and al-Ḥifnī. The Egyptian administration wished to revive the musical past, guard the musical present, and uplift the music progressively into the future, while maintaining its own character and attributes (ibid.:52). The minister, however, ended with a pragmatic and practical word of advice. He stressed that since the researchers did not have obvious musical clues from the distant past "they will be obliged to put their brilliant minds to the task of inventing and concocting foundations and principles appropriate for constructing the future of Arab music" (ibid.:53).

The organizational procedures of the congress reflected the objectives of its organizers. The labor was divided among seven technical committees: 1) General Issues, 2) Melodic Modes (*Maqāmāt*), Rhythmic Modes (*Īqā*ʿ*āt*), and Composition (*Ta*ʾ*līf*), 3) the Musical Scale, 4) Instruments, 5) Recording, 6) Music Education, and 7) Music History and Manuscripts. The committees were to convene for two weeks, beginning on March 14, 1932, to discuss their topics of concern. The week-long plenary session, beginning on March 28, was to discuss each committee's findings and recommendations before issuing its own recommendations and conclusions.

Participants in the congress, which took place at the Academy of Oriental Music in Cairo, came from a variety of backgrounds. Some thirty scholars, composers, and poets were Egyptian, eleven of whom were members of the specialized committees. From outside Egypt, thirteen representatives came from France and French North Africa, including Baron Carra de Vaux, an Orientalist and specialist in Arab theoretical treatises; Alexis Chottin, a Moroccan music specialist; and others affiliated with the Guimet Museum and the National Conservatory of Paris. The six German scholars were Wilhelm Heinitz (Hamburg University), Georg Schünemann (who was represented at the congress by Paul Hindemith of the Hochschule für Musik, Berlin), Erich M. von Hornbostel (director of the Phonogram Archive, Berlin University), Robert Lachmann (National Library, Berlin), Curt Sachs (director of the Museum of Musical Instruments, Berlin University) and Johannes Wolf (director of the Music Section at the National Library, Berlin). From the University of Vienna came Egon Wellesz (medievalist and Byzantine music scholar), and from Italy, Colonel Bizanti (an Orientalist) and Gusto Zampieri (professor of music history at the University of Pavia). Representing Turkey were Rauf Yekta Bey of the Istanbul Conservatory and Masud Jamil Bey (son of the celebrated Tanburi Jamil Bey) of the Radio Association of Istanbul. Béla Bartók came from the Music Academy of Budapest, Hungary, and Adolfo Salazar, a music critic and director of the music section of the Lyric Theatre of Madrid, represented Spain. From Great Britain came Henry George Farmer, a renowned medievalist, historian of Arab music, and an associate at Glasgow University. Composer Alois Hába, known in Egypt for his use of quarter-tone tuning in his compositions, was connected with the Music Academy of Prague. Representing Syria was the music theorist Father Xavier Maurice Collangettes, who was affiliated with St. Joseph University in Beirut, and from Lebanon came Wadīʿ Ṣabrā, a French-trained composer who directed the National Music Conservatory of Lebanon. In addition to these guests, others arrived with delegations from Syria, Lebanon, Iraq,

Algeria, Morocco, and Tunisia, bringing with them traditional musical ensembles and celebrated performers such as the Iraqi singer, Muḥammad al-Qubbānjī.

Issues and Perspectives

Recording. The Recording Committee, under Robert Lachmann, was concerned with the selection, recording, and documentation of local music. Attempting to lay the ground work for subsequent recording by Egyptians, the committee was dominated by Westerners, particularly comparative musicologists. In a commentary published one year after the congress, Bartók stated that he enthusiastically joined the Recording Committee because of the opportunity that recording provided for direct contact with musicians (Bartók 1933, in Suchoff 1976:38). The fourteen committee members (including Bartók, Chottin, and Hornbostel) had access to music from Egypt, Iraq, Tunisia, Algeria, Syria, Turkey, and Morocco. In Cairo they also attended Mevlevi and Laythī *dhikr* performances and a Coptic Church mass, and recorded selections from these and other repertories.

Selection of the material generally complied with the criteria and field recording procedures that had already been established by European comparative musicologists and folklorists.[3] As a matter of principle, it was decided that items of special importance should be recorded on two wax matrices for added safety. At Bartók's suggestion, the committee requested that two recordings be made and pressed of each item, in order to compare two versions of one piece by the same performer. Meanwhile, the committee decided that recording should not be restricted to pieces of "artistic" interest, but should include examples representing the salient features of various traditions. This criterion applied as well to the repertories presented by performing ensembles at the congress. Furthermore, the committee found it appropriate to avoid "music that does not adhere to Eastern melodies" and "which emulates objectionable European music in its worst form, because recordings of such music are unfit to appear in an academy whose most important goal is education" (KMMʿA 1933:49). The report added that collectors should abandon "everything that contains the features of superficial imitation of foreign and Western music (*mūsīqá ajnabiyyah*), and has no roots and no individual character in its musical construction" (ibid.:101).[4]

Preoccupation with "authentic" representations took many forms. The committee stressed that each ensemble should provide a comprehensive illustration of one multi-part form (for example, a *nawbah* or *fāṣil* or religious ceremony) so that samples of all parts would be identified and recorded. Furthermore, special emphasis was placed on folk music: "Next to the refined music of the cities, there is another simpler one. It is the music of rural groups or nomadic tribes, songs by individuals who are not musicians, but whose music is connected with their work (songs of manual labor, sailors' songs, street vendors' songs commonly found in Cairo). These songs are well-known and amidst the present rapid evolution are likely to be lost" (ibid.:95). In its report, the committee maintained that folk and tribal musics, handed down over many generations, are basic material for historical understanding of the oldest "classical" music.

Offering step by step procedures for collecting and documenting folk and tribal music, the committee recommended that further research be conducted by persons familiar with local dialects and traditions. It was also suggested that Egyptian students should receive musicological training in Europe. Europe could offer "comparative musical expertise" gained through research in various world traditions, while Egypt could provide European scholars with information about "Oriental" music (ibid.:96). On a more practical level, the committee gave explicit advice on recording equipment and appropriate ways to select and document the recorded material.

Education was also to occur through specially administered public listening sessions, in which extreme care was to be exercised in handling the fragile 78-rpm disks. The committee suggested periodic radio broadcasts of the disks and supported Bartók's idea that the congress recordings be sold without profit for the purpose of educating the public at large. In the interest of protecting the disks, the committee did not recommend their use for school instruction but explored the possibility of making available extra, specially documented renditions for teaching young students. In short, the work of the Recording Committee, which resulted in over 175 disks (recorded on a special label by His Master's Voice of England) was considered the first step toward reconstructing Arab music in its presumably ancient, uncontaminated, and distinctive form.

Melodic and Rhythmic Modes and Composition. The Committee for Melodic and Rhythmic Modes and Composition, chaired by Rauf Yekta Bey, held nineteen sessions, two of them joint sessions with the Committee for the Musical Scale. Addressing topics of prime interest to Near Eastern theorists, the committee responded to an immediate concern for systematizing the Arab modes and compositional genres in current use. Among the outstanding contributors to these reports were Shaykh ʿAlī al-Darwīsh and Baron d'Erlanger, who because of illness was unable to attend the congress.

The committee's primary interest apparently lay in the *ḥaṣr* (limiting or restricting) and *tartīb* (organizing or systematizing) of the material (ibid.: 134). The committee narrowed down the number of Egyptian *maqāmāt* to fifty-two, arranged these modes according to the fundamental note or "tonic" of each one, and analyzed them in terms of *ʿuqūd* (trichord, tetrachord, and pentachord clusters). Comparing the modes and compositional genres of various Arab countries, the committee specified the material commonly shared, thus treating "Arab music" as one broad category whose features of consistency and diversity needed to be identified and codified.

Also expressed was an interest in the process of *tabsīṭ* (simplification). One report by an Egyptian committee member, Aḥmad Amīn al-Dīk, called for reducing the number of melodic modes, as the committee attempted to simplify "the confusing multiplicity" of rhythmic modes, providing an appropriate analysis of each and illustrative musical examples in some cases (ibid.: 136).

The Musical Scale. Chaired by Father Collangettes, the Musical Scale Committee was charged with accurately determining (*taḥdīd*), a scalar model consistent with performance practice, one that could be adopted as a standard systematic reference for Arab intonation. Such a scale would be comparable to Ṣafī al-Dīn's thirteenth-century scale of seventeen intervals (limmas and commas) to the octave, or with the twelve equal semitones of the modern European chromatic scale.

The committee thus provided a comparative list of measurements in which the seven notes of the mode *rāst* appeared in both the natural and the equal-tempered quarter-tone scales. In the deliberations of the Committee for Modes and Composition, some Egyptian members passionately advocated the use of the equal-tempered scale of twenty-four quarter-tones, which had already been expounded in some Arabic writings (e.g., Arian 1924). The two Turkish participants, however, rejected the quarter-tone system on account of its arbitrary nature and inappropriateness for the accurate measurement of Near Eastern pitch.

Music Education. The Committee for Music Education, under al-Ḥifnī, addressed both practical and conceptual issues. Its tasks were to prepare detailed statistical reports about the status of music education in Egypt and to recommend modern pedagogical methods suited to the needs of Egyptian students. The committee was alarmed by figures showing that more Egyptians studied Western music than Arab music:

2,384 students of European music and 1,789 of Arab music, (a ratio of 1.33:1). The committee found that there were only three native teachers of music in Egypt for every five foreign music teachers.

The committee was "horrified" by the endemic use of pianos and Western wind instruments and by the diminishing popularity of such native instruments as the *ʿūd* and *qānūn*. The committee, however, did not see Arab and Western music as mutually exclusive. On the contrary, it recommended that the study of Arab music be a prerequisite for those students who would eventually take up Western music. At the same time, during their last year of study, students of Arab music were to "become familiar with the landmarks of Western classical music, appreciate the features of beauty in European music, and recognize the extent of Europe's musical wealth" (KMMʿA 1933:347).

In its discussions of the educational duties of composers, the committee drew up basic rules. The Egyptian composer had an obligation to derive artistic material from the local musical art and to draw inspiration from indigenous contexts rather than from the foreign sources of the West. "He should not borrow from a Western art which has already matured and completed its development, but instead he must cultivate the art of his own country, uplift it, and move with it toward higher stages of evolution" and "escort the local art along its own path of progress" (ibid.:347–48).

Such protectionism notwithstanding, the committee still looked to Europe as the source for systematic solutions and the provider of theoretical expertise. The basic assumption was that European methods and musical techniques, considered the most "evolved" and "scientific," had to provide the form for Arab musical content in its path toward "progress" (ibid.:349).

Music History and Manuscripts. The eight general sessions and six branch meetings of the Committee for Music History and Manuscripts, under Farmer, addressed six main issues: 1) surveying Western and Near Eastern writings that discuss the history of Arab music, 2) finding ways to publish scholarly works in Arabic on the various epochs of Arab music history, 3) preparing a report on the history of the Arab musical scale and its "evolution," 4) locating the most important Arab manuscripts on music, 5) identifying the manuscripts that have been published and finding the means to publish others, and 6) determining the extent to which Arab countries might benefit from a program to publish manuscripts on music. Muḥammad al-Hajjāj of Egypt stated that the study of old manuscripts would make it possible to understand the phases through which Arab music had passed in its "evolution" and would help in ascertaining the status of this music during its flourishing medieval period (ibid.:381).

Musical Instruments. The Musical Instruments Committee, headed by Curt Sachs, dealt with concerns that proved to be both popular and controversial: a) to decide what instruments should or should not be used in Arab music, b) to evaluate some proposed organological innovations, and c) to recommend modifications of instruments already in use. Perhaps the key issue of the committee's debates was whether or not European musical instruments should be utilized in Arab music along with local instruments.

One opinion, held mostly by Westerners within the committee, was that instruments were determined by local musical styles and aesthetics: "as history shows from 5000 years ago to the present" each musical tradition has instruments that suit its style and expression, which could only change as the music itself changes (ibid.:393). These members contended that most Western instruments were bound "to disfigure the beauty of Arab music" and should be prohibited. A contrary view favored the assimilation of European instruments, on the premise that these presumably more "advanced" and "scientific" instruments "will advance the renaissance of Arab music and move it forward toward progress" (ibid.:393). Protagonists of all opinions however agreed that European instruments that had fixed twelve-semitone tunings and lacked the appropriate microtonal modifications were unsuited for playing Arab music.

The committee approved some modifications in the manufacture of indigenous instruments and recommended encouraging the use of such neglected instruments as the classical Turkish *tanbur* and *kemençe,* both of which had been used earlier in Egypt.[5] The committee also supported Sachs's earlier suggestion that a national museum for Near Eastern instruments be established, and urged that Sachs be entrusted with its organization by virtue of his expertise in this area.

In regard to the European instruments already used in Egypt, the committee saw no point in criticizing the inclusion of the violin among local traditional instruments, given its widespread use in the Near East. However, the committee discouraged the use of the cello for enriching the lower-octave registers "because the excessive pathos and sentimentality as well as the domineering quality of its sound make it incompatible with Egyptian instruments" (ibid.:395).

Among the most debated issues throughout the congress was the role of the piano in Arab music. Many Egyptians at the congress regarded the piano as the instrument most emblematic of European civilization and contended that the piano could help standardize intonation. If properly retuned, it could assist in fixing an agreed-upon Arab scale, especially the one consisting of twenty-four equal-tempered quarter tones. Wadīʿ Ṣabrā of Lebanon felt that a basic Arab scale fixed through a keyboard instrument would be a progressive step in music education and would contribute to the future development of some form of Arab polyphony (ibid.:418). Thus, through its stable tones, polyphonic possibilities, and history of equal temperament, the piano was regarded by many Egyptians as an indispensable instrument of progress in Egyptian and, more generally, in Arab music.[6]

The committee's report did not conceal the disagreement between the Europeans, who expressed misgivings about the Arab use of the piano, and the overwhelming majority of the Egyptian participants, who voiced their enthusiasm for the instrument. Failing to reach a consensus on the issue, the committee resorted to voting on two rather diplomatically phrased motions. A proclamation that keyboard instruments in their present formats were unsuitable for Arab music carried the signatures of Masud Jamil, Wadīʿ Ṣabrā, Sachs, Hornbostel, and Hindemith. A second motion stated that, although unsuited for Arab use in their present configuration, chromatic keyboard instruments could become a medium for Arab music if modified to play microtonal intonation in accordance with the scale to be determined by the congress. This motion was supported by Muḥammad Fatḥī, Najīb Naḥḥās, Aḥmad Amīn al-Dīk, Alois Hába, Farmer, and Cantoni. Because the vote did not exhibit a clear majority (five to six), the piano issue was tabled for further discussion in the plenary session.

General Issues. The Committee for General Issues consisted of ten members from varying scholarly backgrounds, including Farmer, Hornbostel, Lachmann, and Sachs, who all worked under Baron Carra de Vaux, the committee chairman. Responsible for addressing encompassing issues and concerns, the committee decided to wait for the specialized committees' findings to come out, and to comment on these findings during the plenary session of the congress.

The Plenary Session. The plenary meetings in which the individual committee reports were presented and debated involved larger and more diverse groups of participants. The Recording Committee's report, presented at the first meeting, on March 28, was unanimously and enthusiastically approved. The second session, on March 29, featured the report on modes, rhythmic patterns, and compositional genres, followed by individual commentaries, mostly by Egyptians. These comments generally expressed dissatisfaction that the Committee for the Musical Scale had failed to produce a "definite" and "exact" theoretical scale, supposedly indispensable for precise measurements of the various modal scales. The third session, on March 30, devoted to the musical scale, began with a presentation by Carra de Vaux, the chairman, defending the committee's work: there was no such thing as a simple underlying theoretical scale applicable to all modes, and the scale of each mode was to be ascertained separately, as the committee had done, while bearing in mind that such modes differed tonally from one Arab country to another.

In the fourth session, on March 31, the report of the Committee for Music Education was favorably received. Farmer, Sachs, and others suggested ways to make the study of Arab music history more accessible in Egypt. The fifth session, on April 1, featured the report of the Committee for Music History and Manuscripts, which was accepted and followed by a few further suggestions from al-Ḥifnī.

The sixth session, on April 2, was devoted to the report of the Musical Instruments Committee, read both in Arabic translation (by the general secretary of the congress) and in French (by the chairman, Curt Sachs). A climactic point of the session, and perhaps of the entire congress, was reached in a carefully prepared speech by Muḥammad Fatḥī, an Egyptian member of the committee. He thanked the chairman for his fair handling of the diverse and often conflicting views among committee members and for his recommendation to bring unresolved issues, primarily the piano controversy, before the plenary session for further consideration, adding that this was the only such case of deferral in the congress. Addressing the Western scholars who had objected to the use of Western instruments on the basis that they were incompatible with the delicate sound and monophonic qualities of Arab music, Fatḥī advanced the view that depriving Oriental music of the benefits of tonally fixed instruments "will gravely threaten the future of our music and may even bring about its demise" (KMMᶜA 1933:425). He argued that instruments, like scientific inventions, transcend culture and nationality, and that since European instruments were scientifically advanced tools, they could aid the advancement of Arab music:

> Before you pronounce the verdict that our music should be confined to its distinctive style, let us appeal to your own conscience. If we were to ask you to exchange our music with what you consider charmingly beautiful in your own music, would you willingly accept this exchange? You see in our music a structural beauty comparable to the beauty of arabesque design, but in your views it is a beauty devoid of meaning. You would refuse to apply the same perspective to your own music, which conveys a meaning much more noble and lofty than its structural beauty, namely

> its spiritual meaning and the strength and inspiration it embodies. (ibid.:435)

Fatḥī offered his European counterparts three further points to consider:

> First, do not judge our music with your own ears or through your own feelings and emotional criteria. It is imperative that you judge it through our own ears and to use our own feelings as criteria, because every nation has its own sentiments and feelings.
>
> Second, you should not judge our music on the basis of its present condition. If you find in it faults here and there, the flaw is not in our music but in most of those who work with it and in the dire need for true study in both artistic and scientific respects, and in this realm you honorable Western gentlemen can offer us the greatest service.
>
> Third, you should not judge our music by the nature of its instruments, which out of polite flattery you consider to be tender and delicate but which are in fact weak and fail to satisfy all the desirable goals of the music. (ibid.:426)

In his statement, Fatḥī addressed the specific "inadequacies" of Arab instruments, stating that these artifacts were suited only for one type of human emotion. He expressed profound regret that the trademark of Arab instruments was the emotion of love and romance: "that is why our instruments are imbued with the qualities of whining and pining" (ibid.:427).[7] Fatḥī mentioned that during the Middle Ages, Europe had borrowed Eastern instruments that became the ancestors of modern European ones: "if your instruments had developed from ours, today we would like to develop our instruments from yours, so do not be stingy toward us. Someday, we would like to return them to you with the highest level of perfection" (ibid.:427).

Among the European participants, Lachmann challenged a view advanced earlier by Naḥḥās about the emotional limitations of Arab instruments. Lachmann maintained that expressing varying sentiments did not depend upon the construction of the instruments. Farmer, on the other hand, largely agreed with Naḥḥās's assessment and warned that, if the congress did not approve the use of an Eastern version of the piano, Egypt would be compelled to use the Western piano instead, regardless of this or other congresses. He maintained that the introduction of such an instrument would help to curtail the endemic use of the Western piano in Egyptian homes and would assist in the preservation of traditional music (ibid.:433).

In the seventh session, on April 3, the chairman of the Committee for General Issues, Carra de Vaux, explained why his committee's work had been deferred to the plenary session. He reintroduced the committee's main task of addressing the question, "What are the best means to be followed for the systematization of Arab music, making it civilized so that it can fulfill all the goals expected of music in general, while maintaining its own individual quality?"

In this session another major presentation, by Robert Lachmann, constituted a sort of philosophical finale for the congress and underscored the obviously strong profile of Western, especially German, musicologists. His presentation addressed in part the arguments leveled by Fatḥī against the ideas of Sachs and his committee on instruments. Lachmann argued that the differences separating Arab music from European music did not make the latter more advanced. He also distinguished between borrowing European science and copying European music: while "chemical terminology applies whether in Egypt or in Europe," art and particularly music "is the spirit of a nation and can change only when such change emanates from the depths of the very source of that music" (ibid.:439).

Stressing that traditions must be nourished and supported, Lachmann introduced broad crosscultural views characteristic of his orientation as a comparative musicologist. He stated that one way to preserve music is to demonstrate how it has developed in different nations, bearing in mind that in each nation music has maintained its own individual character. He added that the authorities should encourage musical preservation through public performances on solo instruments and by giving prizes in schools. Referring to the findings of his Recording Committee, he noted that research had shown each separate area to have its own individual music, which was not to be destroyed for the sake of any other music. Finally, he offered an overview of the musical scholar's work: "In our concern for the future of Eastern music, we are not interested merely in the artistic level of the professionals and the benefit of the listeners but also in the people's musical feelings, whose manifestations frequently emanate spontaneously throughout daily life" (ibid.:440).

The session concluded with a terse official statement formulated through discussions among Rabaud, Wellesz, Hindemith, Hornbostel, and al-Ḥifnī: "The Congress members, who unanimously appreciate the beauty of Arab music of the past and present, object to all forms of blind imitation of Western music. While recommending the need to avoid all that impedes the advancement of Arab music, a free advancement in all respects, the group stresses that the musical education of Egyptians must take place in accordance with the traditions of Arab music and with the decisions made by the sixth committee, the one for music education, and with the decisions approved by the Congress" (ibid.:442).

The plenary session took place concurrently with a series of concerts by various local and visiting groups. Extending from March 15 to April 2, the concerts were arranged by the Recording Committee (Wolf 1932:122) and attended by the public as well as by members of this committee. Members of other committees did not attend, reportedly because they were too busy holding discussions and writing their reports (KMMʿA 1933:443).

Historical Premises

We have seen that the deliberations and decisions of the congress were linked to broader ideologies. Although we cannot assume uniform ways of thinking within each participating group, patterns of debate and interaction highlight a basic rift between Egyptians and Europeans, and to some extent among the Europeans or the Egyptians themselves.

The Egyptian views of music history were deeply influenced by the West. European musical concepts and attitudes may have entered Egypt through various channels, among them the European musicians and music teachers who came to Cairo after the Napoleonic invasion. Western musical outlooks and criteria may have gained further ground through the deliberate cultural reforms of modern rulers such as Muḥammad ʿAlī and Ismāʿīl (Racy 1983:164), while the concepts of social Darwinism and the notion of Western musical supremacy must have gained special momentum during the Victorian era, and during Britain's colonial domination of Egypt from 1882 to 1922. The Egyptian assumption that music "is one of the most important manifestations of civilization among nations" (KMMʿA 1933:23) may remind us of the idea that "if architecture is the king of the arts, music is the queen" (Gilman 1909:532). However, it may also contrast with Edward Lane's observation that early nineteenth-century Egyptians, though fond of music, considered it utterly frivolous and "unworthy to employ any portion of the time of a man of sense" (Lane 1973:353).

One basic Egyptian premise was that there were two historical realities, corresponding to two basic world entities: the "Orient" and the "Occident." In the nineteenth and early twentieth centuries, numerous travelers, missionaries, and "Orientalists" wrote books treating the Orient as the exotic counterpart and cultural antithesis of the Occident (Said 1979:1–2). Similarly, many Arabs and Near Easterners referred to their own world as the "Orient" and established historical dualisms between, for example, *mūsīqá sharqiyyah* (Oriental music, that of the Arabic-speaking world and the Near East) and such contrasting categories as *mūsīqá gharbiyyah* and *mūsīqá ifranjiyyah* (both meaning Western music).

Although at the congress the word "Oriental" was sometimes replaced with "Arab" or even "Egyptian," the binary view of world music history was expressed in some basic ways. The title of "The Academy of Oriental Music," which hosted the congress, implied this duality. More explicit were the frequent comparisons made by Egyptian and other Near Eastern participants between the two musical worlds and the ideological motto that Arab music should reach the historical level of achievement of its Western counterpart. The local planners considered a congress attended by both Near Easterners and Westerners to be an international event and a music curriculum of Arab and European music theory and history to be complete and ideal.

The Egyptian assumptions echoed countless nineteenth- and early twentieth-century writings by Western travelers and Orientalists. Descriptive works by such Western travelers as Flaubert (Steegmuller 1979:9), Warner (1887), and Lynch (1890) had made disparaging remarks about Arab music and musical instruments. Many European musical scholars (including Parry 1889; Wallascheck 1893; W. Pratt 1907) had contended that the "primitive" music of Africa and Asia and the "semi-civilized" music of "Oriental or high civilizations" were similar to the early and less-advanced historical manifestations of European music. Some Western writers who dealt specifically with Egyptian or Arab music history had also presented their material in linear and progressive evolutionary formats. Salvador-Daniel had claimed that, historically, modern Arab music was still at the level of the European troubadour and minstrel (1915:48); Jules Rouanet subsequently discussed the origins of Arab music in a step-by-step scenario beginning with functional magic in pre-Islamic Arabia and leading to aesthetic and theoretical creations at the height of medieval Islamic civilization (Rouanet 1922:2800).

The Egyptian belief in Western historical superiority within a dualistic world context led to the acceptance of Western music as the ideal referential model. However, the linear concept of historical evolution was modified by the realization that in the Middle Ages Arab music had already reached a zenith of development culminating in the sophisticated musical life of the ʿAbbasid courts and in a wealth of musical treatises. Accordingly, Arab music and culture were historically sophisticated and capable of entering a new cycle of growth after a long phase of "decadence." By 1932, Khedieval Egypt had already gained independence from the Ottomans and the British. Egyptians had experienced major nationalistic movements, including a popular uprising in 1919 against the British occupation, and they had seen the formation of influential political parties associated with such political leaders as Musṭafá Kāmil (1874–1908), Saʿd Zaghlūl (1856–1927), and others (Zāyid 1973:21). Having witnessed a series of reforms under its modern Western-minded rulers and having maintained close contacts with Europe, Egypt was often described as a progressive country and a leading proponent of the modern Arab musical renaissance.

The congress planners and local participants envisioned musical rebirth along the evolutionary patterns outlined by Western historians. Since evolutionary change meant growth or "progress from simple to complex" (Allen 1962 [1939]:287), monophonic Arab or "Oriental" music had to become polyphonic, the aurally transmitted music had to yield to "scientifically" notated music, the single sentiment of love supposedly predominant in Arab music had to be supplanted by a wide range of sentiments and dramatic means, small ensembles had to become larger, and local instruments had to become more numerous and varied in their timbres and tessituras. Since evolution also meant proceeding from unsystematic diversity to simple uniformity, the role of the congress was to render such entities as scales, modes, and intervals more concise, systematized, and standardized. In the process, Egypt had to emulate and borrow from Europe, which the congress planners accepted as representing the most advanced stage of evolutionary progress. As one Egyptian participant put it, imported forms would enhance the music without impairing its inner expression. Meanwhile, there were apparently no clear ideas about such issues as: how would European music make Egyptian music more advanced without making it less Egyptian; what were the exact boundaries or inalienable components of Egyptian music; and how, if at all, were modernization and progress different from Westernization?

The Oriental-Occidental dichotomy was not alien to the comparative musicologists (see Lachmann 1929). However, these scholars' historical visions differed significantly from the dualistic worldviews of the locals. They believed that all cultures were historically related through distant evolutionary common grounds (Nettl 1984a:36), although Europe's music was in some definite ways unique. Furthermore, their historical conceptions of world music recognized the individual musical traditions, including both the Egyptian and the European, as unique and discrete entities rather than open-ended domains on a single continuum.

The evolutionary thinking of the comparative musicologists contrasted sharply with the revolutionary attitudes of the local scholars and bureaucrats. At the congress, the comparative musicologists encountered local music theorists, critics, administrators, piano designers, and some theoretically minded musicians, as well as a diverse group of other Europeans, conservatory teachers, music historians, and avant-garde composers. This heterogeneous body of thinkers and artists was concerned with local musical "reform" directed toward "inventing and concocting" the foundations for Arab music (KMMᶜA 1933:53). To the comparative musicologists, this aim may have posed an interesting challenge, partly because it implied the creation of practical and experimental solutions in the form of applied comparative musicology. However, "reform," as construed by the local participants, emphasized cultural obsolescence rather than permanence and promoted a type of modernization that went against the historical worldviews of these Western scholars.

In the overall evolutionary scheme of the comparativists, musical change was organic and deeply rooted in a people's character and experience. The view of music as a racial expression permeating both folk and art music appeared in Hornbostel's reflections on his visit to Cairo: "The foreigner is struck by the characteristics of the race because they are so unusual: by the feather-light strides and gestures, by the metallic and dusky texture of the voice, whether a boy hawking his wares, or a child sobbing. These characteristics return unmistakably both in song and in art music. Art song can further develop physical characteristics, but cannot suppress racial characteristics" (1933:17). At the same time, Hornbostel acknowledged that non-Western singers had successfully emulated Western singing techniques. In reference to the artistry of Egypt's celebrated singer Umm Kulthūm, who performed in an evening concert at the congress, he remarked that at one point the singer "no doubt intentionally switched to a European *bel canto* style," adding that " 'the barbarians' also know that style and know how to sing it" (ibid.).

The comparativists regarded induced change as a form of tampering with the natural flow of history and as a somewhat futile or counterproductive endeavor. Historiographic notions that cultures could become "too old" or "too stagnant," or that a "flowering civilization" could simply replace a "decadent" one, did not seem to play a significant role in their thinking. This distinguished them from the classicists, Arabists, and philologists (Farmer, Carra De Vaux, and Collangettes), who treated the concept of music with reference to a "golden" past and with particular attention to the speculative and historiographic aspects of musical research. The comparative musicologists accepted the past as a package and looked at it in its entirety as a foundation for the music of the present.

A further conception held by the comparative musicologists was that historical development was objective and individually relative to each culture. Thus, in a poetic analogy, Sachs likened Egypt to a mother with eternal youth, and stated that the "agelessness" and "eternity" of Egypt's music and culture did not diminish its youthful image (KMMᶜA 1933).[8] In his climactic congress presentation, Lachmann addressed the Orientals' misunderstanding of the concept of civilization and their misconceptions about the meaning of progress (ibid.:439). He maintained that Arab music "has a wealth of melodies and modal material and has no need for harmony," and warned against unjustifiable and harmful changes that would cause the music to lose some of its integral characteristics and instruments, an outcome "for which we cannot allow ourselves to be responsible" (ibid.:439–40).

This relativist outlook was connected with a strong interest in "authentic" musical expressions, especially those emanating from unique and prolonged evolutionary processes. By comparison with the Egyptian modernist rhetoric of the 1920s and early 1930s, the language of the European scholars at the congress featured a plethora of conservationist and purist labels, ranging from "music that emulates objectionable European melodies" (ibid.:49) to music that was "most genuinely traditional" (ibid.:95). In a 1932 article about the congress, Sachs seemed disturbed by the stringent measures of Westernization taken by the Turkish "dictatorship" but spoke positively of the Egyptian people's noticeable adherence to their musical traditions (Sachs 1932:28). However, in the following year Hornbostel bemoaned the threats of "imported European art forms" to the indigenous musical expressions of the Arab world: "One is reminded of the replacement of the Arab violin by ours, a replacement which is virtually complete in Islamic countries. This might signify nothing other than an improvement in tonal color and fullness but that is a mistake, for with the instrument comes our technique, our vibrato, and, horrors, our sentimentality" (1933:17).

The comparativists' emphasis upon the presumably older and less-contrived genres was also reflected by their strong interest in rural music. While the Egyptians and most other participants focused their attention upon urban secular music and its history, rather than the "archaic museum of folk songs" (KMMᶜA 1933:393), these Western scholars saw regional and folk repertories as pure and dignified. In his 1933 commentary on the congress, Bartók wrote: "It is my belief that city-Arab music generally is far behind Arab peasant music with regard to animation and originality (I had the same opinion nineteen years ago, during my study-tour of Algeria). The urban music frequently sounds stilted, affected, and artificial; the peasant music, on the other hand, gives the impression of being a far more spontaneous and vivid manifestation despite its primitiveness" (Bartók 1933, in Suchoff 1976:38).

In light of the comparativists' historical worldviews, musical reform had to be self-generated and locally inspired. Accordingly, musical rejuvenation had to rise on the basis of legitimately indigenous models and through reversal of the undesirable trends of modernization and Westernization. While the historians, educators, and philologists sought reform models in books, manuscripts, and curricular plans, the comparative musicologists focused their attention on the music itself and hoped that the congress and future recordings would make the academy a key archival establishment capable of using the recorded material to instruct future generations. These scholars' prescription for reform was in essence an application of the theories and research methods of Western comparative musicology.

Conclusion

Aimed at implementing reform in Arab music in general and Egyptian music in particular, the Cairo Congress of 1932 enabled participants from Europe and the Near East to work in small, specialized teams and larger groups, and to discuss music with reference to the wider issues of historical change, cultural identity, and progress. I have focused on the various historical premises expressed at the congress in an effort to gain further insight into early ethnomusicologists' historical concepts.

Advancing their goals in the form of a modernistic cultural and political ideology, the Egyptians explained the entire idea of the congress in reference to their views of world history and their Arab and Egyptian self-image. They defined their historical world reality in terms of two unequal entities: the Western world, whose history had reached a mature stage of progress and civilization, and an Eastern or "Oriental" world, whose history had reached a peak in the distant past and had been disrupted by a lengthy epoch of "decline" and "stagnation." Accordingly, in order for the Orient to "catch up" with Western civilization, it had to turn to Western models. The predominant Egyptian approach to reform was expedient and practical-minded. Evolution was conceived of as a phenomenon that could be deliberately activated and caused to move in leaps and shortcuts; musical progress could be "concocted" through administrative "recipes" and resolutions by committees of local and Western experts.

The comparative musicologists and some other Europeans at the congress approached musical reform with different historical paradigms. Their musical worldview was global rather than dualistic. At the same time, they recognized history as an indisputable and inviolable determinant of culture, stressing that, since world historical processes were complex in their own unique ways, musics of the world were discrete and distinctly different. Their pluralistic attitude was combined with a relativistic openness, as they attempted to challenge the Egyptian belief in European musical superiority in favor of a nonjudgmental and nonutilitarian perspective that deemed all local musical profiles legitimate and equally valid. Furthermore, in contrast to most other congress participants, who based their concerns on such historical distinctions as "golden age," "cultural decline," and "progressive awakening," these scholars accepted local histories in their totalities as individual and organic processes. Considering folk music to be the purest manifestation of history and a living embodiment of the collective "spirit" of the people, the comparativists regarded induced change as artificial and the imposition of one musical system upon the other as futile tampering with local history. Instead, reform was approached through emphasis on permanence and continuity, with the aim of restoring what was considered the truthful and historically determined character of the indigenous music. More specifically, the local music had to retain its quaint and individualistic qualities, criteria that were conceived with European music as an antithetical standard of reference. In practical terms, reform had to be instituted systematically through fieldwork, recording the "authentic" music, and using the recordings as models for "reviving" Egypt's music and for educating future generations of musicians.

In this study, my attempt to reconstruct historical worldviews must be read and understood in relative terms. My own interpretation of history has been restricted and shaped by the nature of my data. The congress minutes and reports were offered in Arabic or French largely as impersonal and formal renditions, with individual statements possibly condensed or edited. Although I have attempted to use different types of sources, including the post-congress commentaries of European and Egyptian participants, the reconstruction of past modes of thinking remains, like other historical pursuits, an interpretive activity.

Keeping in mind that ethnographic insight and revealing introspection demand more than first-person narratives (Feld 1987:190), I am aware of the difficulty of accurately assessing my own biases in writing this synopsis. My interest in the subject may have been influenced significantly by my Near Eastern background and my involvement with some of the issues discussed at the congress. In some ways I identify with the role played by an individual such as Maḥmūd al-Ḥifnī, whose background and education derived from both Near Eastern and Western scholarly traditions. Yet my own historical worldview is also that of a late twentieth-century ethnomusicologist who cannot escape the cultural and historical premises of his own discipline.

Similarly interpretive would be the tasks of ascertaining whether or not the European views changed the minds of Egyptians about musical reform, and what impact, if any, the Egyptians made upon the European comparative musicologists or upon the history of ethnomusicology. The congress as a whole made some contributions to local music research and education, while the comparative musicologists and other Europeans who shared some of their attitudes provided ammunition to a few traditional-minded Egyptian writers (see Rizq 1936:109; Mansī 1965:26). In addition to the formation of record and instrument collections in conjunction with the academy, the role played by such local scholars as al-Ḥifnī seems to have gained momentum. In 1935, the academy, known then as the Royal Academy of Arab Music, fulfilled one of the recommendations of the congress by issuing a journal that presented the congress policies and views, *al-Mūsīqá,* or *La Musique,* edited by al-Ḥifnī. In addition to presenting articles in Arabic on Egyptian music history and theory, and on major European composers, the journal published excerpts from the congress reports in French. It also included articles in English and French by Western scholars including Hans Hickmann, A. H. Fox-Strangways, and Helen Roberts. Furthermore, al-Ḥifnī and his fellow educators in Egypt appear to have succeeded in implementing one of the policies of the congress by arranging that the national radio station of Egypt (established in 1934) broadcast congress recordings with commentaries during the year 1935 (Iqtirāḥ 1935:38).[9]

In retrospect, however, the direct impact of the comparative musicologists upon Egyptian thinkers seems to have been minimal, if one considers that the Oriental-Occidental worldview continues to underscore the musical policies of local governments and institutions. The ideology of modernizing and Europeanizing Egyptian music while maintaining its local identity has prevailed at subsequent musical conferences (see *al-Ḥalaqah* 1964:7). Meanwhile, the concept of *taṭwīr* (to develop or to cause something to evolve) is still widely idealized as the aim of all serious musical endeavors, and Western music, commonly referred to as *mūsīqá ʿālamiyyah* (international music), is still commonly accepted as a superior artistic expression (see Racy 1981:11). The idea of introducing quarter-tone keyboard instruments has by no means died out.[10] The congress field recordings are seldom heard, or heard of, and appear to be of much greater interest to curious Western archivists and researchers than to Arab theorists, let alone music students and professional musicians. "Folk" and "tribal" genres do not constitute a topic of prime concern for local theorists and musical scholars.

One may also associate the schism between the two groups with broader differences in scholarly orientations. While comparative musicologists combined their high esteem for history with basic concepts from the social sciences (Nettl 1984a:38), the Egyptian thinkers based their diachronic ideas and attitudes upon musical historicism. As described in the congress reports, the Egyptian premises seemed more compatible with those of Western historiographers and Orientalists than with those of the social scientists. It is noteworthy that al-Ḥifnī's primary interest, as demonstrated by his congress committee work and by his publications (see el-Hefni 1956), was not comparative musicology but historical musicology, a phenomenon that may have rendered his work more in line with the favored Arab and Egyptian modes of scholarship. Today, in addition to translations of major European music histories, there is an impressive number of Egyptian biographical studies of local artists and general historical surveys that present late nineteenth- and early twentieth-century stylistic development in characteristically progressive chronological formats.

To the Western scholars, the visit to Egypt provided a number of challenging thoughts and observations. In Cairo, these visitors saw pyramids, temples, and other vestiges of ancient civilizations standing next to modern edifices and an opera house of the finest European standards. During the evening concerts they listened to the highly respected singer Umm Kulthūm, whose style was not devoid of European influences. Her accompanying orchestra members are shown in photographs wearing black tuxedos and bow ties, as well as the traditional Near Eastern *fez* (red round hat). In Cairo, these guests were, as they put it, very graciously treated by a king and an administration that had no qualms about seeking Western solutions to their national quests. At the congress they also found that some Near Eastern scholars had been well exposed to European music and musical thinking, but held historical worldviews different from their own. During the plenary session, they heard one Egyptian who was an ardent believer in Western superiority, but whose plea for Egyptian music to be judged by Egyptian ears now reminds us of contemporary ethnomusicologists arguing in favor of the insider's vantage point.

It may be impossible to assess the impact of such a mixed bag of ideas and suggestions upon scholars who appeared to hold tenaciously to their historical beliefs, but who also had distanced themselves from the ethnocentric and judgmental attitudes characteristic of European music historians of the early twentieth century. Hornbostel wrote that "it was certainly a privilege for the European guests to hear Arab music in its full liveliness and natural surroundings, although the extent to which we can understand a foreign music is questionable. . . . Most difficult to understand, and likely impossible, is the expression of feeling of foreign music" (1933:16–17). In similarly general terms, Sachs observed that "aside from the deep impressions of the country, we European advisors have learned much and brought home with us a surfeit of musical perceptions, which otherwise will hardly ever be offered to us" (Sachs 1932:449).

It is conceivable that coming into contact with extreme views about Western superiority and modernization at the Cairo Congress and comparable East-West encounters may have caused these scholars in the long run to distance themselves even further from the implications of "evolution" and "progress" (see Sachs 1965:210). At the same time, it is likely that the endemic forces of change and the irreversible trends of modernization brought about further flexibility and moved comparative musicology closer to the ethnomusicological values currently proclaimed. In one of his later works, Curt Sachs (1881–1959) expressed his historical attitudes in such statements as: "neither do I praise the past nor do I chide the present"; "I do not exalt the primitive or despise the Westerner"; "I do not want to exchange what we possess for what we have lost"; and "I do not trade the B minor Mass for an Eskimo melody" (1965:221).

The comparative musicologists at the Cairo Congress were a group of researchers with an ideological identity that distinguished them from a large number of European and Near Eastern music theorists, composers, and historians. In view of the historical links between these pioneering comparative musicologists and modern ethnomusicology, we may wonder about the distinctive nature of our own historical paradigms and about the manner in which we apply our present ideologies in worldwide scholarly encounters.

NOTES

1. In this article, information about the congress is derived primarily from this Arabic work printed in 1933. I am thankful to Virginia Danielson for helping me obtain a copy of this source. In some cases, the French version was also consulted (*Recueil des Travaux du Congrès de Musique Arabe 1934*). Quotations from Arabic sources are translations by myself. I am grateful to Atesh Sonneborn for his assistance in translating German works and to Ergun Tamer for his help with the Turkish articles of Rauf Yekta Bey. I also thank Anne Rasmussen, Barbara Racy, and others who helped in the preparation of the manuscript.

2. The word "recording" here was a translation of the general Arabic

concept of *tasjīl*, which means "to take down" or "to document," as well as "to sound record."

3. The strong impact of the comparative musicologists on the congress procedures appears clearly through the close and almost verbatim resemblance between some passages in the congress proceedings and prior published statements regarding fieldwork, for example by Bartók (see Suchoff 1976).

4. The word *ajnabī* means "foreign" but largely implies "Western" or "European." In this essay it has been consistently translated as "foreign," although the reader needs to be aware of its distinct Western connotations.

5. The *tanbur* and *kemençe* were played in nineteenth-century Egypt, probably by Turks (see Villoteau 1823:246); however, these two instruments are virtually unknown in Egypt today. The tanbur was favored by some committee members for its rich and enchanting sound, and because its fretted long neck was useful for devising a standard theoretical scale.

6. In the 1920s, many Egyptian songs were specially transcribed for the piano, and in 1932 no less than 3,232 pianos were imported from Germany and Switzerland and sold in a store on ʿImād al-Dīn Street (Berque 1972:332). Yet ironically, today the piano may be the least attractive instrument for Arab musicians and exists in Arab homes primarily as a Western instrument. On the other hand, electronic keyboard instruments that have been adjusted microtonally have been widely used.

7. The opinion that Arab music was preoccupied with amorous themes had broader implications. Rauf Yekta Bey recalled that during a congress-related visit to the office of the under-secretary of education, Mr. ʿAbd al-Fattāḥ Ṣabri, the official maintained that Egyptian families were complaining about the excessive sensuality of popular song texts, and for that reason preferred that their children listen to Western songs instead (Sürelsan 1972:6).

8. Sachs's cleverly chosen analogy may have been inspired by the popular Egyptian proverb, "Miṣr umm al-dunyā," literally "Egypt [or Cairo] is the mother of the world," which could refer to both the wonderful quality of the city or the country, and the old age and dignity of Cairo or Egypt, both of which are sometimes referred to as *Miṣr* or *Maṣr*.

9. A commentary in *al-Mūsīqá* was very critical of the chaotic way in which these records were broadcast. Reportedly, single disks from Turkey, Iraq, Tunis, and other areas were presented in juxtaposition, thus providing a scattered and unsatisfactory impression of the musical styles represented (Iqitirāḥ 1935:38–39).

10. At the congress, the Committee for Instruments examined about half a dozen pianos featuring various "Oriental" tunings. These pianos were made by inventors such as ʿAryān (Émile Arian) and Hába. The committee reached a generally unfavorable conclusion, largely because of the impracticality of playing them. However, as recently as 1975, one Syrian woman submitted a quarter-tone piano of her own design at an international music conference I attended in Baghdad.

PART TWO

Authority and Interpretation

The Interpretation of History and the Foundations of Authority in the Visnupur *Gharānā* of Bengal 5

Charles Capwell

In musical traditions that invest individuals or a repertory with an aura of authority, the significance of history lies in its ability to establish and recount the origin, acquisition, and transmission of that authority. In the history of the establishment of the various *gharānās* of Hindustani music, for example, lies an affirmation of the ultimate authority of the musical tradition stemming from the Mughal courts of the fifteenth and sixteenth centuries. A kind of conspiracy in which the individual conspirators accept special status by affirming that of their fellows, this kind of history is a cultural artifact of a Great Tradition. The history of the way in which an individual gharānā has received that Great Tradition, however, may reveal cultural patterns of a more regional kind.[1] In examining the history of the Visnupur gharānā, we will see how this artifact of the Great Tradition of Hindustani music also expresses cultural patterns of a peculiarly Bengali sort.

The part of South Asia known as Bengal now actually constitutes two entities: the sovereign state of Bangladesh and the provincial state of West Bengal within India. Bengal lies near the northeastern extremity of the South Asian cultural area, and through it, the sacred Ganges River exits via many mouths into the Bay of Bengal. Despite being constantly blessed by this holy asperges, the area has always been viewed with something like contempt and suspicion by the descendants of the ancient invaders who settled to the north and west. The invaders who settled in this latter area came to think of it as the "Aryan heartland" because they considered their language and culture to be noble or "Aryan" in comparison to that of the indigenous peoples. Bengal has always been at the periphery of this Aryan heartland, if not beyond its pale.

The contemporary equivalent of Aryavarta is Hindustan, and the style of art music in this region, the *hindustānī paddhati,* remains the musical emblem of this cultural area. Two of its greatest and most widely known exponents are the Bengali instrumentalists, Ravi Shankar and Ali Akbar Khan. Despite the unparalleled eminence of these two Bengalis in the "Life of Music in North India"—to borrow the title of Daniel Neuman's book (1980)—the *hindustānī paddhati* is, in a sense, an alien art in Bengal, although, like some other components of the culture of Aryavarta that have been imported and imposed, it has been willingly adopted there.

Neuman states a conviction that "Delhi is the birthplace, ancestral home, and historical center of North Indian music culture. Other areas, important as some have now become, are nevertheless derivative from Delhi tradition" (1980:12). Indicated in the phrase "important as some have now become" is the fact that some of the areas deriving their art music from the Great Tradition of Delhi became, themselves, great centers for the dissemination of musical culture, though geographically distant from its original locus and surrounded by different local traditions. Other areas remained Little centers of the Great Tradition. A succession, preferably biologically based, of disciples and students—a *gharānā*—maintained, developed, and preserved the tradition, often taking the name of the court where it had been patronized. Bengal has had but one such gharānā, that associated with Visnupur, a court town situated in the area closest to the Aryan heartland.

While the musical tradition patronized by the Visnupur court was the one legitimate indigenous connection with that tradition dispersed from Delhi at the decline of the Mughal empire, Bengal has had far more significant connections with the musical life of Hindustan than this fact would indicate. A powerful connection was established, for example, in the middle of the nineteenth century—at the time when the newly established gharānās were vying for prominence—as a result of the deposition of Wajid Ali Shah, King of Avadh, who moved the remnants of his cultured court from Lucknow to Motiyaburuj, near Calcutta. The musicians patronized by Wajid Ali, like many of those employed at the palaces of wealthy Bengali landlords and minor princes, were Hindi/Urdu speakers trained in upcountry gharānās to the north and west of Bengal. Today, such famous Bengali musicians as Ravi Shankar and Ali Akbar Khan also trace their professional lineage upcountry. With the growing prominence and dispersal of their disciples, there has arisen a tendency to refer to this discipular tradition as the Allauddin gharānā, referring to Allauddin Khan, the charismatic father and teacher of Ali Akbar and teacher and one-time father-in-law of Ravi Shankar. In this way, Bengal has acquired a more significant and active role in Hindustani music than it once had.

Allauddin also had teachers, of course, and he studied with the most important of them, Wazir Khan, at the court of Rampur, outside Bengal. Although no stranger to Bengal, Wazir Khan was one of the many upcountry musicians who made Calcutta an important center of Hindustani music in the late nineteenth century (he lived in Calcutta from 1892 to 1899). At this time, Calcutta was still the capital of British India and a natural center of attraction for musicians and their wealthy potential patrons. Wazir Khan was a direct descendant from the near-legendary musician Tansen, who, near the end of his career, became attached to the court of the Emperor Akbar at the close of the sixteenth century. This fact gave the Rampur gharānā particular majesty, as it could claim a genealogical connection with the man who was looked upon by most gharānās as First Teacher. While Tansen probably remained a Hindu all his life, his descendants became Muslims, and the stress placed by Muslim families of professional musicians upon the necessity for a disciple to be a family member if he were to receive the full teaching of the family tradition ensured that the Rampur gharānā would have special importance due to its genealogical as well as its discipular connection to Tansen.

Not being a member of Wazir Khan's family, Allauddin was not at first fully accepted by his teacher, but as he has related in his orally dictated memoir, after the death of his teacher's first son, he was finally accepted and taught as though he himself were Wazir's son (Ālāuddina 1981:56). Thus, the gharānā currently in the process of formation and carrying Allauddin's name has one of the strongest claims to authority as a *Seniya* gharānā, that is, one stemming from Tansen's heritage.

The Visnupur gharānā is nonetheless considered the one true gharānā in Bengal by virtue of the antiquity of its status as a Seniya gharānā. Like many things Bengali, though, there is something ambiguous in its nature. As a Hindu tradition, for example, it is distinguished from other gharānās. Neuman finds: "There is no evidence that music was a hereditary profession among Brahmans in the pre- and early Islamic era. . . . [T]he professionalization of art music as a hereditary occupation apparently began only with the coming of the Muslims. With two qualified exceptions, all gharanas have been founded by Muslims. The only Hindu hereditary traditions are the Banaras baj (style) of tabla playing and the Vishnupur gharana of dhrupad singers (and later) instrumentalists. In both these cases, the Hindu founders learned their art from Muslim ustads" (1980:105).

The Visnupur gharānā derives its name from the town where the Mallo family held court for over 1,250 years and where its descendants still live. Founded in 694, the kingdom was known as Mallobhum until the reign of Bir Hambir (1587–1620), a notorious dacoit, or bandit.

In the middle of his reign, a party of pilgrims passed through his kingdom carrying a precious cargo from the sacred, upcountry town of Brindaban to the kingdom of Gaur in Bengal. The pilgrims were devotees of Caitanya, a sixteenth-century Bengali saint who founded a still-flourishing emotional cult of devotion to Krishna, incarnation of the God Visnu, and to his consort Radha; Caitanya was himself considered a double incarnation of both Krishna and Radha. The precious cargo carried by the pilgrims was the newly formed literary and theological canon of the sect, but Bir Hambir assumed it to be material wealth and attacked the party. Whether through remorse over his greedy act or chagrin at his foolish mistake, he became a convert of the new cult, and his court was known thereafter as Visnu's City, Visnupur (Mukhopādhyāya 1980:26; Östör 1984:15–20).

A century later, Visnupur achieved its greatest importance and glory in the reign of Raghunath II, fifth in descent from Bir Hambir. Thereafter it rapidly declined in political significance, land holdings, and wealth until India's Independence in 1947. The musical gharānā flourished during this period of hard times, producing a succession of accomplished musicians. As usual in Bengal, however, things were a little different from the way one might expect them to be elsewhere. We have already noted Neuman's observation that, while the founder's teacher was a Muslim, the founder and his successors were Hindus. A further anomaly exists in that the founder's family was not the one whose lineage came to be most strongly associated with the gharānā. The openness with which all comers were taught in the Visnupur gharānā is, in fact, considered one of its distinguishing features, as Naomi Owens points out in her comparison of two musical families in Bengal (1969:62, 79).

Another distinguishing feature of the Visnupur gharānā is the fact that most of its significant performers were also composers who, in accordance with their inherited tradition, specialized in composing *dhrupads* (Mukhopādhyāya 1980:38). The texts of these compositions were often in Sanskrit or Bengali as well as in the more traditional Brajbhasa of upcountry dhrupads. The performing practice of these *dhrupadiyās* was recognized as exceptionally plain and lacking in the heavy trills or *gamak,* the portamenti or *mīṛ,* and rhythmic permutations of text phrases or *bol bāṁṭ* that are featured in most dhrupad styles (Mukhopadhyaya 1980:38, 130–31, 140).

Besides being composers and performers of a unique style, many of the Visnupuri musicians were scholars as well. This is not surprising if one considers that for generations before the gharānā was founded, the founder's family predecessors had been Sanskrit pandits (ibid.:101–102). Unlike the typical Muslim gharānā, in which musical performance was the only specialization, the Visnupur gharānā was as well known for its output of books on musical history and theory and for its published notations as for its musical performances. Among the publications, perhaps the most important and interesting are those of Ksetromohan Goswami, who first devised a system of notation for use by a native orchestra in a dramatic performance in 1858 (Capwell 1986:144, 148) and in 1867, helped to organize the first music conference in modern India under the auspices of Jotindro Mohun and Sourindro Mohun Tagore, the latter being his student and patron. One result of this conference, at which many important musicians were gathered, was the publication two years later of Ksetromohan's *saṇgītasāra* (1879), the first modern Bengali musical treatise (Mukhopādhyāya 1980:36).

This emphasis on learning and general education as a distinctive characteristic of the Visnupur gharānā is neatly captured in Naomi Owens's work. Noting that the Dagar family of dhrupadiyas emphasized the heroic nature of their routine of practice and its very early establishment in their childhood, she points out that the Bandyopadhyay family of Visnupur practiced less, in comparison, and put primary emphasis on general education in youth. Most tellingly, she mentions the lack of printed matter other than some popular journals in the Dagar home and the plethora of books of all sorts in the home of Satyokinkor Bandyopadhyay, one of the last professional musicians of the Visnupur Bandyopadhyay family (Owens 1969:19–24, 45–50, 84–88).

Since all the Indian members of the Visnupur gharānā appear to have been Hindus, they have normally venerated their gurus upon being accepted as students in the conventional Hindu way, with offerings of sweets and flowers, but they have never employed the *nāḍā bandh*—the ceremonial tying of a thread around the wrist—that Muslims use to signify the tie between master and disciple. This, too, differentiates them from other gharānās (ibid.:50–51, 75–76).

Having considered some of the distinctive features of the Visnupur gharānā, let us return to the question of its foundation. Daniel Neuman records that the founder of the Hindu Visnupur gharānā learned his art from a Muslim ustad (1980:105). According to the origin myth, this ustad was named Bahadur Khan and was eighth in descent from Tansen via his son Bilas Khan (Rāycaudhurī 1984:168–70; Mukhopādhyāya 1980:79). At the apogee of the Visnupur court, Raja Raghunath II induced Bahadur to leave the tumultuous life of the Mughal capital to become his court musician. Bahadur's successor as court musician, his unrelated Hindu student, Gadadhar Cakraborty, was the teacher of Krishnamohan Goswami, who passed the tradition on to

Ramsankar Bhattacarya (Mukhopādhyāya 1980:55ff). In his book on the Visnupur gharānā, however, Dilipkumar Mukhopadhyay has demonstrated the unlikelihood of this initial discipular succession (ibid.:75, 83): Raghunath II reigned from 1702 to 1712, when he was murdered during an insurrection, and the two descendants of Tansen named Bahadur were active only after the middle of the eighteenth century. The origin myth, according to Mukhopadhyay, has gained acceptance, in part because the text of a notated dhrupad of the tradition—published in 1893 and attributed to Bahadur himself—mentions the connection between Bahadur and Raghunath, and in part because the story is included in a book entitled *viṣṇupur* by Romescandra Bandyopadhyay, a noted member of the family in which the gharānā settled, so to speak (ibid. 1980:67, 60). Mukhopadhyay noted, however, that Romescandra's account of the early succession was sketchy and confused—in several places he even gives different versions of who was the pupil of whom—but the confusion continues only up to Ramsankar Bhattacarya, about whom there is substantial information, as there is about everyone in the succession thereafter (ibid.:101ff). Naomi Owens also quotes Romescandra as having written in a program note about the gharānā that Raghunath toured Hindustan in 1761 to search for a court musician and came upon Bahadur then (Owens 1969:55); as we have seen, Raghunath's death in 1712 makes this impossible.

After a series of painstaking deductions from circumstantial and substantial evidence, Mukhopadhyay concludes that Ramsankar Bhattacarya was in fact the founder of the Visnupur gharānā. Why else, he asks, would the people of Visnupur venerate him as the town's Sangitguru or Music Master each year during the great fall festival of Durgapuja (1980:99)? Ramsankar was the first Visnupur resident to establish a tradition of dhrupad performance in a characteristic style that was passed down in an unbroken discipular succession. While Ramsankar was not the disciple of Tansen's descendant Bahadur or of any of his supposed disciples, as asserted in the origin myth, he did, of course, have a teacher; according to Mukhopadhyay (1980:107), a manuscript memoir dictated by Ramsankar and preserved in his family identifies this teacher only as Panditji, a pilgrim who stopped in Visnupur, like so many others, on his way from Mathura-Brindaban to Puri.

The question that arises here is, why was Panditji ignored in the origin story in favor of the even more shadowy figure of Bahadur as the ultimate source of the gharānā's tradition? We may be prompted to think again of Bengal's peripheral status in relation to the Aryan heartland and of how its claims to legitimacy rested on receptivity to the culture of its western neighbors; but this does not resolve the problem, since Panditji and Bahadur were both from upcountry. Let us consider, then, another well-known example of imported cultural authority being welcomed in Bengal. This example involves the explanation for the peculiar nature of Bengali caste, which is founded on only two of the four classes of Aryan society—namely the Brahmin, or priestly, and the Sudra, or servant/serf, classes. Among these latter classes, there is an exalted subgroup of castes known as *kulīn;* the Kshatriya, or warrior, and Vaisya, or merchant and farmer classes, are altogether missing.

In his book *Marriage and Rank in Bengali Culture,* Ronald Inden documents the cause of this state of affairs with help from a Bengali religious text, the *Bṛihaddharmapurāṇa* (1976:51–53). It seems that once upon a time an evil Bengali king, Vena, forced the castes to intermarry and thereby confused the organization of society. He was destroyed by the Brahmins, who magically created his son Prithu. King Prithu then commanded the Brahmins to reestablish order; they did this by declaring all the mixed castes Sudra, reducing the four-class division of Aryavarta to two classes. Thereafter, as genealogists of the Bengali Brahmins record, the paramount Bengali ruler Adisura found himself in a predicament in the year 984, when he wished to perform a Vedic sacrifice that was beyond the competence of his now degenerate Brahmins; consequently he invited to his kingdom five holy and learned Brahmins from upcountry in order to carry out the sacrifice. The arrival of five Brahmins attended by their five Sudra servants saved the day. As a result, the foreigners took up residence in Bengal and through marriage and propagation established the highest ranks among the Bengali castes, passing on to their progeny the charisma of an upcountry origin (ibid.:53–60).

Why then was Panditji incapable of passing his similarly derived charisma to Ramsankar Bhattacarya, the founder of the highest ranking musical lineage in Bengal? Evidently, the aura from the west was still necessary, since Panditji was eclipsed by the immigrant Bahadur Khan and not by some indigenous teacher; but the geographical aura had to be combined with one that was derived from a special knowledge as well. While Panditji was knowledgeable, his knowledge did not possess the aura associated with the Muslim professional courtly tradition. In the eighteenth century, only a Muslim ustad carried the necessary authority of upcountry musical culture needed for the proper establishment of a professional lineage, just as in the tenth century only the upcountry Brahmins had the authority to restore the efficacy of sacrifice and the purity of caste in Bengal.

The story of the five upcountry Brahmins was discussed by Inden as the third stage in the development of Bengali caste. A fourth stage took place after the advent of Islamic rule in Bengal. The resulting state of disorder in Hindu society required new adjustments to accommodate the changed circumstances, as in the days of King Adisura. These changes, says Inden, "made it possible by the fifteenth century, for Muslims and Hindus to honor or respect one another. . . . Muslim rulers began to show respect to Hindus by giving them offices in their revenue administration and landed estates as well as titles such as Khan. Reciprocally, Hindus began to show respect to the Muslim King of Bengal. . . . Like the former Hindu King, he becomes characterized as a 'great king' (*mahārājā*)" (ibid.:75–76).

The age-old Bengali habit of looking outside Bengal to the north and west for prestige and status in culture, combined with several centuries of mutual Hindu/Muslim accommodation in Bengal, made it possible for the professional musical lineage of Visnupur, unlike all others but that of Banaras *tabliyās*, to remain comfortably Hindu while paying homage to the precedence of Islamic musical tradition and, incidentally, reaping for itself the prestige of claiming connection with the Seniya succession. Although Panditji was overshadowed by Bahadur Khan in this process, his memory was not totally obliterated, as his rehabilitation by Dilipkumar Mukhopadhyay shows. Perhaps the Visnupuris have always remembered that Tansen himself was a Hindu, though he served the Mughal Emperor.

NOTE

1. The concept of the "Great and Little Traditions" was developed, with reference to India, by Robert Redfield and Milton Singer in their article "The Cultural Role of Cities" (1962); first published in 1954, it has continued to engender reconsiderations and developments while remaining a useful tool for examining cultural traditions. In their view, "a great tradition describes a way of life and as such is a vehicle and standard for those who share it to identify with one another as members of a common civilization" (1962:339). There are four means by which such a standard is "universalized": 1) its embodiment in "sacred books"; 2) establishment of a group of specialist interpreters and performers; 3) identification of leading personalities; and 4) creation of a "sacred geography" (1962:343–44). In terms of Hindustani music theory, these might be seen to correspond to: 1) a canon of repertory and theory; 2) establishment of a discipular tradition; 3) a hagiography of great teachers and performers; and 4) the particular courts where traditions were founded and patronized.

Sufi Music and the Historicity of Oral Tradition

6

Regula Burckhardt Qureshi

Unlike the historian of Western art music, the historically oriented ethnomusicologist is inevitably confronted by the oral nature of his or her sources and indeed of their subject, music itself. For the ethnomusicologist, historical inquiry perforce means to engage with the ongoing life of the musical community, thereby embedding the "diachronic" quest in the "synchronic" reality of social and musical processes. From this results the salutary insight that the phenomenon of "history" emanates from historical perspectives put into the service of those who shape and partake in those processes, reflecting their collective and individual interests. History thus emerges as a process among processes rather than a story, even if it takes narrative form.

For the music historian in search of "the historical record" this implies that the inquiry into a people's musical past is predicated on an understanding of their present engagement with that past. This of course is as true for written as for oral history; oral traditions only make the fact more immediately compelling. For unlike the written artifact, the oral historical datum is accessible only via the filter of its sociocultural milieu: history appears as an artifact of historicity, the starting point and key to an inquiry into the validity and depth of oral historical data.

The oral historian focusing on music faces the additional challenge of the fluid nature of his or her datum; it exists only in the articulation of its makers. At the same time, the extent to which musical communication is structured makes it possible to discern consistencies and variation in this articulation across space and time, providing an independent channel for measuring kind and degree of change, and supplying potential clues to historical processes. The challenge for the ethnomusicologist is to interpret this purely musical dimension with reference to the nonmusical parameters of historical inquiry, integrating these parameters into the research process and thereby enriching the oral historian's enterprise.

In the generalized realm of music history, such a contextualized inquiry into oral musical history can also contribute, both in substance and perspective, toward what has been the mainstay of musicology worldwide: the study of codified art music systems in complex societies with traditions of written history. In particular, the orally shared knowledge of hereditary specialist groups contains an essential body of potentially relevant data for that larger enterprise. The special challenge here is to generate an expanded sociocultural perspective that can account for the particular context of such oral data in relation to other musical contexts and traditions.

The Sufi oral tradition presents historians and ethnomusicologists with the need to face this entire complex of issues. This essay is a first foray around the central question for any level of inquiry into the historical significance of Sufi music: what kind of validity should be accorded to this body of traditional knowledge? I will discuss issues and provide a sampling of musical data, leading to several tentative assumptions that make reference to the Sufi musical repertory.

In the Indian subcontinent—as in the entire Islamic world—the Sufi religious tradition has accorded to music a significant role integral to its ritual practice. Indic Sufism has developed a special musical idiom and a performing tradition, *qawwālī,*[1] that is controlled by its own hereditary musicians, *qawwāls*. With wider implications in mind, I shall focus specifically on the local tradition and repertory of the *qawwāl bachche* performers who are attached to the Nizamuddin Auliya Shrine in Delhi. There is general agreement within the Sufi community that this is the most authentic heritage and that the Nizamuddin Auliya Shrine is a major Sufi center, second only to the shrine in Ajmer of Khwaja Muinuddin Chishti, founder-saint of the Chishti lineage in the subcontinent. The sources used are recordings of repertory and discussions with qawwāl bachche, with Chishti *sheikhs*, and with knowledgeable Sufis.

The historicist stance that characterizes Muslim cultural hegemony in India is well documented as being rooted in the fundamental tenets of Islam (see Hardy 1958). A considerable body of written and pictorial accounts documents Indo-Muslim historiography; at the same time, oral traditions coexist as carriers of historical consciousness as well as source materials. For specialized bodies of knowledge such as music, these traditions are located in endogamous communities of hereditary specialists and are controlled through oral transmission; but they are also embedded within meaning systems that draw from both oral and written sources.

Well established by the thirteenth century, when it began to be institutionalized around saintly shrines with endowments and the hereditary succession of spiritual leadership, the Sufi tradition has enjoyed remarkable continuity. Contemporary scholars of Indian music and of Muslim cultural history have accorded significance to Sufism and its music as a manifestation of the Muslim encounter with Indian musical practice. Accordingly, Sufi music is considered a potential source for the historical investigation of classical music. In particular, the concern of musicologists has centered on the quest for understanding the origin and special character of *khayāl* and other currently predominant North Indian classical forms that were introduced at Muslim courts since at least the seventeenth century (Gosvami 1957:130f; Brhaspati 1966:55f). More specifically, it has been suggested that qawwāls were instrumental in the development of khayāl singing, or were at least linked historically with the introduction of certain musical procedures distinctive of khayāl and other related forms (H. Powers 1980:88). Historians of Indo-Muslim culture have pointed to the significant place of music within Sufism and to the musical dimensions of the "oblique cultural link between the Sufi heritage and the court" (Aziz Ahmad 1969:144; also Haidar Rizvi 1941; Eaton 1978). These claims rest on the assumption of a historically distinct identity for Sufi music, allowing that it could in fact become a source of innovation in art music.

A more specific focus of interest has been the literary and musical contribution of Amir Khusrau, the thirteenth-century Indo-Persian Sufi poet and chronicler, and favorite disciple of Nizamuddin Auliya.[2] Traditional consensus credits him with initiating Indo-Muslim syncretism in North Indian music, including the specific invention of many ragas. Khusrau's own writings indicate his competence in music theory, and several chronicles testify to his eminence as a performer and a musical innovator (Amir Khusrau 1974, vol. 3; Mirza 1974). Because of his intimate connection with Sufism, the Sufi claim of his playing a founding role in the establishment of Indic Sufi music is generally taken seriously (Brhaspati 1969; Sarmadee 1975).

In sum, there is agreement as to the historical significance of the Sufi musical tradition. But the actual role of Sufi music in the shaping of Indo-Muslim culture and classical music remains to be defined, due to a general lack of clarity—both inside and outside the Sufi community—as to what that "tradition" consists of in concrete terms. The obvious reason for this is the paucity of written source material pertaining specifically to Sufi music. For unlike Sufi poetry, Sufi music has not been recorded in writing, and the considerable body of Sufi writings refers to music mainly in very general terms.

At the same time, Sufi oral tradition preserves a body of music and a set of historical notions surrounding the oral tradition. A more direct approach for inquiry into the historical significance of Sufi music would involve a careful examination of the musical heritage, noting any claims to its historicity. What is its foundation, what particular musical evidence of historical continuity does it contain, and on what basis can that evidence be evaluated as to its contribution to the history of Hindustani music? An investigation of Sufi music as a religious musical genre (Qureshi 1986) has shown that in the religious context, historicity is not assigned primacy as a characteristic of the music or of its ritual significance. At the same time, both Sufis and qawwāls see their musical tradition as an integral part of the centuries-old Sufi heritage in India, and there are written records by Sufis from the eleventh century onward (Sijzi 1884; Habib 1950; K. A. Nizami 1958, 1974). This literature, supported by the oral tradition transmitted within the Sufi community, holds that the institution of *samā*ᶜ (the "listening" to spiritual poetry in song for the purpose of attaining spiritual ecstasy) gave rise to a hereditary class of Sufi singers who were closely attached to Sufi sheikhs and their hospice and shrine establishments. Preeminent among such musicians in South Asia is the lineage of the *qawwāl bachche* (qawwāl offspring), said to have originated with two young brothers who were trained as singers under Amir Khusrau.

The qawwāl bachche lineage, or *brādrī*,[3] is centered in Delhi, where they continue to enjoy the exclusive hereditary right to sing collectively at the Nizamuddin Auliya Shrine, every member being entitled to a share in the income from offerings made during the singing. They have similar rights at other, less-prominent shrines throughout Delhi. By virtue of this right they are also entitled to sing at Chishti shrines across the subcontinent, including Pakistan. Other members of the qawwāl bachche remain in Hyderabad (Deccan),[4] where the entire brādrī had migrated following the 1857 rebellion and subsequent destruction of the Delhi Mughal court. Since 1947 a number of qawwāl bachche have migrated to Karachi, Pakistan.[5] So far, continuing contact through travel and intermarriage has ensured the continuity and consistency of the qawwāl bachche heritage that remains preserved in oral tradition. This heritage consists primarily of a body of song texts and melodies, along with the appropriate rhythmic cycles for accompaniment. A second and no less important part of the heritage is the performing tradition appropriate to the very special needs of a samāᶜ audience, which requires that a performer share in the ideological background of Sufism and in the structure and dynamics of Sufi practice. Sufis rely on hereditary qawwāls for the samāʿ performance idiom while also monitoring its proper preservation through the patronage and censorship that the social structure of Sufism permits them to exercise over qawwāls.

What makes music essential to Sufism is the samāʿ, the central ritual of "listening" to mystical songs—poems set to music—as a means of spiritual advancement. The musical repertory of qawwālī, then, consists of a large body of poems, with tunes for singing and metric patterns for drumming, usually on the barrel-shaped *dholak.* These poems are sung by a group of qawwāls led by one or two solo singers and supported melodically by the portable harmonium that has superseded the indigenous *sarangi* or *sitar.* Handclapping by the singers intensifies the rhythmic accentuation. Ensemble structure and performing style make possible extended singing, a strongly articulated musical meter, and a flexible structuring process adapted to the changing spiritual needs of the samāʿ listeners.

The repertory of poems falls into three language categories: the poetry of classical mysticism in Farsi, the poetry of devotional Sufism in classical Hindi, and the more recently composed poetry in Urdu. With the exception of many Hindi poems, this poetry exists in print and can be authenticated; however, it is a memorized repertory.

The Farsi poetry of Sufism, mostly composed by Persian and Indian poet-mystics and dating from the thirteenth century onward, is of course preserved in writing, both in collections of samāʿ poems (e.g., *Naghmat* n.d.; Idris Khan 1973; K. H. S. Nizami 1973) and in the printed works of individual poets, above all those works of the Persian literary classics.[6] The few printed samāʿ collections are very scarce, even among qawwāls, and individual poetic works are hardly used by them. Furthermore, neither type of source contains an adequate text inventory of samāʿ poetry. Both Sufis and qawwāls use such sources only as a reference or backup to their memory, and it is in this sense that they identify poetry and music as two contrasting domains of knowledge: *ʿilm-e-safīnā* (knowledge of the written page) and *ʿilm-e-sīnā* (the knowledge of memory).

Samāʿ poetry in classical Hindi is comprised in a predominantly oral repertory, for it stands somewhat outside the literary tradition of devotional Hinduism (*bhaktī*) from which it clearly derives. Urdu poetry for samāʿ, of recent origin, is represented in the printed collections, but the repertory is fluid and is controlled essentially by oral transmission (including recordings).

Qawwālī musical settings are drawn from many sources, including

North Indian and Pakistani classical, folk, and popular music, in addition to individual composition. But there is a standard repertory of traditional tunes that are passed down in qawwāl families and are well known to all the regular samā' participants. These include songs attributed to Amir Khusrau, songs used for special shrine rituals, and also some "old" qawwālī tunes that belong to the Persian Sufi classics but which are movable to the other poems as long as their metric pattern fits.

A good number of qawwālī tunes are identified by qawwāls with classical ragas, most of them attributed to Amir Khusrau or to the Persian Muslim influence in general. Among the metric cycles, too, classical talas are identified, and also patterns specific to qawwālī; all of them are articulated with much accentuation to invoke *zikr,* the repeated name of God. The performance style of qawwālī is built on a principle of free musical structuring by rhythmically repeating and recombining any text units, down to the individual word, and by inserting extra verses to further enhance such a text unit.

It needs to be stressed that neither qawwāls nor Sufis consider all the musical traits of qawwālī important in historical terms. This is especially true for most movable qawwālī tunes: old as they are recognized to be, they are not held sacrosanct. Musicians say they sing them *muhabbatan,* i.e., "out of affection," but they may also substitute smart modern tunes. What is claimed to be historically important—by performers and Sufis—is a certain number of particular song tunes, their ragas, and a few talas. Furthermore, the syllabic performing style of repeated Persian phrases is linked to the classical genre of the *tarāna,* another Persian Muslim introduction.

In order to evaluate any of these specific musical claims, one must start with the larger context of the Sufi oral tradition. A historical orientation is built into Indic Sufism, which as a whole is hierarchical and based on seniority. This implies a historical dynamic as a structuring principle for both Sufi ideology and its social organization: the spiritual lineages linking the devotee to saints, Prophet, God, and *buzurgī* (the spiritual seniority acquired by the Sufi over time).

A historiographical frame of reference is in fact recognized by every Sufi sheikh, but it does not inform the Sufi tradition consistently. A sheikh may quote a thirteenth-century account to prove a point, but Sufism truly lives through a body of traditions that are oral and cover all aspects of Sufi thought and practice. Sufi oral tradition emanates from those in spiritual authority (the sheikhs) but circulates among all participants in Sufism, including lay devotees and service professionals like the qawwāls. These secondary carriers depend on the primary carriers for information and authentication. The oral tradition provides a kind of spiritual currency, articulating both the ideology and the social structure of the Sufi communities. This currency is used to articulate and pass on what someone in spiritual authority has said.

It is the sheikh's prime function to uphold and disseminate this oral tradition. His spiritual status authenticates what he says. At the same time, his command of the Sufi tradition reinforces, if not legitimizes, his authority. In this dynamic interplay the body of tradition can become a malleable tool, especially where it serves to enhance the individual status of a sheikh or saint. Thus, there is sometimes little consistency in hagiographical or genealogical sources, whether oral or written.

It is in the area of ritual, however, where the oral tradition of Indic Sufism articulates norms that are remarkably consistent and congruent with the classical Sufi writings. This includes the standard conception of the samāʿ ritual; indeed, the principles laid down between the eleventh and fourteenth centuries serve as a charter for the present-day samāʿ practice (al-Ghazali 1979; al-Hujwiri 1970). At the same time, conventionally accepted modifications of this charter are referred back to early contact with Hinduism and with the need for Indic Sufism to cater to a non-Muslim population. This notion, too, is consistently maintained.

Music clearly falls within the ritual domain of Sufism; more specifically, within the concept of the samāʿ. This very concept ("listening") implies a concern with the effect of music on the listener rather than with music per se. This explains why the Sufi oral tradition deals with music primarily in the negative, in the form of caveats and prohibitions aimed at preventing a "wrong" effect on the listener. Excessive melodiousness is to be avoided, as is the use of beardless young singers. Similarly, the appropriateness of certain instruments has been subject to controversy throughout the history of Sufism. More generally, samāʿ implies listening not to music per se, but to the musically embellished mystical poetry. Hence for samāʿ music, texts are primary; musical features may enhance, but may never obscure them. At the same time, samāʿ music also articulates *zikr,* the ceaselessly repeated name—and thus remembrance—of God. On this basis, the accentuational emphasis of drumming and of handclapping has been accepted as a positive feature of samāʿ rhythm. Indic Sufism has consistently asserted the legitimacy of the *daf,* a frame drum said to have been used in the Prophet's time, and the only musical instrument sanctioned by *ḥadīs* (Roychoudhury 1957:68ff). The presence of the dholak and of various melodic supporting instruments is seen as an acceptable concession to a music-permeated Hindu environment, having been sanctioned by the founder saint in India, Mu'inuddin Chishti (Begg 1960).

The Sufi tradition at large, then, yields very little direct evidence that could shed light on the historical continuity of musical features. Indirectly, the insistence on music serving the articulation of words is suggestive in relation to one Sufi musical genre (which is hardly in use today), the *tarāna,* and to the contention that the repeated syllables derive from spiritual phrases in Farsi (Amir Khan 1966). Likewise, the legitimacy accrued to the daf indirectly supports the Sufi assertion that the more historically authentic Sufi music exists in the exclusive samāᶜ rituals held at some shrines where only a daf accompanies special local repertories.

The fact that music as such is "bracketed" out of the standard Sufi tradition suggests rather an open field for the Sufi musician. Indeed, the domain of music is considered the preserve of a functionary, the musician, as long as he adheres to the requirements of the samāᶜ ritual. Separated from spiritual involvement, the qawwāl is likened by Sufis to a mere bearer of gifts from above: a medium, not an agent (Idris Khan 1973:Introduction)

Sufi sheikhs recognize the expertise of their musicians concerning the purely musical knowledge that is a prerequisite to performing, but that is not required of the listener. Thus the musician has his own specialist oral tradition, also passed on through generations. His authority over this tradition differs in two important ways from that of the Sufi sheikh over his. First, it is not backed up by written sources, for, as previously mentioned, music has always been considered an ᶜilm-e-sīnā, unlike poetry, which is an ᶜilm-e-safīnā; and second, the musician's authority, even though based on exclusive knowledge, is "merely" musical—musical authority is superseded by spiritual authority.

Thus it is important to see the specialized musical knowledge of the Sufi musician as he sees it himself: always in reference to a larger body of Sufi tradition that is authenticated and controlled by the sheikh. This view is reinforced by the way oral tradition defines the qawwāl's own identity. Professionally, his identity is articulated in terms of descent and heredity, and socially, it is articulated in terms of a patron-client dependency with the sheikhs.[7] Both methods serve to define the qawwāl as a functionary attached by hereditary right to a saint's shrine and providing local Sufis with the required musical service.

This identity gives the musicians the exclusive right to perform ritual songs specific to "their" saint, so that they in essence become the exclusive keepers of this special repertory. Their control of these ritual songs is important in validating their position vis-à-vis outside performers who compete with them for Sufi patronage in the samāᶜ assemblies at large but have no access to the special shrine rituals. The shrine brādrī is in charge of these *panchāyatī gane* through its leaders, the *panch.*[8]

Of course, the more important the saint and shrine, the more crucial is its special musical repertory to the identity of the performer. The qawwāl bachche of Nizamuddin Auliya epitomize such performers; their shrine has for centuries been a spiritual center of the Muslim empire's capital, resulting in a mighty alliance between spiritual and worldly authority, and in patronage, some of which continues even today.[9] This situation has resulted in close contact of the musicians with secular music-making opportunities, implying their acquaintance with secular musical repertories and tastes. Amir Khusrau himself was both the favorite disciple of Nizamuddin Auliya and an outstanding courtier to three emperors. Five centuries later, during the reign of Muhammad Shah, performers are reported moving between court and shrine (Dargah Quli Khan 1982), and in the nineteenth century Tanras Khan, outstanding qawwāl bachchā of Nizamuddin Auliya, was the court singer of the emperor Bahadur Shah Zafar (Imam 1959:19). Even today, few qawwāls of any shrine survive entirely by performing for spiritual occasions.

Finally, the qawwāl's exclusive oral tradition includes his teaching tradition. It is functional—teaching is for those who cannot learn on their own—and thus characterized by a reluctance toward abstraction, so that qawwāls are not always consistent in identifying even such basic musical features as raga and tala. Some qawwālī songs, on the other hand, are always referred to with their raga or tala label. Also, since teaching is not associated with establishing artistic pedigree, reference to historical precedent is not relevant as an explanatory tool.

Considering the character and function of the Sufi oral tradition as a whole leads to certain assumptions regarding the issue of historicity in Sufi music. I will take up what I consider to be the principal assumptions, establish them as hypotheses, relate them to the musical repertory, and test their potential applicability to concrete aspects of the music. Specific musical examples will furnish evidence of the process used here.

Special authentication for my conclusions comes from Nasiruddin Khan Gore, the senior qawwāl bachchā of Nizamuddin Auliya, who is recognized as the most knowledgeable member of the brādrī. He also supplied important musical information about the ritual repertory of Nizamuddin Auliya. To counter the inevitable danger of circularity in such a procedure, the conclusions are also examined in light of limited external evidence derived from two independent historical sources pertaining to Sufi music. One is the 1739 account of Delhi musical life by Dargah Quli Khan (1982), a Hyderabad noble and courtier of

Muhammad Shah, and the other is the 1856 account of music in Lucknow by Hakim Muhammad Karam Imam (1925, 1959), a courtier of Wajid Ali Shah.

Historicity appears to emerge from the presence of two essential factors: capacity and motivation. Capacity in oral tradition is essentially linked to memory. While the memory of past generations cannot be measured, there is diverse but not unreasonable indication (Vansina 1965:31ff) that the presence of a stable chain of transmission set within a social monitoring unit such as a professional lineage is favorable to oral knowledge being handed down through generations with a minimum of distortion. Both senior qawwāl bachche and classical musicians assume this; Nasiruddin Khan Gore calculates that such knowledge could pass through one or two persons per century to reach the present with the fewest possible agents of distortion.

The crucial element is that of motivation: for what knowledge is such preservation essential? In the case of Sufi music there exists, in response to Sufi listening needs, a motivation for change and innovation that is musically shaped by religious and secular influences. More specifically, Sufi music has had much interchange with secular music, starting with Amir Khusrau in the thirteenth century. This is supported by both the 1739 and 1856 accounts of the qawwāls performing secular music. The claim that Sufi musical features and processes found their way into classical music is therefore a reasonable one and it should be taken seriously. But given the client position of the musician who must cater to the patron's tastes, the converse must also be assumed, namely that secular tastes found their way into samāʿ assemblies and influenced Sufi singing. This is supported by the 1856 source and by the memory of today's senior qawwāls. Senior qawwāl bachchā Meraj Ahmad, a direct descendant of Tanras Khan, somewhat bitterly explained how in principle the sheikh in charge demands tradition and authenticity from the singer, yet at any time may supersede himself by asking for a "light" performance under some pretext, such as the untutored preference of special listeners or of his womenfolk behind the purdah.

It follows from the above that the abstractable musical features of qawwālī, even if specifically labeled as Sufi, cannot automatically be assumed to be of Sufi origin. This is primarily and directly relevant to the two major Indian musical constructs identified as raga and tala. A number of traditional qawwālī songs with "old" tunes are identified melodically as being set to special "Muslim" ragas. Examining the melodic structure of these songs yields some inconsistency or outright divergences from the standard version—or versions—of the raga that represents the consensus of traditional musicians. What complicates the assessment is that even in classical music, composed songs—the *chīz* of khayāl—sometimes include features unusual for the raga.[10] This is accepted by classical musicians as part of what is "given" in a composition handed down by masters of the past, but it does not affect the consensus on the raga rules for improvisation.

From the historian's point of view, this raises the question of whether the inconsistencies found in Sufi songs represent creative freedom or are a manifestation of a consensus from an earlier time. The second possibility suggests itself more powerfully where a song exhibits a consistent divergence from the raga it is said to represent. But the fact that there is rarely more than one Sufi song in any particular raga makes it difficult to assess just what these songs represent in terms of past norms and practice.[11]

What further complicates the inquiry is the fact that qawwāls today accept their own inferior status vis-à-vis classical musicians. They look up to classical raga norms and sometimes even attempt to "correct" a qawwālī song to bring it in line with such norms. Nasiruddin Khan Gore provided an example when he made a recording for classical music expert Acharya Brhaspati of the qaul "Man kunto Maulā" in correct raga *shudh kalyān,* claiming that other, less musically literate qawwāls have distorted what is in fact the universally sung version of the song. Thus, a Sufi song may constitute an original version of a raga, but it may also simply be given a raga label post-facto to enhance its "classical" value.

Example 1. Qaul: Man kunto Maulā

a) standard version

b) correct *shudh kalyan* version

The picture is not much clearer in the area of the Sufi metric patterns. Talas associated with light music predominate, including one that bears the name *qawwālī tāl,* although they are articulated in drumming in a style unique to qawwālī (Qureshi 1986:60). A few songs are set to classical talas; this is deemed by qawwāls a sign of both antiquity and artistic status. Of special interest are several talas with

Farsi names; in particular *sul fākhta* and *dozarbī* or *dobahar*. Both occur in songs that have a special status and that are performed very rarely and under special conditions. Therefore, very few qawwāls are able to perform them, but they attempt to substitute a more standard pattern that will fit the overall count—e.g., dozarbī can be replaced with *pashto*, since both have seven pulse counts (see Example 2). That these rare talas were in more general musical use, at least in the nineteenth century, is clearly indicated in Imam, as is the use of Farsi tala names (Imam 1925:194f).[12]

One facet of tala patterns that is treated in a unique manner by some qawwāls is their scanning. Essentially, verbal scanning is a tool for qawwāls to teach rhythmic cycles with an extended duration; there is thus no rationale for applying it consistently, since the shorter standard talas are taught directly as drum patterns and can easily be remembered by simple counting. Two talas were scanned by qawwāls in a way different from the standard classical norm, by moving the *sam*—the principal accent or downbeat that indicates the beginning and conclusion of each cyclical pattern—to a different count in the cycle. Possibly to accord with the fitting of standard Farsi poetic meters, this variant conception of tala organization is also found in Imam's account of nineteenth-century music, but there these versions bear distinct tala names. Whether the Imam labels are significant is yet to be investigated; in any event, diverse scanning patterns appear to be a historical fact, covered up—as is much variation in oral tradition—by the powerful trend toward the definition and standardization of musical norms that started early in this century.[13]

In sum, no conclusive evidence can be drawn from the oral repertory regarding features of raga and tala that may be specifically identified as originating with Sufi music, but the few parallels between some presently archaic Sufi features and past classical use are suggestive. The question is, suggestive of what? Do they indicate a lag in the modernization of Sufi music, or a more fundamental stability in the repertories that contain those archaic features?

In order to address this question, what first needs to be assessed is the criterion of stability. Based on the functionality of stability in Sufi practice generally, musical stability should be looked for in Sufi ritual songs and not in those sung in standard samā^c assemblies, which are more subject to musical variability due to variable performance needs. This points to the exclusive local rituals whose stability is functional: to legitimize local shrine authority through the authenticity of the repertory, words, and music. Tied to the shrine's very particular locale, these songs specifically address the saint and his representatives, and not a general Sufi audience. All major shrines have such rituals. Best known and preserved among these is the *band samāʿ* (literally: closed listening) of the Gesudaraz[14] Shrine in Gulbarga, held in a small cell within the shrine walls at every *ʿurs* (anniversary celebration) of the saint. Only the saint's descendants are present to listen to the shrine's own qawwāls, who alone know the band samāʿ songs. What these rituals at different shrines have in common is that each has an exclusive repertory of songs that is specific to its saint and his tradition, and that is marked by some textual and musical features that express its antiquity and provide historical authenticity.

At the Nizamuddin Auliya, the ritual repertory is quite extensive, including Arabic qauls (sayings of the Prophet), a few Farsi ghazals (incuding poems by Amir Khusrau, Nizamuddin Auliya, and Faridud-din, his saintly guide), and a number of Hindi songs, all attributed to Amir Khusrau for both text and music. Outstanding among these is the set of songs associated with the yearly *basant* ritual, which commemorates a special event in the saint's life. Amir Khusrau, seeing his sheikh, Nizamuddin Auliya, in desolate seclusion over the death of his nephew, continued to sing songs of spring (basant) and spiritual love at his door until the sheikh responded and joined in the basant festival.

It is for these samāʿ performances that the performers as well as the Sufis stress correctness in observing the tradition; for here the prime purpose is to validate the presence of the saint and his representatives by showing the authenticity and historical continuity of the songs. This gives shrine performers the important privilege and onus of preserving, performing, and transmitting this special—and purely oral—repertory, since they are its exclusive keepers. The same general rule also applies to the special obligatory hymns—the qaul "Man kunto Maulā" and the Hindi *rang*—that are always sung by the shrine performers at the beginning of samāʿ assemblies. For all other samāʿ singing, local qawwāls as well as visiting performers may get a "turn" (*bārī*) to perform.

Thus it would seem that performance of these special ritual repertories serves the specific function of articulating authenticity for the saint through his representatives, and thereby conferring authenticity on the latter as well. That this continues today is evidenced by two examples of sheikhs using ritual songs creatively for just such a purpose. Some years ago, in his quest for recognition as the chief representative of Nizamuddin Auliya, one sheikh introduced a band samāʿ as part of the saint's ʿurs celebration, although no band samāʿ tradition exists at Nizamuddin Auliya. Instead, local shrine songs were performed in a closed cell without drumming, in specific reference to Nizamuddin Auliya's own reported opposition to the use of instruments in the performance of samāʿ (Lawrence 1983:94ff).

The second example, a performance of a song from the basant ritual of Nizamuddin Auliya, took place two decades ago in the gateway of the tomb that the great Chishti sheikh Baba Zahin Shah had built for his own preceptor in Karachi. On hearing the phrase, "at the door of Nizamuddin years went by," he entered a state of ecstasy that lasted for two hours. The basant song, and this phrase, served to articulate the spiritual authenticity of a newly established saint in Pakistan, for its performance evoked a direct analogy of equivalence between the new saint and Nizamuddin Auliya, their shrines, and their respective disciples, Baba Zahin Shah and Amir Khusrau.

The special use and controlled transmission of these ritual songs suggest a potential for consistency somewhat more promising than the song repertory in use at regular samāᶜ assemblies. The fact that for this general repertory the quality of historicity is not deemed of central importance serves to highlight the functionality of such a quality in the songs of the special shrine ritual. In other words, the evidence of functionality accords with—and even explains—the evidence of the consensus among Sufis and qawwāls regarding "age" and authenticity, and regarding their place in the context of spiritual significance. While this evidence is still only inferential in nature and cannot be substantiated in the absence of an independent (written) historical record, it provides a reasonable basis for focusing on the ritual song repertories as a whole in the quest for identifying possible clues to earlier musical norms.

Of the number of ritual song repertories associated with different shrines, that of the qawwāl bachche would seem to be of greatest potential significance musically, due to their consistent proximity to the Delhi court that set cultural standards for courtly India.[15] The following brief review of four songs, all attributed to Amir Khusrau, will indicate what kinds of musical features appear characteristic of this special repertory and might thus be considered worthy of special attention. In proposing to examine the repertory as a whole, stress is being placed on consistency of features as an indicator of historical stability. Thus, rather than looking for individual traits indicative of historical association, interest is focused on identifying a complex of features that can suggest a coherent stylistic profile. Such a profile could then provide a basis for comparison with already existing scholarly hypotheses about past musical usage, and could be used for evaluating individual instances of historically suggestive oral evidence.

The first two songs are core songs of the basant ritual, each consisting of a single verse that is sung repeatedly at each stage of the proceedings. The first song in Farsi, "Ashk rez," is set in a raga with the double name *megh-ushshāq,* consisting of *megh,* a traditional Hindustani raga with seasonal association, and of *ushshāq*, a Farsi-derived maqām of probably Turkish origin (Sarmadee 1975:56). The melodic structure of the song represents a transpositional method of creating a raga by replicating the melodic pattern in a higher tetrachord. Termed *that lautana* (inverting the mode), this melody-making procedure is considered a qawwālī tradition going back to Amir Khusrau; seen from the perspective of the Brahminical music scholar, it is a "deplorable Muslim practice" (Brhaspati 1969:9).

The other notable feature in "Ashk rez" is the tala identified as dozarbī or dobahar (Example 2). Both are hybrid Hindi-Farsi terms representative, as is the raga, of the contact situation between Farsi and Indian culture in which the Muslim elite and its artists found themselves.

Example 2. Tala Dozarbī (Dobahar)

counts:	1	2	3	4	5	6	7
drum syllables:	ka	dhe	te	dha	te	te	ta
accents:	x			x			

The second song, "Auliyā tere dāman" (Example 3), features the same tala; this setting also shows the ambivalence between the song's natural accents and the location of the sam, since the natural accents of the song do not really coincide with the accents of the tala. The raga of this melodically less elaborate song is *sarparda,* another Persian-derived melody with affinity to the Hindustani raga *bilāval,* which accounts for the alternative use of the double name *sarparda-bilāval.*

Example 3. Basant Song: Auliyā tere dāman (raga: sarparda, tala: dozarbī)

The same raga is also found in the third song "Āl-an-Nabī" (Example 4), a qaul in Arabic based on a saying of the Prophet Muhammad and

Example 4. Qaul (Gul): Āl-an-Nabī (raga: sarparda)

Ā - lan Na - bī wa sa - la - vāt ul - lā - he wa - sa - lām - hū a -
lay wā - le - hī Al Fā - ti - ma to baz hat - o
min nī

also identified as *gul*. This song, like all qauls, has the rhythmically marked repetition of syllabic tune material. These are ingredients of a compositional principle associated with Sufi zikr practice and identified in Hindustani music as tarāna.

Closer to the tarāna practice in classical music is the application of this musical principle to a Farsi composition, the *hawā* (Example 5). Here the final line acts as a refrain to be repeated, the highly meaningful text constituted of some of the very syllables that most classical musicians employ without attaching meaning to them. The song also exemplifies how longer Farsi verses are inserted between principal statements of the tarāna, a refrain principle that finds universal expression in the Sufi musical practice of verse insertion (*girah;* see Qureshi 1986:237, 164ff). Classical singers also employ it in the rare tarāna or *ṭhumrī.*[16]

Example 5. Hawā: Āṅ roz (tarāna)

Text of the refrain line: Dar tan dar ā dar namī āmad dar tan

Collectively, these songs exhibit features that are also found in certain Sufi songs outside the ritual repertory, as has already been indicated. The more consistent appearance of these features in this more unified and historically relevant set of ritual songs endows them with more potential historical validity, even within the ritual repertory. This result would make a cautiously reasonable starting point for the kind of inquiry envisaged at the beginning of this essay.

At the same time, looking at the historical potential of the Sufi musical tradition as a whole, my conclusions regarding the evidence so far presented are of necessity double-faced. In this first step toward assessing this oral tradition, I have tried to introduce the use of internal evidence in the historical study of the music. Two contradictory points have emerged: that one must beware of assuming historical causality, for the Sufi samāʿ music is highly variable, and that one must give serious consideration to the historical implications of the limited and special ritual song repertories that appear to have largely escaped this variability. The resulting historical information points to specific areas of plausible Sufi musical influence on Indian classical music that are congruent with, though more limited than, claims made by some Indic musical scholarship.

Finally, the issue of historicity in this oral tradition inevitably leads to a consideration of historical depth. It is not likely that the thirteenth-century figure, Amir Khusrau, is the actual originator of the present-day Sufi musical features; his personage more likely serves as a metaphor for their distinct Muslim origin. The fact that he is also widely regarded as the inventor of the much younger sitar and tablā supports this contention. On the other hand, to reinforce Vansina (1985), we must not underestimate the power of memory in an oral musical tradition or the self-knowledge of an endogamous, hereditary, musical community. Clearly, we need not only to place these data against the wider cultural and sociopolitical horizon, but also to acknowledge the dialectical interplay of oral and written history, of fact and metaphor mirroring each other. Only then can the evidence of oral history begin to make its full contribution to the study of music.

NOTES

Basic ideas in this paper were first presented at the 1983 annual meeting of the Society for Ethnomusicology, held in Tallahassee, Florida.

1. *Qawwālī* is a generic term for the primary South Asian genre of Sufi music; it also denotes the standard occasion of its performance.
2. Amir Khusrau is buried in the Nizamuddin Shrine and venerated in his own right, although he is not a saint.
3. Today the *qawwāl bachche* are actually an intermarrying group of three lineages identified by the small towns near Delhi that were their respective traditional residences (Dasna, Sikandarabad, Hapur). Prominent qawwāls among them are Meraj Ahmad and Hayat Ahmad (Dasna lineage), Inam Ahmad (Hapur lineage), and Mahmud Ahmad (Sikandarabad lineage).
4. Prominent among them are the late Aziz Ahmad Khan Warsi, Iqbal Husain Khan, and Wasiuzzaman.
5. Prominent among them are Manzur Niyazi and Bahauddin Ahmad.
6. Best known among them are the works of Jami and Amir Khusrau.
7. Encapsulated in the paired idiom *mashaikh* (singular, *sheikh*)/qawwal.
8. The terminological and organizational parallel with Hindu occupational castes is worth noting.
9. Ironically, this particular shrine was founded on an opposite premise,

since Nizamuddin Auliya eschewed both influence and patronage from the imperial court (K. A. Nizami 1974:240ff; Aziz Ahmad 1963).

10. This may well account for the fact that a number of songs in the comprehensive Bhatkande collection (1951–57), some of which are also featured in Kaufmann (1968), are slightly inconsistent with the strict raga outlines and are therefore not always suitable as prototypes of raga illustration.

11. This stands in contrast to the much larger number of classical song compositions that are agreed to be of historical stature.

12. Interestingly, one of them, *sul fākhta* (actually *usul fākhta,* see Sarmadee 1975:60) has been revived recently in solos by the most famous representative of a Muslim tablā gharānā, Alla Rakha.

13. Motivated by cultural nationalism and the anticolonial movement, some of its manifestations are All-India Music Conferences, music colleges, and printed music collections.

14. Gesudaraz was the last Chishti founder saint in India; one of his direct descendants has described the ritual (Husaini 1970). I had the special privilege of recording a band samā^{c} performance from outside, through a small lattice pattern in the thick stone wall.

15. Lucknow, which took over that role in the nineteenth century, does not have a single dominant shrine, although the region abounds in smaller saintly establishments.

16. An example is the well-known tarāna in "Yār-e-man be-ā, be-ā."

The History of a Peruvian Panpipe Style and the Politics of Interpretation

7

Thomas Turino

Interchange between members of the urban-Western and rural-indigenous societies in Peru has affected the evolution of Andean musical practices in fundamental ways since the colonial era. The history of a particular rural panpipe style and its diffusion to the city illustrates the circular interaction between these spheres as well as the musical consequences of asymmetrical power relations among various Peruvian ethnic and class factions. The creation of this rural style in the district of Conima (Huancanè province), in the southern department of Puno, was inspired by *indigenismo,* an urban-based ideological movement of the early twentieth century. In the 1970s the style was adopted by Puneño migrants in Lima and other Peruvian cities. The urban panpipe movement subsequently raised the prestige of the style, thereby influencing the musical activities of young peasants in rural Puno. However, rather than viewing this history and the Conimeño panpipe style itself as one phenomenon, we should interpret the style as a symbolic fulcrum to which quite disparate meanings have been attached in specific temporal and geographical contexts, according to the needs and status positions of particular actors within Peruvian society.

Although panpipes are played in various highland and tropical forest regions, Puno is the primary center for the large-ensemble, double-row panpipe traditions in Peru. Each of the four major ensemble styles using double-row panpipes is associated with a specific repertory and dance of the same name: *sikuris* (accompanied with *bombos,* large double-headed drums); *ayarachi* (accompanied by *cajas,* large indigenous snare drums); *chiriguanos* (without percussion as performed in Puno); and *sikumorenos* (with Western snare drum, bass drum, and cymbals). The first three are rural indigenous traditions, while *sikumoreno* refers to an urban-mestizo style distinguished from the others by its livelier rhythm, stylized urban costumes, distinct repertory, and slicker choreography. All four types feature a manner of performance in which the two panpipe rows (each containing alternate pitches of the scale) are divided between a pair of musicians who perform the melody in interlocking fashion. The ensembles are frequently comprised of between twelve and sixteen pairs of musicians.

The *ayarachi* and *chiriguano* styles use three different-sized panpipes played in parallel octaves, whereas *sikumoreno* ensembles usually have only the two lower voice parts in parallel octaves. The *sikuris* style, performed by the Aymara of Huancanè province and the Quechua in the province of Puno, traditionally used three (or more rarely four) parallel octaves, or three voice groups of two voices, each tuned in parallel fourths, fifths, and octaves.

At the end of the 1920s, the sikuris style that concerns us here emerged in Conima, Huancanè, and included nine voices in parallel thirds. Local oral history suggests that the innovation resulted from a mestizo *indigenista*'s involvement with, and intervention in, the indigenous Aymara musical culture. The Conimeño style later gained popularity in Lima and through the advocacy of migrant and university panpipe organizations in the capital it has since been widely diffused to different cities and rural areas in the southern highlands.

The meanings of a musical style are frequently constructed to serve given social ends in political struggles over the creation of identities and the maintenance or challenging of positions in a social hierarchy. This process of construction may be supported by a reinvention of the style's history that can then bolster and legitimize the agendas of the particular social groups. People create history in a double sense: through concrete action in specific circumstances, and through the subjective interpretation of past occurrences according to needs, dispositions, and social conditions at the moment of reconstruction. The new Conimeño sikuris style became an emblem of three different identities: the regionalistic-nationalistic position of its mestizo creators since the 1920s; "indigenous Conimeño culture" for the local peasantry and for Conimeño migrants in Lima; and "the indigenous masses" for the politicized vanguard of the urban-panpipe movement in the late 1970s and early 1980s. My reading of the style and its disparate meanings involves yet another level of construction that underlines issues of asymmetrical social power, and concerns the fact that parallel thirds are a fundamental feature of mestizo musical culture in Peru—whether or not this is recognized by the specific actors.

The different uses of the Conimeño sikuris style can be treated in a single account because each of these groups is situated within the same social, economic, and political hierarchy. This is made more or less explicit, depending on who tells the story. In each case, motivations, musical choices, and subjective meanings hinge on issues of identity, power, and different types of social controls, ranging from external economic incentives to an internalized "social consensus"—*hegemony,* in Gramscian terms (Gramsci 1971). A comparison of the rural and urban groups who perform the Conimeño panpipe style suggests that the dominant "social consensus," when really internalized by members of subordinate factions, becomes a more fundamental form of control, directing cultural choice precisely because its impact is not recognized, whereas the effects of external controls cease when the incentives are no longer applied.

Aymara Musical Culture in Conima

Conima, a rural Aymara district on the northern shore of Lake Titicaca, is located between the district of Moho and the Bolivian border. It is part of Huancanè, one of the two Aymara-speaking provinces in Puno (along with Chucuito to the south of the lake). The district of Conima is divided into six indigenous *ayllus* (political, geographical, religious community units), which are often further subdivided and are primarily supported by subsistence agriculture.

The town of Conima serves as the administrative and trading center for the district. It is largely inhabited by mestizos who maintain a national-cultural orientation in contrast to the localist Aymara, and there is a major sociocultural schism between the two groups. Mestizos have long exhibited a marked social prejudice against the Aymara. Mestizos call themselves "the notable people" or "the decent people" in contrast to the lower-class Indians, while among themselves the Aymara refer to mestizos as *q'ara* (a negative term used to denote outsiders). The strained relations between the two groups are exemplified by stories of Aymara peasants being physically ejected from stores in town upon the entrance of mestizo *vecinos* (townsmen).

Before Velasco's agrarian reform (1968–75), the superior power of the local elite was based on larger landholdings and wealth through commerce. The mestizo group also manipulated the support of the police force and judicial system. Landlord-serf relations existed in the three Conimeño communities where *haciendas* were established, and even the independent peasantry entered into different types of patron-client relationships with the local elite. Ritual "co-parent" (*compadrazgo*) relationships have been, and remain, a primary mechanism by which peasants seek aid and protection of the wealthier mestizos. Although the mestizos' power has diminished in recent years, relations between the two groups remain asymmetrical and strained.

The egalitarian social relations and the value of group solidarity within Aymara communities afford a striking contrast, and they have generated many cultural patterns. Social interaction is nonconfrontational, and speech styles are quiet and indirect. Individuals do not like to stand out, or be singled out, in group interactions, and priority is given to collective over individual identity. Public criticism or correction of individuals within the group is rare, and if a conflict emerges that cannot simply be ignored (the usual way of dealing with problems), factionalism results.

Equal access to opportunity is stressed above individual competence for specific tasks. The political and religious offices of each ayllu or subdivision rotate equally among adult males regardless of personal aptitude for a given post. Each social unit also has its own musical ensemble, which acts as its primary public representative for the community during fiestas. While certain men in the community are recognized for their greater dedication and knowledge in musical matters, any male[1] is welcome to perform with his community ensemble during fiestas, without concern for musical competence, or even proper tuning of the instruments in his possession.

Conimeños articulate a definite set of aesthetic ideals for musical performance (Turino 1989). However, since no one is turned away from participating and since publicly correcting or commenting on an individual's playing within the group runs counter to basic Aymara social mores, the realization of the ideals is sometimes socially constrained. Stated another way, equal access to participation and congenial community relations have priority over the quality of the musical sound.

Five basic instrumental traditions are currently performed by the community ensembles in Conima. These include: *sikuris;* five-hole *pinkillus;* six-hole *pinkillus* (cane duct flutes); *tarkas* (carved wooden duct flutes); and *pitus* (side-blown cane flutes). Each instrumental tradition is performed only for the specific fiesta occasions with which it is associated, and most older Aymara can play all the instruments on the rotating basis that context requires. These are large-ensemble (between ten and fifty players) and nonspecialist traditions. Only wind instruments of the same type are performed together, and all are accompanied by specific types of percussion.

The History of Qhantati Ururi and the Conimeño Sikuris Style

The ad hoc community ensembles just described still represent the mainstay in the ayllus of Conima. In the late 1920s, however, a new type of musical ensemble was organized by a local town mestizo, Natalio Calderón. A series of musical innovations grew out of Calderón's involvement with the local Aymara traditions, apparently including the harmonic change for sikuris ensembles that concerns us here.

Prior to the early decades of this century, members of highland rural elites held the indigenous culture in disdain, precluding any creative involvement with musical practices. By the 1920s, a few liberally minded rural-town mestizos began to take an interest in the local indigenous culture due to a sociopolitical movement known as *indigenismo,* which was centered in Lima and highland cities among upper- and middle-class intellectuals, writers, and artists. The movement had several facets. For some it grew out of a concern for national identity and unity vis-à-vis Europe and North America. Aspects of Andean culture were symbolically selected—and thus given greater legitimacy—since they provided a clear point of contrast. Members of the movement with leftist leanings began to fight for the rights of Indian communities in cases of land snatching and overt exploitation.

In the southern highlands the situation was somewhat distinct. In Puno, the expansion of the international (primarily English) wool trade and the increased control of the region by coastal and Arequipeña exporting firms threatened the less powerful members of local elites. In this context, certain mestizos in rural areas took the side of the indigenous communities, largely in the spirit of regionalistic solidarity in the face of foreign and coastal exploitation. Again, aspects of indigenous culture were used as identity emblems, involving mestizos directly with such cultural manifestations for the first time.

Natalio Calderón, a mestizo landowner in Conima, was a leftist indigenista who was associated with members of this movement in the city of Puno and with others, such as V. Mendoza, of the provincial capital of Huancanè. In April of 1928 (or 1929; oral sources differ), during a visit by Mendoza to Conima, these men decided to organize a sikuris ensemble comprised of indigenous players. According to Calderón's son, Augusto, the purpose of forming this ensemble was to defend their rights:

> To defend their land they also had to stand up for the *zampoñas* [panpipes], and the zampoñas were their homeland. They were defending their homeland, because according to my father, to defend your music is to defend your homeland. [There was also] the idea that one should not allow the use of metal [brass band] musical instruments—which were starting to be used at that time. He said, "We should not buy even one metal instrument because to do so was to fill the pockets of the rich with money." (interview tape no. 85, transcription, p. 8)

Typical indigenista sentiments include the use of the indigenous panpipe as an emblem of the homeland and the need to defend themselves against the imperialism of outsiders ("the pockets of the rich"). The symbolic importance of musical instruments is clearly shown in the contrast of the panpipe with brass band instruments.

The musical group organized by Calderón, which was to become known later as Qhantati Ururi (Dawning Star), differed significantly from traditional community ensembles. Calderón and Mendoza decided to choose the best indigenous players from all the ayllus in order to form a group of "superior" quality, as defined by their own mestizo standards. The idea of a pan-ayllu ensemble must have been strange for the Aymara at the time, since it contrasted fundamentally with their normal mode of community-based organization.

A peasant who joined the ensemble in 1931 indicated that in order to organize the group and maintain stable participation and discipline (i.e., control), economic incentives were offered to the Aymara musicians, including preferential treatment in regard to land access. Natalio's son stated that *compadrazgo* (co-parent) ties between his father and various peasants were also involved in organizing the ensemble. Their greater wealth enables mestizos to form large networks of *compadres,* which are used to elicit services from Aymara in return for promised aid or protection. In short, while more specific information is unavailable, it is clear that the mestizo founder of Qhantati Ururi used economic incentives and his higher social position to form this rather atypical group and to direct its future course.

In addition to its pan-ayllu "all-star" character, mestizo ideas and values guided other aspects of the musical organization. The traditional ad hoc structure of ayllu musical ensembles was replaced by relatively fixed personnel, and the heightened stability aided in creating a "superior" musical group as the musicians became a well-rehearsed unit. Moreover, the ensemble rehearsed on a more regular basis than traditionally occurs. During rehearsals under the mestizo's direction, musicians were made to play alone or in pairs to check performance quality, and those who did not come up to standard during these examinations were not allowed to stay with the ensemble.

Clearly, the singling out and testing of individual players as well as restrictions on participation ran counter to the basic Aymara sociomusical modus operandi. The major musical change involved, however, was that quality control over musical sound production was given priority over the equality of social relations among participants. Such an alteration, which imposed a hierarchical structure on the Aymara musicians, was possible only because of the asymmetrical power relations between the mestizo and the indigenous peasants. Stated simply, only a mestizo could get away with such behavior in Conima, and then only because certain types of incentives and social pressures were used.

Calderón's impact on the indigenous musical culture did not stop here, however. According to various local sources, Calderón was directly involved in the creation of the Conimeño sikuris harmony using parallel thirds. As told to me, Calderón was a harp player who used to perform duets with a church organist. Inspired by the organ's sound and based on his knowledge of harmony from harp performance, he thought of placing the *octavin,* or *bajo,* voice a third below the major melody-carrying voice (the *malta* or *ankuta*) so that a sikuris ensemble "would sound like an organ." Under Calderón's direction, the Aymara peasant who "cut" the panpipes for Qhantati began to make the style of *tropa* (consort of instruments) with parallel thirds.

The harmonic change involved may be seen in Figure 1a. The distinct voices (each with its own name: *suli, malta,* etc.) are created by cutting the tubes of each panpipe type to different lengths so that each voice sounds in specific harmonic intervals with the other voices. With the addition of the bajo voices in the Conimeño style (compare Figures 1a and 1b), the *contra* voices were lowered a whole step so as to avoid the parallel second. The harmonic arrangement of the Conimeño tropa is conceptualized by peasant musicians from the center malta voice outward, not in terms of stacked root position triads. The pitches given refer to the lowest tone of each panpipe; the remaining twelve tubes of each panpipe maintain the same harmonic relationships (the pitches given are relative).

Figure 1a: Parallel 4ths, 5ths, 8ths

Suli	E5
Contrasuli	B4
Malta	E4
Contramalta	B3
Sanja	E3
Contrasanja	B2

Figure 1b: Conimeño Style

Suli	E5
Bajosuli	C#5
Contrasuli	A4
Malta	E4
Bajomalta	C#4
Contramalta	A3
Sanja	E3
Bajosanja	C#3
Contrasanja	A2

Although there is not complete unanimity regarding Natalio Calderón as the creator of this harmonic style, people both within and outside the district identify Conima as the place of its origin.[2] It is also generally agreed that the local community ensembles performed in parallel octaves, or with fourths, fifths, and octaves, until the beginning of this century. Because tertian harmony is so obviously linked to mestizo/criollo tradition in Peru, the cited oral history provides the most likely explanation for the harmonic innovation. Other issues suggest that a mestizo with some knowledge of Western harmony was involved. For example, Aymara panpipe makers in Conima conceptualize siku voice relationships in terms of tube size rather than harmonic intervals and, by the best maker's own statement, they are unable to create new harmonic voicing except through the economically prohibitive practice of trial and error.

With the formation of a sikuris ensemble under his direction Calderón had both the knowledge and the medium through which to realize a new tropa voicing. Apparently, no other individual was in such a position, and no other explanations for the creation of the Conimeño sikuris style were forthcoming during my investigation. It is clear that the *bajo* voice was in place by 1931 according to a Qhantati member who joined in that year. All statements indicate that Calderón's ensemble was responsible for diffusing the style.

Under *vecino* (town mestizo) direction, the ensemble performed in fiestas both in Conima, and, through Mendoza's promotion, in Huancanè. With mestizo initiative and sponsorship, the ensemble traveled to Lima in 1939 to perform at the "folklore" festival of Amancaes. Through these activities Qhantati began to gain recognition and began to diffuse its new style of sikuris harmony. In 1965, Qhantati returned to Lima to perform under mestizo tutelage, and on this occasion the group recorded an LP record. Due to the scarcity of sikuris recordings, this publication ensured the group wide recognition and a place of honor when interest in panpipe music began to mount among young people in Lima after 1970. It is probable that the group's acceptance by a wider audience—including mestizos and people in urban centers—was aided by the use of parallel thirds as well as by the dependence of its playing style on a mestizo's conception of polished performance.

When Natalio passed away his younger brother Lucho assumed the directorship of the group, and it remained a disciplined performing ensemble guided by mestizo aesthetics. As before, the repertory included the best dances and musical genres that the different ayllus had to offer. The ensemble maintained the Aymara practice of performing all the different Conimeño wind instruments (pinkillus, pitus, etc.), and this was reflected on the 1965 record. For "folkloric" festival and stage performances, however, the various costumed dances (associated with different times of year) were performed sequentially to add variety to the stage show.

Lucho's death marked the end of mestizo direction and sponsorship for Qhantati. Under the current leadership of an Aymara *guia* (consensually chosen guide), the ensemble has changed in major ways. Rehearsals are only held immediately before performance events, as is traditional, and the examinations have been dropped. During rehearsals and performances the Aymara custom of not commenting on other peoples' playing has been reinstituted among the older players, and hence sound-quality control has diminished. Another major change has taken place in regard to personnel. The participating members no longer hail from all over the district, but are primarily from Ayllu Sulcata, the guia's home, or nearby. Thus, within district fiestas, Qhantati has basically come to represent a subdivision of Ayllu Sulcata, and in keeping with traditional ensemble organization, it has basically become an ad hoc ensemble.

Some mestizo critics claim that since the passing of Lucho the discipline of Qhantati has decreased and with it the quality of performance. In my estimation, what has happened is that the group has returned to functioning as a traditional community ensemble. With this transformation its sound has changed as well, due to Aymara sociomusical priorities.

This return to the traditional mode of ensemble organization raises important issues. The innovations in the group under mestizo direction were instituted largely by external incentives. However, the changes in values and modus operandi were not internalized or internally generated by Qhantati members but were dependent on mestizo direction and discipline. Once this influence disappeared, so did the mestizo innovations that conflicted with the basic style of Aymara communal relations.

Significantly, the innovation of the harmonic style was not only maintained but spread to all the Conimeño community ensembles by 1984. Several reasons for the maintenance of the harmonic change may be cited. At the most practical level, the guia who currently makes the panpipes for Qhantati learned to do so from (and uses the measuring sticks of) his predecessor, who made the tropa with parallel thirds. According to the guia, it is the only way he knows. Perhaps equally important, and as an explanation for the style's diffusion, Qhantati's fame and popularity outside the district raised the prestige of this type of tropa. It therefore began to be adopted by other groups in Conima until it became associated with the district as a whole, and it is now considered the "traditional" Conimeño style.

Such sound changes are easier to institute in Conimeño musical culture than are innovations that require alterations in basic modes of social behavior. In fact, the guia of Qhantati told me that he potentially favors radical sound changes (such as the creation of totally new sikuris voicing) because such innovations would make his ensemble distinct. On the other hand, if an Aymara guia attempted to give examinations, restrict participation, or correct individual players, he would not be tolerated and would forfeit his leadership role.

The history of Qhantati and of the musical changes described here provide various points of contestation and different ranges of meaning for Conimeños according to their ethnic/class position and agendas. For example, the people most apt to reject Calderón as the creator of the Conimeño consort type were rural peasants who invariably attributed the fundamental aspects of their musical practices to their ancestors, due to the importance of music as an identity emblem and the antagonism felt toward mestizos. Conversely, those who had the most investment in stories of the mestizos' role in Qhantati's former glory and quality of performance were from the mestizo faction, the obvious implication being that for something of worth to be established, mestizo leadership would have to be involved. The political motivations underlying the act of historical interpretation in this instance, as in so many others, are clear. Whether or not one accepts Natalio Calderón as the actual innovator of the consort with parallel thirds, his role in the creation of Qhantati Ururi and the diffusion of the style seems indisputable. He made history—but on the basis of political-economic conditions, the indigenista ideology, and internalized Western/mestizo aesthetics *not* of his own making.

Regardless of the given historical interpretation, no one I spoke with in Conima was aware of the issue of parallel thirds or the fact that this is a primary feature of mestizo musical style in Peru. Contemporary peasant performers only know that their sikuris style has gained wide popularity outside the district and has spawned many imitators: a source of fierce pride that has made them all the more eager to claim the innovation as their own. At the same time, they disparage outside imitators. Ironically, then, while the vanguard of the urban-panpipe movement adopted the style to identify themselves symbolically with the indigenous peasantry, Conimeños in the ayllus regard this as the unauthorized theft of a paramount identity emblem: new points of contestation emerge.

The Urban-Panpipe Movement and the Diffusion of the Conimeño Style

Until the 1970s, the Conima sikuris style remained largely localized in the district. By the 1980s it had been diffused to the cities of Lima,

Arequipa, Cusco, Juliaca, and the city of Puno, as well as to other rural areas in Puno. By this time it had become the most widely known sikuris style in Peru. Qhantati's sojourns to different cities and their 1965 record partially explain this. The national diffusion of the style, however, must be understood in the context of a musical movement among Puneño migrants in Lima that began in the 1970s.

By the late 1960s the intense sierra-to-Lima migration had resulted in the advent of increased performance of indigenous musical traditions in the capital by highland migrants (Turino 1987, 1988). This contrasts dramatically with the previous situation in which lower- and working-class migrants were reluctant to perform their indigenous musical traditions in Lima because of social prejudice and the "shame" or "embarrassment" that they felt in regard to their highland heritage (see Arguedas 1985:8; Schaedel 1979).

Currently, for Puneños and other migrants, musical ensembles and activities are largely organized in the context of regional associations whose prime criteria for membership are based on common place of origin and, often, socioeconomic class; the character and functioning of the clubs differ according to both region and class. As early as the mid-1950s there were several lower/working-class Puneño regional clubs in Lima that played panpipes as well as tarkas and pinkillus. Although they occasionally played in public-stage contexts, for the most part these club-based ensembles performed at their own private fiestas behind closed doors.

In 1985, I counted sixty-nine sikuris and sikumoreno ensembles performing publicly in the capital, and I am certain that my count is only partial. Fifty-seven of these groups are based in Puneño regional associations of the working and lower classes, and twelve are comprised of middle-class university students, largely non-Puneño. On practically any Sunday afternoon during 1985 there were sikuris performances in several locations around Lima. By 1985–86, panpipe ensembles were given pride of place in a number of "folkloric" parades and events in central Lima that had been organized by the city and national governments, and this music was becoming well known and even popular with some Limeños. Among the urban sikuris groups, the Conimeño harmonic style was the most common.

What took place between 1960 and 1985 that led to the dramatic rise of sikuris performance, visibility, and importance in Lima? At a general level, the demographic explosion of highlanders in the city—and a consequent change in economic and political power relations that led to a shift away from the prior assimilationist tendencies among migrants—is fundamental. The widespread public performance of panpipe music in Lima, however, began after 1970 with a middle-class Puneño students' movement and with the activities of a particular regional organization in the capital: the Asociación Juvenil Puno (AJP). By nearly all accounts, AJP was almost single-handedly responsible for the current popularity of panpipe music in Lima and in other Peruvian cities.

According to several of the early founders, AJP had its beginnings in a rather informal social club consisting of middle-class Puneño students who, for the most part, had come from the city of Puno to study in Lima. Affected by "culture shock" and homesickness in the capital, the members of "Centro de Estudiantes Puno" began meeting in various homes in 1970 to socialize and, on occasion, to sing and play music with guitars.

As the group evolved in 1970–71, they sought a focus for their activities and they decided upon music. One of the founders stated that they wanted to perform a type of music that would differentiate them from the mestizo string ensembles (*estudiantinas*) used by Puneño clubs of the highland elite. Another early member noted that the panpipe was considered particularly appropriate, given the leftist and regionalist orientation of the group, since the instrument was associated with the indigenous peasantry (i.e., the "masses") in Puno.

On June 27, 1972, an event in the city of Puno further radicalized the group politically and inspired them to activity. During a protest against a visit to Puno by the wife of the Peruvian president, Juan Velasco, a number of students and workers were wounded and some were allegedly killed by government troops. The Puneño students in Lima were scandalized by the way the event was presented in the media. The organization, by then called Asociación Juvenil Puno, thus used the name "Sikuris 27 de Junio" for their performing panpipe ensemble, in honor of the martyrs in Puno. They also took it upon themselves to inform Puneños and other groups in Lima about the truth of the affair. Using panpipe music as their medium for gaining public attention and access, the group began to perform at union meetings, in squatter settlements, on the streets, and in the theaters. It was in this context, through the activities of radicalized middle-class students from urban Puno, that panpipe music began to be widely performed in Lima for the first time.

At this point in its history, AJP played panpipes in the urban-mestizo sikumoreno style. According to early members, this was the type they were most familiar with as urban Puneños. Also during this period, they continued to refine their cultural-political ideology. Based in nationalistic/regionalistic, neo-indigenista, and leftist sentiments, AJP members argued that the siku was the most appropriate revolutionary emblem for Peruvians. For AJP, the very act of playing the siku, involving the communally oriented hocket technique traditional in

Puneño panpipe performance, was a demonstration of solidarity with the oppressed indigenous population, a rejection of foreign cultural imperialism, and an icon for leftist collectivism.

In 1976 and 1977, AJP traveled as a group to perform sikumorenos in the fiesta of Candelaria (February 2) in the city of Puno. At that time in urban Puno only peasants or lower/working-class people played panpipes, and only the sikumoreno, not the indigenous sikuris style, was used. The performance of sikumorenos by the middle-class students of AJP—who enjoyed a certain prestige because they lived and studied in Lima—was a great novelty. During these trips, they planted the first seeds of their "cultural politics" in the departmental capital, and raised questions about urban-Puneños' prejudices against what was then considered a cultural expression of the "*bajo pueblo*" (low-status people).

Regarding these trips, one of the founders of AJP notes: "We were identified [in Puno] as being from Lima, regardless of our [Puneño] origins. Through our publicaton *Jake'e Aru,* leaflets, and the media, we diffused the idea of the necessity of revitalizing the most genuine expression of Puno to the youth. In the years that followed, new panpipe groups appeared that consisted totally of young people, reaffirming our faith in the vitality of our people" (Vilca 1982:63). After their 1977 trip at least three sikumoreno groups sprang up among the middle-class youth and university students in the city of Puno, and more were to follow.

Likewise during the 1975–80 period in Lima the activities of AJP inspired the formation of migrant panpipe ensembles. By 1970 a large number of lower/working-class Puneño regional clubs were already in existence in Lima, but most were involved with sports rather than musical activities. After 1975, increasingly more lower/working-class migrant clubs began shifting their focus from sports to music and dance, many specifically to panpipe performance. AJP had direct input into this process. For example, when asked about the formation of their panpipe ensemble, one member of a working-class Puneño club noted: "We formed the group in 1976. Well, we had seen this group of young people [AJP] playing in the streets, we saw them playing in schools, here in Lima. 'Well, then,' we said to ourselves, 'if this group of young people who play so badly but with such enthusiasm, can perform panpipes [here in Lima], why can't we who are old experienced players?' " (field tape no. 63).

In Lima, the young men of AJP consciously worked to alter the prejudicial attitudes and feelings of inferiority internalized by working-class migrants regarding panpipe music and their Puneño heritage. To this end, in 1978 AJP began organizing public performance events for the Puneño groups in the relatively prestigious public locale of Campo de Marte, near downtown Lima. Also during this period other Puneño and non-Puneño university student groups began forming sikumoreno ensembles directly following AJP's lead. While the more conservative lower/working-class clubs tended not to adopt AJP's political ideology, the university groups saw their musical activities in a nationalistic, neo-indigenista, and leftist light.

Significantly, during 1978, AJP changed over from sikumorenos to the more indigenous sikuris style. After their participation in the Puno Candelaria fiesta in 1977 a number of AJP members traveled to Conima with the express purpose of making contact with traditional panpipe musicians. This region was probably chosen because Qhantati had already popularized the Conimeño style through its LP record and performances in urban centers. Dante Vilca, a founder of AJP, specifically mentions that the AJP delegation met the musicians of Qhantati Ururi in Conima: "the cultivators of one of the most successful and beautiful sikuris styles of the Aymara region in Puno" (1982:63).

Through increasing familiarity with the musical traditions of Puno, the members of AJP came to realize that for their purposes of demonstrating solidarity with indigenous people and culture, the sikuris style was more appropriate than the urban-mestizo sikumorenos. Although some members of AJP stated that they much preferred sikumoreno music personally—because of its livelier rhythm, among other factors—the ideological importance of the change took precedence over such aesthetic considerations.

Of central importance to the present discussion, AJP specifically adopted the Conimeño harmonic style. In addition, much of their repertory was (and still is) comprised of pieces composed and performed by Qhantati Ururi, which were learned from cassettes recorded by AJP members in Conima. When the affiliate branch of AJP was formed in the city of Puno in 1979, they also adopted Qhantati's style, repertory, and even the costume featured in the photo on their 1965 record jacket (which they no longer wear).[3]

Once again AJP acted as the vanguard for the urban-panpipe movement. Following their adoption of the Conimeño sikuris style and repertory, student and migrant groups in both Lima and the city of Puno began to change over to sikuris and, in disproportionate numbers, to the Conimeño style. Moreover, new sikuris ensembles—often incorporating the parallel thirds harmony—were formed as the popularity of this music increased. Even during my two years of research (1984–86), sikumorenos ensembles continued to decline both in number and visibility while sikuris ensembles were on the increase.

Feedback to Rural Puno

Important ramifications of the urban-panpipe movement were also felt in the rural zones of Puno. Legitimized by the newfound popularity of Puneño panpipe music in the cities, young mestizos in rural towns such as Moho and Huancanè, Rosaspata and Conima, began to form sikuris ensembles, and again the style initiated by Qhantati Ururi was taken as the model. The impact of the movement among rural-town mestizos was all the more pronounced since they could take pride in the fact that music from their own region had gained national recognition.

This phenomenon, in turn, has had dramatic consequences among the youth of indigenous communities. In contrast to their parents, and since the 1960s, young people in the ayllus of Conima have increasingly turned to urban-national culture, values, and worldview. This is the result of migration and return migration, increased access to public education, and the advent of the transistor radio. Consequently, many young people of peasant families in Conima have ignored the majority of indigenous musical instruments (such as pinkillu, tarka, and pitu), and these community traditions are dwindling for lack of the youths' participation—as the older players point out. It is significant, then, that the young peoples' participation in Conimeño sikuris ensembles is thriving (even the local high school has its own panpipe ensemble), and this can only be attributed to the legitimization of this tradition by the urban-panpipe movement and by the local town mestizos. A similar trend is evident in other Aymara districts in the province of Huancanè.

Conclusion

The circular cultural interchange between the Western-oriented dominant society in Lima and indigenous rural people is clearly evident at all stages of the history presented here. Like the indigenista ideology in earlier decades, the urban-panpipe movement was diffused from Lima to highland cities, and finally to the rural sector of Puno, while at the same time these movements utilized rural cultural resources. Paradoxically, the prestige of urban society led to a revitalization of rural-based sikuris music among the Aymara youth, while they continued to ignore the other instrumental traditions that had not found support in the cities.

The types of controls operating in situations of asymmetrical power relations may explain processes of cultural resource selection and musical innovation, as well as the stability and meaning of such innovations. The participation and cooperation of the indigenous members of Qhantati were brought about through the mestizo director's greater social power within the situation and his use of economic incentives. When the leadership of Qhantati passed from mestizo to peasant hands the most significant changes in the group were dropped. This example demonstrates that internalization of innovations—and of the values that generate them—is central to their longevity, whereas the effect of external controls is dependent on their constant application.

In choosing a musical emblem that expressed their solidarity with indigenous Puneños, it is significant that AJP—the leaders of the urban-panpipe movement—selected the Conimeño sikuris style. Several questions need to be addressed. First, why was the panpipe chosen over other indigenous Puneño flute traditions? Second, in making the conscious choice to switch from the mestizo sikumoreno tradition to an indigenous style, why, out of all the possible choices, did they select the one that had been most affected by mestizo musical culture?

In both cases my interpretation involves the dominance of urban-Western aesthetics and attitudes internalized by these actors. It is clear, as a number of candid Puneños suggested, that in contrast with the loud, high, shrill sound of pinkillus, pitus, and tarkas, the softer, smoother timbre of the siku is much more acceptable within the dominant-urban society.[4] The Conimeño sikuris style, with its inclusion of parallel thirds, is also the most Western—in obvious contrast to other more "exotic," and indeed, more traditional-sounding indigenous panpipe styles. Because of AJP's conscious opposition to *criollo* (of Spanish heritage) society and culture, I can only assume that their selection of the siku and the Conimeño style was based on the ideological "correctness" of these emblems for their leftist, neo-indigenista position, while at the same time they provided the next best fit with AJP members' own Westernized musical values—after the sikumoreno.

Understood in the context of the asymmetrical power relations between the dominant criollo society and highland migrants, and the goals and identity needs of the latter, the adoption of the Conimeño sikuris style is clearly a case of strategic choice. But at the same time, the dominant "social consensus"—when internalized by members of subordinate social units—becomes a fundamental form of control directing cultural choice (Gramsci 1971). The influence of internalized Western aesthetics among AJP members, which even conflicted with their stated ideological goals, is a clear case in point.

This example sheds additional light on Richard Waterman's (1952) hypothesis regarding heightened syncretism of "like" musical styles. That is, in choosing an identity emblem to distinguish a subordinate group, members may select the one from their "own" tradition that is closest to the style of the dominant society due to their internalized acceptance of the superiority of that society and its musical values and resources. The selection of such similar styles also offers the path of least resistance while still serving an identity-marking function.

Internalization of the idea that urban-Western society and culture are somehow superior to indigenous culture has also taken place among many young peasants in Puno, largely since the 1960s, and this explains the somewhat paradoxical results of the urban-panpipe movement's influence in the rural zone. Conversely, the older indigenous players of Qhantati have not been greatly affected by the hegemony ("internalized social consensus") of the national society; consequently, when external controls ceased, most of the musical innovations that they wrought also passed away.

As a final point, it should be mentioned that when I explained my interpretation of AJP's initial selection of the Conimeño sikuris style to members of the group, with few exceptions, they aggressively rejected it. They also rejected the idea that it was somehow more Western in style and, like Conimeños, seemed unaware of the meaning of parallel thirds as a marker of mestizo musical culture in Peru. For AJP members, sikuris music is an index of indigenous society, and its history must be traced to "their" ancestors, not to a mestizo indigenista's intervention. The "what really happened" of past occurrences is fluid and becomes a point of contestation, depending on the position and needs of the speaker. History—like identities, or the meanings attached to musical resources—is constantly being appropriated and reconstructed for contemporary political use and, in this sense, it is always modern.

NOTES

This research, conducted in Puno and Lima, Peru between November 1984 and July 1986, was supported by a Fulbright Fellowship, which I gratefully acknowledge.

1. Women do not play musical instruments in Conima. They participate in fiesta performances by dancing, or by singing on the relatively infrequent occasions when songs are included.

2. The fact that this harmonic style originated in Conima is supported by the fact that groups from other regions, who later adopted it, cite Conima as the source. Given the degree of regional chauvinism in the sierra, and the usual custom of claiming important innovations on behalf of any given speaker's home, Conima's claim to the sikuris harmony with parallel thirds seems assured.

3. By 1985, AJP in Lima had also begun to perform the sikuris style of Taquile, Puno in addition to the Conima style, which represents a continuing search for "more indigenous" types of musical expression.

4. The idea that sikuris music is more palatable than the other wind instruments for urban listeners was also reinforced for me by playing recordings of the various Conimeño traditions for Limeños. Consistently, my listeners would state a preference for sikuris over the pinkillus, tarkas, and pitus, largely due to the harmony used, the softer timbre, and the less shrill ensemble sound. As another example, in the district of Moho, the pinkillus tradition was more important, traditionally, than sikuris. For this reason, a member of a Moheño regional club in Lima commented that they really should play pinkillus rather than sikus to mark their regional identity. I asked him why they did not, and he replied that Limeños do not like pinkillus, and that people might even laugh if they played them.

Music Institutions and National Consciousness among Polish and Ukrainian Peasants

8

William Noll

With the gradual rise in national consciousness that began in the late nineteenth century among rural populations of Central and Eastern Europe, new musical practices became increasingly common in villages. By the early twentieth century, many of the new practices were supported by national or international networks that linked rural and urban populations. The networks made it possible to distribute music as either commercial product or national symbol. In some regions, urban political activists established a network of village institutions in which arrangements of rural music were explicitly presented as national in character.

Although they have antecedents, such networks and institutions are most characteristic of the twentieth-century state, and they are now found in many parts of the world. They often support images of cultural homogeneity that seem to belie the extreme regional variety of the recent past, and in many areas, even of the present. For the most part, the music practices of these networks are less than 100 years old, and they are largely of urban invention.

This essay examines the music of one ethnically mixed region, tracing some of the cultural exchanges that have taken place between urban and rural populations. In the Przemyskie region of southeastern Poland (current borders), Polish and Ukrainian populations have shared a common domicile for several hundred years.[1] The main city of the region is known in Polish as *Przemyśl* and in Ukrainian as *Peremyshl';* hence the region's name: *Przemyskie* in Polish, and *Peremyshchyna* in Ukrainian (see Figure 1).[2] In the nineteenth and early twentieth centuries, part of the music of these two groups was shared, another part was similar, and still other aspects of music were different

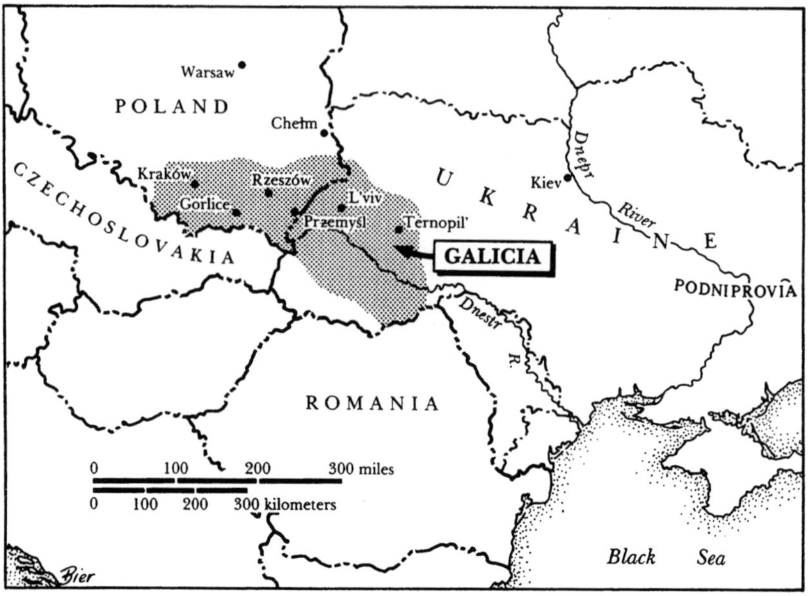

Figure 1. Map of Poland and the Ukraine

for the two groups. The older music practices were largely village-based and regionalized. The new practices were urban-derived and nonregional; they reflected cultural norms of national or international distribution.

Many music practices of rural populations in Poland, the Ukraine, and the rest of Central and Eastern Europe reflect a long-standing diversity of regional culture, a heritage of dozens, even hundreds, of distinct rural mini-cultures. Some cultural "regions" cut across ethnic territorial lines, and the boundaries of nearly all have shifted through time. Although more pronounced in rural culture up to the early twentieth century, this regionalism remains evident today in some areas, as many scholars have noted (e.g., Bojko 1980 for Ukrainian regions; Elschek 1985 for Slovak regions; and Stęszewski 1981 for Polish regions).

It is generally true that "[n]ational identity is not an innate characteristic of people, but the result of social learning" (Krawchenko 1985:2). Well-established, recognizable differences between Ukrainians and Poles were nonetheless articulated in religious practices and in other areas of life. The new circumstances created by the nineteenth-century national movements allowed for development of a secular identity that corresponded to those differences.

Music and the Social Spectrum in the Late Nineteenth Century

Having lived together for several hundred years, the Polish and Ukrainian populations of Przemyskie carried many similarities in culture. These included aspects of language: for the most part, the Przemyskie dialects of the two groups were mutually intelligible.[3] Both groups constructed village residences and barns in generally the same way; food preparation was similar; and the same can be said of dozens of other cultural elements. Many, but not all, musical elements were also shared; these involve metro-rhythmic norms, scales, aspects of repertory, instrumentation of ensembles, and musical contexts. Elements that were more common west of Przemyskie can be called "Polish," and those that were more common east of Przemyskie can be called "Ukrainian."

The Polish ethnographer Oskar Kolberg (1814–90) conducted fieldwork in Przemyskie in 1865 and again in 1883–85 (Kopernicki 1964[1891]:xi).[4] He described the population as having long been "a mixture of various ethnic groups [*rosnoplemienna*]; besides Poles . . . [there] live here Ukrainians [*Rusini*], Germans, and Jews" (Kolberg 1964c[1891]:3). The criteria that Kolberg may have used to establish ethnic identity are problematic, as this was a time before accurate census taking.

More important, it was an age before large numbers of peasants carried a national consciousness; very few associated themselves with a national entity. Most were probably unaware of much territory beyond their own and contiguous villages and the nearest market town or towns. A peasant author spoke as follows, with reference to rural Polish regions in the late nineteenth century: "As for national consciousness . . . [the peasants] lived their own life, forming a wholly separate group and caring nothing for the nation. I myself did not know that I was a Pole till I began to read books and papers, and I fancy that other villagers came to be aware of their national attachment in much the same way" (Slomka 1941[1912]:71–72). A similar lack of national consciousness was characteristic of peasants in western Ukrainian regions: "[The Ukrainian peasants of the nineteenth century were] unsure of where they fit in the East European mosaic of nations. Centuries of serfdom and enforced ignorance had not allowed a sense of national identity to crystallize. Some Ukrainians thought they were a branch of Poles; others that they were Russians; still others that they were . . . Ruthenians or Rusyns . . .; others recognized national kinship [with a larger Ukrainian entity]" (Himka 1984:433).

It seems likely that Kolberg regarded religious rite as the primary measurement of peasant identity in Przemyskie. He carefully noted the presence in a village or town of either Roman Catholic or Greek Catholic parishes, or both (Kolberg 1964c[1891]:2–10).[5] Kolberg's approach can be said to reflect the way the Przemyskie population of the time regarded itself. As national ties became increasingly significant in daily life, this division by religious rite became the main line of ethnic demarcation between Ukrainians and Poles. Most Roman Catholic peasants of the region would later embrace Polish national culture, and most Greek Catholic peasants of the area would embrace Ukrainian national culture.

In his Przemyskie monograph, Kolberg (ibid.:54–126) describes parts of the peasant wedding sequence and its music from four villages, all of them Ukrainian. The music reflects a mixture of "Polish" and "Ukrainian" elements, as defined above. Many of the transcriptions have a triple meter and the $\frac{3}{8}$ ♬ ♩ ♩ ♫ ♩ or similar *mazur* rhythms (ibid.:55–120, nos. 65, 67, 75, 85, 105, 138, 139, 140, 144, 147, 159, 172, 178, 180, 186, 187, 188, 195, 197, 206, 209, 216). These "Polish" elements were well-established norms in the Polish regions to the west and northwest of Przemyskie, but they were not as common in the Ukrainian lands to the east. Example 1 (ibid.:59, no. 75) illustrates the mazur rhythm used by both Roman Catholic and Greek Catholic peasants.

Example 1. Mazur Rhythm

Other musical features are unquestionably of Ukrainian origin. The *dumy* (historical epics) and the *kolomyjka* (a social dance genre), both of which are transcribed by Kolberg (ibid.:127–41, 193–98), are not common in the Polish regions to the west of Przemyskie. These genres were spread over a wide area of the Ukraine, as noted by Ukrainian ethnographers one generation after Kolberg (Kolessa 1910a, 1913; Hnatiuk 1905:102–54). Since at least the mid-nineteenth century, and to some extent even today, both Polish and Ukrainian villagers in Przemyskie have played the kolomyjka as a matter of course. It is one of several genres that have long been a mainstay of peasant musical practice in the region.

The scale types or modes of several wedding songs that Kolberg transcribed also belong to a widespread Ukrainian music culture. Here again, a Ukrainian musical element has long been present among the Poles of Przemyskie and elsewhere. These scale types are rare among the Polish rural populations that are far removed from contact with Ukrainians, but they are common to virtually all Polish rural populations who live in close proximity to Ukrainians. Example 2 shows three of these scale types, and Example 3 is one of the melodies transcribed by Kolberg (1964c[1891]:112, no. 205). These scales include a minor third in conjunction with either a raised sixth, or the more characteristic raised fourth, or both. The same scale types are used by both Polish and Ukrainian populations in another region, around the city of Chełm/Kholm (see Kolberg's *Chełmskie* monograph, 1964b[1890]:22, no. 87; 245, no. 131; 263, no. 177; 306, no. 273; 308, no. 280; 328, no. 348; 334, no. 363; 336, no. 368; 338, no. 373; and 339, no. 380).

These examples and the transcriptions cited from Kolberg's monographs reflect a mixture of Polish and Ukrainian genres—both mazur

Example 2. Scale Types

Example 3. Melody from Kolberg

and kolomyjka, for example—in the village repertory. Kolberg does not describe this mixture in greater detail, noting only that the ensemble played both Polish and Ukrainian melodies (ibid.:121). On the subject of ensemble instrumentation, again Kolberg is not specific, although a fiddle and *basy* or *bas* (large bowed lute about the size of a cello) seem to have been common among all ethnic groups of the region (ibid.:118, 120, 121). The ensemble sometimes included a hammered dulcimer (*cymbały/tsymbaly*) and by the late nineteenth century often a clarinet as well.

Finally, the Polish and Ukrainian peasants of the second half of the nineteenth century shared several significant features of the wedding sequence, the main context for most of the village ensemble music. A wedding was a two-to-seven day series of events that required the ritual enactment by a wide range of dramatis personae (characters/roles assumed by villagers) of orations, incantations, songs, and monetary payments (to name a few), as well as rituals in which music and dance figured prominently. Many events included specific texts and melodies that were heard exclusively in that event, or in a very few others. The ritual actions and music were executed in a sequential order that was partly of local origin and partly of regional (or wider) distribution (Kolessa 1910a:226; Bystroń 1960:80).

An extremely large ethnographic literature from the nineteenth and early twentieth centuries details the complexities of the wedding sequence in its many regional varieties.[6] If we compare Kolberg's description of the sequence in four Ukrainian villages of Przemyskie with accounts from ethnographies of other regions, we do not find regional or local differences in Przemyskie that are any more unusual or striking than those found in other regions. In other words, local varieties of wedding practice were part of the regionalization of cultural elements that was typical among peasants throughout Central and Eastern Europe.

The Przemyskie wedding sequence is noteworthy for its mixture of Polish and Ukrainian elements. The particular "cap ceremony" (*oczepiny* in Polish) practiced in these Ukrainian villages is more common west of Przemyskie, in Polish regions, than east, in Ukrainian regions. Nevertheless, the names of the characters who performed the ceremony are Ukrainian: *bojary* ("groomsmen"), *molodyj* ("groom"), and *moloda* or *kni͡ahyni͡a* ("bride"). The term for bridesmaids is shared by Polish and Ukrainian villagers in this and many other regions: *drużka/druzhka* (Kolberg 1964c[1891]:55, 111, 126). Once again, similar mixtures of Polish and Ukrainian elements are common in most regions where the two groups have lived for a long period in contiguous domicile (see Kolberg's *Chełmskie* monograph, 1964b[1890]:192–342).

To summarize, musical elements that were common to Roman Catholic and Greek Catholic peasants in nineteenth-century Przemyskie include metro-rhythmic norms, aspects of repertory, scale types, ensemble instrumentation, and musical context. It was not unusual for certain cultural elements to be shared in a region inhabited by two or more ethnographically distinct population groups. This began to change in the late nineteenth century as new institutions were established in villages, bringing new cultural elements to rural areas along with an ever-expanding feeling of national identity.

The Institutionalization of National Networks

Throughout the nineteenth century, both Polish and Ukrainian regions were parts of larger zones of partition that constituted provinces of the absolutist empires. Poland was divided among the Prussian, Russian, and Austrian states; the Ukraine among the Russian and Austrian states.[7] The Austrian (Habsburg) zone of partition of Poland and Ukraine was Galicia, which included Przemyskie.[8] Polish and Ukrainian national movements became increasingly active from the 1860s to the birth (or rebirth) of both nations at the end of World War I.

Such national movements could be found in nearly all of those regions of Europe that by 1918 would become Poland, the Ukraine, Czechoslovakia, Hungary, Romania, Yugoslavia, and Bulgaria. "Before and after liberation of each country, there was a continuous effort made by national . . . leaders [of a wide political spectrum] to convince the peasantry that they were not merely members of a village or a region, but rather members of a nation" (Sanders 1958:46). Urban intellectuals realized that if national political entities were to emerge from partition and occupation, it was necessary to bring the peasants (at least 80 percent of the population in southeastern Poland) into a participatory role (Kieniewicz 1969:204). The establishment of institutional links between urban and rural communities was central to this effort.

In both Polish and Ukrainian lands, literate urban activists called for the establishment of village libraries and social clubs in which peasants could learn to read, or at least have read aloud to them, newspapers, journal articles, and books that would increase knowledge of personal hygiene, promote improved agricultural techniques, and teach the history (mostly urban, military, or aristocratic) of the Polish or Ukrainian nations. By the 1880s, journals were published in Galicia for distribution in villages, primarily to increase literacy. Agricultural associations were begun to assist peasants in financing capital improvements on the land (Narkiewicz 1976:38–64).

Priests, journalists, teachers, ethnographers, and folklorists attempted to propagate a sense of national identity among rural dwellers. These groups fanned out over the countryside, bringing their message to hundreds of thousands of peasants. They took up the problem of how to disseminate specific cultural elements among a regionally diverse rural population in ways that would create a distinctive and common cultural heritage. Some of the new music institutions established in the early twentieth century transmitted practices that had been little known, or even unknown, to rural populations, but which could now be learned and propagated as "theirs," as part of a national heritage.

Music in the Polish Village of the Early Twentieth Century

In Polish regions of Galicia during the early 1900s, efforts to promote a national vision of music practice were centered in the city of Kraków. These urban-based efforts, with ties to the romantic nationalism of the nineteenth century, were mounted primarily by the small group of intellectuals commonly known as the "Young Poland" (*Młoda Polska*) movement. It included playwrights, actors, poets, and novelists, as well as composers and performing musicians. For these urbanites, all things peasant were the fashion. Drawing upon a national cultural vision of aristocratic origin, they incorporated selected aspects of village culture in their works. The authors Stanislaw Wyspiański (the play *Wesele*, "The Wedding," 1901) and Władysław Reymond (the novel *Chłopi*, "The Peasants," 1904–1909) wrote on peasant life. In art music, the use of rural musical themes in concert works—already common in the early nineteenth century—became far more common at this time. Two composers who drew upon village music practices were Grzegorz Fitelberg (*Polish Rhapsody*) and, especially, Karol Szymanowski (*Piano Variations*), who utilized music from the highland region Podhale, south of Kraków. Such efforts were not aimed at rural audiences, and there was little concerted effort to create a direct institutional link between urban and rural areas. These compositions were intended primarily for urban audiences, the occasional use of rural themes notwithstanding. Village music remained a separate culture (or, rather, a group of regional cultures). The distinction between *kultura pańska i chłopska* ("the elite and peasant cultures," Burszta 1980:488) is otherwise known in the literature of social science as the "great and little traditions" (Redfield and Singer 1962[1954]). This urban-rural split was, and remains, a common state of affairs and reflects the ethnographic reality not only of Poland or even of Europe, but of most of the world. In all but a few cases prior to the twentieth century, literate composers of art music have had little impact (and have not attempted to have an impact) on rural music practices. They might draw on rural practices, but they generally did not attempt to influence them directly. This general rule, however, has not held true in the twentieth century.[9]

The national music institutions that emerged in Poland after independence, at the end of World War I, were part of a broad campaign to establish a wide variety of national organizations in rural areas. Largely through the agencies of the Polish Republic (1918–39), illiteracy in rural areas was greatly reduced, village libraries became common, peasant participation in national political life was established, national holidays were celebrated by all, and the peasant had available the institutions, explanations, and rationale for participation in a broad-based national culture. Local musicians included patriotic melodies and marches in their repertories (e.g., "Boże Coś Polskę," "Marsz Pierwszej Brygady," and "O Mój Rozmarynie"). Farmers' sons and daughters received higher education at a number of rural colleges, some including choirs with national repertories. Newly established regional museums—in Łowicz, Pułtusk, Plock, and elsewhere—sponsored regional song and dance ensembles, consisting largely of village or small-town youth (Burszta 1980:492–94). On rare occasions, villagers might organize an ensemble for stage performance; in the Przemyskie village of Grodzisko Dolne during the 1920s, for example, stage performances of regional peasant music were usually given on national holidays (Linette 1978:180).

The small amateur dance movement of the 1920s consisted largely of urban-born and small-town performers who created stylized, staged versions of regional music and dance. Such ensembles were not numerous and remained unknown to most rural dwellers; they probably had a limited effect on rural music culture. A few villagers may have seen such performances in movies and newsreels. The efforts of the choreographers were partially funded and promoted by state and other national organizations, including the Ministry of Religious Affairs, the Association of Rural Universities, and the Union of Folk Theater and Folk Choirs (Dąbrowska 1981:191–92).

The greatest changes in village music practice among Poles in the 1920s and 1930s did not stem from patriotic customs or from song and dance troupes, but from the newly established recording industry, and especially from the radio. More than ever before, urban music affected the practice of the village musician in conclusive and dramatic ways. Although village music had probably always been subject to constant (if slow) processes of change, the rate of change accelerated drastically in the 1920s, when the village musician entered into a kind of competition with the radio. In some regions, either he became a participant in the newly emerging musical styles, or he became an anachronism. Elsewhere the degree of change was less drastic, and long-standing peasant regional practices remained dominant. But urban music—including genres, styles, and melodies from America and Western Europe—became a fact of daily life almost everywhere.

A village musician in southeastern Poland near Przemyskie describes this process by noting that those in his village who could afford to do so would hire musicians for a wedding from the nearest small city (in this case, Rzeszów), because their repertory and style were the latest and most fashionable. In order to compete successfully, many village musicians had to alter their practices: "It should be emphasized that some village musicians, not only from younger but from older generations as well, managed to adapt from the old style of playing to the new. They learned the new melodies, the new rhythms and, above all else, the new instruments" (Kotula 1979:38). Learning to play the new instruments was crucial to the village musician's adaptive strategy. In some locales the musicians nearly abandoned the older instruments entirely. For example, instead of playing cymbały (hammered dulcimer) in an ensemble, a musician would learn and most often perform on trombone or accordion. The most common ensemble in southeastern Poland before World War I was fiddle and basy, perhaps with a second fiddle, or perhaps with cymbały and/or clarinet. By 1930 this had changed to *harmonia* or accordion and drum set, perhaps with a fiddle, often with a contrabass, and when available, one or more wind instruments (even three or four) such as trumpet, trombone, and saxophone. For the most part these changes were brought about by the influx of urban dance crazes: tango, fox-trot, rumba, beguine, and somewhat later *bugi-ługi* (boogie-woogie). The regional dances declined, as did the ritual wedding sequence. Increasingly, villagers adopted urban fashions in music, dance, and wedding practices. Even today, among elderly village musicians who were active in the 1930s, the tango melodies are especially favored. The dance itself, however, is rare.

The musical practices of Polish rural dwellers in the 1920s and 1930s edged closer to urban practices in genre and form, although they remained more distinct (and still do today) in ensemble instrumentation and overall style (e.g., tempo, ornamentation, use of harmony). Some new musical practices of the time entered village life through agencies of the state: for example, music of national/patriotic holidays, organized and stylized ensembles, choirs, and a small amateur dance movement. But the radio and recording industry were the most powerful instruments for disseminating national and international norms, especially with respect to new musical instruments, new dances, and urban wedding practices.

Music in the Western Ukrainian Village of the Early Twentieth Century

Some of the musical practices described above for Polish regions were also present among Ukrainian peasants of Galicia in the 1920s and 1930s. For example, various patriotic and martial melodies became widely known during the eight years of warfare from 1914 to 1921 (World War I, revolution, civil war, the Polish-Soviet War, and partisan guerrilla warfare). Many of the same urban influences from radio and recordings greatly affected the music of rural Ukrainians, and many Ukrainian village musicians also adopted the urban musical instruments, dance crazes, and wedding practices. Ukrainian urban composers of the late nineteenth and early twentieth centuries who incorporated folk themes into their works included Mykola Lysenko in eastern Ukraine, and Ostap Nyzhankivskyj and Filaret Kolessa (the last also a distinguished ethnomusicologist) in western Ukraine. As among Poles, however, the works of these urban literate Ukrainian composers were unknown to, and had little or no impact on, the vast majority of rural dwellers.

Rural Ukrainians in Galicia, including Przemyskie, participated in one music institution that had no counterpart among Poles. It was directly tied to the emerging national movement and brought villagers into contact with musical practices that had been partly or wholly foreign to them.

After the Polish-Soviet War of 1920, some regions of eastern Galicia were internationally recognized as a part of the Polish state. This meant that a large number of Ukrainians lived in the Polish Republic, constituting approximately 14 percent of the total population (Rothschild 1974:35–36). In most rural areas of eastern Galicia, Ukrainians were unquestionably the majority and in some regions constituted 80 percent or more of the population. The ethnically mixed Przemyskie region was one of the westernmost reaches of the Ukrainian population. Urban Ukrainian intellectuals of Galicia, especially those in the city L'viv, had long realized that, for a viable Ukrainian political entity to emerge in Galicia, the peasantry must be brought into the national fold. The problem was how to do this, especially how to link urban and rural areas. The Ukrainian urban population was small; the population of most Galician cities and towns was Polish and Jewish.

In 1868 a group of young intellectuals in L'viv founded the *Tovarys-*

tvo Prosvita ("The Society for Enlightenment"—henceforth referred to here as Prosvita). The statutes called for the publication and dissemination of Ukrainian songs, fables, stories, history, etc.; in short, anything that might help distinguish and disseminate knowledge of a national culture. Over the next twenty years or so, the membership became increasingly interested in promoting literacy among rural dwellers through village schools and libraries (Doroshenko 1959:9–14). In many respects the aims of Prosvita were similar to those of other broadly based social movements of the time that were common in much of Europe. One of the distinguishing characteristics of Prosvita was its longevity: while Poles, Czechs, Hungarians, Romanians, and others had state institutions after 1918 within which to promote national cultural norms, the Ukrainians of Galicia did not. Prosvita gained in importance as a social movement in the 1920s and 1930s. It may have been the most important de facto western Ukrainian national institution of the time. Among Galician Ukrainians, it was certainly one of the most influential and powerful cultural institutions with respect to music.

Above all, Prosvita was a particularly significant block in the building of a popular mass movement in eastern Galicia from the 1870s to 1939. The founding branch in L'viv developed contacts with and sent representatives to other cities; most important, dozens of branches were established in small towns and villages. Each branch helped to establish large numbers of village institutions, soon numbering in the thousands and scattered over much of Ukrainian Galicia. Although each village was different in terms of its activities, some of the most common institutions promoted by Prosvita were reading clubs, temperance societies, church brotherhoods, cooperative stores, communal granaries, loan funds, schools, choirs, theater troupes, gymnastic clubs, volunteer fire brigades, and, in a few locales, wind ensembles (Himka 1979:5–6).

Village reading clubs met in local community centers, often the property of Prosvita. In later years, these centers housed musical activities in addition to the reading clubs and libraries. If no such village community center existed, they would meet in private homes, schools, or even cemeteries. The number of reading clubs in Galicia steadily increased, from about 233 in 1895, to more than 1,500 in 1905, and almost 3,000 by 1914. In 1939, Prosvita had over 1,600,000 members in Galicia (Doroshenko 1959:24). Both the literary and the (later) musical activities were designed to promulgate a national vision among the peasantry: "by joining the reading clubs, peasants joined the nation" (Himka 1979:8).

Apart from encouragement of fieldwork and collecting by urban professionals, the musical activities of Prosvita were limited until about 1910. Prior to that time, there was little distribution of musical material that could directly affect village music culture, except in a few scattered locales where choirs were established in the late nineteenth century. The reasons for this were the same as in most regions of East Central Europe: at the time there were few or no national institutions through which this could be accomplished. In 1909, at the first Prosvita Congress in L'viv (the proceedings of which were published the following year), several speakers noted the need to establish direct music-related links between the main Prosvita branch in L'viv and the villages. Their program explicitly called for the promotion of an arranged music, published in and distributed from L'viv, to be utilized by villagers all over eastern Galicia (still a province of the Austro-Hungarian Empire). Most speakers suggested a prescriptive approach that would encourage participation in newly formed music organizations without proscribing existing practices. For example, the composer and ethnomusicologist Filaret Kolessa (1910b:235–36) acknowledged the cultural/musical influence that Poles and Ukrainians had exerted upon one another over centuries of contiguous domicile in parts of Galicia. For him, and for many others at the Prosvita Congress, the new music institutions being proposed were to add another element to village musical life; they were not intended to supplant what already existed. To the contrary, Kolessa felt that if long-standing rural musical norms were to survive, villagers would need to see their existing regional practices as symbols of a greater national entity. He doubted that could happen; hence he proposed wide-ranging activities that might help to create a national musical practice as an addition to village practices. Another Prosvita Congress participant, Zakhariivo, felt that certain village music practices should be actively discouraged and made to resemble urban music as much as possible (1910:215–16).

The congress discussed not only music but also the need to increase the number of village theater groups, libraries, and dance activities (Kryni͡akevych 1910:201), all of which was to take place primarily under the auspices of the Prosvita village reading clubs. Urban members from the L'viv branch were encouraged to spend one or more years in villages to promote these as well as other institutions among the peasantry (Skvarko 1910:174).

Kolessa put forward the most extensive proposal for creating a link between village and urban music:

1) to conduct yearly courses in music transcription for directors of village choirs, so that they could help in collecting rural music;

2) to send urban students to villages to collect and transcribe music, and to have them stay in villages to help establish village choirs in the already existing reading clubs;

3) to publish popular (easy to read) theoretical books on music transcription;

4) to publish arrangements of songs for use in village schools; and

5) to publish a series of selected rural-derived songs with "light harmonization," especially melodies from the eastern regions of Ukraine known as Podniprovia͡ (i.e., from what were then regions of the Russian Empire, those that would shortly become part of Soviet Ukraine); these would be used by village reading-club choirs and, where they existed, instrumental ensembles (1910b:238).

All of these activities were to be supervised by a "music section" of the central L'viv branch of Prosvita, where urban musicians would select material collected in villages for notation, stylization, and eventual dissemination among village populations of Galicia. The plan called for the implementation of a Ukraine-wide repertory that would be stripped of many of its region-specific characteristics and arranged after the fashion of urban music. This would promote a musical idiom that could be easily notated and thus widely distributed in all regions. In addition, it would create a practice derived from nationwide, not just "statewide," materials, i.e., from both western and eastern Ukraine. Significantly, Kolessa called for western Ukrainians to give special attention to eastern Ukrainian music (e.g., from Podniprovia͡). Ultimately, this would create a music in which both urban and rural dwellers could participate. Such a music practice can be seen as part of a cultural meeting ground for people with diverse backgrounds and habits. It was not a spontaneous development but was to be created, even invented, by a specific group of people.[10]

While conducting fieldwork in Poland in 1980–83, I interviewed several people who participated in village Prosvita activities in Przemyskie and contiguous regions in the 1920s and 1930s. Their accounts of Prosvita activities confirm that the above program, at least in part, was implemented after World War I in that part of Galicia. They report that Prosvita expanded its activities in the early 1920s, adding to some of those mentioned above. Various sections of the village clubs were developed for youth, young adults, women, the elderly, and children. With respect to music, most larger villages had at least one choir, and many had two. One of these would be for church services and the other for secular occasions (such as the festivities commemorating the birth and death of the Ukrainian poet Taras Shevchenko), secular holidays, and concerts. These usually featured the choir a cappella. The local choir director was often Prosvita-trained in courses that were especially designed for village choir directors. These lasted a month or more and took place in L'viv. The village director received no compensation for his musical activities. He purchased for the choir musical arrangements written by urban professionals. Each arrangement was submitted for publication, and individual choir directors chose the material for their groups. Materials could be ordered through Prosvita, which acted as a kind of clearing house. The money to purchase notated music came from the same general village fund that paid for the reading club, etc. Each Prosvita member had to pay an annual (or more frequent) fee. Tickets had to be purchased for some occasions, e.g., for entry to concerts or theatrical performances. Much of the general fund came from membership fees and ticket revenues. The musical arrangements were mostly SATB and often featured melodies of recognizably rural origin, although region-specificity was apparently not often a major consideration in the choice of choral repertory.

Village choirs commonly rehearsed in the facilities of the local reading club, which, in the 1920s and 1930s, was often a building owned and maintained by the local Prosvita organization. Only paying members could use the facility, which was open nearly every day in the autumn, winter, and spring. In summer, because of the heavy agricultural work, it was open less frequently, but at the very least on Sundays. The facility had a library as well as space where people could gather for various activities: to play chess, tell tales, rehearse a drama or a choir. Awards in the form of plaques were given to outstanding individuals for their contributions to local Prosvita activities. These awards, and in general any recognition for services, carried a high degree of prestige among a large percentage of the village population. Service to the village and service to the Ukrainian nation were strongly linked.

Correspondence courses were also available through the main Prosvita branch in L'viv. Various subjects of study could be pursued, including choral music, agronomy, and teaching. A person who wished to start or assume directorship of a choir but could not study full-time would use material sent through the mail, then attend a month-long seminar in L'viv when he or she was able to do so. Such courses were organized and taught by urban professional educators.

Dance classes for both children and young adults were also held in the village Prosvita facilities. In the summer, kindergarten classes were organized by young women, usually in their late teens, who had taken a special Prosvita course for this purpose in a county or provincial capital, e.g., in Przemysl. There they learned how to teach what were then emerging as the national dances, primarily choreographed versions of kolomyjka and *kozak,* and their variants such as *hutsulka.* Versions of these dances had become widespread over a large part of eastern Galicia by the mid-to-late nineteenth century, but styles and general dance steps differed greatly from region to region (Harasymczuk 1939:13–176). The fixed choreographed sequences that were learned and then taught by the young women under Prosvita auspices helped to introduce a stylized version of dance to the village. This attempt to create national symbols in music and dance was part of a general effort by rural dwellers to fix among themselves a national allegiance. After learning the dances, the young women taught them in day courses for children, and in some locales in evening courses for young adults. Virtually every village had at least one, and often up to four or so such people who were active in the national dance movement. In some places song and dance performances were given by locals. By the 1930s, much of the music that accompanied the dances was recorded rather than live—recorded most often by urban professional musicians who performed notated arrangements in large orchestral formats.

The village musicians who played in the traditional small regional ensembles did not usually take part in most of these activities. They were first and foremost farmers, and secondarily village musicians who earned cash for musical services rendered at weddings, social gatherings, and other performance contexts. Most of them seem to have had neither the time nor the inclination to take part in the creation of stylized ensembles that would perform arrangements of the emerging national repertory. Very few stylized ensembles were formed in villages; those people whom I interviewed were not aware of a single one. Village ensemble practice, particularly that of the wedding sequence, was considered a thing apart. The changes that took place among village instrumental musicians resulted more from the linking of urban and rural areas through radio and recordings. Such changes among Ukrainian musicians of Przemyskie and contiguous regions are virtually identical to those described above for Polish instrumental musicians of these regions: the introduction of new musical instruments, the popularity of a series of urban dances, and the adoption of urban wedding practices.

The instrumental musical activity that was put into place through institutional urban-based concerns was the wind ensemble, mostly brass and single-reed instruments along with percussion. These were not common in villages, although they did exist in a few locales; they were mainly organized in small towns. Some were sponsored by Prosvita, and musical arrangements and costumes were purchased with funds from the local Prosvita branch. Small-town wind ensembles were sometimes invited to give concerts in villages. More commonly they traveled to villages to play at the funeral of a local Prosvita activist. Musical activities on such occasions included a procession through the village, accompanied by funeral music, with patriotic Ukrainian melodies played at the graveside. For these performances, members of the wind ensemble were typically dressed in a kind of stylized national costume that was by no means widespread in these regions before World War I: red boots, cossack pants, and an elaborately embroidered shirt.

Conclusion

The institutionalization of new musical practices among Poles and Ukrainians of Przemyskie in the early twentieth century was largely due to commercial and national networks formed through a widespread economic and political process. This is evident in the ever-increasing prominence in the village of urban lifestyles, as various urban practices were promulgated over the radio, through movies, and on recordings. It can be seen as well in the use of music as a national symbol. Among Poles this took the form of patriotic and martial melodies as well as a small amateur folk dance movement. Among Ukrainians of Galicia, a network of cultural institutions brought a set of national music practices to the village.[11]

According to those I interviewed who were Przemyskie residents in the interwar period, neither the radio-derived music nor the development of national music institutions completely altered the music culture of the village. On the contrary, much of the established repertory that was common before World War I continued to be performed. Both Poles and Ukrainians continued to play kolomyjka, to use the $\frac{3}{8}$ meter and mazur rhythms, and to utilize melodies with the scale types described above in the wedding sequence. Indeed, all of these elements can still be heard today in the music of some residents of Przemyskie, mainly those who became adults before World War II.

Some of the music institutions of the early twentieth century had different consequences for Poles and Ukrainians. The Polish peasant became a participant in national state institutions (holidays, schools, government-financed village community centers, museums, etc.). His or her adoption of the national music was part of his or her activity both as a citizen and as a member of the dominant ethnic group of the state. For Ukrainians the situation was different. They were one of several minority ethnic groups of the interwar Polish state, and their most important national cultural institutions were self-financed and administered. Galicia was covered by a network of thousands of village-level institutions, within which a national vision of music was promulgated to link villagers culturally (and in a de facto sense, politically) to a greater Ukrainian entity.

The institutionalization of certain musical practices in rural regions of southeastern Poland proceeded along lines that resemble those of similar processes in other parts of the world. Over a short time period of one or two generations, music practices tied to specific contexts often seem able to coexist, without necessarily impinging upon or negating one other. Over a longer period of time, however, certain practices become less context-specific; styles and fashions mix and blend to become a new entity. Today this process can be observed in many lands: notated music and national symbols have converged in several parts of the world over the last few decades to help create what has become a predictable and widespread style of music.

NOTES

This paper is based on fieldwork conducted from 1980 to 1983 in several regions of Poland, including Przemyskie/Peremyshchyna. The research in this region involved making recordings and conducting interviews among Polish and Ukrainian residents as well as former residents who now live in other regions. I was assisted by grants from the Wenner-Gren Foundation for Anthropological Research, the Polish Academy of Sciences, and other organizations.

1. The rural population of this area was predominantly Ukrainian and Polish. The settlements were in a hodgepodge of intricate and overlapping sections of ethnic groups. In most of these, Ukrainians were the majority, in some, Poles were the majority, and in still others there was an indescribable, interwoven mixture of the two. Settlements of rural Jewry were scattered throughout the area, and there were isolated colonies of German-speaking farmers. This mosaic of ethnic groups is too complex to discuss here. One interpretation of this demographic labyrinth is shown on a map in Davies (1984, 2:507), from compilations published in 1921. Of note, however, is that Polish immigration to these regions increased in the late nineteenth and early twentieth centuries, thus affecting the ethnic mix in some regions where, until that time, Ukrainians had likely been a larger percentage of the total population than in 1921.

2. Henceforth the names of regions and cities are referred to in accordance with how they are known in their current state. The primary region under question is today in the Polish People's Republic, therefore: Przemyskie, and not Peremyshchyna. Formerly a predominantly Polish city, L'viv is today in the Ukrainian SSR and only the Ukrainian form of the name is used here, regardless of the time period in question. The population of this city was, until World War II, primarily Polish-speaking, with a significant Yiddish-speaking minority as well as a Ukrainian-speaking group. The city is known in Polish as Lwów, in Yiddish and German as Lemberg. On most current maps available

in North America it is shown in Russian, L'vov. Today, L'viv is an overwhelmingly Ukrainian city, and is widely regarded as the cultural capital of western Ukraine. It was a major, if not the, dominant cultural and political center of the national movement in western Ukraine in the nineteenth and early twentieth centuries.

3. In Przemyskie, the Roman Catholic and Greek Catholic peasants in the nineteenth century spoke regional dialects that had borrowed much, especially lexically, from each other over the centuries. Although they were in large part mutually intelligible, they carried recognizable differences. As older residents of the region described it to me, when a Roman Catholic peasant spoke with an educated Pole (e.g., a priest, a teacher, a noble), he or she might attempt to speak a more literary Polish. When a Greek Catholic peasant spoke with an educated Ukrainian, he or she might attempt to speak a more literary Ukrainian. When among themselves, the peasants of one group seem to have easily conversed with those of the other, each in their respective dialects, probably largely because each had incorporated many lexical items from the other.

4. From the 1840s to the 1880s, Kolberg conducted field research in various regions that were then part of the German, Austrian, or Russian Empires, and that are today part of East Germany, Poland, Lithuania, Bielorussia, the Ukraine, and Czechoslovakia. His monographs have recently been collected and edited into fifty-six volumes. These as well as his collected letters, music compositions, etc., are part of a series published since 1961 by *Polskie Towarzystwo Ludoznawcze* ("The Polish Ethnographic Society"). The regional monographs are especially valuable and include over 25,000 transcriptions as well as detailed descriptions of music context and ensemble instrumentation.

5. In 1596, at an ecclesiastical gathering in Brest, a group of the Orthodox united with Rome. This was the beginning of what has become today's Ukrainian Catholic Church, known in the nineteenth century by various names; the one used here is Greek Catholic. Generally speaking, most Eastern Rite Catholics live in western Ukraine, while mostly Orthodox live in eastern Ukraine. The Eastern Rite Catholics retain liturgical practices that stem from Byzantium. Their hierarchy is integrated into that of the Roman Catholic hierarchical structure.

6. From the Polish language literature, among dozens of others can be mentioned Sarna 1896, Kolberg 1964a[1889] (vol. 22 *Łęczyckie*), and Ryś 1972. From the Ukrainian language literature, among many others can be mentioned: Hrysha 1899 [collected in 1885], Lytvynova-Barosh 1900:70–173, and Shubravs'ka 1982.

7. The Ukraine is conventionally divided into two cultural zones of unequal size. The western zone is smaller, approximately 20 percent of today's Ukrainian SSR. Most western regions were part of Polish states or the Habsburg Empire for more than 500 years, and were never a part of any Russian state until 1939. Regions of the larger eastern zone were a part of various Ukrainian, Mongol, Ottoman, Polish, and Russian states, and were incorporated into the Soviet Union in 1920.

8. In Polish this zone was known as Galicja, and in Ukrainian as Halychyna. In what was commonly referred to as "western Galicia" (roughly from Kraków to the Przemyskie region) lived primarily, but by no means exclusively, a

Roman Catholic peasantry. In what was commonly referred to as "eastern Galicia" (roughly from Przemysl to the Ternopil' region) lived primarily, but not exclusively, a Greek Catholic and Orthodox peasantry.

9. For example, see Chepeliev 1979:35 for a description of an active but highly proscriptive use of urban art music among rural dwellers in Soviet Ukraine in the 1920s and 1930s.

10. It seems to be an almost universal rule, that in the development of national institutions anywhere, a small group of people take upon themselves the tasks of establishing and entrenching widespread institutions that have an impact on a much larger population group (cf. Sugar 1969:43).

11. The establishment of a cultural network of sorts also took place in eastern Ukraine after its incorporation into the Soviet Union in 1920. Although this network on the surface seems to resemble that which was undertaken in Galicia, in fact the aims, content, and organization of the Soviet Ukrainian network were quite different; see Chepeliev 1979.

PART THREE

Brokers and Mediators

Ravi Shankar as Mediator between a Traditional Music and Modernity

9

Stephen M. Slawek

Bruno Nettl has noted the existence of a "curious disparity" in the field of ethnomusicology: in spite of the personal interaction between researchers and their informants or teachers during fieldwork, the literature contains relatively few studies centered around the individual in music (Nettl 1983:278). Studies of North and South Indian classical musics are an exception. Here, scholars have consistently referred to the musical practices of particular musicians in attempting to better understand musical production. More often than not, each field researcher of an Indian classical tradition becomes closely connected with a particular musician or group of musicians, and while he or she may observe and interview musicians from outside this tight circle to approach broad issues in the study of music as culture, most of the researcher's knowledge of musical practice will be secured from the immediate teacher and fellow students. Although this knowledge may be reported without emphasizing its source, most major publications concerning one of these traditions acknowledge the researcher's indebtedness to individually named teachers. When musical examples are included for the sake of illustration or analysis, the performers are often identified (as in Wade 1984).

Although it is not unusual for ethnomusicologists to work with a limited number of informants, the peculiarity of the relationship between classical Indian music scholars and their informants raises several issues of a specifically historical nature. A reader may reasonably question the objectivity of studies written by researchers who have collected their data through the intimate relationship of *gurū* and *śiṣya* (student).

The present study relies on information gleaned from interviews with my guru and principal informant, Pandit Ravi Shankar. He is centrally concerned with the musical and social components of a musical tradition, that of the Maihar gharānā, which he has presented to me in the twelve years since I became his student in 1977. I continue to meet him whenever the opportunity arises. Unless otherwise noted, whatever I attribute to Shankar in this essay has been conveyed in the context of my studies with him.

Upon entering into a *gurū-śiṣya* relationship, the researcher gains access to knowledge that might not otherwise be available, but he or she also acquires the responsibilities entailed by this complex social relationship. For example, while Shankar does not hesitate to modernize his pedagogical methods, he maintains a very orthodox attitude in the relationship of student and teacher. He insists (as do musicians of the "old school") on performing the *gandā bandhan* ceremony, imposing certain responsibilities and restraints on the student. Yet he encourages students to tape lessons so that a maximum amount of information can be taught in the time available (or at least "given" and stored for learning at a later date). While he generously imparts his knowledge to his bound students, he imposes strict limitations on the rights to this knowledge. He restricts access to recorded lessons to the student who makes the tape, and, particularly in my case, asks that explanations of less accessible, esoteric aspects of performance practice not be published. This proscription causes me no problems as a performer of Indian music; one tends to guard jealously the inside secrets of one's trade. However, it does sometimes create dilemmas in my scholarly activities. My difficulties in deciding which materials acquired in private discussions and lessons may be used in writing indicate the depth of commitment engendered by the gurū-śiṣya relationship.

During my long period of study with Shankar, I have had to confront conflicting perceptions and evaluations of Shankar's musicianship and stature in the Hindustani tradition. Musicians of lesser fame and members of rival schools often dispute the authenticity of his repertory, sometimes going so far as to suggest that the quality of his musicianship is not commensurate with his fame. However, he is often singled out by others as the instrumentalist with the greatest raga knowledge, the strictest maintainance of raga purity in performance, and the steadiest command over rhythm—the most basic criteria by which Hindustani musicians are judged. Placing such contradictory data into proper perspective is sometimes easy (e.g., an obvious case of sour grapes), and other times quite difficult. The authenticity question is especially hard to resolve because, in such a dynamic tradition as Hindustani music, what is innovative beyond the bounds of tradition for one musician may readily satisfy another's criteria of authenticity. Whether working within or outside a gurū-śiṣya relationship, researchers must recognize the potency of subjective interpretations of music history, as Hindustani musicians negotiate their relative positions in a collectively constructed past, present, and future. The interpretations are part of what drives the dynamic system; they are versions of the past that can guide us toward a plausible reconstruction of history.

The present essay examines Shankar's impact on the recent history of North Indian classical music. I hope to shed light on the singular role Ravi Shankar has played as a mediator between the traditional musical culture of which he is a part and the modern cultural spheres within which he exists. I will also examine the social dynamics of the Maihar gharānā, whose members share the values that inform Shankar's musical practice. Discussion of an experimental work in the final section of the paper illustrates how traditional musical materials are incorporated in modern musical contexts, and how the life of the piece in performance contributes to the mediation process that brings this individual's tradition into the modern world.

Since the early 1950s, Shankar has stood as a role model for numerous Hindustani musicians of the younger generation. This has resulted not only in his playing style becoming one of the most widely emulated, but also in the adoption of certain stage mannerisms and other behavioral traits by young musicians as they form themselves in the image of this eminent performer.[1] Shankar has shown a remarkable versatility in shifting between the various guises he has assumed and the roles he has fulfilled during his illustrious career. He has described himself as multifaceted, as a chameleon able to assume a stylistic attitude appropriate to the context in which he must function. First and foremost, he is a performer of North Indian classical music in the strictest and most traditional sense; second, he is a composer working in other milieus—writing "serious" art music ("concertos" for sitar and orchestra, pieces written for performance by Western ensembles), scoring music for both Indian and Western films (*Charly, Gandhi, The Apu Trilogy,* and *Mirabai*), and experimenting in avant-garde, electronic, and fusion music (The Ravi Shankar Project, a collaborative effort with the minimalist composer Philip Glass, and his *Svar Milan,* a work combining various Indian ensembles with several Soviet ensembles). A creative artist who reaches out in so many directions could easily lose touch with his tradition's roots. However, most of Shankar's collaborations are, in essence, a projection of his Indian musical self into new contexts, and the substructural compositional process (like the individual) remains Indian at the core.

Bonnie Wade (1978:31) has posed the question, "Why Ravi Shankar?" Why was it that Ravi Shankar became the catalytic agent in setting into motion the "Indian music movement" in the Western world in general and the United States in particular? Why was he the one who succeeded in becoming the primary mediator for his tradition?[2] The answers to these questions reside not only in the individual but also in his family's history and in the political transformations that occurred during the first half of the twentieth century.

Passage to America

Shankar was the youngest son of Pandit Shyam Shankar Hara Chaudhuri. Shyam Shankar, a member of a Bengali Brahmin family, received his first major employment as headmaster in the court school of the Maharajah of Ghazipur. In 1906 he became attached to the court of the Maharajah of Jhalawar (in present Rajasthan) as foreign minister and advisor (*jāgirdār*). In 1911 he traveled to England in the service of the Maharajah. He apparently was so taken with the West that he proceeded to extricate himself from direct service to the Maharajah and remained in London to pursue advanced degrees in law while he continued in foreign service as an independent agent. He participated in the Indian *svadeśī* (independence) movement, albeit thousands of miles from India's border, and he staged several theatrical productions for the entertainment of wounded Indian soldiers conscripted by the British in World War I. Whatever the reasons behind his separation from his family, it appears to have been amicable and intermittent, for Ravindra Shankar Chaudhuri was born in 1920, the same year that his eldest brother Uday joined their father in London to pursue studies in art and painting.

Ruth Abrahams has recognized in Pandit Shankar many of the qualities that enabled Ravi Shankar to endear himself to Western audiences: "His success on behalf of the war casualties was due, in part, to the uniqueness of the entertainment he offered and to his own professional success with and acceptance into British society, which subsequently supported these projects. Pandit Shankar's association with the Maharajahs, his intellectual acumen and scholarly training, his personal achievements, his knowledge of the arts and his obvious facility with the English language opened doors into Europe's otherwise tightly enclosed enclaves" (1985:32). First to benefit from this entrance into British society was Uday Shankar. Through his father's circle of friends and professional associates, Uday Shankar eventually came to meet Anna Pavlova. The Russian ballerina was so impressed with Shankar's dancing ability (she considered him a "natural" and referred to him as such when requesting financial support for projects in which he would star) that she virtually wrenched him from his career in art and launched him into what was to become an international career in dance, the theatrical arts, and film.

It was as a performer in his brother's dance troupe that Ravi Shankar was first introduced to the Western world and to Ustad Allauddin Khan, the famous disciple of Wazir Khan who became Shankar's revered guru. During those most impressionable adolescent years Shankar's future as a stage artist was determined, and during the same time he developed both an admiration for the West and a strong sense of Indian nationalism and Bengali identity. Shankar's autobiography describes his craving for knowledge of his own culture during his years with the dance troupe and his sensitivity to the misinformed criticisms voiced by musicians and composers who frequently visited the Shankar house in Paris to meet Uday: "I was both hurt and infuriated when I heard what some of these Western artists had to say, and I was sorry they could not understand the greatness of our music" (Shankar 1968:68). Still, his travels in Europe and the United States at that early age provided him with a broad cultural experience and a deep understanding of the Western mind that would not be available to other Indian musicians for decades.

Shankar has expressed his indebtedness to his older brother Uday for his aesthetic education: "He appeared, really, like a god, and when he danced he was almost a god, filled with an immense power and overwhelming beauty. To me, he was a superman, and those years with him did a great deal not only to shape my artistic and creative personality, but also to form me as a total human being. It was Uday who taught me to understand and appreciate our ancient traditions in art and all our culture, and my apprenticeship under him in stagecraft, lighting, set design, and general showmanship was of great value to me many years later" (ibid.:65). And elsewhere, he has credited his experience with his elder brother's troupe for his distinctive stage presentation: "Uday was a great influence on me in the way to *present* something. It has nothing to do with the music. In fact, I sort of started this idea of performing on a proper dais, with a proper carpet, proper lighting, and proper way of sitting, and now everybody's following it. It used to be very shabby. People sat in a strange way and there was no decorum. I believed in having good visual effect. If you call that 'show business,' perhaps it is; but I think it is very good to have pleasant visual surroundings"(Landgarten 1979:34). When we ask why it was Ravi Shankar who first stimulated Western interest in India's musical culture, the answer must begin with Pandit Shyam Shankar Chaudhuri's opening the doors to the West for his sons, a family aptitude for showmanship and stagecraft, and the powerful effects of extensive cross-cultural experiences.

The growth of Western receptivity to Indian culture certainly facilitated Shankar's mission. In the 1930s, the critical response of many Western listeners to Indian music emphasized its "monotonous, repetitive" nature and lack of harmony and counterpoint (Shankar 1968:68). The faddish interest in Indian music in the 1960s, resulting from Shankar's association with the Beatles, touched a far greater number of people. Western youths, particularly members of the counterculture, came to associate Indian music with instant enlightenment and tied it to experimentation with mind-altering drugs. What Shankar terms the "Great Sitar Explosion" of the 1960s continues to produce repercussions in the musical culture of India. In the West, the fad passed as quickly as it had started, leaving behind the carcasses of sitars and tablas and the incongruous products of Indian musical ideas in popular compositions.

Historical perspective reveals the "Great Sitar Explosion" as a short-lived diversion. Scholars of India's musical culture had begun intensive field research before the fad erupted. In 1961, upon his return from Madras, Robert Brown began a program in the performance of South Indian classical music by hiring the late mridangam virtuoso, T. Ranganathan, to teach at Wesleyan University. Ranganathan was subsequently joined by his brother T. Viswanathan, flutist and vocalist, and intermittently by their sister Balasaraswati and other South Indian musicians (Brown 1988:277). Several North Indian musicians (Laksmi Ganesh Tewari, Ramdas Chakravarty, and Sharda Sahai) later complemented the Wesleyan program. Harold Powers started to plan the visit of Dr. Lalmani Misra and Jnan Prakash Ghosh to the University of Pennsylvania several years before their arrival in 1969. On the West Coast, the American Society for Eastern Arts in San Francisco maintained an active program while preparations were underway for the establishment of the Ali Akbar College of Music in nearby Marin County. Clearly, serious interest in Indian music was in place and would have continued without the infusion of Indian exoticism in the popular culture of the 1960s. The reasons for this interest stem from the contacts between scholars and Indian musicians that took place under the British Raj, the contacts between Western composers and Indian musicians fostered by the presence of Uday Shankar's dance troupe in Paris and its tours of Europe and the United States during the 1930s, and the initial concert tours of Western countries by Ali Akbar Khan and Ravi Shankar in the late 1950s.

Neuman (1984:13–15) has discussed the efflorescence of Indian music on the world stage and the increased interaction between Indian musicians and the West. He correctly notes that certain characteristics of the Indian tradition have facilitated its adaptation to a Western niche: among these are its high cultural standing in its homeland; its "symbol repertoire which speaks to all manner of religious interests"; the improvisatory nature of the music itself allowing for performances tailored to suit its audiences; and a small ensemble tradition allowing for mobility and inexpensive performance production. The growth of a support system in the West, whose members are drawn from a growing South Asian immigrant population and sympathetic India-philes, has ensured the continued existence on Western soil of India's classical musical traditions. Keeping all of this in proper perspective, we must also remember that at the center of the expansion of Indian music's geographical borders has been the presence of Ravi Shankar.

Because of his success in creating new contexts for his tradition, Shankar has often been regarded as nontraditional both by Indians and by non-Indians. Thus, Hansen (1987:3) writes: "Ravi Shankar we might say was the great modernizer . . . , experimenting with different concert environments and styles. Vilayat Khan on the other hand was a traditionalist. . . . Nikhil Banerjee avoided both the flamboyance [of Shankar] and the courtly self-consciousness [of Vilayat Khan]." Hansen labels Banerjee "a purist," implying that Shankar is not. The *Sunday Observer,* an Indian newspaper, carried the following from Amjad Ali Khan, one of India's most famous sarod masters: "I hope to God that Ravi Shankar lives for at least 200 years so that he sees for himself what good and what damage he has done to our classical music. . . . Ravi Shankar has contributed a lot to our music. Out of this, what is good and what is bad, surely he must be knowing" (Kumar 1984:1). These remarks led to a justifiably heated response from Shankar (also carried by the *Sunday Observer*). Shankar views himself as a pioneer who cleared the way for those Indian musicians who later enjoyed and profited from the audiences he had cultivated.

While it is true that Shankar has experimented, he has also kept his traditional style sequestered in an insulated part of his inner self, and it is from there that his music springs forth when he performs. To refute the criticisms against him he has striven in the past fifteen years to regain an unquestioned position of pure classicism in the eyes of his countrymen. Partly because of this effort, the school of which he is a prime representative has become formalized to a greater extent than it would have been if he and Ustad Ali Akbar Khan, the other major representative of this school, had not traveled abroad so extensively. The musicians who share Shankar's immediate tradition have come to identify themselves during the last twenty years as the Maihar gharānā, and it is this tradition that Shankar has introduced to the modern world. The emergence of the Maihar gharānā as a major school of instrumental music in North India is closely intertwined with the modernization of India and the concomitant forces brought to bear on its musical culture. Its history provides us with knowledge of the sources of Shankar's repertory and with insight into his role as conservator in a rapidly changing tradition.

The Sources of the Tradition

The Maihar gharānā is said to originate with Ustad Allauddin Khan Saheb, an outstanding twentieth-century musician recognized particularly for his mastery of the sarod. Allauddin Khan was known to his disciples and followers by the nickname Baba which, to Bengalis, implies both a father figure and a religious man, particularly an ascetic. While Baba is recognized by his disciples as the founder of the Maihar gharānā, he did not think of himself as such. He was a disciple of Ustad Wazir Khan, the great *dhrupadiyā* and master of the *bīn* at the Rampur court of Nawab Hamid Ali Khan.[3] Although documentation is lacking, Hindustani musicians generally recognize Wazir Khan as a direct descendant of Tansen, the legendary court musician of Emperor Akbar, through the *bīnkār* lineage of Tansen's daughter, Sarasvati, and son-in-law, Misri Singh.[4] Baba saw himself as one member of an extension of the Tansen gharānā that he is said to have referred to as the Rampur bīnkār gharānā, a school recognized for its expertise in instrumental performance of the *dhrupad ālāp*.

But Baba learned with Ustad Wazir Khan only after an extended odyssey in his quest for music instruction had brought him in contact with several musicians. Table I lists his teachers, what he learned from each, and the approximate dates of his study. Baba's musical education was extraordinary in that he was trained in practically every genre of performance in the classical tradition. He learned dhrupad and *khayāl* from Nulo Gopal, various types of instrumental *gat* from Ahmad Ali Khan, and, among other practices, the bīnkār approach to raga ālāp from Wazir Khan. We can also assume that Baba had absorbed many of the light classical genres of singing (*ṭhumrī, gazal,* and other folk-derived vocal forms) through his association with the Calcutta theater world. Baba's eclecticism is one of his main contributions to the music culture of North India. In contrast to the strict caste-like specialization of most musicians of the late nineteenth and early twentieth centuries, Baba's eclectic approach to performance seems to presage the value subsequently placed on pluralism in Indian society under an independent government.

Baba's success in popularizing his amalgam of styles was partly a result of the legitimacy he gained as a disciple of Ustad Wazir Khan. Studying under the doyen of the Tansen gharānā, Baba gained access

Table 1. The Teachers of Allauddin Khan

Approximate dates	
1889–99	Nulo Gopal (Gopal Chakravarty) [Gopal was trained by Haddu and Hassu Khan of the Gwalior gharānā of khayāl], dhrupad and khayāl.
1899–1911	Habu Dutta (Amritlal Dutta), violin. Dutta encouraged Baba to learn with other teachers during this same period. These included:
	Lobo Prabhu, bandmaster at the Eden Garden, Calcutta, Western violin.
	A Bengali Brahmin (name unknown), clarinet.
	Hazari, śahnāī.
	Nandlal Babu, tablā and pakhāvaj.
1911–14	Ahmad Ali Khan [trained in the *rabābiyā* style of sarod playing], sarod.
	Abid Ali Khan [Ahmad Ali's father; taught Allauddin sarod for a short time after Ahmad Ali discontinued teaching him].
1914–17	A son-in-law of Kutub-ud-Daula, dhrupad.
	Muhammad Hussain Khan, sarod.
	Raja Hussain Khan, dhrupad.
	Karim (Kalu) and Hafiz Khan, sitar.
1917–26	Wazir Khan and his son, Sagir Khan; sarod, sursiṅgār, rabab.

After Bhattacharya 1979; Ghosh 1982; and Shankar, personal communication, 1987.

to the *khās tālīm,* the rigorous, systematic method of imparting instruction for which this school was known, and he became intimate with the most prestigious lineage of North Indian musicians practicing at that time. Most accounts of Baba's life view his early teachers as stepping stones to the revered Ustad. While the knowledge he received from these individuals undoubtedly contributed to the formation of his mature style, it was the training he received from Wazir Khan that made the greatest impact on the community of musicians who were to judge him.

After completing his training under Wazir Khan in Rampur, Baba was appointed chief musician at the court of the Maharajah of Maihar in what is now Madhya Pradesh. Except for the few years he spent touring Europe and North America as a musician in the dance troupe of Uday Shankar in the early 1930s, Baba spent the rest of his life in Maihar, teaching the many students who enrolled in the music conservatory he established on the palace grounds. He became well known for his experiments with producing new sounds on traditional instruments and for creating new instruments on which traditional music could be played. He expanded the range of the sarod and added a supplemental set of drone strings to increase its sonority (Bhattacharya 1979:121). His reputation as a versatile musican and a great teacher grew with the success of two brilliant students, his son Ali Akbar Khan (the present *khalīfā* [leader, chief] of the gharānā) and Ravi Shankar. His musical lineage now extends to a third generation and beyond. Ali Akbar's son, Ashish, and Ravi Shankar's son, Shubhendra (by his first wife, Annapurna, the daughter of Allauddin Khan), confirmed this by performing together in a concert arranged by the Ravi Shankar Music Circle in Los Angeles in October 1987. The lasting impact of Allauddin Khan and his protégés on North Indian instrumental music is undeniable. The controversies generated by gharānā rivalries, and intensified by the high value placed on innovation in the competitive music scene of the modern world, have obscured the musical changes resulting from this impact. By naming their alliance the Maihar gharānā, Baba's disciples honor him as an innovator whose creative efforts have taken root in the Hindustani tradition.

The Style

Scholars almost always define gharānā in terms of its social and musical components (see Neuman 1980:146; Wade 1984:2–5). A gharānā is said to encompass a group of musicians linked through familial relationships and/or discipular lineages, who share a style or approach to performance practice that sets them apart from other gharānās. Because the Maihar gharānā embodies a confluence of so many different musical streams, the existence of a core musical style throughout its membership may be less apparent than in other gharānās. It is not dominated by performance on a particular instrument, in contrast to other instrumental schools. While he was particularly renowned for his expertise on the sarod and violin, Baba played many other instruments, some of which he invented. Moreover, many of his students specialized on instruments he did not play: for example, his daughter Annapurna Devi specializes on the *surbahār,* and the late Pannalal Ghosh introduced the bamboo flute to the Hindustani concert stage. Ustad Ali Akbar Khan has trained Brij Bhushan Kabra, who plays a modified Western guitar with a slide in typical North Indian instrumental style, and Ravi Shankar has students of *vichitra vīṇā,* guitar, flute, and voice.

A further impediment to isolating a common stylistic core is the value placed on innovation in this gharānā. Its most illustrious members are recognized as the foremost innovators in the contemporary Indian musical scene. Their creative endeavors have led to a proliferation of individualized styles that, on the surface, appear to be somewhat different. The value of innovation has introduced an air of competitiveness not only between Maihar gharānā members and musicians of other gharānās, but also among themselves. This drive toward individualization has progressed to the point that one well-known musician, regarded by Ali Akbar Khan and Ravi Shankar as a gharānā member by virtue of his discipleship under Annapurna Devi, has presented himself as "a free spirit. A man without a traditional *gharānā,* without artistic prejudices, without a prima donna complex" (Badhwar 1987:65). Another direct disciple of Baba, the late Nikhil Banerjee, created such a distinctive sitar style that his students and others speak of the "Nikhil Banerjee style" as distant and detached from the Maihar gharānā. Banerjee himself claimed that his originality was instilled in him by his guru: "I've been asked, 'You and Ravi Shankar being disciples from the same person, why are both your styles and approaches to music different?' This is because my teacher understood. The first time when I went to Maihar, the first thing my teacher said, 'I will channelize you in a different way, I will put you in a different way than Ravi Shankar. There will be no similarity.' Of course, the basis is the same, about the rag and how we will handle the treatment of the rag—it is all the same, but the exposition is different, the style is different" (Landgarten 1987:14).

Despite the internal and external forces working against stylistic unity in this gharānā, one can still discern common features of performance practice that mark the group as a whole. As Ravi Shankar has said: "In spite of the fact that there seem to be great gulfs of approach between Ali Akbar Khan, Bahadur Khan, some of their students—you see, they may not be identically—what is the word?—clones—but they have the basic training originally from Baba" (personal communication, New York). A few descriptive examples may illustrate what I perceive as the central features of the style prepared by this basic training.

First, the Maihar gharānā stresses the bīnkār approach toward ālāp. While ethnomusicologists and Western admirers of Indian music are quite familiar with the Indian ālāp, certain aspects of the instrumental performance of ālāp in the bīnkār style have remained hidden. Those scholars who have also studied Indian music through performance will agree that the secrets of ālāp performance are among the most heavily guarded in the instrumental repertory. Traditionally, ālāp is taught only after a student is judged to be worthy of this most exalted form (see Hansen 1987:6). The determination is often arrived at through tests of varying severity that measure a student's loyalty and perseverance.

The bīnkār ālāp has been described as consisting of several *aṅgs*, or parts: the *sthāyī* and *antarā* aṅgs are primarily registral distinctions, and the rarely played *sañcārī* and *ābhoga* aṅgs are distinguished by rhythmic pace, ornamentation, and contour. Sections in the pulsed *joṛ* are differentiated by the traditional tempo ranges of *vilambit, madhya,* and *drut*—or slow, medium, and fast—and the *jhālā* is said to contain several aṅgs, such as *laṛī, laṛ guthāv, katar,* and *tār paraṇ,* that are distinguished by their rhythmic character (see Slawek 1987 for descriptions). Traditionally, these were played during the final section of the joṛ-ālāp with *pakhāvaj* accompaniment and were modeled on various types of *paraṇ,* the long strings of stroking patterns played on that drum. While these aṅgs have become archaic as formal elements, or separate subsections, senior members of the Maihar gharānā claim them as a valued part of their heritage from the Rampur bīnkār gharānā. According to Shankar, these aṅgs are reserved for performance before an exceptionally knowledgeable audience.

The style of the bīnkār ālāp is defined by what it excludes as well as by what it includes. The exclusion principle relates to what Shankar has often described to me as the "fine line between dhrupad and khayāl." Certain embellishments characteristic of khayāl singing are to be avoided in the traditional bīnkār ālāp. The urgent and dramatic expression of romantic impetuousness found in khayāl (and encapsulated in the Indian term *raṅgīlā*) should not impinge upon the devotional serenity, or *bhakti,* of a bīnkār dhrupad ālāp. The bīnkār ālāp is like the deepest river that flows most smoothly. There should be no splashy turns of phrases as the melody proceeds in continuous lines of extended portamenti, the wonderful *mīṇḍs* that are so characteristic of bīn technique.

A special repertory of instrumental *gats* also lends cohesiveness to the musical tradition shared by Maihar gharānā members. Among these we find one type, played in a slow tempo, that differs from the more widely practiced slow gat by starting not on the twelfth, but, in the fashion of many dhrupad compositions, on the first beat of *tīntāla,* the predominant 16-beat rhythm cycle of Hindustani music. Ravi Shankar has taught me several such gats, sometimes referring to them as *navāb-pasand* gats (gats composed for the "nawab's pleasure"), and he has played such a gat in raga *khamāj* with Ustad Ali Akbar Khan in a duet (*jugalbandi*) released by the Gramophone Company of India (n.d.; see also Allauddin Khan's recording of *kaushi bhairav*, also on a Gramophone Company of India recording, n.d.).

Other characteristics of the Maihar gharānā are an emphasis on complex rhythmic manipulations and an ability to play in numerous difficult talas; the inclusion of arithmetically contracting *savāl-javāb* (question-reply) sections at the ends of performances, an innovation of Ravi Shankar's based on the model of percussion solos in South Indian *pallavis*; and an interest in the orchestration of Indian music, creating new instrumental ensembles and musical instruments in the process. Allauddin Khan had his own Maihar Band; Shankar is known for his experiments with ensemble music, first for All India Radio and later in film scores, concertos for the sitar, and experimental electronic music; and Ali Akbar Khan has reincarnated his father's idea with the New Maihar Band, presently at his college of Indian music in California. Maihar gharānā musicians are credited with adding several newly created ragas to Hindustani music (among them *Hemant, Naṭ Bhairav, Ahir Lalit, Māñjh Khamāj, Tilak Syām, Parameśvarī,* and *Jogeśvarī*).

The Gharānā Concept in This Tradition

Having established that the Maihar gharānā possesses a body of knowledge and practices constituting a stylistic core that is developed through individual creativity, I will now explore the gharānā concept as a force that directs this musical process. I will draw upon my discussions with Ravi Shankar about what gharānā means to him and what membership in a gharānā does for him.

From Shankar's own statements it is clear that both musical style and shared lineage, as they pertain to his tradition, are fluid concepts. While gharānā is marked by a shared style, this style is always in a state of flux: "First, it is very pure, something very strongly characteristic; then after a few generations, as I said, if there is a very creative musician from this gharānā, he adds or does a lot of new innovations—he calls it the same name, but it does become a little different. That is how it has been always. And after three or four generations, then a new name is taken" (personal communication, New York). Thus, the establishment of a gharānā appears to certify that musical change has taken place and to legitimize those changes. The gharānā also contains much of what is old: in this case the style, according to Shankar, is derived directly from that of the Rampur bīnkār gharānā.

The fluidity of shared lineage in the gharānā concept is related to the practice of learning or borrowing from musicians outside the tradition of the khalīfā. Thus, in Shankar's opinion, the late Nikhil Banerjee transgressed the invisible boundary of the Maihar gharānā by emulating the singing style of the late Amir Khan and by absorbing certain stylistic traits of Ustad Vilayat Khan, the leading exponent of the Imdad Khan gharānā (whose members are regarded as the main rivals and challengers of the Maihar gharānā). Simply absorbing outside influences is not the crux of the problem. After all, Baba had studied with so many different teachers, and even Shankar characterizes his own style as a mixture of his training with Allauddin Khan and influences from other musicians whose styles appealed to him.[5] According to Shankar, it is not bad to imitate others if, at the same time, you can maintain your own purity of style. From this we may infer that the source of the borrowed materials is of greater import than the nature of those borrowings. The severity of proscriptions against borrowing appears to vary according to the degree of rivalry. Indeed, Ravi Shankar has asserted that he and Vilayat Khan have indirectly influenced one another's stylistic development by seeking to avoid what the other was doing.

An unstated notion of allegiance appears to be central to the concept of gharānā. This is supported by the fact that a few musicians who have received instruction from Allauddin Khan's disciples have also rejected the gharānā concept because they wish to expand their range of musical sources without the constraints imposed by gharānā membership. The renegade behavior of these few annoys senior members of the Maihar gharānā because it weakens the alliance. Shankar conceptualizes gharānā as a mechanism through which one's musical status can be preserved. The stronger the alliance, the higher and more stable the status. Weaken the alliance and you create conditions that will allow the propaganda of rival groups to be taken for historical fact.

We also see in Ravi Shankar's comments a distinction between musical knowledge and musical performance. The issue of musical knowledge is encapsulated in the concept of khās tālīm (special training). For Shankar, a gharānā musician is one who has received khās tālīm, the rigorous education imparted to a student in the traditional gurū-śiṣya relationship. As Shankar states, khās tālīm makes the musician sturdy like a strong oak tree that will not budge under the influence of other styles. Those who learn not by tālīm, but, for example, with the aid of pirated recordings, might become virtuoso performers, but they will lack the orally transmitted theoretical knowledge so necessary to the preservation of tradition. In his own attempt to modernize the classical system of music training, Shankar has established The Ravi Shankar Institute for Music and Performing Arts in Benares, where he periodically gives "crash courses" in the performance practice of his tradition to his most advanced and devoted students:

> I give master classes for six or seven days two or three times a year, and my students—most of whom are already established professionally—come from all over North India. . . . The classes are like a refresher course, but very deep. It's a great place, and we have the traditional atmosphere there. To be with those students for seven days is like spending seven months or even two years with a new person. I still am living the life of my guru then with my old students. But most of the time it is very different, and that is partly our own fault, the musicians of my generation. When the gurus are living this jet set life, it is hard to preserve the old ways. (Rockwell 1981)

Thus, while even he has described himself as chameleon-like, able to change his stylistic colors and shadings to meet the demands of his performance context, he implies that the knowledge of the old and the orthodox imparted to him by Baba in the khās tālīm in some way grants him the privilege of such flexibility in performance practice. Knowing the rule and breaking it is acceptable, but breaking it in ignorance harms the tradition. Shankar periodically reveals his command over the old and the orthodox by performing an exceptionally austere ālāp and joṛ, such as his recording of raga Parameśvarī, in which he structures his ālāp in the archaic sthāyī-antarā-ābhoga-sañcārī form of the Rampur bīnkār gharānā, or his recent recording on compact disk of ālāp and joṛ in raga *Pūriyā Kalyāṇ,* in which he plays a joṛ set to *cautāla,* the dhrupad tala of twelve beats. In his demonstration of this archaic style of performance, the effect of an accompanying pakhāvaj is produced on a tablā tuned an octave lower than usual. In the same vein, he takes pride in displaying in his teaching a knowledge of the archaic forms of such ragas as *Bhairavī* and *Pīlū,* ragas that are no longer known to most musicians other than in liberated ṭhumrī-style expositions.

Ravi Shankar's conceptualization of the form and significance of his tradition can be summarized as follows: 1) the gharānā serves both as guardian of the tradition and as an internal mechanism by which musical change is socially recognized, legitimized, and, to a certain extent, fueled; and 2) it serves as a force promoting social cohesion and conformity of musical style, yet provides the legitimization a musician requires in order to have the freedom necessary to develop his or her individual style. Possibly because of his particular role as a mediator in bringing traditional Indian music into the modern world, gharānā serves Shankar's purposes more fully in the realm of legitimization. To counteract charges of breaking tradition and to reassert the conformity of his own musical knowledge with that of other orthodox Indian musicians, Shankar has increasingly embraced the concept of the Maihar gharānā as a refuge of authenticity.

The Modernity of a Traditional Repertory

Shankar holds in his personal repertory both the core of what can be considered one of the most authentic performance traditions in Hindustani instrumental music and a body of musical styles, genres, and pieces that includes folk melodies of Uttar Pradesh and Bengal, light-hearted melodies of the ṭhumrī tradition, South Indian ragas, and even melodies borrowed from the countries he has toured since the age of ten. The eclectic nature of the repertory imparted to him by Ustad Allauddin Khan certainly contributed to Shankar's success in meeting the challenges presented to a traditional musician by the modern world. It allowed Shankar the versatility required of musicians who would compete successfully in a rapidly changing cultural system. He also possessed the political acumen and foresight to work in collaboration with South Indian musicians, bridging cultural gaps that exist in his homeland, to become a truly national musician.

The survival and present well-being of North Indian music in an environment that is vastly different from the one in which it developed must be credited to the many individuals who worked for its continued existence and growth. But leadership, a quality that emanates from the individual, must also be recognized. Leadership in the expressive arts implies that one has had an impact in setting stylistic norms and has opened new avenues of expression through innovation. Shankar's artistic leadership has transformed the configuration of symbolic meanings carried by his tradition. This is especially apparent in some of his less orthodox endeavors.

Shankar's second concerto for sitar and orchestra, *Rāga-Mālā,* is innovative in content, medium, context, and symbolic meaning. The work was commissioned in 1979 by the New York Philharmonic Orchestra, partly because the conductor, Zubin Mehta, had long desired to collaborate with Shankar. Shankar composed the bulk of the piece in the summers of 1979 and 1980 during temporary residencies in New York City. The process entailed in its production displays his adaptability and creativity in surmounting the obstacles that stand in the way of translating an oral tradition into one that relies upon notation.

Shankar first wrote the individual parts of this piece in his own version of the syllable notation promoted by V. N. Bhatkhande in North India early in this century. Once this stage of the work was completed, he began to work with members of the orchestra to teach them their individual parts. Special attention was given to those musicians who would play the numerous solo parts featured in the piece. Shankar enlisted the aid of José-Luis Greco, at that time a graduate student in composition at Columbia University, to begin the process of transcribing the piece into Western staff notation, and he discussed aspects of its orchestration with another composer, Fred Teague. Once the parts were in Western notation, Shankar, who is unable to read staff notation, consulted the various musicians with whom he had been working to ensure that the transcriptions conveyed his intentions, especially with respect to rhythmic groupings, tempo changes, and ornamentation.

Typically, Indians dislike Shankar's efforts at joining the sitar and the Western orchestra because the results lack the type of interactive improvisation that they expect in authentic performances of their music. Western composers and music scholars object to the "misuse" of the orchestra, the thin textures, the lack of harmony and counterpoint, and so on. Yet, his *Concerto No. 1* continues to be well received by audiences throughout the United States and Europe. *Rāga-Mālā* has not been performed many times since its premiere (April 23, 1981); a recording was issued by Angel in 1982. Shankar himself has difficulty keeping the complete work in his memory, hence making rehearsals particularly stressful since he cannot use the notated score to help find his place.

The tonal vocabulary of *Rāga-Mālā* is based entirely on traditional ragas, but the forms used for their manifestation are not entirely traditional. The first movement contains an elaborate and elegant ālāp-joṛ in *Lalit,* a raga traditionally performed in the early morning, that is very similar in construction to what normally transpires in a traditional performance; differing, of course, in the presence of the orchestra to amplify the phrases played by Shankar. However, this ālāp is preceded by a substantial introduction by the full orchestra that is characterized by heterometric rhythmic organization and florid passages running over several octaves in the strings. Several sections following the joṛ also have no counterparts in the Indian tradition and occasionally call to mind symphonic textures and harmonies not unlike those characteristic of Aaron Copland's works. Here, Shankar seems to have broken the boundaries of genre. In my opinion, the first movement of *Rāga-Mālā* stands as the finest of all his collaborative efforts with Western musicians.

The remaining three movements of *Rāga-Mālā* also juxtapose sections that seem to reflect traditional genres and practices with sections that fall outside the classical Indian tradition. Whereas the first movement is composed entirely in one raga, each of the succeeding movements contains several ragas: five in the second movement, three in the third, and nineteen in the fourth. These are all presented in unified sections, some very short (especially in the last movement), others well developed along the lines of a traditional form such as the madhya *laya* gats in ragas *Yaman Kalyāṇ* and *Desḥ* that frame a section in raga *Mārvā* in the third movement. The last section of the fourth movement is composed in the light, semi-classical ṭhumrī style, using the raga *Pañcam se Gārā* (Gārā is a raga used solely for lighter forms; pañcam se indicates that the tonic is rotated to the fifth scale degree to create this variety of Gārā).[6] The movement concludes with a jhālā, but not before the expected savāl-javāb (question-reply) section that Shankar has popularized in the traditional performance context. Here, however, the savāl-javāb assumes grandiose proportions as it is set antiphonally, making use of the entire orchestra.

Innovation in both medium and context is apparent when Shankar combines the sitar with a Western orchestra and performs these pieces in concert halls on programs that contain other items of traditional Western symphonic literature. What is not obvious is the value that Shankar places on this activity. If we recall Shankar's experiences in his early childhood in Paris, it becomes apparent that, beyond securing new venues within which to realize his creative impulses, he is effectively proving that Indian music is able to share equal footing with Western music. The symphony orchestra and the concert hall are two of the most powerful symbols of Western music. By sharing the same stage with the Western orchestra, Shankar projects his own tradition (however severely modified it must be to enter that context) against a backdrop that automatically imprints legitimacy and authenticity. Beyond exploring new avenues for creativity, Shankar has also displayed his ingenuity in manipulating symbols for the benefit of his traditional music. By reaching into these unconventional areas of experimentation, he has opened himself to harsh criticism from purists at home and in the West. Yet, the prominence he has helped to secure for Indian music around the globe will continue to provide an expanded audience, and expanded patronage, for the tradition whose recent history he has shaped.

NOTES

1. The widespread acceptance of Shankar as one who defines a style became apparent to me in 1971 after my first performance on the sitar at the Banaras Hindu University. I was told that I played in the "Ravi Shankar" style, this despite my having studied for two years with Dr. Lalmani Misra. This seemingly contradictory incident attests to the stylistic coherence of the Maihar gharānā. Dr. Misra often proudly confided that he was strongly influenced by the style of Ali Akbar Khan.

2. Wade cites three reasons for Shankar's catalytic role: 1) he purposefully assumed the role of a musical missionary; 2) he made systematic modifications to his performance format in order to surmount the "basic difficulties that Western audiences might have with Indian music"; and 3) he broadened his potential for exposure by accepting nonclassical concert contexts for his performances (1978:32).

3. While it is generally recognized among Hindustani musicians and in histories of Hindustani music written by South Asian music historians (see Chaudhury 1975:209; Chaube 1977:52–59; and Garg 1978:546) that Ustad Allauddin Khan was one of the most illustrious disciples of Ustad Wazir Khan, even this most basic fact can be asserted only on the basis of oral information. To my knowledge, there exists no written declaration by Ustad Wazir Khan that Allauddin Khan was his disciple. Nor is there direct documentary evidence to show that Ustad Hafiz Ali Khan also learned from Wazir Khan, or to prove that Ustad Vilayat Khan learned anything from his father, the late Ustad Enayat Khan, who died when Vilayat was a young boy. While it is not uncommon for musicians to claim false links to luminous teachers as a means of self-promotion, all of the above musical relationships are generally accepted as fact. This did not prevent Daniel Neuman from publicly questioning the relationship of Allauddin Khan to Wazir Khan at a meeting of the Society for Ethnomusicology at Ann Arbor, Michigan, in 1987. While he was simply making the point that we are dependent on our informants' historical accounts when working with oral traditions, it happens that the Hindustani musicians with whom he formed close alliances are of the Imdad Khan gharānā, to which Vilayat Khan belongs. Neuman, in all likelihood, was motivated to declare his skepticism by the subjective interpretations to which he had been exposed during his close association with these musicians.

4. See Garg 1978:545 and Chaube 1977:52–59 for exemplary writings on the topic. The late historian, Kailashchandra Deva Brahaspati, challenged Wazir Khan's account of his family lineage to V. N. Bhatkhande, the lawyer turned musicologist/musician who obtained many dhrupad compositions from Wazir Khan at the command of the Rampur Nawab Hamid Ali Khan in the early twentieth century. Brahaspati's method can be questioned since he accepted as fact written records contradicting the information of oral sources even though the written "facts" were created only slightly before the oral records (see Brahaspati 1976:204–208). Even if Wazir Khan related a lineage fabricated by his ancestors for personal gain of wealth and prestige, as Brahaspati claims, the musical facts prove that his tradition is one and the same with the prestigious dhrupad tradition, and it is widely believed that he was indeed descended from Tansen. Be this as it may, the impact on the dynamic of the tradition remains the same.

5. The musicians (apart from Allauddin Khan) whom Shankar cites as having influenced his stylistic development include Rameshsvar Pathak and Yusuf Ali Khan, two well-known sitar masters of the early twentieth century, and the vocalists Faiyaz Khan, of the Agra gharānā, and Behere Wahid Khan, of the Kirana gharānā.

6. The rotation of tonic pitch within a scale-type (sometimes drawn from the South Indian *melakarta* system) to effect modulation from one raga to

another is a device commonly found in Shankar's composed works. His *Three Ragas in D Minor* for Western chamber orchestra begins in the scale-type of the South Indian raga *Hemāvatī* (incorporating scale-degrees 1 - 2 - flat 3 - sharp 4 - 5 - 6 - flat 7), rotates tonic to scale degree 5 to modulate to raga *Kīrvānī,* and ends the piece with a section in which the tonic is again rotated to scale degree 2 (of Hemāvatī) to modulate to raga *Basant Mukhārī.*

An Eighteenth-Century Critic of Taste and Good Taste

10

Amnon Shiloah

Only in the last few years has Charles Fonton's *Essai sur la musique orientale comparée à la musique européenne*—one of the earliest and most important studies of Turkish music by a European—received the attention that it merits. Fonton's manuscript (Bibliothèque Nationale, n.a. 4023), dated 1751, contains a wealth of information, with drawings of instruments and six examples in musical notation. It was preceded only by the work of the converted Pole Albert Bobovsky, alias 'Ali Beg (d. 1675)[1] and the Romanian Prince Demetrius Cantemir (1673–1723),[2] to whom Fonton refers several times with the utmost reverence. Yet Fonton's work never received the approbation and esteem accorded to La Borde's *Essai sur la musique ancienne et moderne* (1780), which includes chapters on Arab and Turkish music, and to the subsequent writings of Villoteau (1823, 1826) and Kiesewetter (1842).

In 1838, the *Revue et Gazette Musicale* printed a short summary of the contents of Fonton's essay, prefaced by the judgment that his work had lost all value upon the appearance of Villoteau's contributions to *La Description de l'Égypte* (Villoteau 1823, 1826). This editorial comment was repeated in Fétis's short entry on Fonton in his *Biographie universelle des musiciens* (which may have been drawn, as well, from Michaud 1856): "A French Orientalist, lived in Constantinople in 1751, as indicated by the date affixed to the two manuscripts found in the Bibliothèque Impériale. The author seems to have been little versed in the matter he treats; his work, as a matter of fact, became valueless after the publication of Villoteau" (1874:291). Nearly a century later, Alexander Ringer remarked upon the importance of Fonton's "virtually unknown account of Turkish instrumental music," which "not only draws attention to the rhythmic patterns of Arabic music but also makes some pertinent observations concerning the inadequacy of Western notation for the transcription of Eastern melodies" (1965:116). Not until 1985 was the full French text of the manuscript published, with extensive critical notes, by Eckhard Neubauer (Neubauer 1985–86). Most recently, the Turkish musicologist Cem Bahar (1987) has published a Turkish translation of the essay, with an important introduction on Fonton and his times. In Bahar's work, the value of this early source is assessed by an expert who is native to the culture treated by Fonton.

Three reasons may have been instrumental in consigning Fonton's work to oblivion. (1) He was neither a professional musician nor a recognized musicographer and therefore may not have been taken seriously by experts in the field. (2) The essay deals basically with questions related to performance practice and its theory. Consequently, it is not conceived in a rigorous, systematic manner and excludes more ordinary theoretical aspects such as scales and modes. It may therefore have been considered merely a curious, rather amateurish endeavor. (3) Last but not least, particularly in its initial pages, Fonton's essay contains harsh and cogent criticism of what may be called ethnocentric European views with regard to Oriental musical cultures in general.

These are the very attributes that imbue this work with great value for us. For example, to inculcate better understanding, Fonton recommends what modern terminology would call an "emic" approach. The freshness of the text, the personal stamp it bears, and the pertinent observations resulting from the author's long exposure to Ottoman musical culture make the essay much more important for us than the types of ethnomusicological observation that are included in the anthology compiled by Frank Harrison (1973).

Fonton provides invaluable information on musical practice during the first half of the eighteenth century in the flourishing center of Constantinople. His chapters on rhythm and rhythmic modes, as well as the extensive organological notes, offer painstakingly accurate analysis of a subject the author knew well. Fonton was in all likelihood proficient in handling an instrument; Cem Bahar assumes that he had learned to play the *tanbur*. From an ethnological point of view, Fonton's argument with his contemporaries' flawed approach and misjudgment of non-Western musical cultures is most significant and revealing. The present essay thus concentates mainly on this aspect and attempts to illuminate it against a broad background.

Fonton was officially sent to Constantinople as a *jeune de langues* (literally "youth of languages"), a translation of the Turkish *dil oglan*. The institution of jeunes de langues had been decreed in 1669 by Colbert, to prepare *drogmans* (interpreters) to serve with the French diplomatic and consular corps in the Levant. According to the provisions of the decree, six French youths of nine to ten years were to be sent to the Capuchin monastery in Constantinople to study Oriental languages and cultures. The cost of their education, which amounted to 300 pounds for each child, was defrayed by the Marseilles Chamber of Commerce. This explains the fact that Fonton's essay, written as a dissertation to prove that he had fulfilled his obligations and was qualified to work in the profession, was addressed to Monseigneur Rouille, Ministre de la Marine. The covering letter suggests that Rouille was particularly interested in the state of the arts and sciences among the Orientals, but the real reason for the choice of subject matter was in all likelihood Fonton's own penchant for and proficiency in music and his knowledge of the musical scene of his time.

According to Gustave Dupont-Ferrier (1921:420), Fonton was born on December 4, 1725. He was admitted to the Parisian school of Jeunes de Langues attached to the Collège Louis-le-Grand, which was then run by Jesuits. He graduated in 1746, in natural sciences, and was sent the same year to Constantinople for five years. From 1753 to 1778, he served in Aleppo, Cairo, and Izmir. The date of Fonton's death is unknown, but we do know that his son followed in his footsteps and also became an interpreter.

For an understanding of the original views that Fonton elaborates in his introductory prologue it is important to note that his arguments bear directly on the major ideas and concerns surrounding the operatic rivalry in France and the impassioned controversy over French and Italian opera. However, although he argues on the same ground and uses the same idiom as his contemporaries, Fonton reaches different conclusions.

In three concise sentences at the beginning of his prologue, Fonton clarifies his fundamental approach to the two facets of the art of music, the universal and the particular. This opening is the point of departure for a discussion of the cultivation of an appropriate attitude toward non-European musical traditions in general and Oriental musical traditions in particular. Fonton's initial sentences formulate his principal ideas:

> The divine art of music, which need only be named to be acclaimed and extolled, has as many followers in the world as the world has people. Its empire encompasses all who breathe, and there is no clime, be it ever so barbaric, where music's sweetness and charm are not recognized. Each nation has its own music, and the taste for it is as particular to each as it is general to all. Being a divine art, music should be looked upon as a revelation common to all human beings; all share equally its delight and effect, as through its medium all seek to satisfy the same basic needs. And yet, when it comes to taste, there is wide divergence with respect to that which is innate to each particular nation.

The concepts of "taste" (*goût*) and "good taste" (*bon goût*) were at the center of a lively debate among Fonton's contemporaries. Fonton speaks only once of "good taste," perhaps trying to avoid the value judgment it connotes. In the course of his prologue he is probably referring to contemporary theories about musical taste in the context of the controversy regarding French and Italian music.

Fonton's remarks may have been inspired by a well-known work, the *Traité du bon goût en musique* by Le Cerf de la Viéville, Seigneur de Freneuse (excerpts translated in Strunk 1950:489–507). This treatise forms part of the sixth dialogue of the *Comparaison de la musique italienne et de la musique française,* written between 1704 and 1706 in answer to Raguenet's attack on Lully, whom de Freneuse ardently admired. In the framework of a learned discussion about the best way of judging things, one of the Seigneur's protagonists enumerates the following criteria: thorough knowledge of and long familiarity with the matter under consideration; how it compares with other things of its kind; and, above all, good taste. The latter is said to be formed by the union of "our inward feeling" and "rules" or "established precepts." Such an approach, wherein good taste is conceived as superior judgment comprising experience and observation, inward feeling and codified rules based on intellectual processes, makes no explicit claim to be absolute and therefore applicable to all men. The question of whether individual norms might vary in response to diversity of taste remains open.

Fonton's answer to this question may be compared with that of his contemporary, Johann Joachim Quantz. In the final chapter of Quantz's *Versuch einer Anweisung die Flöte traversière zu spielen,* paragraphs 52 and 53, we read "The divergence in taste which asserts itself in all the various nations that take any pleasure at all in art has the greatest influence on musical judgment. . . . Every nation, unless it belongs among the barbarians, has in its music some one quality which pleases it pre-eminently and above all others" (1752, XVIII, in Strunk 1950:592). We still do not know exactly who the barbarous nations are, but as we read on, it becomes clear that "all the various nations" eventually narrow down to two that were the outstanding arbiters of good taste in music: "In recent times, however, two nations have not only acquired special merit through their improvement of musical taste, but have also, in following their innate temperamental inclinations, come to diverge pre-eminently from one another in this respect. These nations are the Italian and the French. The two peoples have been seduced into setting themselves up as arbiters of good taste in music and for several centuries they have been the musical lawgivers" (ibid.). Further on, Quantz undertakes to characterize the music of the Italians, French, and Germans, and to show how their distinctive tastes affect their treatment of parallel themes. Are these ideas meant to convince us that not all nations have musical taste or are privileged to enjoy the sublime quality of "good taste"?

The above opinions are the general background against which Fonton presents his argumentation. He pits himself against the egocentric views and warped attitudes of his European colleagues toward the music of the "other." His point of departure is Quantz's discussion of divergent taste. Fonton contends that this diversity actually applies to all nations and to all of the arts; consequently, it is not the exclusive property of a few European nations. Art asserts itself in all nations and reflects their respective values, norms, manners, feelings, and ways of thinking. Hence it does not and cannot comply with the abstract norms and contentions of what is known as "good taste." It is repugnant for any given culture to conclude that others do not have art, or take no pleasure in art, merely because it does not conform to certain rules and is contrary to that very culture's logic and rules of good judgment. In so doing, the European arbiters of good taste rely on false impressions and prejudices, that is to say, on the more aberrant of "inward feelings." This approach is recognized as wrong when applied to Western music but is used to condemn inexorably the music of the "other." Such prejudice, leading inevitably to baseless conclusions, becomes even more deplorable when combined with partiality and misjudgment.

Fonton goes further and openly accuses his contemporaries of permitting themselves to be guided by self-love, which we would now call ethnocentrism. He writes: "One imagines, and this surely comes from judgment dictated by self-love, that the alien nations, chiefly those who dwell outside Europe, are deprived of any sort of knowledge and are immersed in the deepest, darkest ignorance." He rebels against such an insulting generalization but, as he says, he refrains from arguing with it, to avoid digressing from his main theme. Then, turning to the music itself, he declares dramatically that he can already hear the excited outcry of his critics who will accuse him of debasing and dishonoring this noble art in ascribing it to "barbaric, crude people who are totally incapable of appreciating its value." These are probably the very same "barbarous nations" whom Quantz excluded from those that "take any pleasure in art."

Expressing himself boldly and harshly, Fonton continues to put into the mouths of his critics a concentration of the worst conceivable stereotypes used to describe the alien music of the "other": "How can we, they would say, make so light of the word music as to apply it to a motley collection of untuned instruments, dissonant voices, graceless movements, unrefined songs, bizarre mixtures of low and high sounds, ill-assorted, disparate, cacophonous tunes, in brief, a monstrous symphony designed to inspire aversion and horror rather than to evoke captivating pleasure? This is the prevalent concept of any music that is not European, an entirely erroneous perception founded on universal prejudice that passes judgment without due examination and condemns without knowledge." Fonton's scathing censure reaches a climax here, as he accuses his European colleagues not only of prejudice fed—albeit in good faith—by ignorance, but also of partiality and misjudgment nourished by ethnocentric views.

May he not have been exaggerating to sharpen the thrust of his argument? Perhaps not all of his contemporaries were so arrogant, intolerant, and egocentric. Indeed, let us examine the case of one who supposedly sympathized with his views. The European composer and musicographer Blainville, who spent some time in Constantinople and even learned to handle Turkish instruments, wrote as follows in a chapter devoted to Turkish music: "A Turk told me that if he could make use of our beautiful musical pieces, he would soon abandon their insignificant Turkish airs and *chansonettes*." Blainville concludes philosophically, "Yes, Plato would have persuaded this people that good, beautiful music is always to be preferred." Then he goes on to state that the Turks have neither art nor science, and at the close of the section devoted to Turkish music he says: "I will not mention Persian, Mongol, or Indian music here at all; they are of the same genre as Turkish music, all are more or less the same" (Blainville 1747:63–65).

Having let off steam and expressed his contemptuous irritation with the narrow, biased intolerance of his contemporaries, Fonton turns to a more constructive way of explaining diversities of taste. He states that within its own genre, Oriental music has its own beauty and its own criteria for judging that beauty. He admits that an ear that is not naturally attuned to a different type of music would certainly suffer upon hearing it for the first time. This holds true for the Orientals as well: "They will be as insensitive as rocks to the harmonious accents of the Lullys and the Tartinis." Long exposure and experience as well as the willingness to be exposed to and to admit that the "other" too has an art, will help to reveal the unique beauties particular to a different culture. Diversity of taste is due to the different influences impinging on each individual as a result of "the climate he is born into, the nature of the air he breathes, the various things that affect him, the diverse impressions that generate different penchants and inclinations, different ways of thinking, feeling and behaving." The nature of a given taste, then, is determined by the physical and sociological environment; its norms are determined by the culture, based on maximum uniformity and on those attributes of taste common to its adherents.

Turning to the then-accepted definition of good taste, Fonton says, "But this definition would not fit the tastes of different nations when compared to each other. French taste is entirely different from Italian, Italian from German, and German from English. Nevertheless, each of them, moving in different, even opposing, directions, claims to follow good taste. It would be impossible to decide among them." He then concludes that the most desirable state would be to belong to no country at all, that is, to appear on the face of the earth without having been born into any one of these four countries.

Fonton is aware that his argumentation can be refuted by the claim that rules defining the beautiful, the good, and the true are general and common to all, because they obey the dictates of reason that are shared by all people. He agrees that reason is the supreme, infallible judge, but adds that, in effect, most things are subject to relative and arbitrary considerations. Reason, as part and parcel of the Divine intelligence, is indeed the same in all creatures, but once planted in the human being it becomes the captive of the body that envelops it and the recipient of all the impressions and perceptions of exterior objects transmitted to it by the senses. This divergent perception of objects leads to different ways of thinking that in turn generate different ideas, implying that the norms of judgment are relative and culture bound. Fonton formulates this as follows: "A thing is not beautiful until it is seen within the context of the genius of each nation."

Nevertheless, most people have the potential capacity to listen appreciatively to alien sounds after several hearings; the ear that is naturally pained the first time it hears strange music may, upon better acquaintance, find it delightful. Some ears, however, are so constructed as to be irreversibly attuned to a single, familiar musical genre, and may categorically reject any new vibration. It is not to such organs that Fonton's essay is addressed, nor does he consider it his task to sing the praises of Oriental music and to strive by all possible means to gain advocates. To render his presentation more explicit and accessible to the European reader, he chooses to use a special method of comparison: in comparing Turkish with European music, he endeavors to emphasize the differences between them rather than to parallel their beauty.

In his prologue, Fonton provides a synopsis of the four chapters that comprise his essay, stressing that his observations are based on musical practice and not on theoretical sources. He maintains that he was unable to find good, authoritative examples of the latter.

The first chapter of the essay deals with the Oriental view of the origin of music. In this connection Fonton records a number of legends and presents a pseudohistoric, "emic" interpretation, indicating what he considers credible and what should be seen as anecdotal. A short "historical" survey relates the chain of succession from the Persians to the Turks, ending with a fifteenth-century "reformer" named Hodjia (*sic*), who restored the musical art and to whom Fonton devotes several pages of anecdotes. This is followed by an account of the flourishing court of Sultan Ahmet III, in the period immediately prior to Fonton's own time. He mentions Greek, Arab, and Jewish musicians, as well as the Romanian Prince Demetrius Cantemir.

The second chapter provides a brief characterization of Italian, French, and German music before describing comparable attributes of Oriental music.

The third chapter deals with the general rules governing Oriental music. Criticizing the weakness of the Orientals with respect to systematic theory, Fonton nevertheless extols the merit of the musicians who are "more skilled connoisseurs and observers than the Europeans . . . and have a sure ear." Remarks about intervals, scales, the absence of a notational system, and the inadequacy of Western notation for the transcription of Eastern melodies are followed by an important description of the Turkish rhythmic system and twenty-eight rhythmic modes (*usul*). Equally important is the subsequent treatment of the musicians' artistry and creativity with reference to major forms such as the *peshref* and *taqsim,* and to the ethical connotations of a musical performance.

The fourth chapter deals with the tremendous power the Orientals ascribe to music. "This is perhaps the only chapter," says Fonton, "in which their views coincide with ours." To illustrate this point, he contents himself with one example gleaned from a Turkish treatise on music, recording a fictional story about the famous theorist Safī al-Dīn (d. 1294). Safī al-Dīn is the only figure from an earlier historical period whom Fonton mentions. Fonton provides appendices that include very important organological notes on the *ney* (flute), tanbur (long-necked lute), *miskal* (panpipe), and *kaman* (fiddle). Each entry is accompanied by a sketch drawn by another jeune de langues, Jean-Baptiste Adanson. He added a final drawing depicting an ensemble that includes the aforementioned instruments plus a drum.

The aim of this essay has been to draw attention to the original ideas that Fonton elaborated in his introductory prologue, some of which are strikingly similar to the major concerns of modern ethnomusicology. Further exploration of Fonton's essay and its appendices must be reserved for another occasion.

NOTES

1. Albert Bobovsky was *drogman* (interpreter) to the Sultan Mehmed IV. He wrote a book on Turkish music (Bibliothèque Nationale, ms. turc 292) in which he included a large number of Turkish compositions recorded in Western notation.

2. Cantemir acquired an extensive knowledge of Turkish music and, according to Fonton, was a dextrous *tanbur* player who performed for the Sultan Ahmet III. He wrote a treatise on Turkish music and transcribed 150 compositions using a notation that he invented. One of these compositions is included among the notated examples reported by Fonton.

Arzelie Langley and a Lost Pantribal Tradition

11

Victoria Lindsay Levine

The abundant recordings of musical sound preserved in archives and private collections throughout the world pose a formidable historical challenge for ethnomusicologists. Many recordings, especially those made before the 1950s, lack adequate documentation. Fortunately, it is sometimes possible to identify oral and written sources that can help to reconstruct the historical context of early recordings. Our consultants and collaborators may offer indispensable assistance, relating their family histories and serving as mediators between the sources and their own experience of past and present.

I confronted such a challenge when Claude Medford (1942–89) invited me to examine his collection of Louisiana Indian songs. My interpretation of the repertory was hampered at first by the paucity of published ethnographic data on Louisiana tribes. Fieldwork was not a solution, as most of the singers are deceased, and the songs have not been performed publicly for fifty years or more. The key to interpreting the recordings proved to be the songs and biography of Arzelie Langley, Medford's grandmother by marriage and one of the singers represented in his collection. She recorded seven songs during an interview with the linguist James Crawford in 1970, at which Medford assisted as an interpreter. Family history regarding Arzelie Langley, as related by Medford, offered personal insight into the experience of Louisiana Indians.[1]

Medford, of Choctaw Indian descent, though assimilated in outward appearance and behavior, devoted his life to the study and preservation of Louisiana Indian cultures. After attending college, Claude held a variety of jobs, from service in the U.S. Navy to work in the off-shore oil industry. He studied Southeastern split-cane basketry in his free time and gradually acquired national acclaim as a basketmaker and basketry expert. He supported himself through basketry in the last decade of his life. Claude was also a dedicated family historian with good collecting instincts. His deep interest in Louisiana Indians motivated him to salvage traditional songs. He did this from 1959 until his untimely death. He originally collected the songs for his own personal use, but in the early 1980s he decided to make his collection available for study in the hope of stimulating scholarly interest in Southeastern Indian musical cultures. From the time that I first met Claude in 1983, he shared with me his field recordings and extensive knowledge. In 1985, he guided me through the intertribal communities of Louisiana and east Texas, introducing me to some of those who still remember songs or song fragments.

Claude clearly understood the significance of his song collection, which greatly enlarges the slender sample of Louisiana Indian music that survives.[2] The eclectic nature of the collection, and Claude's ability to mediate between source and experience, have led to a new interpretation of musical interaction among the southern tribes. Claude was fascinated by the numerous song cognates he had recorded. When I suggested to him in 1985 that the repertory reveals the existence of a local pantribal music, he concurred enthusiastically and urged me to undertake the analytical and historical work necessary to support this interpretation. Claude read an earlier version of this paper a month before his death. In his usual upbeat manner, he praised my efforts and then proceeded to correct several details, reminding me that this is "just the tip of the iceberg."

The singers whom Medford recorded resided in three communities: Marksville and Kinder, Louisiana, and Livingston, Texas. Each of these communities had become a center of intertribal and interethnic contact by the early twentieth century (Drechsel 1979:158), and the singers identified themselves as Coushatta, Alabama, Tunica, or Choctaw Indians. Information on Kinder and Marksville in the early twentieth century survives in the unpublished fieldnotes and correspondence of two ethnographers, John Swanton and Stuart Neitzel. Texts collected in Marksville by the linguist Mary Haas in the 1930s (Haas 1950, 1953) provided further clues concerning the language of intertribal songs. The biography and the songs of Arzelie Langley help bring into focus these diffuse historical materials.

Arzelie Langley and the Louisiana Choctaw

Arzelie Langley was a woman of power, a Choctaw herbalist and seer. Her skill as a medicine woman earned her a place in the folklore of native communities throughout Louisiana and east Texas. This remarkable woman spoke several languages, including Choctaw, Coushatta, Alabama, English, French, and the Mobilian trade language. She danced in the ceremonies retained at Kinder well into the twentieth century. Some say she was more than 100 years old when she died in 1975. Medford narrated the family's early history in 1983.

> CM: Arzelie Langley's [maternal] grandfather was a veteran of the War of 1812; he was among the Choctaw that fought with Andrew Jackson down in the Battle of New Orleans. After this was over, he had gone back up into Mississippi. And as the years passed, these two brothers, Arzelie's grandfather and her uncle, they kept moving ahead of the settlers. They would move to a new area of dense forest and they would build a new house, and in a few years, the settlers would come and build a new town. And so they moved all the way through Louisiana and went out into Texas. The Comanches were still moving around in their traditional manner and these two Choctaw men went and lived with the Comanches for awhile. But they said there was too much sky and it felt like it was falling on 'em. So they came back to Louisiana and they said we're not going to move anymore. They just made up their mind no matter who moves in now, this is it, we're not movin'. So they built their houses and established their community. Other Choctaws moved in, and finally the Coushatta moved into that area.

Nineteenth-century documents lend credence to the story of Langley's grandfather and uncle. John Sibley, then the Indian agent at Natchitoches, reported in 1806 that there was "a considerable number" of Choctaws settled in villages as well as "rambling hunting parties of them to be met with all over Lower Louisiana" (Sibley 1852:1097). Originally, the Choctaws resided primarily in Mississippi but had begun to migrate westward prior to the Louisiana Purchase. In time, they became the largest immigrant tribe in Louisiana (Drechsel and Makuakāne-Drechsel 1982:21). Sibley also described the "Conchattas" (i.e., Coushatta or Koasatis), who lived some eighty miles south of Natchitoches. He mentioned that "a few families of Chactaws [*sic*] have lately settled near them from Bayau Beauf" (Sibley 1852:1086). This community, located on Bayou Nez Piqué (near Basile, Louisiana), is the village in which Langley's grandfather settled permanently (Hiram Gregory, personal communication, 1989).

> CM: Arzelie was born and raised there. Her father was pure Choctaw and her mother was mostly Choctaw, but she had a little bit of Biloxi. Arzelie's first husband was a Frenchman, and she had several children by him in her twenties. And then the Frenchman died. So years later, she married a Coushatta man, [she moved to the vicinity of Kinder, and she] had two sons and a daughter. Her second

> husband, he was a logger. He died maybe sixty years before her death, and she never remarried. And so she made buckskin like her father; she was a cane basketmaker and a pine needle basketmaker, and she did cure people. Made medicine for 'em. And that's how she supported and raised her second family.
>
> She was a medicine woman, and she treated people among the Alabama in east Texas, and . . . she treated among all the Choctaw communities that once were in Louisiana. Plus the Tunica and Biloxi community in Marksville. Everywhere that I've been in Indian Louisiana, in Texas, in parts of Oklahoma, they knew her or knew of her. And she treated many people of all races and she was successful in her treatments. Many people were cured.

Langley's biography suggests that fusion typified contact among Louisiana Indians during the nineteenth century, when a series of events promoted intertribal consolidation (see Drechsel and Makuakāne-Drechsel 1982). Beginning in the 1830s, the removal of the southern tribes initiated a period of increased mobility and demographic fluctuation for the entire southeastern culture area. In Louisiana, many of the small indigenous bands had already joined dominant tribes such as the Natchez or Caddo, and these for the most part removed to Indian territory (Swanton 1946:106). Eighteenth-century immigrants to Louisiana, such as the Tunica, Biloxi, Ofo, Alabama, and Coushatta, resisted removal by retreating into backwoods areas. Throughout the nineteenth century their numbers swelled incrementally with the addition of new arrivals, including the Avoyel and Choctaw.

By the century's close, the remnants of diverse tribes had either assimilated into neighboring white or black communities or had joined forces with one another, gradually merging their cultures. This process of amalgamation produced the intertribal communities of Marksville, Kinder, and Livingston. Marksville was inhabited by Tunica, Biloxi, Ofo, Avoyel, and Choctaw Indians; Coushatta, Alabama, and Choctaw-Biloxi lived near Kinder, while Alabama and Coushatta settled near Livingston. Within these communities discrete traditions dissolved, exemplified by the virtual collapse of Louisiana Choctaw culture.[3] Yet traditional music and dance survived in these communities, newly manifested as an aggregation of formerly distinct practices. It is impossible to pinpoint when Louisiana pantribalism began, but one report suggests that intertribal dances occurred as early as the middle of the nineteenth century.[4] By the end of the century, the residents of Marksville, Kinder, and Livingston frequently attended one another's pantribal events (Drechsel 1979:158).

Lousiana pantribalism developed as an accommodation to rapid changes in demographic and socioeconomic domains. It was not necessarily a reaction against white domination; rather, it emerged gradually as the traditionalists among the tribes redefined themselves and reinterpreted their cultures in the face of intense change. Louisiana pantribalism was the kind of movement that Hazel Hertzberg describes as essentially optimistic and based on two underlying assumptions: that the survivors among the various tribes constituted a cohesive Indian community, and that this Indian community would endure (1971:315). Notes made by Swanton, Neitzel, and Haas profile the social contexts in which Louisiana pantribal music was performed.

Louisiana Pantribal Gatherings

Intertribal gatherings among Louisiana Indians in the late nineteenth and early twentieth centuries occurred in two main social contexts: performance of the annual Green-Corn Ceremony and intermittent Stickball Game/Night Dance events. The Green-Corn, or Busk, Ceremony appeared throughout the southeastern area (cf. Speck and Broom 1983; Swanton 1928, 1946). The ceremony heralded the ripening of new corn in the summer. Ritual activities carried out over several days included purification rites, prayers, orations, sacred dances, social dances, recreation, and feasts. Some Louisiana tribes had discontinued the Green-Corn Ceremony in the nineteenth century; these included the Atakapa (Gatschet and Swanton 1932:23–24) and the Chitimacha (Densmore 1943:10). Nevertheless, the Indians at Kinder and Marksville continued to perform the Green-Corn Ceremony well into the twentieth century.

Swanton visited Kinder in 1910 and 1930; on both occasions he worked primarily with Arzelie Langley's brother-in-law, Jackson Langley (Swanton 1930, 1946). He entered this description of the Kinder Busk Ceremony in his field notes:

> All came together in one place like a camp during the afternoon. They brought the food there all cooked ready to eat but did not eat until next morning. They stayed there all night, sang and drank coffee but did not dance. Then all men, women, and children went down to the bayou and sat down in the water up to their necks. Then the chief, who had not gone in, brought pieces of roasting ears which he distributed and they ate right there in the water. Chief went in afterwards. Then they dived under water four times and then changed their clothes at home. Came back all together again and ate some breakfast (having their feast). Next night they danced. (Swanton 1910)[5]

Neitzel carried out fieldwork in Marksville in the 1930s, at which time he probably worked with Joseph Pierite, according to an undated letter to Frank Speck. Pierite was a community leader at Marksville until his death in 1976 and is another singer represented in Medford's recordings. Neitzel's description of the Marksville Green-Corn Ceremony indicates marked similarities between the ritual performances at Marksville and Kinder, despite regional variations.[6] They involved comparable purification rites, including the fast and immersion in the bayou, although the Marksville men also scratched the calves of their legs with needles. The new corn was first tasted in or near the water in each case, prior to the communal feast back in the village. Furthermore, the dance in each locale began at night after the purification rites and corn tasting. Ceremonial practices differed between the two areas primarily in that the people of Kinder sang all night during the fast, and in addition, the ceremony at Kinder emphasized the number four while the number three may have been emphasized at Marksville. The latter point remains open to question (Hiram Gregory, personal communication 1989). The use of the number three, symbolic of the Holy Trinity, would correspond to other Catholic influences found in the Marksville ritual.

The second context for intertribal gatherings in Louisiana was the ball game and night dance cycle. Many Southeastern tribes played some form of stickball (cf. Swanton 1931:140–55). During ball play, the men formed two opposing teams and played stickball all day; the night dances began after a communal supper at sundown. The cycle repeated over a variable time period. Swanton's field notes from 1910 furnish the following account of the ball game cycle at Kinder, where it was called a Horned-Owl Dance.

> [The Horned-Owl Dance] lasted four nights and played ball all day. Did not sleep all this time. Men cooked the meat and the women bread during this dance. At supper time all sat down to eat cross-legged around the fire. Four men cooked and brought meat and put it in front of the women. Four women cooks brought bread and set it down in front of the men. After that the chief talked and then all sang, men and women. They sang the song of the Horned-Owl Dance. Then the chief talked again and told them, "Now get up." The women picked up the meat and the men the bread. Then they went to another place (the dance ground) and mixed the food all up and then they ate. After that they danced all night. If before four days a man was found sleeping, they took him and blacked him all over with soot.

Neitzel did not describe the ball game, but linguist Mary Haas recorded this text at Marksville in the 1930s: "I went to a Choctaw ball and danced for three nights. We played ball for three days. They danced every night" (Haas 1950:163). Here again, the ball game/night dance events at Kinder and Marksville appear similar, except that the event lasted four nights in Kinder and three in Marksville. Swanton's description of the elaborate food ritual, oration, and sleep deprivation suggest that the ball game, like the Green-Corn Ceremony, involved both social *and* religious aspects. This duality of purpose typifies the Busks and ball games of other Southeastern tribes, as well (cf. Levine 1990; Schupman 1984).

Neitzel's field notes provide a few additional clues as to the style and structure of the night dances associated with pantribal gatherings at Marksville. The dance repertory, inventoried in Table 1, included a relatively large number of individual dances. The dances tended to move counterclockwise, in a circle around a pole that may have been a stickball goal post. Then men and women formed segregated dance lines for many of the dances, and the dance steps included a "walk," "shuffle," and "trot." Male dancers wore red and blue suits with white shirts; the color combination symbolized the American flag. Evidently, the dance events consisted of two main segments during which a sequence of dances was performed, rather like analogous events among the Choctaw (Levine 1990), Creek (Schupman 1984), and Cherokee (Speck and Broom 1983). The available ethnographic data

Table 1. Louisiana Pantribal Dance Inventory*

Alligator Dance	Horse Dance
Bear Dance	Little Bird that Stays in the Woods Dance
Bed Dance	Midnight Dance
Biloxi Dance	Old Buffalo Dance
Bird Dance	Old Dance
Blackbird Dance	Old People's Dance
Buffalo Dance	Pumpkin Dance
Chicken Dance	Quail Dance
Crow Dance	Rabbit Dance
Daybreak Dance	Raccoon Dance
Double-Head Dance	Round Dance
Drunk Dance	Sheep Dance
Duck Dance	Skunk Dance
Eagle Dance	Snake Dance
Fish Dance	Squirrel Dance
Fox Dance	Tick Dance
Four Dance	Tree Frog Dance
Friend Dance	Turkey Dance
Garfish Dance	Turtle Dance
Horned-Owl Dance	Wolf Dance

*This inventory has been compiled from the dance titles of the available recordings as well as from those given in Haas (1950, 1953), Neitzel (1930), and Swanton (1910).

suggest that night dance events were generally similar to those of other Southeastern tribes.

But the Louisiana pantribal gatherings also manifested some of the traits James Howard noted in Oklahoma powwows (1955, 1983). For example, powwow participants use a lingua franca, English, to facilitate intertribal communication. Participants in Louisiana pantribalism also used a lingua franca: the Mobilian trade language, a pidginization of Western Muskhogean with other Southeastern and European languages (Drechsel 1979:191; see also Crawford 1978). Intermarriage often occurs among tribes that participate in Oklahoma powwows, and this certainly took place in Louisiana, as illustrated by Langley's biography. Above all, Oklahoma powwows combine modified tribal customs, reworkings from white culture, and new elements peculiar to the powwow movement itself (Howard 1983:71); this combination of traits also applies to Louisiana pantribalism. Louisiana pantribalism differs in a significant way, however. Howard insists that pan-Indian movements focus either on secular or religious domains; the Louisiana tribes did not sharply distinguish between the two in their gatherings. In addition, the associated musical repertory was unique to Louisiana. This sketch of Louisiana pantribalism establishes a context for the interpretation of its music.

Louisiana Pantribal Music

The songs in Medford's collection illustrate the Louisiana pantribal musical style. The selections sung by Charlie Boatman for the Smithsonian also belong to this repertory and are included with the inventory of the sample in Table 2. His connection to this genre is confirmed by Swanton's census of Kinder, where Boatman's name appears with the residents of Alabama descent (Swanton 1910). All of the songs in this sample were necessarily performed out of context and are therefore very brief renditions. In some cases the singers could only recall a fragment of the song, and one item, Langley's "Old People's Dance," is too inaudible for use. Nevertheless, it is possible to characterize generally Louisiana pantribal music. For the most part, these songs use anhemitonic pentatonic scales, and their ambitus is usually an octave or less. Melodic contours descend or undulate with a descending inflection. Rhythmic patterns tend to be repetitive but involve frequent metric changes as well as unmetered solo introductions in some songs. Song texts consist mostly of vocables with words occasionally inserted; Haas found that Mobilian was used in these cases (Haas 1950:165). These renditions feature a soloist or two singers in unison. But originally, the predominant choral style was call and response; a male

Table 2. Recordings of Louisiana Pantribal Dance Songs from Claude Medford's Collection*

Song	Singer(s)	Date
Alligator Dance	Charlie Boatman, Kinder	1934
Bear Dance	Irene Abbey, Livingston	1969
	Nathan Barbry, Marksville	1964
	Charlie Boatman, Kinder	1934
Biloxi Dance	Joseph Pierite, Marksville	1964
Buffalo Dance	Irene Abbey, Livingston	1969
	Charlie Boatman, Kinder	1934
	Arzelie Langley, Kinder	1970
Chicken Dance	Nathan Barbry, Marksville	1964
	Charlie Boatman, Kinder	1934
Daybreak Dance	Clementine Broussard, Marksville	1969
Double-Head Dance	Arzelie Langley, Kinder	1970
	Joseph Pierite, Marksville	1964
Drunk Dance	Joseph Pierite, Marksville	1964
Duck Dance	Irene Abbey, Livingston	1969
	Nathan Barbry, Marksville	1964
	Charlie Boatman, Kinder	1934
	Arzelie Langley, Kinder**	1970
Eagle Dance	Irene Abbey and Isobel Robinson, Livingston	1969
Horse Dance	Irene Abbey, Livingston	1969
	Charlie Boatman, Kinder	1934
	Clementine Broussard, Marksville	1969
	Arzelie Langley, Kinder	1970
	Joseph Pierite, Marksville	1964
Midnight Dance	Carrie Barbry, Marksville	1972
	Carrie and Sam Barbry, Marksville	1964
	Clementine Broussard, Marksville	1972
Old People's Dance	Arzelie Langley, Kinder	1970
Rabbit Dance	Carrie and Sam Barbry, Marksville	1964
	Charlie Boatman, Kinder	1934
	Arzelie Langley, Kinder	1970
Snake Dance	Arzelie Langley, Kinder	1970
Tree Frog Dance	Irene Abbey and Isobel Robinson, Livingston	1969

*All of the Louisiana pantribal songs recorded by Claude Medford from 1964 through 1972 are included in this Table. Medford's tapes have been deposited at the Louisiana Folklife Center of Northwestern State University of Louisiana, Natchitoches. Also included on this table are the songs performed by Charlie Boatman for Mr. Folsom-Dickerson; these recordings are deposited in the National Anthropological Archives of the Smithsonian Institution, Washington, D.C.

**Langley's Duck Dance is actually a variant of the other Chicken Dances.

soloist led and the male dancers responded in unison, doubled at the octave by the women when appropriate.[7] Some songs were accompanied by a small water drum, played by the leader who carried it at the head of the dance line.[8] Some of the songs conclude with a formulaic call of indefinite pitch.

Louisiana dance events opened with the performance of the Double-Head Dance, called *Talawanoskobotukulu* ("Two-Head Dance") or *La Danse de Têtes* at Marksville[9] (called "Back-and-Forth Dance" by Langley). The two surviving Double-Head songs, Examples 1 and 2, are musical cognates of the Stomp Dance songs of other Southeastern tribes. The Double-Head Dances feature short, symmetrical phrases. The leader would have repeated—or improvised variations on—two or more calls, which contrasted with one another in rhythm, vocables, and melodic contour. The male dancers would have responded with a fixed phrase throughout, using a vocable pattern derived from one of the calls. There may have been several songs in this category, all referred to by the singers under one name and all used to accompany one generic choreography. Each song would have been short, lasting

Example 1. Double-Head Dance song. Joseph Pierite, Marksville, Louisiana. Recorded in 1964 by Claude Medford.

mm ♩ = 70
call
response (etc.)
ke wa ka na ke ho ke ne – wa hi yo wa hi ya ha
wa hi yo wa he wa hi ya hi ye wa hi yo wa hi ya ha
ke wa ka na ke ho ke ne wa hi yo wa hi ya ha
wa hi yo wa he wa hi ya hi ye wa hi yo wa hi ya ha
ke wa ka na ke ho ke ne wa hi yo wa hi ya ha
wa hi yo wa he wi hi ya hi ye wa hi yo wa hi ya ha

Example 2. Back-and-Forth Dance song. Arzelie Langley, Kinder, Louisiana. Recorded in 1970 by Claude Medford.

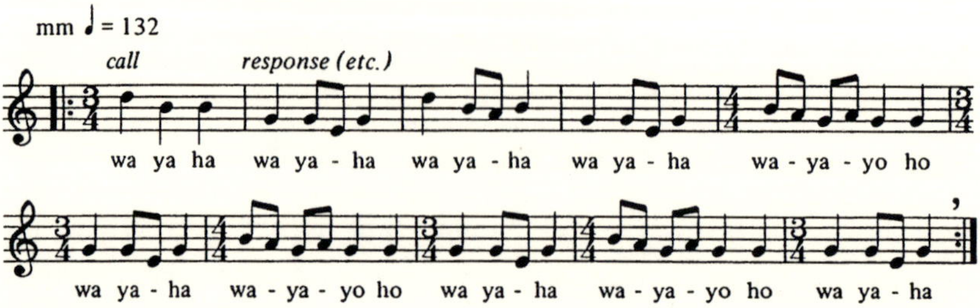
mm ♩ = 132
call
response (etc.)
wa ya ha wa ya - ha wa ya - ha wa ya - ha wa - ya - yo ho
wa ya - ha wa - ya - yo ho wa ya - ha wa - ya - yo ho wa ya - ha

about a minute, but the dance would have been performed for a few hours with a continuous succession of Double-Head songs. Joke songs in Mobilian could be inserted between the dances (Drechsel 1979:149) and, in addition, animal dances could be alternated with Double-Head Dances for the sake of variety.

All of the animal dances in this sample feature a strophic form also found elsewhere in the Southeast. The Rabbit Dance in Example 3 illustrates this form. The song opens with a two-part introduction; the leader would have performed the unmetered solo, and all of the dancers, including the women, would have joined in on the call-and-response section. The strophe proper also divides into two sections; the first section may have been sung entirely in unison, while the concluding part, which resembles a Stomp Dance song, would have reverted to call and response. These frequent textural changes coincided with alternations in the drum pattern, tempo, phrasing, vocables, and melodic contour. Each resultant musical section signaled a different dance step.[10] The strophe would have been repeated unvaried as many times as necessary for the dancers to complete one full circuit of the dance ground; hence the song probably lasted five minutes or more. Each animal dance had its own choreography. The animal dances together with the Double-Head Dances constituted the opening half of a pantribal night dance event.

The second half of the event, beginning at midnight, appears to have been devoted to Midnight Dances (called *Talawa Lohara* at Marksville) and Daybreak Dances. Neitzel described the Midnight Dance as follows: "At twelve midnight, the men and women form in opposing lines to one side of the pole and revolve like spokes of a wheel. The men dance backwards and . . . the steps are short and shuffling" (1930). The Midnight Dance appears to have been a cognate of the Choctaw Drunk Dance (Howard and Levine 1990); if so, there would have been several different songs in this category, each used to accompany one standard choreography. One of the surviving Midnight Dances is in

Example 3. Rabbit Dance song. Charlie Boatman, Kinder, Louisiana. Recorded in 1934.

*Inserted on the repeat by analogy with other renditions of the same song.

strophic form. The other two, as well as the Daybreak Dance, seem to employ what I call chant form in Choctaw music (ibid.). Chant-form songs feature call-and-response texture but the phrases are longer, more tuneful, and often asymmetrical in length, compared to Stomp Dance songs. Chant-form songs are sectional; the song leader improvises variations while the chorus sings with one fixed chant throughout any particular section. The leader changes the chant to begin a new section; once he changes the chant, he does not reuse previous chants. Each song has a number of chants arranged in a fixed order; the chants differ in regard to vocable and rhythmic patterns, melodic contours, phrase lengths, and beat groups. The song leader decides which and how many chants to include in a given performance; in other words, chant-form songs involve some degree of spontaneous composition based on predetermined musical materials, and each performance of a chant-form song differs from the last. The Daybreak Dance in Example 4 provides the best illustration of this form in the Louisiana repertory. It uses two chants that contrast slightly in rhythmic and vocable patterns, and its asymmetrical phrases are somewhat longer and more tuneful than those of the Double-Head songs.

Example 4. Daybreak Dance song. Clementine Broussard, Marksville, Louisiana. Recorded in 1969 by Claude Medford

In summary, the style elements of the Louisiana repertory correspond to those of other Southeastern musics (Nettl 1954), although the available sample indicates somewhat simpler rhythmic and melodic structures in Louisiana music. The Louisiana singers use moderate vocal tension, as do other Southeasterners, but employ fewer vocal ornaments than do Creeks or even Choctaws. I suspect that the preponderance of strophic forms in the Louisiana sample reflects Creek influence; in the seventeenth century, the Coushatta lived among the Creek and the Tunica lived among the Natchez, close relatives of the Creek (Swanson 1946:27, 30). The Alabama originally lived near the Chickasaw, a group also related culturally to the Creek (ibid.:822), and the one Chickasaw song recorded employs precisely the same form as that of Example 3 (Howard and Levine 1990). By contrast, the Louisiana Double-Head songs closely resemble the Choctaw Double-Header (ibid.), rather than Creek Stomp Dances, and like the Choctaw, Louisiana Indians did not wear shell shakers for this dance category. Louisiana music displays a further affinity with Choctaw music in the use of chant form, the Choctaw song structure par excellence. In fact, the first chant in Example 4 replicates the initial chant of a Choctaw War Dance song, which suggests an actual borrowing from the Choctaw repertory.

Louisiana pantribal music, then, probably derived from Coushatta, Alabama, and Tunica traditional musics, shaped through contact with the Creek, and gradually expanded by accretion from Choctaw and other musical cultures. On the basis of the ethnographic evidence, it must have been a rich repertory, containing, as Swanton noted, "too many [songs] to be finished in one night" (1910). And on the basis of the musical evidence, it was a diverse repertory, possessing a variety of forms and compositional devices derived from sources throughout the Lower Mississippi basin. Arzelie Langley's recordings provide the decisive evidence that this repertory was truly pantribal. Even though she identified herself as a Choctaw, her songs fall squarely within the Louisiana style and repertory. She offers the aural proof that individuals in Louisiana relinquished their discrete tribal musics to adopt a collective, intertribal musical identity. That she was not alone in this is confirmed by Swanton, who remarked after his first visit to Louisiana that "*all the tribes had the same songs*" (Swanton 1910, italics in original).

A Lost Tradition

The Indians of Marksville, Kinder, and Livingston discontinued their pantribal gatherings by the 1940s; several circumstances contributed to the demise of this tradition. The loss of the timber industry, the drought, and the Depression wreaked economic havoc on the intertribal communities. A series of letters exchanged between Swanton and Caroline Dormon attest to the conditions at Marksville as well as to Swanton's anguish at his inability to offer significant financial assistance (Swanton 1930). By analogy with other tribes, I would guess that the advent of World War II further disrupted Louisiana Indian communities, as the young men moved away to enlist in the armed forces or in search of wartime jobs. Above all, the pantribal gatherings may have engendered negative or even hostile reactions from the local white residents, ultimately posing a threat to the continued existence of the Indian communities.

Yet the early optimism that buoyed Louisiana pantribalism was not unwarranted. Indian communities at Marksville, Kinder, Livingston, and elsewhere in Louisiana have survived. Today, the residents of these communities retain their native languages and many traditional crafts, especially basketry. But few people remember the pantribal gatherings of half a century ago and fewer still can recall the songs associated with those events. Those who do remember do not discuss them with outsiders, preferring to preserve a sense of cultural privacy. Musical life in these communities now revolves around Western traditions. Arzelie Langley's Coushatta sons, for example, became award-winning Cajun-style fiddlers. Others, such as some residents of Livingston, adopted Southern Plains powwow music and dance. Louisiana pantribal music, therefore, will probably remain imperfectly documented. Nevertheless, the knowledge that this musical tradition existed contributes toward a fuller picture of the Southeast as a musical area, and the use of musical data in studying the history of interaction and exchange among the Louisiana tribes may hold important implications for Southeastern ethnology.

NOTES

This project was partially funded by a grant from the University of Illinois Graduate College. I wish to acknowledge the Archives Division of Watson Library, Northwestern State University of Louisiana, for the use of Swanton's letters in the Dormon Collection. I am grateful to the anthropologist Hiram Gregory, Northwestern State University of Louisiana, who alerted me to the archival materials used here and who provided hours of stimulating discussion. Above all, I wish to acknowledge the help of the late Claude Medford, my friend, consultant, and collaborator.

1. I obtained the biographical information on Arzelie Langley presented here from Claude Medford. Langley is also discussed by Crawford (1978), Drechsel (1979), and Kniffen, Gregory, and Stokes (1987).

2. Other recordings of Louisiana pantribal music exist in various archives. Mary Haas, a linguist who worked in Marksville in the 1930s, recorded several songs performed by Sesostrie Youchigant; these tapes are deposited at the Archives of Traditional Music, Indiana University, Bloomington. Recordings of Charlie Boatman made by Mr. Folsom-Dickerson in 1934 are deposited in the National Anthropological Archives of the Smithsonian Institution, Washington, D.C. Another tape made of Arzelie Langley during the 1960s is archived at the Center for Cajun and French studies, the University of Southwestern Louisiana, LaFayette. Recordings of Charlie Thompson (Livingston, Texas) are deposited in the Archive of Folk Culture of the American Folklife Center at the Library of Congress.

3. John Peterson (1975) points out that a few Mississippi Choctaw families continued to migrate into Southern Louisiana in the early years of the twentieth century. These families established small enclaves of traditional Choctaw culture, documented by Bremer (1907) and Bushnell (1909), but they gradually assimilated to some degree into white society (see also Colvin 1978). In contrast, at least one Choctaw community in Northern Louisiana neither assimilated into white society nor participated in the pantribal movement

(Gregory 1977); the members of this community still speak Choctaw and retain many aspects of traditional culture but have lost Choctaw music and dance.

4. In *Twelve Years a Slave* (1853), the autobiography of a black northerner who was kidnapped and enslaved in the south, Solomon Northup amusingly describes a "Chicapee" intertribal gathering:

> On one occasion I was present at a dance, when a roving herd from Texas had encamped in their village. The entire carcass of a deer was roasting before a large fire, which threw its light a long distance among the trees under which they were assembled. When they had formed a ring, men and squaws alternately, a sort of Indian fiddle set up an indescribable tune. It was a continuous, melancholy kind of wavy sound, with the slightest possible variation. At the first note, if indeed there was more than one note in the whole tune, they circled around, trotting after each other, and giving utterance to a guttural, sing-song noise, equally nondescript as the music of the fiddle. At the end of the third circuit, they would stop suddenly, whoop as if their lungs would crack, then break from the ring, forming into couples, man and squaw, each jumping backwards as far as possible from the other, then forwards—which graceful feat having been twice or thrice accomplished, they would form in a ring, and go trotting round again. The best dancer appeared to be considered the one who could whoop the loudest, jump the farthest, and utter the most excruciating noise. (Northup 1968[1853]:72–73)

Since there was no Chicapee tribe, Hiram Gregory infers that Northup actually encountered a Choctaw-Biloxi band, due to the geographic location mentioned, as well as the linguistic clue that *chik api* means "our body" in Choctaw. The "roving herd from Texas" may have been an Alabama band (Gregory, personal communication, 1985).

5. It is important to point out that Jackson Langley had strong ties to Marksville through his wife, Alice Picote (Ofo), who came from that community. Hence Langley may have been describing to Swanton a version of the Tunica water ritual (Hiram Gregory, personal communication, 1989).

6. The following is Neitzel's description of the Marksville Green-Corn Ceremony.

> Whoever finds that his corn has arrived at the roasting ear stage informs the chief or head man. A date is set one or two days ahead at which time everyone goes to his field and gets an ear of corn.
>
> It is roasted in the husk and the grains stripped from the cob, in the evening. At midnight a fast is started which is broken at noon the next day. Right at sunrise the people proceed to their mutual burial plot and the corn is placed in saucers or bowls by the graves, such as they can find, of their relatives. Pieces of paper may also be used for receptacles and are discarded or never used again. The man attends to his wife's relatives as his own. Crosses are at the foot of the grave and heads are to the east. The corn is placed by the cross.
>
> They all proceed to the bayou, the men in one group and the women in

another. Undress and go in. They dive or duck three times facing the east. Afterwards they can swim around if they like.

On getting out they dry themselves and the head man takes an ear of the roasted corn and bites off a few kernels, passing it to the next man. The corn is thoroughly chewed and some is taken in the hand and the sign of the cross is made, Catholic fashion. The remainder is spit out, none is swallowed. Afterwards they proceed home or to a central meeting place or visit around waiting for noon at which time fast is broken. The older men usually get out of the water first—at least the first to land follows the head man in the sacrament.

That night is when the dancing starts. (1930)

7. Two ethnographic sources suggest that call and response was used. In his field notes on the Double-Head Dance, Neitzel wrote that "the leader sings a question and all the men answer." This is confirmed by Joseph Pierite, who, after his rendition of the Double-Head song, remarks "when you hear me say 'wa hi yo wa hi ya ha,' well that's the men right there in back supporting [the] singer." In addition, of course, the music itself implies call-and-response texture.

8. Neitzel describes the drum in his field notes as a "pot covered deerskin and tied drum," adding elsewhere that "it was the Tunica custom to place fragments of broken dishes or large garfish scales in the drum to serve as rattles for the dances. The heads of the drums must be wet before they give the proper tone and have resonance" (1930).

9. The following is Neitzel's complete entry on the Double-Head dance.

It takes place at dark on the night of the day on which the New Corn Ceremony has been performed. The leader, a man or chief is first, alternated and followed by women and men in a circle around a pole. They move counterclockwise with their left sides to the pole. The leader sings a question and all the men answer; the women are silent. He may change the question and the others know the proper responses—the words have no meaning. The head man holds the drum in his hand while singing. The steps are trotting steps. They usually sing until tired, but stop sometime before midnight. . . . The Twelve O'clock Dance starts at midnight, but between it and *Talawanoskobotukulu* other dances such as the Horse Dance, Chicken Dance, or Coon Dance were performed for variety. (1930)

10. That the different sections of music accompanied different dance steps is suggested by Sesostrie Youchigant's description of the Rabbit, Bear, and Raccoon Dances (Haas 1950:165), by Neitzel's field notes, and by analogy with current practice among other Southeastern tribes.

Music and the History of Tribe-Caste Interaction in Choṭanāgpur

12

Carol Babiracki

The Muṇḍas are one of the larger aboriginal or tribal groups living today in the Choṭanāgpur Plateau, a multiethnic region in northeastern Central India.[1] Like other large tribes of Choṭanāgpur, they have persistently maintained their linguistic and cultural integrity despite centuries of contact with other tribes, Hindu castes, and small numbers of Muslims. These diverse communities today represent all three of India's major language families: the Austro-Asiatic (Muṇḍāri and other tribal languages), the Dravidian (Kūṛukh, the language of the Oraon tribe), and the Indo-Aryan (languages of caste communities, and the area's lingua franca, Sādāni).[2]

Because of its long and central role in Muṇḍāri life, music is an ideal source for information about the historical change and cultural interaction of the Muṇḍas. More Muṇḍas devote more of their time throughout the year to singing and dancing than to any other expressive activity. Historical evidence suggests, moreover, that it has been this way for centuries. This central role in Muṇḍāri life has empowered music to symbolize Muṇḍāri cultural identity, which itself has been challenged by the influences of numerous other cultural groups—other tribes, nontribal caste outsiders, and dominant national cultures. The music of the Muṇḍas traditionally acts as a cultural mediator, absorbing some external influences while resisting absorption by them. Muṇḍāri music, therefore, encodes this history of intercultural contact, becoming by extension a chronicle of the tribe's own history.

The dual roles music plays as a barrier against absorption and as a mediator of change belie the usual historical explanations of Muṇḍāri culture and many other tribal and minority cultures. Those explanations stress the process of assimilation, seen as leading inevitably to the disappearance of Muṇḍāri culture and society within a larger regional and national culture. Music, in its central relation to other Muṇḍāri activities and values, reveals quite different responses to national and regional pressures. Muṇḍāri music and culture have not become less Muṇḍāri. It is possible, then, that Muṇḍāri music will enable us to write an entirely new history of the Muṇḍa past and present.

The dynamics of change in Muṇḍāri culture and society have been neglected in traditional historiography because historical documentation and ethnography have stressed the early isolation of tribal societies in Choṭanāgpur and have tended to overlook their extensive intertribal contact (Man 1983[1857]; Roy 1912, 1915; Elwin 1939). The literature concerning tribe-caste contact is greater, but, as the product of a nontribal national culture, it naturally portrays the tribes gradually subsumed by a dominant caste society (Bose 1941; Ghurye 1943; Sinha 1959; Mathur 1972). Despite this literature about tribe-caste interaction, we still understand little about the contribution of that interaction to the development of India's tribal and regional cultures.

Reconstructing a Muṇḍa music history over the last several centuries is not without its problems. In an oral musical tradition such as the Muṇḍas', it is impossible to date individual songs, genres, or even musical styles with any assurance. But, then, dating is the tool of a different historiography, namely an older Western model of music history that calibrates change by relying on the convenience of controllable artifacts. In this essay, I am less interested in dating musical change than in establishing its relation to other types of change—religious, cultural, political. It is only in this way that music can demonstrate its fullest potential as a tool for examining the modern music history of the Muṇḍas.

Muṇḍas and Others

For centuries, the pattern of Muṇḍāri life in the subcontinent has been influenced by their contact with others and their response to that contact. As Indo-Aryans advanced into their homelands in the Gangetic Plain, the Muṇḍas migrated southward into Choṭanāgpur, probably sometime between 800 and 500 B.C.E. (Roy 1912:118; Fuchs 1973:28–33). Once in Choṭanāgpur, Muṇḍas pushed aside smaller groups of Indo-Aryans and Austro-Asiatic tribes, such as the Asuras, to claim the land for their villages and rice fields (Fuchs 1973:157).[3] With the influx of other tribes sometime after 500 B.C., the main body of Muṇḍas moved even further into the hills of what is now Ranchi district in the state of Bihar (ibid.:164). Many ancestral Muṇḍāri villages are still intact there, and the area is recognized as the heartland of Muṇḍāri language and music culture.

Despite their reluctance to live among non-Muṇḍas, the Muṇḍas of Choṭanāgpur gradually allowed small, marginal artisan castes to settle in or near their villages in exchange for specialized services. The artisan blacksmiths, basketmakers, weavers, musicians, and the like have contributed to the relative economic and cultural self-sufficiency of Muṇḍāri villages. Men of the musician caste, the Ghāsis, for example, provide instrumental music on drums, *śahnāi* (double-reed wind instrument), and *bhẽr̤* (long trumpet) at Muṇḍāri weddings, funerals, and other life-cycle rituals.[4] Scattered in small settlements throughout the area, Ghāsis, like other artisans, serve not only the Muṇḍas but other tribes and Hindu castes as well. A few artisan communities have probably descended from offshoots of Austro-Asiatic and Dravidian tribes and are still recognized as tribals by the government. The majority, however, including the Ghāsis, are considered low-status castes and in all probability are descendants of the area's ancient Indo-Aryan speaking communities.[5]

Artisan castes such as the Ghāsis, even when they live and work among the tribes, identify culturally and linguistically with a larger community of nontribals called Sādāns. Sādāns, specifically, are those Indo-Aryan speakers whose ancestors settled in Choṭanāgpur anywhere from several centuries to two millennia ago. They are a diverse and stratified sub-society, with the artisan castes occupying the lowest ranks, and farm laborers, traders, and landholders filling out the upper strata. The Sādān castes are unified by their adherence to a localized variety of Hinduism and by their Indo-Aryan language, Sādāni. Residents of the region are careful to distinguish Sādāns from the *diku* (outsider, alien, exploiter)[6] Hindu castes that began settling in Choṭanāgpur some 300 years ago. It is likely that the tribes and Sādāns coexisted in relative harmony and cooperation for centuries under the hereditary leadership of landholding tribes such as the Muṇḍas (Singh 1966:12). With the intrusion of the dikus, both Hindus and Muslims, that relationship began to change.

Beginning in the seventeenth century, the indigenous tribal and Sādān populations found themselves increasingly threatened by outsiders: first, by the agents of Delhi's Mughal rulers, then by high-caste Hindus from other parts of Bihar and Bengal, and finally by the British (Roy 1912:150–82). No longer able to avoid the more powerful foreigners, Muṇḍas began losing their land and authority, despite their often hostile resistance. They, like the other tribes, came to know the intruders and their descendants as diku, an exogenous group set in opposition to themselves, whom they call *hor̤o* (human being, mankind). Dikus have the power to exercise economic and political control over the tribes, and all are considered potential troublemakers, thieves, and deceivers. *Zamindārs* (landlords), moneylenders, petty rajas, upper-caste immigrants (Brāhmins, Baṇiyas, Rautias, Marwāris, Muslims) and many upper-caste Sādān landholders and traders are all diku to the tribes (Sinha et al. 1969). Even a Muṇḍa may come to be regarded as a diku if he or she acts like one, abandoning his or her language and culture, taking on diku attitudes and habits (Hinduizing), or exploiting his or her own people. The recognition of a diku out-group is one of the distinguishing features of the tribes of Choṭanāgpur.

Like each of the other large tribes of central India, the Muṇḍas have also distinguished themselves from others musically. Although Muṇḍas contract the Ghāsis, a Sādān caste, to provide background music at their life-cycle rites, Muṇḍas perform their own communal songs and dances with and for themselves alone. Furthermore, the traditional or indigenous core of these communal repertories is uniquely Muṇḍāri in content and style. By contrast, the numerous Sādān castes share a common, Indo-Aryan music culture in which solo stage performance occupies a prominent place. Dikus and high-caste Sādāns do not participate in communal singing and dancing at all. The lower-status artisan castes, as might be expected, are closer to the tribes culturally, and some do perform their Sādāni songs in group dances. Unlike the tribes, however, caste women and men are usually segregated in separate arenas. Communal singing and dancing, unsegregated by gender, underscores the cultural differences between tribe and caste in Choṭanāgpur.

As the feudal system took hold, Sādāns came into greater and more profitable contact with the newcomers. Dikus were a new source of patronage for the artisan castes, and their linguistic affinities encouraged contact, as did the hope of upward social mobility. Dikus and Sādāns are now united, to varying degrees, by a common religion (Hinduism) and social structure (caste) and the beliefs and practices associated with each. The Sādāni village dialects have been refined and standardized into four regional Indo-Aryan languages, each with a thriving literary and musical tradition. Two have had an impact on the Muṇḍas: Nāgpuri in the western uplands and Pāncpargania in the eastern plains bordering Bengal. Each Indo-Aryan musical tradition has become the expression and emblem of a regional culture that unites all Indo-Aryan speakers, both diku and Sādān.

The small populations of Sādān artisan castes that still live in or near Muṇḍāri villages are more marginal culturally than those who live and work among other castes. Although they are not considered diku by the Muṇḍas, they are also not hoṛo and are not treated as the social equals of the Muṇḍas and other tribes. They have been absorbed into the Muṇḍāri village world, but as a separate, segregated entity. At the same time, they keep social and cultural ties, especially marriage ties, to Sādāns elsewhere in the region. With a foot in each world, so to speak, the artisan castes have acted as culture brokers between the Muṇḍāri and caste worlds.

Ghāsis, the Sādān caste of musical specialists, have had a special role in mediating between Muṇḍāri and caste music cultures, serving as they do both Muṇḍāri and caste patrons. Many Ghāsis are also among the most popular stars of regional musical stage and radio performances and are at the forefront of regional cultural movements. These professional musical activities mark them as caste, but village Ghāsis are also the Sādāns most likely to keep their own *akhaṛa* (dancing ground). Although Ghāsi men and women don't often dance together in public, when they do so in the privacy of their own akhaṛas they appear little different from tribes like the Muṇḍas. Moving easily between caste and tribe, Ghāsis have facilitated musical exchange between the Muṇḍas and diku castes that would not have taken place otherwise.

Another culturally marginal group, mendicant devotees and gurus of the Hindu Vaiśnava sect, have also been important musical brokers between the Muṇḍas and castes. They began passing through and settling in Choṭanāgpur as early as the sixteenth century, seeking to win converts with their poetry, singing, and dancing. Despite their egalitarian religious message, the Vaiśnavas were products of an Indo-Aryan caste society. They were loyal supporters of the upper castes and have enjoyed the patronage of the diku landlords and rajas. Their religious mission made little headway among the Muṇḍas, but their songs, set to regional Nāgpuri and Pāncpargania tunes, were received with enthusiasm (Sinha 1966; Zide and Munda 1970).

The intrusion of Hindu and Muslim outsiders into Choṭanāgpur, beginning some two to three hundred years ago, dramatically changed the relationship between Muṇḍas and Sādāns. The Muṇḍāri kinship-based leadership structure and communal land tenure was supplanted by a caste-based feudal system and a cash economy. There were corresponding changes in Muṇḍa-Sādān musical relationships as well. The pre-feudal period saw the development of a common musical base among the Muṇḍas and Sādāns, traces of which are still evident today. The development of common customs, symbols, and beliefs among culturally different peoples in India is a process Ram Srivastava (1966) has called "cultural approximation." The "musical approximation" (or "musical convergence") produced by early Muṇḍāri-Sādāni interaction involved a gradual evolution of common musical practices, genres, and stylistic traits. As the dikus gained control over land and power, the musical interaction of Muṇḍas and Sādāns changed. Muṇḍas began to introduce songs and dances borrowed from both the Sādāns and the Vaiśnavas into their annual round of communal performances. A direct, unidirectional borrowing superseded the earlier Muṇḍāri-Sādāni musical approximation. Muṇḍas have confined their borrowings within one season, the monsoon, in a repertory they call *karam,* from the Indo-Aryan word *karma.*

Karam has been cited as evidence of the Muṇḍas' inevitable assimilation into caste society, an interpretation of culture change widely applied to the tribes of India (Sachchidananda 1979:303–305). However, a closer look at how Muṇḍas have borrowed the Sādān songs and dances, transforming them and integrating them into their own music culture, reveals another historical process, a traditional and expressly Muṇḍāri pattern of change that has ensured the continuity of what is central to Muṇḍāri culture despite the changes of the last 200 years.

Muṇḍāri Music Culture

In the face of the destabilizing political and economic changes in Muṇḍāri society, their performance of communal song and dance (if not the specific songs and dances themselves) has remained a constant. Communal dance makes real and physical the values of communality and equality that are central ideals among Muṇḍas. These ideals do not always find expression in the political, economic, and social realities of Muṇḍāri life today, though ethnographers like Roy and Hoffmann would have us believe that they once did (Roy 1912; Hoffmann 1950). But these ideals *are* the reality of the communal dance event in the village akhaṛa, a commonly owned arena in the center of every Muṇḍāri village or hamlet.

Muṇḍas have no word in their language that is equivalent to our word "music." Moreover, the closest term, *durang* (song, singing), is not applied to all Muṇḍāri activities that an outside observer might consider music. Only communal musical activity is called durang, and it occupies far more of their time and energy than does any individual music making. Singing and dancing is a weekly activity and is an essential, central part of most Muṇḍāri ritual and festival occasions.

The Muṇḍāri musical and festival year is organized around the three agricultural seasons: spring (planting; April–May), the monsoon (rice transplanting; June–October), and winter (harvesting; November–February), as well as a fourth "season," that of the ritual hunt (February–March). Each season has its own distinct repertory of songs, dances, and drum patterns (Muṇḍāri *khod,* Sādāni *tāl*). Throughout a season, weather and work permitting, Muṇḍāri men and women might gather on one or more nights each week to dance with those of their own village, an extended "family" dominated by one exogamous clan. This weekly dancing is only preparation for the important event, a large festival toward the end of each season, held on a different day in each village to allow boys to visit the akhaṛas of other villages and display their talents before marriageable girls.

Once each year, Muṇḍas from a dozen or more neighboring villages come together to sing and dance in a large, regional fair. In Ranchi district, for example, thousands of Muṇḍas gather each January on top of their highest and most sacred mountain for a public sacrifice of chickens followed by singing and dancing. For a few hours, the long, flat mountain top is crowded with small makeshift akhaṛas, each representing a different village, and all of them alive with simultaneous, but independent performances of songs, drumming, and dance. Just as village dancing unites a clan in communal, expressive activity, the annual fair unites all members of the tribe within a given region. Elsewhere in Choṭanāgpur, Muṇḍas display their singing and dancing at annual multicultural fairs, originally held in honor of and/or sponsored by rajas and zamindārs.

Muṇḍas now reserve the monsoon season for their karam repertory, the repository for their borrowings from the Sādāni and Vaiśnava musical traditions. In tune, text structure, subject matter, and movement patterns, karam songs and dances resemble their Sādān sources more than they do Muṇḍāri traditional songs. Those traditional songs sung during the remaining three seasons (spring, winter, the hunt) are uniquely Muṇḍāri, as different in their structure from karam as they are from Sādān songs.

Whether the songs sung are borrowed or traditional, all are equally Muṇḍāri in performance style and context. For example, all Muṇḍāri song performance is characterized by occasional diaphonic singing in parallel fourths or fifths, and when women respond antiphonally to men in the akhaṛa, they frequently answer at the fourth or fifth. Unless they have learned otherwise from Sādān or diku musicians or media "experts," Muṇḍas do not appear to distinguish this occasional diaphony and bi-tonality from unison singing. To my knowledge, neither technique is present in Sādāni song performance, but both are found in the music of other tribes in Bihar (Parmar 1977:23), Kerala and Uttar Pradesh (Wade 1980:153), and Madhya Pradesh (Knight 1983; Dournon 1980).

Muṇḍāri song and dance performance is probably most distinctive from that of the Sādāns and dikus in its rhythmic organization. Muṇḍas consistently drum, sing, and dance slightly behind the beat, unlike Sādān musicians who tend to anticipate the beat. And Muṇḍas typically subdivide the beat of their songs and slower dances into asymmetrical portions. Although many Muṇḍāri tāls (repeated drum patterns), even those that accompany traditional songs, have been influenced by Sādān patterns, some are highly distinctive. *Jadur,* a spring season song type, is sung to a twenty-beat tāl that falls into asymmetrical subgroups of 6 + 4 + 8 + 2. In its length, it is quite unlike any Sādān tāl in the area (see Example 1). Finally, in all Muṇḍāri song performance, drum patterns, dance patterns and phrases of the song are normally of different lengths and continually out of phase with one another. Sādāns, particularly in stage performances, often attempt to coordinate the phrases of drumming and singing; good drummers are expected to follow the phrases of the song.

Whether the dance songs are traditional or borrowed, Muṇḍāri

Example 1. The Muṇḍāri Tāl for the Jadur Song Type

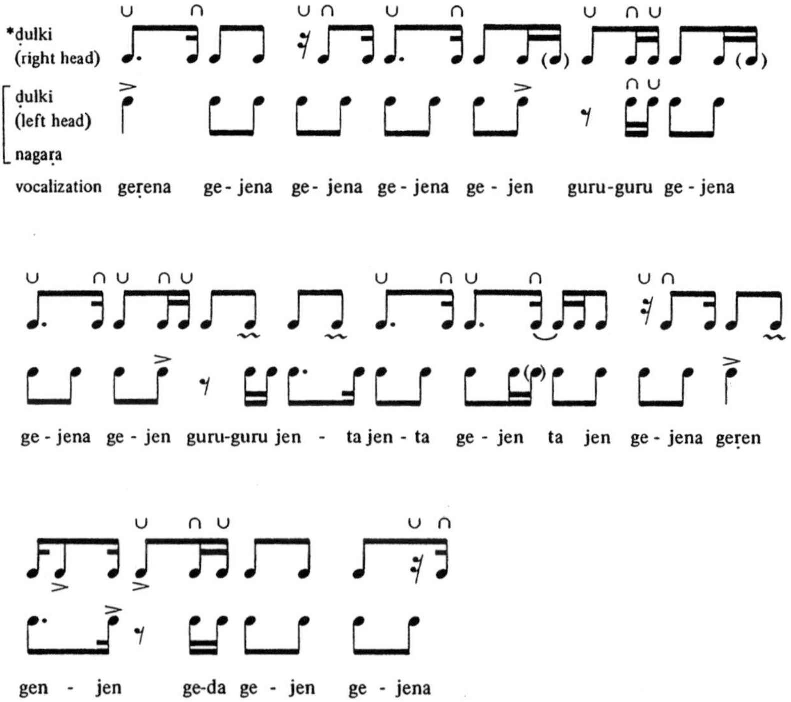

Note: ♫ is always played with the first eighth slightly shorter and the second slightly longer (♫)

*(As performed by Ram Dayal Munda, Dec. 16, 1984)

communal performance is distinct in style, particularly with respect to rhythm. And while small groups of individuals may sing these songs while working or sitting together, their full performance is realized only with dance in the akhaṛa. Despite the changes in the content of Muṇḍāri song repertories, the most striking of which is karam, the communal dance event and its relationship to the seasons, sacrificial rites, festivals, marriage patterns, and values have remained a constant. The point is important; a full understanding of the changes in Muṇḍāri-caste musical and cultural interaction over the last several hundred years must take into account continuity in Muṇḍāri culture as well as change.

Early Interaction: Musical Approximation

For centuries before the establishment of feudalism in Choṭanāgpur, the Muṇḍas and larger Austro-Asiatic tribes apparently enjoyed some degree of economic, social, and cultural dominance over the smaller tribes and Sādān populations. Linguistic studies suggest that the Muṇḍa languages, a subgroup of the Austro-Asiatic family that includes Muṇḍāri, Santāli, Ho, and others, were once spread across a large part of northeastern India (Fuchs 1973:163). According to Kumar Suresh Singh, the Muṇḍas and Sādāns were able to develop an integrated social, economic, and cultural system that was relatively undisturbed by outsiders until the seventeenth century (1966:12).

The long cooperation between the Muṇḍas and Sādāns produced a common cultural base that has since become somewhat obscured by more recent and more radical change. In all likelihood, Muṇḍāri-Sādāni "musical approximation" did not involve radical or sudden change in either Muṇḍāri or Sādāni musical traditions and did not disturb the unique identity of either. The process of musical approximation may still characterize some Muṇḍāri-Sādāni musical interaction in certain settings, particularly within the Muṇḍāri village.

Evidence of musical approximation seems most apparent in Muṇḍāri and Sādāni drums and drumming patterns. Although their drums may be known by different names, they differ only in minor details of shape and size. They include the *māndar* (Muṇḍāri *dumang*), *ḍholak* (Muṇḍāri *ḍulki*), *nāgaṛa*, and *karah* (Muṇḍāri *rabaga*).[7] Most Muṇḍāri tāls also bear a strong resemblance to those of the Sādāns. The *mage* tāl (winter season), for example, is almost identical to the Sādān (Nāgpuri) *phagua* tāl (winter, spring), even though mage and phagua songs are entirely different.

The differences between Muṇḍāri and Sādāni tunes are far greater than the differences between their tāls. Even so, some Muṇḍāri tunes approximate the Sādāni versions performed in villages, particularly in the group dances of women. The unaccompanied women's marriage songs of both groups are sung in the same seven-beat meter (3 + 2 + 2) and to some of the same tunes. This is not altogether surprising. Their marriage rituals as well are another example of approximation.[8] Communal song and dance performance itself was probably the result of cultural approximation between Sādāns and Muṇḍas. The segregation of Sādān men and women in separate akhaṛas came later, influenced by Muslim and upper-caste Hindu notions about the indecency of women dancing in public. Sādāni women's akhaṛa songs can resemble Muṇḍāri traditional songs in both subject matter and text structure. We might consider, as an example, two songs of the monsoon season, a *ciṭid̖* song of the Muṇḍas and an *anganāi* (pre-midnight) song of the Nāgpuri *janāni jhumar* (women's jhumar) repertory (see Example 2).

Muṇḍāri men and women sing ciṭid̖ during the early months of the monsoon. Although they share the season with karam, ciṭid̖ songs almost certainly predate the borrowed repertory and have much in common with the other traditional repertories: most texts are in Muṇḍāri and lack intentional rhyme; texts are "unsigned," that is they do not carry the poet's name; they lack a musical distinction between verse and refrain; and they are sung only by Muṇḍas, even at mixed Muṇḍāri and Sādāni events.[9]

I had heard many anganāi songs performed in Sādān stage performances, but I was not struck by their similarity to ciṭid̖ until I heard them sung by a group of Lohar (blacksmith) women in a village dancing ground. The women repeated the same anganāi tune (Example 2) to different sets of couplets for most of the night, just as Muṇḍas might sing only one or two traditional song types throughout a night of dancing. Both the anganāi and ciṭid̖ tunes are based on a typical Muṇḍāri scale pattern, and their melodic contours and general rhythmic characters are similar. In a Sādān stage performance, this anganāi tune might be performed only once or twice in a night; its melody would be elaborated and its range extended. The two tunes of Example 2 are not similar enough to be considered the same by either group, although Muṇḍa and Sādān musicians have acknowledged their similarity. Their resemblance is further obscured by the fact that they are accompanied by very different tāls, played on different drums. The ciṭid̖ tāl (either ten or twelve beats long) is played on the ḍulki and nāgaṛa, and the anganāi tāl (ten beats) on the māndar and nāgaṛa.

The differences between Muṇḍāri and Sādāni musics are often more apparent than their similarities. Under the patronage of the feudal landlords and rajas, new idioms of Sādān music were developed for solo and small ensemble stage performances. The changes appealed to the new diku patrons, but they moved the Sādāns further away from Muṇḍāri music culture.

Example 2. Comparison of a Nāgpuri *Janāni Jhumar* Song and a Muṇḍāri *Citịḍ* Song

Janāni Jhumar: "kā dose rājā mārali" (Nāgpuri). Recorded in Pundag, Sept. 18, 1984.

Citịḍ: "pisire-pisire gama leda" (Muṇḍāri). Recorded in Gaṇamaṇa, April 10, 1984.

Janāni Jhumar (♩. = 87)
(a)
Verse:
(ni) na me co - ra - nī na ham - e
Citịḍ (♩. = 90)
(b)
pi - si - re pi - si - re ga - ma le - da
ca - ta - nī kā do - se rā - jā mā - ra - lī
(mā - re - la)
ba - ki - ri re le - per a - ṛa?
Refrain:
rau - ra la - gī na ek - ā - da - sī ka - ra - lī re
a e - aŋ - ga ṭu - pa? ka - ji
kā do - se rā - jā mā - ra - lī
(mā - re - la)
ki - ri - a - ña me

Alternate Refrain:

yi hai re
bo - le bo - le bo - le rā - jā e - aŋ - ga
o de re kā do - se rā - jā mā - ra - lī
(mā - re - la)
ṭu - paʔ ka - ji ki - ri - a - ña me

SCALES:

Janāni Jhumar:

Ciṭiḍ:

Tāls (nāgaṛa only):

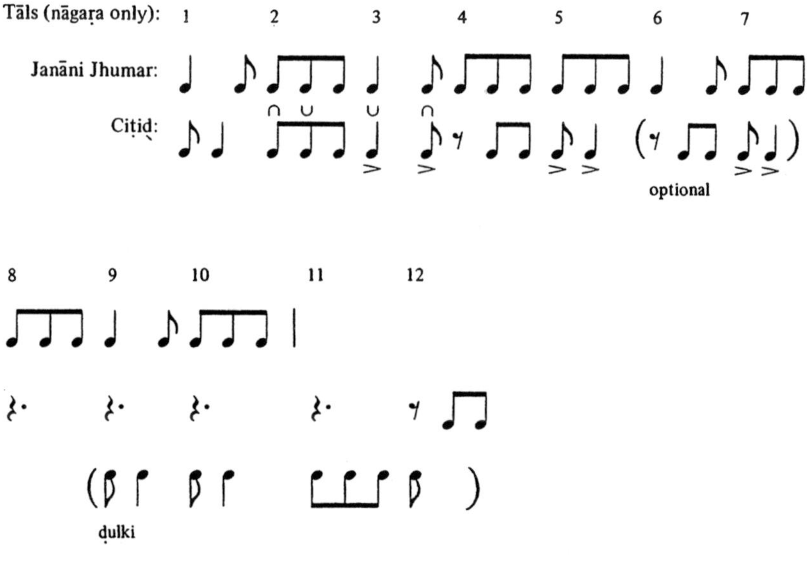
1 2 3 4 5 6 7
Janāni Jhumar:
Ciṭiḍ:
optional
8 9 10 11 12
ḍulki

Text and Translation of Nāgpuri Janāni Jhumar song, "kā dose rājā mārali" (Example 2a).

ode ode re, kā dose rājā mārli,
raur lagīn ekādasi karlī re [refrain]
na ham chorni, na ham caṭni [verse]
kā dose . . .

ode ode re, āb to jīvā jānelā,
charke hārī pānī cuvelā [refrain]

ode ode re, Kausilā re kodāe ḍā̃ṛe ḍā̃ṛe
Rāmcandra khojāe bane bane [refrain]
ḍā̃ṛe re khojāe kahā̃ pāvāe,
Rāmcandra khojāe bane bane [refrain]

āsan pataī chahiyā̃ banāval,
dai re kodāe duiyo bhāi [refrain]
[verse unclear]

ode ode re, dohe re dõgā dubelā,
bacpan kar dosolī moh cutelā [refrain]
rā̃dhlī dāil bhāl, kera ke tarkārī re [verse]
dohe re . . .

ode ode re, māyā jāle kāsāenā,
[—]ka kāer māṭī ne milāe delā [refrain]

Look there, my king, for what fault did you beat me?
I went through fasting [for you]. [lit.: I did the eleventh day] [refrain]
I'm neither a thief nor a glutton, [verse]
My king . . .

Look there, now the *jīvā* [soul] realizes [what life is].
The house is leaking on the veranda [roof]. [refrain]

Look there, [Queen] Kaushila is roaming in the field crying,
She is looking for Ramcandra, her son. [refrain]
She looks for him all over, but where will she find him?
She is looking for Ramcandra, her son. [refrain]

They have made a shed with *āsan* leaves,
[Seated] in there, little brothers weep. [refrain]

Look there, the boat is sinking in deep waters,
The affection of childhood friendship is left behind. [refrain]
I cooked rice and dal [and] banana curry [to go with it], [verse]
The boat is sinking . . .

Look there, to be caught in the Net of Deception,
To lose the youthful body in dust. [refrain]

Text and Translation of Muṇḍāri *ciṭiḍ* song, "pisir-pisire gama leḍa" (Example 2b)

pisir-pisire gama leda, bakiṛire leper aṛaʔ
ho bhala, eaŋga, ṭupaʔ kaji kiriañ me [verse]
bole, bole, bole, rājā, eaŋga, ṭupaʔ kaji kiriañ me. [refrain]

kupul kodoko hijuʔ akana, aṛaʔ begaḍ mā̃ḍio kako jojom,
eaŋga tupaʔ kaji kiriañ me [verse]
bole, bole, bole, rājā, eaŋga ṭupaʔ kaji kiriañ me [refrain]

It rained a little; *leper* [has sprouted] in the backyard.
Young mother, bring me a basket. [verse]
bole, bole, bole, raja [exclamatory], young mother,
bring me a basket. [refrain]

Guests have arrived; they wouldn't eat without vegetables.
Young mother, bring me a basket. [verse]
bole, bole, bole, raja, young mother, bring me a basket. [refrain]

The author wishes to express her deep thanks to Asrita Purti for transcriptions of the texts and to Ram Dayal Munda for translations.

Raja and Diku Patronage

The earliest chiefs in Choṭanāgpur rose gradually from an indigenous leadership structure dominated by the Muṇḍas. According to S. C. Roy, the hereditary leaders of Muṇḍāri villages and groups of villages, called *patti*s, were "chiefs among equals," leaders rather than rulers (Roy 1912:120). They organized militia and headed councils of elders, but they enjoyed no economic advantages over other Muṇḍas. Eventually, there emerged a hereditary line of rulers, the Nāgbansis, who united the Muṇḍas, Sādāns, and other residents of Choṭanāgpur (Sinha 1962; Roy 1912:135–49). Like the patti chiefs before them, the early Nāgbansi rajas apparently functioned primarily as military leaders, for which they were given a share of village produce but no title to village lands. Most Muṇḍas probably had little or no contact with them (Roy 1912:148). In the villages, Muṇḍa-Sādān cooperative coexistence remained relatively undisturbed (Singh 1966:12).

The influx of Indo-Aryan outsiders into Choṭanāgpur began in the early years of the seventeenth century, when the Mughals finally succeeded in reducing the Nāgbansi Raja, Durjan Sāl, to a tributary of Delhi (Virottam 1972:1–6). Durjan Sāl, now proclaimed Maharaja of Choṭanāgpur, and his successors built large palaces and Hindu temples throughout the area west and southwest of Ranchi city, an area that is the stronghold of Nāgpuri language and culture. To serve in his courts and temples, the Maharaja and his family invited Brāhmins, Rautias, Baṇiyas, and other high born Hindus to their courts as advisors and servants. They were followed by businessmen, moneylenders, and lower Hindu service castes. In exchange for their services, the outsiders were granted rights to the produce of tribal villages, and eventually to the land itself. The Maharaja and his subordinate rajas extended their ties to the outside Hindu world through marriages with other ruling families in northern Bihar, Bengal, Orissa, Madhya Pradesh, Nepal, Rajasthan, and Gujarat, among other places.[10]

The final intruders, the British, made the Maharaja of Choṭanāgpur a vassal of the East India Company in the mid-eighteenth century. With the British military and courts backing the new feudal order, the economic and political position of the rajas and other newcomers was strengthened while the status of the Muṇḍas deteriorated. By the early nineteenth century, the traditional Muṇḍāri communal land-tenure system was breaking down, and many Muṇḍas and other tribals found themselves reduced to the condition of bonded laborers.

The status of the Sādāns, particularly the Ghāsi musicians, also changed under the Hinduized rajas and foreign landlords, but for the better. Ghāsis became favored servants, receiving grants of land and revenue for both their military and musical services (Singh 1966:3–4). Those who profited from the patronage of the caste Hindus were regarded with scorn as diku by the tribes. It is not clear when the Ghāsis began serving as musicians for Muṇḍa patrons as well as diku. It is possible that they were only village basketmakers, as their name suggests, before the seventeenth century. Nevertheless, the Muṇḍāri patronage of Ghāsi musicians might reasonably be interpreted as an emulation of the rajas and landlords.

Through their royal patrons, the Ghāsis were introduced to Indo-Aryan music from throughout northern and central India. The rajas brought musicians of *śāstriya saṅgīt* (canonical, art music) to their courts from as far away as Gujarat and Rajasthan. The interaction of the Ghāsis with these outside musicians eventually gave rise to the standardization of Choṭanāgpur's Sādān musics into regional musical traditions, the most widespread of which are the Nāgpuri and Pāncpargania. The differences between the two can be attributed in part to the political and cultural alliances of their respective royal patrons. Descendants of the former Maharaja of Choṭanāgpur believe that it was a Nāgbansi raja, Ragunath Sahadev "Shah," whose reign followed that of Durjan Sāl in 1640 (Virottam 1972:205), who created Nāgpuri music and taught it to the Ghāsis.[11] That, of course, is a claim that Ghāsis dispute, insisting instead that they are the original *ustāds* (masters, teachers) of both Nāgpuri and Pāncpargania musics.

Outside, Indo-Aryan influences on Nāgpuri and Pāncpargania songs are obvious in their language, text structure, subject matter, tunes, drumming patterns, and performance style. Nāgpuri and Pāncpargania musicians, as well as tribal musicians following their lead, now refer to their tunes as rāgs and their drum patterns as tāls. Like the classical rāgs, Nāgpuri and Pāncpargania tunes are not only associated with seasons but also with specific performance times during the evening and night.[12] The adoption of the models and mores of Muslim and Hindu rulers had a particularly strong impact on the role of women in musical performance. Under the influence of the dikus, Sādān women were musically segregated, and new classes of female solo performers were introduced, most of them either concubines (*nacini*) or prostitutes (*kasbi*).[13] As patrons of the Ghāsis and other Sādāns, the Choṭanāgpur rajas became brokers between them and a larger world of Indo-Aryan classical and folk music. Such mediation by ruling classes is a characteristic of the *jajmāni* patronage system throughout India (Wade and Pescatello 1977:279). But it has been marginal groups like the Sādāns (particularly the Ghāsis) and Vaiśnavas who have mediated between tribes like the Muṇḍas and the outside musical world. The Muṇḍas, in turn, have been agents of contact between Nāgpuri and Pāncpargania regional musics, combining both in their karam repertory.

Karam and Muṇḍāri-Caste Interaction

The karam repertory took form gradually during the last 100 to 200 years, following the Hinduization of the Choṭanāgpur rajas, but its widespread popularity is probably more recent. Many songs with Vaiśnava texts date only to the late nineteenth century, and as recently as 1942 it was observed that "[karam] songs are not sung in purely Muṇḍāri parts or very little sung by the Muṇḍas" (Bhaduri 1942). Karam has developed during a period of rapid change in the balance of power in Choṭanāgpur in favor of the caste Hindu outsiders and their Sādān servants. Although the Muṇḍas have remained dominant within their own villages, they have lost much of their earlier political and cultural influence in the region as a whole. The last 200 years have been marked by competition and conflict in Muṇḍāri-caste interaction. Interestingly, the Muṇḍas' concept of diku and their karam repertory both developed during this same period. Today, the concept of diku remains strong, and karam is growing in popularity.

Muṇḍāri karam, as a musical repertory of songs, dances, and drum patterns, is a Muṇḍāri creation, a collection of borrowings from throughout the full range of Nāgpuri and Pāncpargania seasonal genres, combined with new Muṇḍāri creations based on those borrowings.[14] In karam, Muṇḍas have made these borrowings an integral part of their annual cycle of song and dance, not evenly distributed throughout the year as one might expect, but segregated in a separate season, the monsoon.

The association of karam songs with the monsoon, the season of the love-play of Radha and Krishna, attests to the influence of Vaiśnava musicians in its development. Many popular karam songs, in Muṇḍāri and set to Sādāni tunes, were actually composed by Vaiśnava poets of the late nineteenth century. A majority of karam songs, in fact, can be traced to Nāgpuri and Pāncpargania monsoon repertories. The months between the end of the monsoon and beginning of winter (September–November) are a time of good weather and an easing of work, hence a time of fairs and festivals throughout Choṭanāgpur. At the post-monsoon fairs, Muṇḍas have the opportunity to observe the musical activities of other tribes and Sādāns, both in dancing grounds and on the stage, and they are called upon to display their own musical skills. It is not surprising that Muṇḍas choose to perform karam, their version of the regional musical dialect rather than their own, unique repertories, which are neither understood nor appreciated by the non-Muṇḍas.

The word "karam" actually designates much more than the Muṇḍāri music and dance repertory. It is also a tree, the spirit or deity of that tree, and the rituals and festival dedicated to that spirit. The karam deity is worshiped during the month of *bhādo* (August–September), by both tribes and low-status castes, from northern Bihar and Uttar Pradesh southward into Madhya Pradesh (Russell 1975[1916]:29, 117; Mitra 1921). In Choṭanāgpur, tribals and Sādāns usually follow the ritual with a courtyard festival of music and dance. Although the Muṇḍāri repertory takes its name from the tree spirit, the songs themselves and their performance are quite independent of the spirit and its festival. Unlike the traditional Muṇḍāri communal festivals, the karam festival and ritual are optional and personal, performed only by those households that have been bothered in some way by the karam spirit, and then without the sacrifice of chickens that is required in Muṇḍāri rituals.

The attraction of the Muṇḍas to karam songs and dances lies, at least in part, in their musical qualities and in the skill required to master them. Musically, karam songs resemble their Indo-Aryan sources far more than they do the Muṇḍas' own traditional songs. Each of the traditional seasonal repertories is based on just two or three different song types, each one a flexible melody that is adjusted to texts of various lengths. The karam song repertory lacks such homogeneity and simple internal organization. Rather, karam is a large and continually expanding pool of dozens of different songs and tunes, open to as much innovation as the skill of the singers and dancers can support.[15] Karam tunes use a wide variety of scale types and melodic shapes and move rapidly over a wide range, extending at least a third or fourth beyond the octave. Traditional tunes, on the other hand, generally wind around four or five notes, all within one octave. Karam texts also reflect their Indo-Aryan sources. Rather than the traditional Muṇḍāri nonrhyming couplets, most are rhyming verse-refrain forms, with their verses sung in a high range and their refrains in a low. While traditional songs in Sādāni are rare, karam songs may be in Muṇḍāri or Sādāni, and sometimes are in both. Whatever the language, the final verse of a karam song often contains a "signature" line that identifies the poet, an individualistic gesture missing in all traditional songs.

The enthusiasm of the Muṇḍas for the songs and dances of their Sādān and diku nemeses appears less paradoxical when we consider how the Muṇḍas have absorbed karam songs into their musical world. For example, the borrowed Sādāni songs, tunes, tāls, and dance steps have been recombined in karam without regard for their original associations with each other or with season or gender. Thus, a popular Muṇḍāri karam song ("*lega daṛin me*") combines a tune from the Nāgpuri *mardāna jhumar* (men's jhumar) repertory with a dance step that closely resembles the Nāgpuri janāni jhumar (women's jhumar) dance. The tāl is one chosen from the Muṇḍas' own stock of a half dozen or so karam tāls.

Karam songs exhibit their most Muṇḍāri qualities in their performance style and context. The differences in melodic turns, phrase endings, and dance styling between a Muṇḍāri and Sādāni performance of the same tune may seem insignificant to an outside observer, but to the people of Choṭanāgpur these differences mark a performance as Muṇḍāri, Nāgpuri, or Pāncpargania. The rhythmic character of a karam song may also be very different from its Sādān source, usually performed at a slower tempo, with a triple subdivision of the beat even when the Sādān version is sung with a duple subdivision, and always with a characteristic Muṇḍāri asymmetry within the beat.

As karam songs become more popular, they are also becoming increasingly localized. Radha and Krishna of the Vaiśnava text become a simple village couple in the karam text, their names sometimes disappearing altogether. Many Muṇḍāri poets now prefer to compose on specifically Muṇḍāri subjects, such as diku exploitation or heroes of Muṇḍāri rebellions. Their songs are in Muṇḍāri and pointedly omit the foreign "signature" line. Because Muṇḍāri poets also freely alter and recombine tunes, some karam tunes cannot easily be traced back to their Sādān antecedents, although they resemble them in structure. In short, there is some indication that the karam repertory is becoming increasingly distinct from its Indo-Aryan sources.

The karam festival has also been localized, particularly in the Muṇḍa-dominated hill country. In Sādān and diku households, the karam deity or king (*karam deota, karam rāja*) is worshiped by unmarried girls for the well-being of their fathers and brothers. The rituals, performed on the eleventh day of the month of bhādo, include a validating story that is based on Hindu ethical concepts of karma and *dhārma;* they are properly performed by Hindu religious specialists. Only some village Sādāns of the artisan castes might be found dancing in the courtyard following the ritual.

Muṇḍas take little interest in the Hindu version of karam and do not bother to worship the karam tree spirit (*karam bonga*) at all unless it has bothered them in some way. This is because the Muṇḍas regard karam bonga not as a deity but as a modality of one or another troublesome spirit, such as *ikir bonga,* a malevolent spirit who was left behind by the Asuras, the ancient enemies of the Muṇḍas. When karam is celebrated in Muṇḍāri villages, it is often transformed from a household ritual into a village-wide festival. They choose the day of celebration, begin the festivities with a small sacrifice to village spirits, and follow it with a dance including visitors from other villages. Other Muṇḍāri villages might celebrate an identical festival, minus the karam tree, and call it Ras. Although the name is obviously derived from the Hindu Raslila (the play of Radha and Krishna), Ras has little connection with the Vaiśnava version, except as an opportunity for young boys and girls to enjoy each other's company. For Muṇḍas, what is important is ending the season with a festival and dance event that includes Muṇḍas (especially those of marriageable age) of other villages. By transforming a Hindu household festival into a variety of village festivals, the Muṇḍas have created a festival season that resembles the other three in the Muṇḍāri calendar.

Conclusion

Karam is not the simple borrowing of a diku festival with its songs and dances, nor is it a sign of the beginning of the end of Muṇḍāri culture, as researchers such as Roy, Hoffmann, Sachchidananda, and many others would have us believe. Muṇḍas have transformed and integrated both the festival and the music into a bounded Muṇḍāri (hoṛo) world. In the context of their collective song and dance performance, Muṇḍas use the songs of the outsiders to reaffirm Muṇḍāri values of communality and equality and to establish a cultural boundary between themselves and the dikus. By virtue of their context and performance, karam songs and dances are not diku.

As Indo-Aryan culture has spread across Choṭanāgpur during the last two centuries, it has taken into its fold long-time cultural allies of the Muṇḍas, such as the Ghāsis. Karam has been one Muṇḍāri response to the cultural encroachment of the Sādāns and dikus. Muṇḍas consider the karam repertory more difficult and demanding (*hambal*, heavy) than their traditional repertories, requiring a greater knowledge of tunes, drum patterns, and foreign languages. Karam requires courage. It exposes a Muṇḍa to judgment by non-Muṇḍas and to the risk of making mistakes, particularly when singing someone else's "signed" song. As a strategy for dealing with an outside threat, karam is not foreign at all, but typically Muṇḍāri, a means of controlling the foreign by adopting it, transforming it, and absorbing it into the "inside" Muṇḍāri world. In the same way, as Muṇḍas are reminded in their epic tale, their old enemies the Asuras were tricked, subdued, and finally absorbed into the Muṇḍāri world as spirits, subject to the control of Muṇḍāri shamans. Muṇḍas have similarly incorporated marginal tribes and Sādān artisan castes into their village families as fictive kin relations. Like those artisan castes, karam has been incorporated into the Muṇḍāri world as a new entity, segregated from traditional song repertories, but integrated into the social and cultural fabric of Muṇḍāri life. Karam is not diku, but it is not originally Muṇḍa either.

The changes in Muṇḍāri-caste musical interaction during the last 200 years reflect changes in the political and cultural status of the diverse communities of Choṭanāgpur. Before the arrival of the dikus, the cultural distance between the Muṇḍas and Sādān castes was minimal. They developed common musical styles, performance contexts, and instruments, while maintaining separate repertories. With the Hinduization of the Sādāns, the cultural distance between the two groups increased. Musical approximation gave way to the unidirectional borrowing that has resulted in the Muṇḍas' karam repertory. In karam, the earlier pattern of interaction has been reversed. Muṇḍas have adopted the individual songs of the castes but have reinterpreted them in distinctly Muṇḍāri styles and performance contexts. Karam reflects the multiple identities that modern Muṇḍas must negotiate; it is simultaneously regional in its content and Muṇḍāri in its performance.

The participation of India's tribal groups in regional economic and political systems and their cultural borrowings from castes have been widely interpreted by anthropologists and historians as evidence of their gradual social and cultural assimilation into the Hindu caste system (Sachchidananda 1979:303–305; Kolenda 1978:96). In the case of the Ghāsis, this is probably a fitting characterization. Muṇḍāri karam, however, reflects more than a simple borrowing of foreign items, and assimilation does not seem to be an adequate explanation. In their long history of dealing with outsiders, Muṇḍas have persistently preserved the continuity of their own society and culture by absorbing foreign threats rather than being absorbed by them. In karam, we see evidence that this process continues, despite the Muṇḍāri loss of political and economic autonomy. Given the rapid social, political, and economic changes they have faced and continue to face in the twentieth century, the realization of Muṇḍāri cultural ideals in the communal dance event, whether they are dancing karam or a traditional genre, may be vital for preserving the continuity of a distinct Muṇḍāri cultural identity. In the performance of karam, Muṇḍas demonstrate their ability to control and cooperate with the outsiders, while still asserting their cultural autonomy. Rather than assimilating into Hindu caste society and culture, Muṇḍas are continuing to redefine their own world in relationship to the outside.

NOTES

This essay is based on research conducted in Ranchi district in southern Bihar in the fall of 1981 and again in 1983–84, funded by a Fulbright-Hays Dissertation Research Fellowship and a grant from the University of Illinois at Urbana-Champaign. I would like to express my gratitude to the many Muṇḍāri, Nāgpuri, and Pāncpargania musicians who assisted me, and to Dr. Ram Dayal Munda and Mr. Mukund Nayak, in particular.

1. The Choṭanāgpur plateau and cultural region extends across southern Bihar, south of the Gangetic plain, and into adjacent areas of Madhya Pradesh, Orissa, and West Bengal. The highest concentration of Muṇḍas is in Choṭanāgpur Division in Bihar, where they numbered 714,927 in 1971 (Das 1980). Figures for 1981 were unavailable at the time of this writing.

2. The Muṇḍāri language belongs to the Muṇḍa language group of the Austro-Asiatic subsection of the Austric language family. The Muṇḍa language group also includes Santāli, Ho, Khaṛia, Korwa, Asura, and other tribal languages of northeastern Central India (Fuchs 1973:36).

3. The origin and race of the earliest Indo-Aryan speakers in Choṭanāgpur is unknown. Fuchs suggests that they were indigenous tribes that had adopted ancient Indo-Aryan languages prior to the arrival of the Muṇḍas (1973:157).

4. For further information about the instruments of the Ghāsis, see my

articles on *ḍhāk, nāgaṛa, ḍholki, pereṇeḍ* (*śahnāi*), *bhēṛ*, and *narsigha* in *The New Grove Dictionary of Musical Instruments* (Sadie 1984).

5. For example, the Lohara (blacksmith) and Mahali (basketmaker) communities are officially classified as tribes by the government of India, while the Lohar and Teli (oil presser) communities are classified as castes. The classification does not necessarily correspond to any prescribed set of "tribal" or "caste" characteristics.

6. *Diku* is from the Sādāni "*dik dik karna*" (to trouble, to vex) (Sinha et al. 1969:123).

7. The most common drums of the Muṇḍāri akhaṛa today are the *ḍulki*, a double-headed barrel drum; *nāgaṛa*, a large iron-bodied kettledrum; and *rabaga*, a slightly conical, double-headed drum, only the larger head of which is played. The *dumang*, a clay-bodied double-headed drum, has passed out of use in the central Muṇḍāri area, but can still be found in other areas. The ḍulki player, leader of the ensemble, plays the entire drum pattern, a combination of accented strokes (left head) and elaborating patterns (right head). The nāgaṛa drummers play only the accented strokes. For further information, see my articles on these drums in *The New Grove Dictionary of Musical Instruments* (Sadie 1984).

8. Despite the similarity in marriage rituals, Hinduized Sādāns today practice a system of dowry rather than the typical tribal system of brideprice.

9. At a 1984 village performance of Cho (Chau), a folk dance drama depicting tales from the Hindu epics, Muṇḍāri boys circled the performance site aggressively singing ciṭiḍ throughout the performance.

10. Personal communication from Lal Ranvijay Nath Sahadev, of the family of the Maharaja of Choṭanāgpur, 1984, and Gobordhan Bhanj, of the family of the Raja of Seraikela, 1984.

11. Personal communication from Lal Ranvijay Nath Sahadev, 1984.

12. It should be noted that while Muṇḍāri song types are not associated with any specific times of the day or night, they are associated with seasons.

13. The term *nacini* is related to the more common Hindi term *nātchni* (dancing girl, courtesan). *Kasbi,* also in general use in northern India, is from the Arabic *kasb* (prostitution).

14. The Oraons and Santals also have monsoon repertories called karam that have resulted from their interaction with Indo-Aryans.

15. The karam dance step is an exception to this. Women dance only one or two basic karam patterns, derived from Nāgpuri and Pāncpargania women's dances.

PART FOUR

Musical Reproduction and Renewal

Indian, East Indian, and West Indian Music in Felicity, Trinidad

13

Helen Myers

> How small of all that human hearts endure,
> That part which laws or kings can cause or cure!
> Still to ourselves in every place consigned,
> Our own felicity we make or find.
>
> —Samuel Johnson, *Lines Added to Goldsmith's Traveller*

"Well, your ancestors came from India, true?" I asked.

"Yea," Siewrajiah replied. "They come in a big ship that taking three month to reach Trinidad from India; it used to move slow."

The people of Felicity, nearly all Hindus, refer to themselves as East Indians to distinguish their group from other West Indians (all peoples of the West Indies) and from the American Indians (the indigenous Arawaks and Caribs). The forebears of the East Indians—143,000 in number—were brought by the British from South Asia to Trinidad beginning in 1845. Known originally as the "Gladstone Coolies," these people were among the legion of indentured laborers shipped out from India to work the plantations of the Empire: sugar in Trinidad and other colonies of the Caribbean (Jamaica, Grenada, St. Lucia, St. Vincent, St. Kitts, St. Croix, and British Guiana); coffee, tea, rubber as well as sugar in Africa, Asia, and the Pacific (Ceylon, Malaya, Natal, Burma, and Fiji). "They tell them that they going in Trinidad to shift sugar," Doday of Felicity explained. "My grandfather often said they thief some of them an bring them come. Unknowing to their parents, they catch them by the wayside and bring them."

Since the time of indentureship, the villagers of Felicity have adapted their musical repertory to suit their changing social needs and aesthetic sensibilities. The main source of their musical ideas has been their motherland, India. Villagers have a disdain for African culture and have borrowed only sparingly from their Creole neighbors. They sing the occasional Hindi calypso, but these songs tend to be regarded as curiosities. The time-honored theory of acculturation so carefully drawn by Herskovits from his understanding of Afro-American cultures does not apply comfortably to the East Indians of Felicity. A more useful theory is revitalization, "a deliberate, organized, conscious effort by members of a society to construct a more satisfying culture" (Wallace 1956:265). Revitalization is characterized by the deliberate intentions with which people set out to effect changes in their lives and the speed with which they achieve these changes. In Felicity, the process of revitalization can be traced from the earliest years of the East Indian indenture to the 1980s.

The student of musical change cannot avoid the unhappy early historical records, for it is in the ships' logs, amidst recounts of shipwreck, fire, hurricane, epidemic, suicide, and despair that are found the few hints about the original repertory of these people: "Coolies on deck all day, singing and dancing in the evening"; "the Madrassee is a lively, singing fellow"; "Coolies and crew were very subdued, there was no music"; "should be permitted to play their drums till 8 bells"; "getting music up to amuse the Coolies"; "Coolies having some native games and war dances"; "the Coolies are very musical"; "Coolies performing" (Carlile 1859:8–11). Nothing about the steps of the dances, the verses of the songs, the types of drums, the groups of singers; here only the sparsest evidence of cultural persistence and the wonderful image of songs at the very moment that they were transported from one world to another, glimpses so incomplete, so wanting in detail, that, for all they lack, carry us in our imagination across those oceans in those ships with those emigrants; glimpses that tell of the curiosity of white captain and crew hearing traditional North Indian songs sung on deck, and that suggest the wonderment of the passengers themselves hearing songs from other villages, other districts, and in other languages. Did the amalgam that has become the Trinidadian Indian music of today originate on shipboard as new songs were passed from one voyager to the next and strangers learned to dance hand in hand?

The export of East Indian labor was suspended during World War I and legally abolished by Act of Parliament in 1921. The indenture system had little to recommend it over the system of African slavery that it replaced. Greed prevailed, but Lord John Russell (Whig secretary of state for the Colonies), opposing indenture before it began, said: "I am not prepared to encounter the responsibility of a measure which may lead to a dreadful loss of life on the one hand, or on the other, to a new system of slavery" (in Parliament, February 15, 1840). "They wasn't knowing they was coming to be slave here," Doday said.

Indians worked five- or ten-year terms in the fields or cane refineries. They were paid a small salary, and given free return passage to India upon completion of their contract. By 1865 the Indians were allowed to exchange their return passage for a tract of land in Trinidad—mostly swampy savannah land along the western coast of the island. Today about 45 percent of the population of Trinidad is of East Indian descent.

Felicity lies midway along the road leading west from the market town of Chaguanas to the cane fields and the sea. Approaching by car, it is easy to miss the turning on the right, Cacandee Road, and the markerless weedy cemetery on the left, to suddenly find yourself lost on a narrowing lane, all vista save for the sky cut off by the green stalks and the spiky white arrows of mature sugarcane. There, amidst the fields of cane, in the savannah land of central Trinidad, you find the sights and sounds that transport you to an Asian world. It is a long village, some two miles from the junction with its two shops at the Peter's Field end up to the Caroni River on the northern extreme. The land is a treeless and marshy savannah, a region of tall bamboo grass. Houses, shops, and parlors line Cacandee Road on either side, thinning out about half a mile before the river. The riverside is pleasant, cool, quiet, but no one lives there. The girls stroll by the banks in the evening, after the day's cooking, sweeping, and washing are done. The rites of cremation are performed at the southern shore; the little river carries the ashes of the villagers, the Hindu faithful, westward away from the village and out to the sea. I never saw anyone wash clothes in the river, or bathe in the river, or swim in the river. The Felicity folk would not understand India's great Ganges, which serves so many purposes.

Only four years after the founding of Felicity, the Reverend John Morton, first Christian missionary to the East Indians, saw the rice-fields spread across the Caroni savannah. "Imagine over one hundred acres of level land divided into fields of several acres each by a low bank of earth that can be made to serve as a dam to flood the fields when necessary" (Morton 1916:321). And so on—the savannah, the sugar and the cacao, the rice. How little time has changed the face of the land. The villagers—great materialists that they are, owners of pressure cookers and color televisions—still stand barefoot in the mud, as did their Indian forebears and as do their present-day cousins in eastern Uttar Pradesh, planting each seedling by hand. There is no other method; the rice dictates a way of life that the Indian understands.

The world for Felicity folk looks like the old BOAC route maps: Christchurch and Wellington, Georgetown, Toronto, Cape Town and Durban, Karachi, Lagos, Delhi, Hong Kong—the countries shown in red from the 1950s school atlas mildewed on the shelf. Beyond their many parochial concerns, theirs is the world of the BBC external services, and of relaxed afternoons in the shade, listening to the cricket test-match from Islamabad or Melbourne or Lord's. It is the world that hears the Queen's Christmas message and watches the Commonwealth Games, the world of Paddington Bear, Mills and Boon romances, New Zealand cheddar cheese, the eleven-plus exams, Horlichs for tea, and the ubiquitous orange spines of Penguin paperbacks. It is the old Empire, terra incognita for the American, home ground for the English. Ironically, the villagers look with suspicion upon V. S. Naipaul, their best-known spokesman in the West, because he ignored the anglicized side of their lives and their love of the modern, the fashionable, the up-to-date. They resent being portrayed to the outside as the inheritors of Mr. Biswas, leading the life of the Tulsi family in Hanuman House (Naipaul 1961). Naipaul told the world of their hidden treasures, those old Indian ways; he robbed them of their secret, and they never really forgave him as he told how

> India lay about us in things: in a string bed or two, grimy, tattered, no longer serving any function, never repaired because there was no one with this caste skill in Trinidad, yet still permitted to take up room; in plaited straw mats; in innumerable brass vessels; in wooden printing blocks, never used because printed cotton was abundant and cheap and because the secret of the dyes had been forgotten, no dyer being at hand; in books, the sheets large, coarse and brittle, the ink thick and oily; in drums and one ruined harmonium; in brightly coloured pictures of deities on pink lotus or radiant against Himalayan snow; and in all the paraphernalia of the prayer-room: the brass bells and gongs and camphor-burners like Roman lamps, the slender-handled spoon for the doling out of the consecrated 'nectar'. . . the images, the smooth pebbles, the stick of sandalwood. (1968:29)

The brass vessels, the string beds, the printing blocks, these artifacts, "never repaired," "no longer serving any function," were these like the wedding songs of the Felicity ladies, the *godna* (tattoo song) Moon sang, and the *sohar* (childbirth song) Mr. Charran chanted from his great *Ramayan,* "cherished because they came from India"? They "continued to be used and no regret attached to their disintegration" (ibid.:29–30). Were these songs from India's past here locked in time and slavishly reproduced in their Trinidadian exile? "How can I explain my feelings of outrage," Naipaul cries out, "when I heard that in Bombay they used candles and electric bulbs for the Diwali festival, and not the rustic clay lamps of immemorial design, which in Trinidad we still used" (ibid.:36). But the traveler to northeast India will soon discover that the songs, unlike the rustic clay lamps, are not merely marginal survivals of practices that are obsolete in their villages of origin. In Mahadewa Dube, Naipaul's ancestral village near the Nepal border, village singer and traveler alike can quickly match the traditional songs of that village to their Felicity counterparts.

It would be hard to find a villager in Felicity who doesn't like music. Older women usually prefer the traditional Bhojpuri wedding songs; men especially enjoy *tassa* drumming for the springtime Holi festival; teenagers like English songs or reggae or pop music. But everyone agrees that music per se is a good thing. "Whenever music is playing," Suruj Pandit explained, "no matter if you are worried or anything, you just feel a different happiness come into you. Music is a charm. If a person don't like music, they're considered to be half alive and half dead."

"Why sing?" I asked Brahmchari Karma.

"They say that when you sing and you clap, you destroy all the past *karmas*," he replied. "You beat them off."

"Why sing?" I asked Kedar Pandit.

"If music has got in it what Shakespeare said, 'if music be the food of love, then play on,' right?"

"Why sing?" I asked Popo.

"Like to sing," she replied, "and fete naa. I like to sing and fete. Enjoy yourself. To live. Nice."

"Why sing?" I asked Siewrajiah.

"Who could afford to have music make it more beautiful, more pleasure, more happiness."

"Why sing?" I asked Moon.

"I feel I should get more young," Moon replied, "only just for singing's sake."

Most dear to the villagers is what they call "Indian music." Indian music is different things to different people. For the younger generation it refers especially to Indian film songs, for the older to the traditional Bhojpuri folk songs, and for practically everybody to temple songs, such as *bhajan* and *kirtan*. For all, it means a repertory with texts in an Indian language, be it Bhojpuri or Hindi, Bengali or Sanskrit. This special affection for Bhojpuri—what is for the older villagers their mother tongue and for the younger a foreign language—dominates Felicity's culture and music.

The Bhojpuri repertory, the oldest music of Felicity, originated in eastern Uttar Pradesh and western Bihar, and has been passed down in oral tradition in Trinidad since the period of indentureship. It includes *byah ke git* (wedding songs), sohar (for the birth of a child), *khajri* (for the cultivation of rice), as well as bhajans and songs for important Hindu festivals like Diwali and Holi. Songs of this type thrive today in the villages around Banaras, Azamgarh, Gorakhpur, Ghazipur, and Chapra in northeastern India. Those Indian villagers listen with great interest to recordings from Felicity, and can easily identify the type of song, the ritual or social occasion it accompanies, and the text narrative; they often know songs with similar or nearly identical melodic structures, matching texts, and corresponding responsorial forms. In contrast to this lively tradition in village India, however, the Bhojpuri repertory in Felicity appears to be dying out together with the spoken language.

Felicity villagers are almost unanimous in their preference for Indian music—any Indian music—over local African forms or Western music. Calypso, the most renowned song of the West Indies, is not popular in Felicity.

"Calypso have too much robust things in it," Doday explained. "It is evil."

"In calypso," Kamini told me, "they give you the facts of life, you know."

"I Like Indian music," Kassie said. "Is a choice."

"Indian music sounds much sweeter," Channu, a village singer, explained. "Whatever the Indian sing and whatever music they play, they don't do it of a joke. It's a serious thing for whoever understand it. It brings such serious feelings to you. Calypso they only sing. You might hear calypso. You will just feel happy to jump up. But if you hear a real technical piece of Indian music, you might sit down stiff and still, and you might be concentrating so much that you mightn't know when it start or when it finish" (Myers 1984:197–99, 106).

In part, this preference for Indian music is a question of taste, for as Professor Adesh told me, "liking is one's own." And partly it is an expression of Indian ethnic solidarity, provoked and nurtured by their minority status in Trinidad's plural society. "You see, that's *my* culture," Kamini explained. "I born in it. I growing up in it. And I'll keep it. Long time people never bothered about anything much. But now we going back to our own culture" (ibid.:76).

"No one is advocating that we return to India," writes K. V. Parmasad, the Trinidadian writer of East Indian descent, "but it is necessary that we, the Indians of the West—West Indians in the truest sense—should come to terms with what we have here, not discard it. We must dig deep into the farthest recesses of our consciousness as a people and discover our true selves, tapping if necessary the limitless reserve at the source of our culture" (1973). "What is striking," writes John La Guerre, Professor of Government at the University of the West Indies, is "the virtual demise of some of the more crucial features of East Indian culture—of the *panchayat* [village council] and of caste—and the retention of those with more symbolic value" (1974:xiii). Musical history in Felicity follows a pattern similar to that described by Lowenthal for other aspects of East Indian culture:

> Clothing, food, and language display a common sequence of retention, gradual disappearance, then self-conscious revival in ethnic separatism. The elaborate *pagadi* headdresses, the ubiquitous long skirts and *orhnis, dhotis* and *shalwars,* gave way by the time of the Second World War to dress differentiated from Creole mainly by the vestigial head veils of East Indian women and the ceremonial *dhotis* of some men. But imminent independence in India and rising ethnic tensions in the Caribbean impelled many East Indians to adopt imported saris and other items of 'national' dress.
>
> The decline and rejuvenation of Hindi follow the same pattern. Within a generation of their Caribbean arrival, indentured East Indians, save those in Surinam, spoke English and had begun to forget their native Hindi, Tamil, or Telegu. Although many rural Indians in Trinidad and Surinam continue to speak Hindi at home, almost all are bilingual in Creolese. National sentiment reanimated by Indian independence spurred prominent East Indians to advocate Hindi instruction in schools, and Hindi has become an anti-Creole focus for urban Indians, even those whose ancestral tongue it was not. (Lowenthal 1972:154)

The predicament confronting the villagers in the 1980s is the development of a non-Bhojpuri but truly Indian repertory. To this end they turn to India. Despite the thousands of miles, despite the passing decades and the lost generations that separate them from their Indian roots, from the India of their heart and their fantasy and their memory of memories, India ever remains the source of their musical inspiration. For over 100 years there has been continual cultural traffic from India to the overseas Caribbean communities, and the Felicity villagers have used this imported material to enliven their repertory. This process of revitalization is in no way a revival; the villagers have not revived music that once was practiced in the village. The villagers have incorporated into their repertory Indian music that is to them new and unfamiliar. "In India I know I am a stranger," writes Naipaul (1977:xi).

The processes of musical revitalization and exchange are the great fascination of the musical history of Felicity. Seven stages in this history have special importance and illustrate the process of musical revitalization in Felicity.

1. During the indentureship period, thousands of new immigrants from India arrived each year. How curious the established settlers must have been to hear the recruits sing. The core repertory known to both the settled immigrants and the recruits seems to have been

reinforced, and minority tastes (the South Indian repertory, for example) rejected. For the village ladies, every new ship arriving in the harbor of Port of Spain brought new companions to join in the many songs of the life-cycle and the agricultural calendar.

2. During the 1920s, the Trinidad Indian's repertory was enhanced by the songs and chants of Hindu missionaries from Indian reformist organizations such as the Bombay-based Arya Samaj ("Society of Aryans"). These visiting priests reconverted Presbyterian and Catholic Indians in Trinidad back to Hinduism, often in mass gatherings in town marketplaces. They introduced traditional styles of Sanskrit liturgical chant and Hindu devotional songs hitherto unknown on the island. The texts of these chants and songs were published locally, and this music is still performed in the temples of Felicity.

3. In 1935, *Bala Joban,* the first Indian talkie, opened in San Fernando, Trinidad, inaugurating a new phase of musical history in Felicity. The overnight craze for Indian film culture so clearly portrayed on the cinema screen—the colorful saris, the intricate gold ornaments, and the appealing *filmi* songs—soon reached Felicity. By 1936 commercial records of Indian film songs were exported to Trinidad (Ramaya 1974). Local performers learned film songs and copied film-song style. Trinidadian singers imitated the famous playback singers and competed for the title of local "Lata" (Mangeshkar) or (Mohammed) "Hafi" (Vidyarthi n.d.). Today as one walks down Cacandee Road, film songs fill the air—from village juke boxes, transistor radios and hi-fi systems, and cassette players in passing cars and taxis.

4. In 1951, Swami Purnananda of the Bharat Sevashram Sangha, Calcutta, arrived in Felicity. He settled in the village and stimulated something of a religious and musical revival by introducing the most ancient of Hindu services, the Vedic *sandhya* daily prayer and *havan* sacrifice together with new bhajans and styles of devotional chant. He also encouraged the members of lower castes to participate in other Hindu services, undermining the exclusive jurisdiction of Felicity Brahmins over important sacred texts and the performing styles associated with them.

5. In 1966, Professor H. S. Adesh, the first teacher of Indian classical music, arrived in Trinidad. Adesh taught thousands of Trinidadian students the conventional North Indian system of ragas and talas, using a graded syllabus based on Indian pedagogical methods. Lessons were offered in voice, sitar, tablā, and other instruments as well as in music theory, Hindi, and Sanskrit. Adesh has been a harsh critic of local Indian music, arguing that it is a corruption of Indian classical style. His objections were readily accepted by Trinidadians, who tend to denigrate their local culture; for example, the island patois, which

Trinidadians call "broken English." Adesh's top students find fault with local artists who perform *ṭhumrī* and *gazal* in "local classical" style. Students hailed the arrival of Adesh as the beginning of a "cultural renaissance in Trinidad" (Bissoondialsingh 1976).

6. In 1974, within the span of a few months, the inauguration of the Sai Baba religious movement in Trinidad brought a new devotional repertory and musical style to Felicity. The style is characterized by hypnotic repetition of short melodic phrases with accelerando, crescendo, and loud handclapping. The Hindi song-texts are short and easy for English-speaking villagers to memorize. The Sai Baba style caught on in Felicity temples between 1974 and 1975 and has held popularity into the late 1980s.

7. In 1984 and 1985, the popular Indian vocalist, Kanchan, made concert tours of Trinidad. Her first hit was "Kayse Banie," a *chutney* (hot song) composed by Sundar Popo, a popular local Indian singer. To this song, already popular in Felicity, Kanchan added the typically Indian filmi sound with the characteristic style of attack, and light, little-girlish vocal quality. Through these changes she transformed a "local-composed" song into a song "from away." For Felicity villagers, she made the song truly Indian.

On the 1985 tour, Kanchan sang arrangements of three prize-winning West Indian socas from the 1985 Carnival: "Tiny Winy," "Rock It," and "Bust Up Shot." These West Indian pieces, little heard in Felicity, were transformed into Felicity hits through changes in language (English to Hindi); modality (diatonic to pentatonic); and vocal style, including ornamentation, nasal resonance, and style of attack and decay. Most noticeable on the recordings of these songs is the transformation of soundfield. For example, Merchant's West Indian recording of "Rock It" presents an artificial anechoic soundfield, achieved by direct injection of the electronic instruments into the mixing console, by very close miking of the acoustic instruments and loudspeakers, and by reducing the dynamic range to almost nil through electronic limiting and compressing. The recording of "Rock It" by Kanchan presents an equally artificial but highly echoic soundfield created by studio techniques associated with Indian film songs. These include reverb, double-tracking of the vocal line with a right-left bounce ("ping-ponging"), and more extended dynamic range, with limiter and compressor used only to avoid distortion.

This progression of events—from the arrival of new shiploads of immigrants to the advent of Hindu missionaries, Indian films, Swami Purnananda, Professor Adesh, the Sai Baba movement, and Kanchan—has supplied the villagers of Felicity with new musical material from India. West Indian artists have made use of Indian themes in calypso and soca for over twenty years. During the last decade, with the Kanchan arrangements, India has begun to draw musical inspiration from Trinidad—from both its East Indian and its West Indian populations. The traveler can hear Kanchan's "Kayse Banie" playing on the in-house audio system in a cheap hotel in Gorakhpur, only a few miles from the village of Naipaul's grandfather.

In the past, villagers have tended to select Indian models for their temple repertory and for other religious contexts. They have selected Western models, including calypso, soca, and disco, for dance and other entertainment music. Indian-inspired pieces are described as "classical," "from books," "deep" (profound, meaningful), or "from away" (the opposite of local). Western-inspired pieces are described as "make-up," "composed," "local." In the 1980s, Kanchan and other visiting Indian artists have begun to draw on Trinidad Indian sources for pop and entertainment music. In composing new items in the musical repertory, villagers now have a wide selection of models: Indian, Western, local East Indian as interpreted by an Indian performer, and local West Indian as interpreted by an Indian performer. This rich and interesting situation cannot be properly explained in terms of conventional concepts of acculturation. An ethnomusicologist might opt to label new compositions influenced by West Indian music "acculturated" and all three varieties of Indianized music "revitalized." Whatever happened to the notion of "authenticity," so important in folk music studies only a few decades ago? It is not lost, for the villagers would happily apply that term to their Indianized repertory, including the Kanchan songs. But the observer, the ethnomusicologist, might hesitate before concurring with the villagers that these Indianized pieces, borrowed from a twentieth-century urban Hindi culture, are more authentic than the local Westernized repertory, a reflection of their New World heritage.

> In India I know I am a stranger; but increasingly I understand that my Indian memories, the memories of that India which lived on into my childhood in Trinidad, are like trapdoors into a bottomless past. (Naipaul 1977:xi)

Conclusion

The modern music history of Felicity illustrates a number of fundamental issues in ethnomusicology:

First, the deliberateness of musical change and exchange. We sometimes fall into the habit of describing musical change as something that happens to people as opposed to something that people cause to happen. In Felicity, most musical change is conscious and deliberate.

Second, the differential nature of change. Different repertories in a musical tradition often change in different ways. Felicity villagers have tended to Indianize their religious repertory and to Westernize their popular repertory.

Third, the speed of change. In Felicity, new styles and repertories can gain acceptance in a single season.

Fourth, music and ethnicity. The ethnomusicologist might describe the Kanchan songs as acculturated while the villagers would call them authentic. The ethnomusicologist would categorize the local East Indian chutney of Sundar Popo as genuinely Trinidadian, while the villagers think it is "broken," "local," and "made-up."

Fifth, the musical grey-out. Let this brief account of music history in a Trinidad village be added to the evidence that demonstrates that a worldwide musical grey-out, the universal Westernization of the world's music (much feared by ethnomusicologists in the 1970s), is not taking place. Musical change is moving in directions that we did not anticipate.

Sixth, the essential vitality of traditions in flux. Our descriptive terms such as acculturation and revitalization refer not so much to the winding down of traditional styles as to the unleashing of enormous expressive and creative forces. The modern music history of Felicity shows that living traditions are continuously being reformed. As we witness over and again the pervasiveness of musical change and exchange around the world, we must acknowledge that, with such creative acts, the bearers of tradition reinvoke their culture.

Stability in Blackfoot Songs, 1909–1968

14

Robert Witmer

There is general evidence for various patterns and processes of change in North American Native music over the past eight or nine decades. Several scholars have described the attrition and impoverishment of traditional repertories and techniques of composition and performance. We also have evidence of revitalization, and of musical acculturation—both intertribal and interracial.

At the same time, Native musicians have assured a number of fieldworkers over the years that songs themselves do not change over time, and that—particularly in the realm of liturgical music—even the most minute changes would have dire consequences of various kinds. The prevailing Blackfoot view, for example, is nicely encapsulated by Nettl (1983:197) in reflecting on his 1967 fieldwork among them: "the Blackfoot did not appear to feel that songs change very much, seemed rather to regard each song as especially created and essentially unchanged."

Despite the existence of this general body of knowledge and opinion concerning what has been happening to musical repertories and styles in Native cultures over the past century or so, very little concrete documentation yet exists concerning what has happened to subsets or individual items of repertories over this time span. There have as yet been few attempts to seek out and study what would be, by some criteria or other, cognate items of repertory—or concordances—from the century-long history of sound recordings of Native music. This strikes me as a lacuna in North American Native music studies and, perhaps more important, a largely untapped opportunity for studying musical change in general, as the history of sound recording of Native American music is longer than that for any music in the world outside of Western popular and classical traditions.[1]

Two works that present plausible concordances of North American

Native songs and base their conclusions regarding change on evidence gleaned from transcription and analysis of these cognate items are Willard Rhodes's study of the diffusion of the opening peyote song (Rhodes 1958) and Thomas Vennum's "A History of Ojibwa Song Form" (Vennum 1980). Rhodes's essay demonstrates that in the process of diffusion, whether inter-reserve or intra-reserve, peyote songs exhibit processes of variation not unlike those that scholars have noted in various other aurally transmitted musics, i.e., "singing is a re-creative activity providing within certain limitations a wide range of variation and expression to the singer" (1958:44). Vennum provides evidence of what happens to a particular item of repertory in a single Native culture over a fairly long period of time. He illustrates a number of his points with reference to a paradigmatic transcription of what he takes to be two renditions of the same item of Ojibwa repertory—one rendition transcribed from a 1910 recording and the other from a 1971 recording (1980:67). A comparison of these two transcriptions supports a common belief, noted by Nettl (1983:184), that as music changes "it increases in complexity, adding tones to scales, sections to forms. . . ." In addition, in the analogous sections of the two transcriptions presented by Vennum there are considerable divergencies of melodic and rhythmic activity, some of which are along the lines that are encountered among members of a tune family in Anglo-American folksong. In Vennum's two examples, as in any two variant forms of an Anglo-American folksong, few details of the tune are constant through both renditions (to paraphrase Bayard 1954:15).

Following Vennum's lead, this essay discusses two recorded renditions from the same culture group—the Blackfoot Confederacy of Alberta and Montana—and fairly widely separated in time, of what I take to be the "same song." The notion that these two recordings present renditions of the "same song" is solely an etic one: I have not had an opportunity to play these recordings for Blackfoot or Blood musicians and question them on the nature of the interrelationships that I perceive. The transcriptions were initially done by me, then subjected to the scrutiny of younger ears in the person of a graduate assistant, Geoff Somers.

My examples point to different conclusions from those suggested by Vennum's (and Rhodes's) examples. Recorded fifty-nine years apart and unquestionably transmitted aurally, they are (etically) *virtually identical* down to the very smallest of details, a finding that potentially challenges commonly held assumptions about the inevitability of change over time in aurally transmitted musics and that also invites historical interpretation/speculation.

The first rendition to be examined is a Blackfoot Night Love Song performed by Chief Bull and recorded by Joseph K. Dixon for the American Museum of Natural History, at Crow Agency, Montana, in 1909.[2] The second is a Night Serenade Song performed by Bob Black Plume and Willie Eagle Feathers that I recorded in 1968 on the Blood Indian Reserve in southwestern Alberta.[3] The initial apprehension of the (alleged) concordance between these two items was entirely serendipitous, i.e., no formal method was involved: for an earlier study (Witmer 1982) I had auditioned old field recordings of Blackfoot music and had intuitively recognized the 1909 Dixon recording of the Night Love Song as closely resembling a song I had collected on the Blood Indian Reserve in 1968. The analysis of these two songs presented in Witmer 1982:77–81 was based on a literal-minded interpretation of transcriptions, which I now believe to have been wrong-headed.

A study based on a sample of two recordings (and fragments of a few others) is admittedly particularistic, and even the most tentative of conclusions based on the evidence of such a sample must be taken with all due caution. This study is therefore intended as a preliminary probe: affirmation (or refutation, or revision) of its inferences must await further particularistic studies by a number of scholars and, ultimately, broad comparative work. Owing to the size of the available archival holdings, such studies would undoubtedly have to be computer-assisted.

Before proceeding to a discussion of the musical examples, a few remarks about the transcriptions themselves (Figures 1 and 2) and some of the methods used in this study are in order. Rather than notating vocal pulsations with the rough-and-ready device of a series of dots over or under long-note values (as per Abraham and Hornbostel 1909–10:7 and their followers), the pulsations have been notated in a more rhythmically precise and descriptive manner, using eighth notes and broken slurs; and a syllable has been provided for every breath push in the pulsations. (The reason for this procedure will become apparent subsequently.) The transcriptions are in a paradigmatic format and have been transposed to a common "tonic" (C) for ease of comparison. Because I have been unable to detect marked strophe-to-strophe variation in the musical materials, only one strophe of each rendition has been notated. The third phrase of the 1909 rendition includes the one marked musical divergence that is apprehendable to me, and it is noted in the transcription. Strophe-to-strophe variants in vocables, apprehendable in the 1968 rendition but not in the 1909 rendition, are shown stacked.

The method used in investigating strophe-to-strophe congruency of small details in, and between, each of the two renditions shown in

Figure 1 was to work from a "phrase-by-phrase" cassette tape. That is, for the 1968 rendition, which repeats three times, a tape was prepared that has the three instances of phrase one recorded in successive order, and so on. The 1909 rendition, which repeats two times, was also retaped in this manner. Finally, for comparing details of the 1909 and 1968 renditions a tape was prepared that goes back and forth, phrase by phrase, between the two renditions.[4] Despite the ease of aural comparison that such a system of taping provides, the precise vowel sounds on the vocal pulsations of the 1968 rendition continually proved to be elusive: the notation of vocables has been changed a number of times, and the solutions presented here should be considered provisional. (Neither transcriber has had formal training in linguistics, and equipment for a sonograph analysis was not available for this study.)

As to the notation of pitch, the 1968 rendition presented relatively few problems. But the 1909 rendition is much less stable tonally than the 1968 rendition, particularly in the opening statement. I decided not to be too literal-minded about this attribute in the transcription of the 1909 rendition (Figure 1, upper staff), in order to avoid producing a large and microtonal pitch collection, which squares neither with academic orthodoxy nor with my own beliefs concerning pitch systems in North American Native music, past or present. I agree with the argument of Hornbostel (1913) and others that musical systems that are free of overt harmonic (or drone) principles are not as melodically "constrained" intonationally as those that are not.

Arrows have been placed above a few notes to indicate pronounced deviations from the pitches notated. For example, there is a series of high F-sharps near the beginning of the 1909 rendition. At this point it sounds as though the singer is about to raise the tonal framework slightly—neither an unknown nor an unintentional phenomenon in Plains singing, as noted elsewhere (e.g., W. K. Powers 1980:32)—but then the tonal framework returns to where it was, with the D's that follow and precede the raised F-sharp being more or less identical in pitch.[5] In the second system of Figure 1 a few downward arrows have been placed over some C's, most of them in the 1909 rendition; I hear these deviations occurring consistently, which might mean that they are intentional and systemic rather than merely circumstantial. The other microtonal deviations that are audible on the tape have not been shown in the transcriptions, as they do not appear to me to be systemic.

Now we can move on to a comparative examination of the examples shown in paradigmatic transcription in Figure 1. These two renditions exhibit an extraordinary degree of consistency, not only in strophe-to-strophe congruency within each individual rendition, as mentioned

Figure 1. Two Blood/Blackfoot Night Love/Serenade Songs, 1909 and 1968.

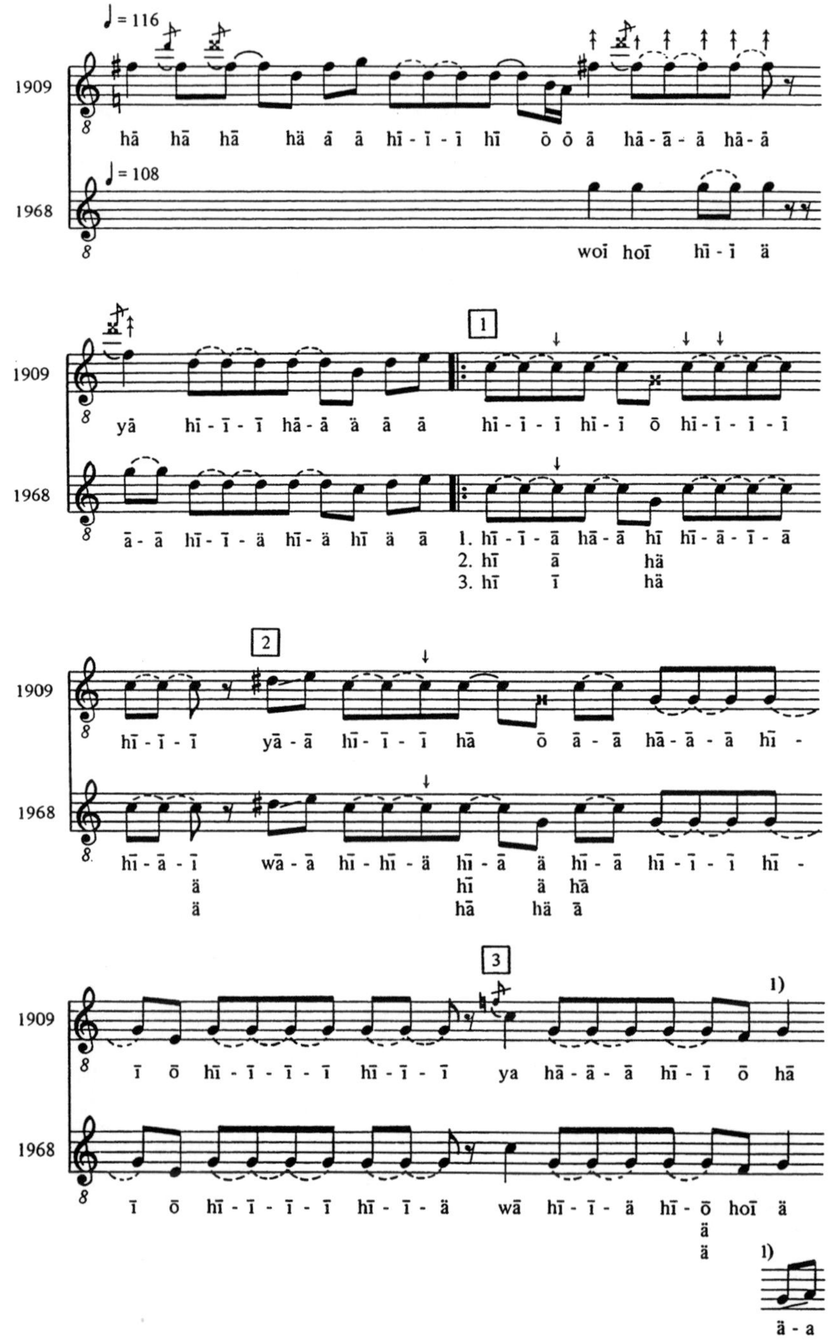

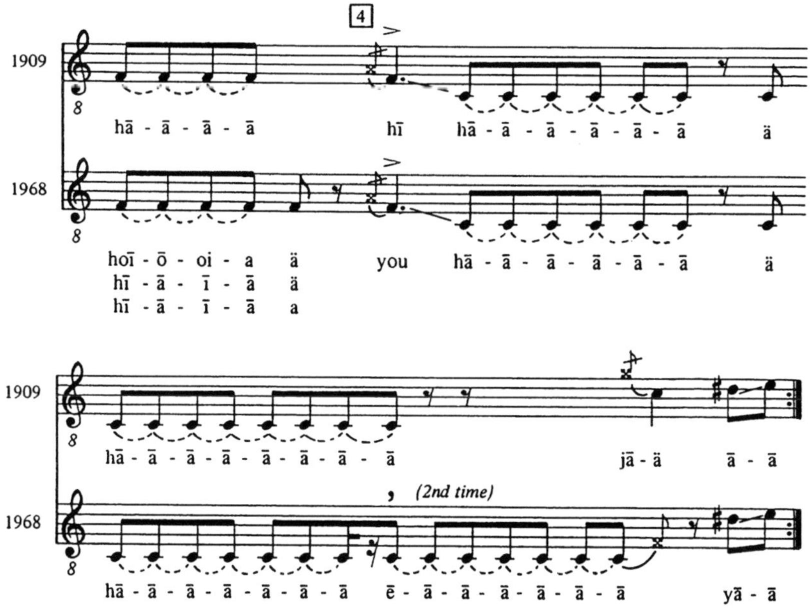

earlier, but also, as depicted in the transcriptions, between the two renditions. In addition to the gross general features, several minute details are consistent throughout, such as the number of vocal pulsations on sustained tones and the rhythmic placement and syllabification of these pulsations. To be sure, there are audible differences in performance style between the 1909 and 1968 renditions that the transcriptions do not adequately describe. Most striking is the increased tonal stability of the 1968 rendition and its dramatically more pronounced pulsations. Other recordings by these musicians and others of their respective generations are consistent on these points.

In the realm of content, as distinguished from style (see Nettl 1983:47–49, 115–17, 189–91), there appear to be only three truly notable differences between the 1909 and 1968 renditions.

First, the opening statements (top system of Figure 1): the 1968 rendition omits the first unit of the opening statement of the 1909 rendition; and the second unit of the opening statement of the 1968 rendition resembles the analogous portion of the 1909 rendition only moderately closely in comparison to the resemblance between subsequent sections.

Second, the length of the ending formulas (marked "4" in Figure 1): the ending formula in the 1968 rendition is longer than the ending formula in the 1909 rendition. But on this point there is evidence for

Figure 2. Ending Formulas in Blood Blackfoot Night Love/Serenade Songs.

flexibility if we refer to other recordings of Night Love Songs I collected from Black Plume and Eagle Plume in 1968. For example, in the four repeats of another Night Love Song recorded by these singers, the ending formulas are of differing lengths on each repeat (see Figure 2), whereas other features of the musical content display the unerring strophe-to-strophe consistency exhibited in the Night Love Song shown in Figure 1.

Third, the closing "yelps" (not transcribed): there are four yelps concluding the 1909 rendition and only two concluding the 1968 rendition. Other 1968 recordings of Night Love Songs exhibit three yelps, possibly indicating that the ending yelps are not a rigidly fixed element of the Night Love Song genre and hence may not need to be consistent in successive renditions of a particular Night Love Song.

Despite these three differences we are still left with a preponderance of exact parallels between the 1909 and 1968 renditions, many of them on the "micro" level. What are we to make of these parallels, or, to paraphrase Gushee (1981:151): what kind of oral tradition is this? One hypothesis, given the startlingly close congruencies of small details between the two renditions, is that Bob Black Plume and/or Willie Eagle Plume have somehow, at some time, assiduously studied Chief Bull's 1909 recording, and that their rendition is essentially, to borrow the argot of contemporary Top 40 groups, a "record lift." Upon initial consideration, it may seem implausible that a 1909 cylinder field recording—by definition, a *unicum,* and a private one at that—may have found its way back to the Native community and into the hands of musicians who then use it as a referent for historically authentic performance. This hypothesis becomes less implausible when we examine the unpaginated report for the Dixon collection in the Indiana University Archives of Traditional Music, which states "[This collection consists of] *Edison commercial reproductions* of Dixon's field recordings taken on the Wanamaker Historical Expedition II to the North American Indians. . . . These cylinders were made by commercial, mass-production methods by Edison *probably for Dixon's private use.* . . . They *may* have been issued commercially, although I do not find them listed in the Edison catalogs in the Archives or in my private collection" (italics added).[6]

At the present state of knowledge, then, we have evidence that the 1909 Dixon cylinders were commercially duplicated in their own day, but no evidence that they were ever commercially available. Even if we were to learn that they were never commercially available, the possibility remains that Dixon himself, or someone else, might have made them available to one or more members of the communities in which they were recorded. Although the Night Love Song recorded by Dixon in 1909 was obtained among the Montana Blackfoot and not among their Alberta kin, the Blood, there is constant social intercourse between the two groups: an artifact such as a cylinder recording could be shared between these two tribes just as readily as other items of material culture traditionally have been. Finally, the notion that traditional Plains musicians could have referred closely to recordings in the assemblage and maintenance of repertory and stylistic norms in the "pre-cassette" age does not strike me as farfetched, given the ubiquity of cassette recordings as song-learning aids among contemporary pow-wow musicians on the Plains, and elsewhere in Indian America. As has been disclosed time and again in the anthropological literature, non-Western societies adopt those aspects of Western technology and material culture they perceive as potentially advantageous to them almost immediately upon exposure. There is no reason to assume that the uses to which sound recordings could be put in the maintenance of their own musical traditions did not quickly dawn on any number of early twentieth-century Native musicians.

It must be admitted, however, that neither Willie Eagle Plume nor Bob Black Plume, nor any of the other elderly traditional Blood musicians whom I recorded and/or interviewed in 1968, ever indicated that they referred to recordings in the learning or maintenance of their repertory and/or style, although I made a point of asking them about song learning and provenance. In hindsight, I should have played copies of the 1909 Dixon cylinders for elderly traditional musicians, alongside such questions as: "Did you ever hear a recording of this one before?"

Of course, other hypotheses can be put forward in an attempt to account for the unerring (etically unearthed and perceived) resemblances between Chief Bull's 1909 rendition and the 1968 rendition of Black Plume and Eagle Plume. Perhaps the most prevalent emic conceptualization regarding stability versus change in Blackfoot music is, in fact, etically viable. The musical examples under scrutiny here may be taken as a modest demonstration (albeit, not as proof) that Blood/Blackfoot musicians are able, as their statements assert, to transmit and preserve items of repertory and elements of performance style in an essentially unchanged form over fairly long spans of time. A close reproduction of the Night Love/Serenade Song may well have occurred without any use of recordings.

Neither of the two hypotheses discussed above seems to me more powerful than the other in explicating the evidence under investigation. Further work along these lines might lead to an accommodation between them. To predict a possible outcome as succinctly as possible,

I would hypothesize the following: Blackfoot musicians—or Native American musicians at large—have the ability, where they have the will and/or cultural imperative, to transmit and maintain items of repertory and elements of performance style in an essentially unchanged form over fairly long spans of time; both this will/imperative and this ability are enhanced and strengthened by the availability of, and recourse to, venerable sound recordings. At present, though, we are left with contrasting views of process in recent Native American music history.

Fortunately, resources to further the work are readily at hand. Since the late nineteenth century, recordings have been made in abundance among the Blackfoot and their Canadian counterparts, the Blood, South Piegan, and North Piegan. Similar recording activity obtains among neighboring Plains tribes with whom the Blackfoot have had long-standing contact. A substantial portion of the recordings made over the years are on deposit in major archives and are thus available for scholarly investigation. For example, the catalog of *Early Field Recordings* at the Indiana University Archives of Traditional Music (Seeger and Spear 1987) lists four collections of Blackfoot material containing in all no fewer than 394 items (subtracting those deemed "unusable")—all predating 1940. Many other Blackfoot recordings, emphasizing more recent collecting activities, are housed in the Indiana University Archives of Traditional Music,[7] and various other archives and museums in Canada and the United States.[8]

The Blackfoot recordings available from archives and museums—along with commercial LP and cassette recordings, which have appeared in increasing numbers since the early 1970s—together comprise a more than adequate sample for the investigation of questions arising out of the present study. Nettl (1989a:174–78) lists forty-one available collections of Blackfoot recordings (field collections plus commercially disseminated collections) spanning the years 1897–1984 and comprising approximately 1,469 items in all. Once the songs have been transcribed and entered into a computer database (a daunting task, admittedly) the questions, historical and otherwise, that can be posed of the repertory will be limited only by the intelligence and imagination of investigators (and, to be sure, the resourcefulness of computer programmers). One could, for example, discover if there are other instances in the repertory of the various types of historical stability in song transmission outlined in this essay (or is my pair of examples the only needle in this haystack?). If it turns out that there are indeed other instances, to what extent can they be correlated with the existence of prior recordings? A multitude of questions concerning less all-encompassing, or less exact, interrelationships among members of the repertory could also be investigated and, in turn, plotted to ascertain the trajectory of possible historical trends.

For large-scale computer-assisted repertory studies of North American Native musics it would probably be best to begin sorting by endings (which are generally agreed to be formulaic) and to refine the groupings by working "backwards" through the form. While lists or data banks of incipits have been used with great success to unearth concordances and melodic interrelationships among items of repertory in other musical domains, e.g., Renaissance chansons and sacred pieces, such a method would obviously not have "flagged" the interrelatedness of the two Night Love/Serenade Songs under discussion here, precisely because their "incipits" are, relatively speaking, distinctive.

Armed with the results of such computer-assisted investigations, and the new questions they would undoubtedly engender, we could undertake further fieldwork with Native musicians, attempting to learn of their perceptions of "same/different/related/indebted to," and so on. The results of inquiries along these lines should ultimately allow more informed and cogent responses to the question posed earlier: "What kind of oral tradition is this?" For any music transmitted by oral/aural means, our ability to respond to that question in an informed and cogent way is a major prerequisite to our addressing the larger question of which it is an integral part: "What kind of a music history is this?"

NOTES

1. The first recordings of non-Western music were evidently made by Jesse Walter Fewkes, who "tested the phonograph as an instrument for fieldwork, in March 1890, by recording songs of the Passamaquoddy Indians in Maine" (De Vale 1986:115). "Recordings made from the first Paris performance of *Parsifal* (1882) are believed to be the oldest preserved" (Miller 1969:666).

2. The copy of this item used for this study was dubbed from the University of Illinois (Urbana-Champaign) Archives of Ethnomusicology (Collection no. 12, tape no. 1, song no. 2), which is in turn copied from the Indiana University Archives of Traditional Music, Collection 54-094-C (ATL 1856.2). The voice announcement on the original cylinder identifies the item as follows: "Night Love Song, sung by Chief Bull, Blackfoot Indian, for the Wanamaker Historical Expedition Number Two to the North American Indians, September 12, 1909, at Crow Agency, Montana." A commercially issued copy of this item may be heard on Nettl 1978b, *An Historical Album of Blackfoot Indian Music* (Folkways Records FES 34001, side A, band 11). At some point in the regeneration history of this recording the speed has been changed: it is substantially faster on the Nettl disk than on the archival tape copy from which I worked.

Judging from the opening voice announcement, I feel that the (slower) archival copy is closer to the "correct" speed.

3. This item is accessioned in the University of Illinois Archives of Ethnomusicology (Collection no. 52, tape no. 17, song no. 3).

4. A similar, or perhaps identical, method is alluded to, though not explicated, in Shelemay 1978 (see especially 90–91).

5. It is also possible that the recordist was having trouble with the spring mechanism at the beginning of this recording, and this could have caused some of the "pitch instability," including the opening F-sharp, which may have been closer to a G as sung, thus further aligning the 1909 rendition and the 1968 version. I offer my thanks to Thomas Vennum (personal communication) for this observation.

6. The last two sentences are attributed to Frank Gillis in the IUATM report. My thanks to Mary E. Russell, librarian of the Indiana University Archives of Traditional Music, for sending me photocopies of this material, and to Anthony Seeger for alerting me to the fact that the Dixon cylinders were commercially duplicated in their own day.

7. For a summary of holdings, see Lee 1979:193–94.

8. For example, the University of Illinois Archives of Ethnomusicology houses Bruno Nettl's 1966 field collection of approximately 160 Blackfoot songs (recorded in Montana) and Robert Witmer's 1968 field collection of approximately 366 Blood/Blackfoot songs (recorded in Alberta).

Of *Yekkes* and Chamber Music in Israel: Ethnomusicological Meaning in Western Music History

15

Philip V. Bohlman

Western music has emerged as a phenomenon of virtually worldwide proportions during the twentieth century. It is seemingly neither confined to Western societies nor excluded from non-Western societies, and its performance takes place in a panoply of cultural settings unimaginable in previous centuries (see Nettl 1985). Not least among the repertories in this dispersal has been Western art music, which thrives as governments throughout the world sponsor orchestras and conservatories, festivals and competitions, all symbols of nationalism and modernity.

Western art music has worn decently well under all this attention. It seems malleable enough to withstand just about any reading or misreading of its standard works; it lends itself to any definition or brand of nationalism that the most pedantic culture minister has foisted upon it; that it measures up to the important symbolic role assigned it is evident in the rather common response of audiences coming back for more. So seductive is the encroachment of Western art music worldwide that one is tempted to wonder whether this is a music beyond specific cultural meanings and outside particular historical moments. Interpreted by Wiora (1965) as the fulfillment of a final phase in the history of world music and understood similarly by others as a form of historical culmination or closure, Western art music should be, in essence, a music without history, or at least a music unaffected by the context of history in the modern world.

Such interpretations of Western art music are hardly unique to its dissemination in the twentieth century, but in fact are symptomatic of a system of values from the nineteenth century. Many historical suppositions and ideological claims have attempted to explain this putatively antihistorical tendency in the nineteenth century (e.g.,

George Steiner's notion of "the great *ennui*" in Steiner 1971), but rather than trying to pick and choose from these for interpretations that might best explain a music-historical stasis, I shall instead identify a thread common to all: the musical text becomes more and more important, until it achieves an independence that twentieth-century scholarship has further transformed into a seemingly unassailable hegemony. We have all witnessed the preoccupation with authentic texts or the "composer's intent." Emanating from the scholarly attention to text are portrayals of Western art music as a canon of "absolute music," of music totally international and purged of any ethnic or historical particularity (cf. Dahlhaus 1978; Kaden 1984:140–70).

No genre epitomizes the ahistorical core of Western art music in its ideal form more than chamber music. The champions of chamber music, whether Ludwig Tieck or Theodor Adorno, believe it to have arisen *sui generis*, motivated only by internal forces that determine structure and delimit audiences. Adorno goes so far as to dismiss the audience, "whom the composer seems at times scarcely to have considered" (1976:85), relegating chamber music to a universe complete unto itself, for "great chamber music could come into being, could be played and understood, as long as the private sphere had a measure of substantiability" (ibid.:86). If Western art music had historically stepped outside of history on the way to the present, chamber music had achieved a privileged position in the barrenness of a world without history.

Idealism and ideology notwithstanding, Western art music, in general, and chamber music, in specific, have come to thrive in a world rich in histories and diverse in cultural meaning. In this essay I examine one community and a historical setting in which Western art music has functioned for almost two centuries as a primary genre of ethnic music. In fact, in the past half century, chamber music has increasingly become the salient form of ethnic music for this community, relying on complex rituals and patterns of social structure for its maintenance and meaning.

Far from being purged of cultural particularity, the practices of Western art music by Israelis with a German cultural background exhibit all the characteristics for which ethnomusicologists search when describing the musical culture of an immigrant community or ethnic group. Interpreted as a complex of performance, repertory, social behavior, and audience and patronage systems, Western art music functions not unlike styles and repertories most commonly accepted as the ethnomusicologist's field, namely folk and non-Western music. This same complex provides Western art music with new historical patterns and constructs, not simply those peopled only by great composers and virtuoso performers. Central European Israelis have, in effect, reinterpreted the cultural contexts of Western art music and the institutions associated with it so that they constitute a historical tradition that lies at the core of their own ethnic community.

The Cultural "Boundaries" of Central European Jewish Society

The ethnic community of Central European Israelis exists within diverse boundaries, some geographic, others metaphorical, some generated within the ethnic group, others erected by outsiders. As described by Barth (1969), Royce (1982), and others, ethnic boundaries can be flexible and permeable, allowing members of the community to determine their own degree of membership and activity. The same flexibility affects outsiders who enter the community for various reasons, such as intermarriage or professional activity. Ethnic boundaries are constantly responsive to changes that occur inside and outside the ethnic group. Cultural boundaries include a preference for the German language, a classic corpus of German literature, and a set of educational values referred to as *Bildung* (Mosse 1985). Religious activity, too, implicitly indicates cultural boundaries, for Central Europeans are on the whole less observant than other communities. They tend, for example, to use the Sabbath for secular cultural activities, such as concerts of chamber music in the home. Perhaps the most persistent cultural boundary is the designation of German-speaking Jews as *Yekkes* by other Jews, thus identifying the ethnic community in contradistinction to many other aspects of Jewish and Israeli society.[1] And finally, there are the ethnic boundaries constantly reinforced by the musical activities of the community.

The cultural boundaries of the Central European community in Israel are not simply products of the immigrant environment. They have demarcated the German-speaking Jewish community at least since the inception of modern emancipation, that is, the liberalization of legal restrictions on the European Jewish community and consequently the more extensive integration of Jews into Central European society. Cultural boundaries gradually supplanted ghetto walls and many legal boundaries. They were, therefore, factors of choice, both from the Jewish community looking for ways to protect its integrity and from the external society hoping to retain certain restrictions while removing others. It was to the advantage of the Central European Jewish community that cultural boundaries were flexible and could be conveniently dismantled and reassembled in Israel. Whereas the boundaries distinguished the Central Europeans from a very different external society in Israel, these same cultural boundaries functioned quickly to increase the chances for interaction between community and external society because of the historical continuity they marked.

The cultural boundaries of Jews in Central Europe had formed during the period of rapid urbanization in the Jewish community, which flourished in the large cities of Germany and Austria. Similarly, the German-speaking immigrants to Palestine during the 1930s, the so-called German Wave of Immigrants (*aliyah germanit*), settled primarily in the larger cities (Jerusalem, Tel Aviv, and Haifa) and quickly reestablished an urban cultural life (Bohlman 1984). Within the cities, ethnic boundaries often paralleled the boundaries of new neighborhoods, thereby affording many different types of contact, such as access by foot to the numerous homes where concerts of chamber music regularly took place.

The best example of this type of Central European neighborhood in Jerusalem is Reḥavia. As a neighborhood, however, Reḥavia is more than just a place where Israelis with a common German heritage live: it contains many, if not most of the cultural institutions essential to the maintenance of this heritage. Hence, the Rubin Academy of Music, the Van Leer Institute (the Israeli Academy of Arts, Letters, and Sciences), the Jerusalem Theatre (home to the Israel Broadcasting Orchestra, the Jerusalem Symphony), the Israel Museum, and the Givat Ram campus of The Hebrew University all lie within Reḥavia or just outside its boundaries. The Central European communities in Tel Aviv and Haifa have somewhat different boundaries, albeit those resulting from the distinctive cultural institutions of these cities, but the musical life of the ethnic communities similarly reflects the active participation in the cultural institutions of the city. In Tel Aviv, for example, the concerts of the Israel Philharmonic and the public chamber concerts at the Tel Aviv Museum have benefited from sustained support in the German-Jewish community since the mid-1930s. The cultural institutions that the Yekkes frequent and support with a fervor bordering on fanaticism thus surround their community, defining its cultural geography. These cultural institutions function as buttresses and vivid metaphors for the cultural boundaries of the entire ethnic community.

Ethnic boundaries determine the cultural activities of a community in three different ways. First, they may be primarily exclusive, preventing the encroachment of external society, especially if they require processes of maintenance and communication that only community members control; language differences are a primary cause for this type of boundary. Second, boundaries may be essentially inclusive, enclosing community activities different from or not present in the external society. This is often the case when religion or ritual is a factor in the choice of boundaries. Third—and seemingly in contradiction to the first two functions—ethnic boundaries may actually facilitate cultural exchange and social interaction between communities by providing a mechanism for contact and the mediation of change. The more complex the social organization of an ethnic group and the external society, the more significant the third function for ethnic boundaries. When boundaries are permeable in a complex society, individuals may choose to take part in several communities, moving freely across boundaries while nevertheless remaining aware of the distinctive demands each community places on those interacting with its members. In the most ethnically pluralistic settings, for example in Israel, boundaries and change are inextricably linked, thereby making it necessary to perceive the ethnic community as a social sphere with considerable mutability. Chamber music has in many ways benefited from this mutability, which has stabilized the attendance at chamber-music concerts by encouraging outsiders to participate, even when it means crossing the community's ethnic boundaries.

The Historical Role of Chamber Music in the Central European Jewish Community

Chamber music has an extensive history of social centrality in the Jewish communities of Central Europe. The rise of chamber music coincided with burgeoning liberalism during the second half of the eighteenth century (Adorno 1976:86), the same economic and political liberalism that yielded and shaped the modern European Jewish community. Closely related historical forces therefore molded this Jewish community and chamber music, rendering it, in effect, the ideal genre of music for the community. During an age of expanding public and professional musical life, chamber music occupied a private and amateur sphere. It flourished not as public spectacle but in the cloistered atmosphere of the bourgeois home, played by musicians of considerable skill whose primary source of income did not come from public performance.

Just as Jews had benefited from the rise of liberalism through the expansion of socioeconomic opportunities, so too did chamber music provide a special venue for musical and cultural interaction outside the religious community. The Jewish home or salon was a place where Jews and non-Jews met in an atmosphere of equality. Chamber music, with its democracy of parts and abrogation of barriers between performers and audience, further symbolized this spirit of equality (ibid.:85). Jews also excelled as members of amateur chamber ensembles in the nineteenth century (and of professional chamber groups by the twentieth century), so much so that the history of chamber music in some German cities transpired largely within the Jewish community from the mid-nineteenth century until the 1930s.[2] Even the liberalization of the German synagogue in the mid-nineteenth century stimulated a similar liberalization of the official musical life in the community by spinning off new ensembles from those already in existence and multiplying the performance opportunities for those musicians, amateurs and professionals, previously restricted to music making in the community's religious life. So pervasive was this role of chamber music in the Jewish community that the *Jüdischer Kulturbund,* the administrative unit permitted by the Nazis as a means for the Jewish community to oversee (and by extension to restrict to the community) its own cultural life, created a separate category within its administrative purview to sanction and support chamber music after the exclusion of Jewish musicians from German society in 1933 (Adler-Rudel 1974:146–48). By the early twentieth century, chamber music had become a preferred, perhaps the preferred, form of musical activity in the Jewish community of Central Europe.

The music most highly valued by the Jewish community was also that most closely identifiable with the canon of absolute music (Dahlhaus 1978:118–27). The work of chamber music was ideally a self-contained composition, in which meaning came not from the composer's need to accommodate the fancies and fashions of the general public, but rather from the dictates of cohabiting voices and layers of sound (Adorno 1976:85). Why then should chamber music acquire so many specific associations and meanings for the Jewish community? Does this not make the claims for absolute music at best paradoxical and at worst untenable? In its most rigid sense, absolute music, being bound to the musical text with its anthropomorphized parts (ibid.), eschews the particularity of history. Viewed, however, from a performative perspective, the absence of specific meaning within the text allows meaning to accrue only upon performance, thus empowering any group—for example, an ethnic community—to shape what it will from absolute music. A gap therefore forms between the content of chamber-music repertories and the style of performance situations. It is within the mutability allowed by style that differences in meaning and function of music arise, thereby transforming chamber music into a genre that can follow numerous historical paths. These paths may be as different as, say, the ethnic associations in Israel and the practices of amateur music making found in many American academic communities. Clearly, such cases reflect different attitudes toward both the repertories of chamber music and the communities that lend the music its distinctive functions and form its different histories.

Style as a factor of performance reveals that many levels of meaning interpenetrate even the most absolute of musics (see Hebdige 1985). Neither a philosophical insistence on self-containment nor a historical interpretation of extreme particularity is right or wrong, implicit or explicit. Chamber music contains associations for the Jewish community at once flexible and inflexible, intrinsic to the text and extrinsic in the performance setting. The various levels of meaning make possible many histories and multifarious constructions of the past and present in the ethnic community.

For the Jewish community, chamber music was particularly enveloped by multiple layers of historical meaning, or, one might also say, ethnic and cultural boundaries. The community retained these boundaries in Israel, even though both the community and the sociomusical life of the external society were unlike those in Europe. The association of chamber music with a Central European history—with Germanness—had become a central tenet of absolute music (Adorno 1976:88–89), transforming a genre regarded by some as specific to Central Europe in general to one rooted in the German-speaking immigrant community. It is not surprising, therefore, to find this association even more evident in Israel, where many make the distinction that Eastern European Jews excel in virtuosic solo or concerto literature, while Central European Jews are content with their predilection for chamber music. Accounts of chamber music's history in Jewish culture emanate from both sides of the cultural boundaries of the German-Jewish community.

Repertory

The repertory of chamber music in Israel is quite specific, thus heightening its symbolic role in the ethnic community. The repertory comprises works from a historical period stretching approximately from the mid-eighteenth to the mid-nineteenth century, roughly parallel to a period initiated by Bach and concluded by the early Romantics, with Beethoven playing a central role in the formation of consciously absolute music at the beginning of the nineteenth century (see Dahlhaus 1978:118–19). For Central European Jews the pantheon of composers reformulating the position of chamber music in European society includes some later figures—Mendelssohn, Schumann, Brahms, Wagner, even Mahler and Schoenberg. Accordingly, the chamber-music repertory in Israel contains works from the late nineteenth and early twentieth centuries, even though the response to the position of such works in the cultural history of the Central European community is far from unequivocal. Wagner, for example, belongs to that history when understood dispassionately as absolute music; Schoenberg's consummating role grows all the more convincing when his advocates claim hidden significance for his Jewishness. Essential to these attitudes, then, is the ability to divorce Wagner's music from his much-debated anti-Semitism and, conversely, to associate Schoenberg's music with his return to Judaism late in life (see Bohlman 1989:1–13).

The historical period in which chamber music first developed and then flourished has special significance for Central European Jews. Whatever historical flexibility their particular chamber-music repertory demonstrates, it never contains works preceding the inception of enlightened liberalism or subsequent to the forced collapse of European Jewish society in the twentieth century. Historically, this was a period of rapid transformation in the Jewish community, a period during which a secular self-awareness virtually supplanted the religious definition of the community. Jewish society had discovered new promise and philosophical resonance in the Enlightenment concept of Bildung, the cultivation of learning and intellectual pursuits as a means of advancing one's position professionally and socially. For Jews, Bildung additionally formed a conduit to the larger society, to the Germany or Austria outside the Jewish community (Mosse 1985:3). Accordingly, Bildung meant something different to the Jewish community, something more precious, than it did to non-Jewish society. Just as Bildung became a sort of secular religion for many Jews, so too did the music of the Classic and early Romantic periods acquire a deeper ethnic significance, a more profound form of cultural power: in essence, this music was one of the most accessible means whereby Jews could enter the Western tradition of civilization, thus coupling their own history with another.

The association of the chamber-music repertory with classicism is also a salient determinant of its symbolic role, for this has meant a dissociation from nationalism and sacred functions for works constituting the repertory. The chamber works of Mozart or Beethoven are therefore not perceived in Israeli society as German or Austrian, but as higher expressions of art signaling value systems that transcend specific nations. Nationalism may even be manipulated in order to include or exclude works from the repertory or to invoke aesthetic dicta for and against new music in contemporary Israel. When subareas in the classicized repertory of the German-speaking community develop, it is to draw attention to individual performers. Several Czech-Israeli pianists, for example, whose cultural background in

Czechoslovakia allied them with the Czech German-speaking community, characteristically add a small, one might say token, group of Czech pieces to their repertories in order to personalize their performances. One rarely hears such pieces other than as encores in a *Hauskonzert,* and never would they assume a central position in a concert. Accordingly, they serve to define even more precisely the core of the repertory itself. Within Central European society a few other genres have functions similar to those of chamber music, the best example being *Lieder,* or German art song.[3]

The official and unofficial exclusion of the German language from Israel has even more resolutely relegated Lieder to the ethnic community, specifying yet another marker of chamber music as cultural turf occupied by the Central European community. The boundaries of the chamber-music repertory are therefore the products of a particular past and present, of an ethnic community that has always been Jewish and yet has always witnessed the confluence of other cultures in its intellectual and musical endeavors.

Ritualization of Chamber Music

The performance of chamber music has become highly ritualized in Israel, with ritual taking place primarily in and around the events attending the Hauskonzert, the concert in the home. The ritual of the concert itself creates various levels of organization, all of which are vital to the role of chamber music in the ethnic community. On one level, the social ritual extends to the evening and events surrounding each Hauskonzert. On a second level, organization characterizes other activities in the ethnic community and the necessity of establishing a regular position for chamber concerts in the community. Ritual therefore characterizes both private and public aspects of chamber music, effecting the necessary link between these aspects. It is because of the ritualization of chamber music that concerts have come to serve as a means of organizing interaction with Israelis and foreigners outside the ethnic community, making it possible for them to attend and participate in an event that is otherwise highly structured and potentially exclusive.

Each ritualized concert contains elements of both stability and change, the structure and anti-structure necessary for the Hauskonzert to maintain its range of historical meanings (cf. Turner 1969). Moreover, the coexistence of these contrastive factors affords ethnicity many different forms, some of them precise, others ambiguous, but together characteristic of continuous processes of negotiation with the outside that have been requisite for the survival of the German-Jewish community for two centuries.[4]

Three types of participants are necessary for a successful evening of chamber music, that is, a complete enactment of the social ritual of the Hauskonzert. The host or hostess is the primary organizer of the concert, and it is in his or her home that the concert takes place. The musicians may or may not play an organizational role, although there is general consensus that performers are ultimately free from direct organizational responsibilities. And finally, the audience is an indispensable participant in the ritual, for it is the audience member who is at the greatest distance from his or her own sub-society during the occasion of the concert. Of these three types, the first comes almost inevitably from the ethnic community, and the third only rarely does not include someone from outside the community. It is not essential that the musicians, the second type, come from the community, though most do. By far the bulk of Israeli chamber players, especially those willfully maintaining an amateur status, come from the Central European ethnic community.

Each evening of chamber music unfolds as a series of specific events or phases, which together may last as long as five or six hours. A Hauskonzert may occur on any night of the week, but those with the largest attendance take place on the weekend, namely on Friday and Saturday evenings, when sufficient time for full enactment of the ritual is available. The performance of chamber music itself usually comprises roughly an hour in the middle of the evening. Framing the concert are other phases, in which various types of refreshment, including full meals, and intellectual discussion are of primary importance, especially to the extent that these make outsiders feel more a part of the ritual. The custom of late-afternoon coffee and cake, called in Viennese dialect—and most often in Israel—*Jause,* initiates the evening, with a full meal, for those few who stay the entire five or six hours, at the close of the evening. All of the framing phases serve in specialized ways to situate the chamber music at the center of the ritual and to provide moments for outsiders to enter this highly symbolic expression of community values.

Ritualization of chamber music in Israel depends on several organizational groups, some specific to the social ritual itself, others more general in function. Of the first type, a core group attached to one home or host is the best example; I refer to the core group as such because its members rarely miss a concert of chamber music in a particular home, thus ensuring considerable audience and ritual stability in that home. The Rubin Academy of Music or the Hebrew University in different ways characterize the second, more general type of organization. Young performers, often the students of teachers from the Central European community, occasionally come to perform from the Rubin Academy; the Hebrew University is often a source of intellectuals familiar with the relation of chamber music to the German-Jewish value system, and it is also a source of the educated amateur musician, on whom chamber music has historically depended. The two types of organization are both necessary because of the dialectic of structure and anti-structure they couple. Together, the two types stem ossification and ensure historical vitality by stimulating and channeling constant change.

The social ritual itself consists of three large stages. In the first, audience members and musicians arrive in the home of the host, gradually passing from the world outside the ritual to the sequestered environs of the event. The first stage is necessary for the establishment of new acquaintances, who come to constitute a social network specific to the ritual. In the second stage, there is a complete suspension of external time, with the only meaningful temporal structures those of the concert itself. In the final stage, participants gradually take leave, albeit in such a way that the break with the ritual is not overly abrupt and that preparation for a future enactment of the ritual is underway.

These three stages reflect a pattern inherent in many of the rites of passage studied comparatively by Arnold van Gennep (1960[1909]) and extended to ritual behavior and social drama by Victor Turner (e.g., 1974, 1984). According to the van Gennep model, the concert occupies a stage called "liminality," in which the group's most sacred values are embedded and expressed. Indeed, this is the case with the second stage of the Hauskonzert, the only time when the audience does not participate actively in the events of the ritual. It is at this moment that the values of the Yekkes are most exposed, when they are stripped bare of other historical and ethnic meanings. Reflexivity between performer and audience is at a crucial intensity during this liminal stage, and even the outsider, so it is hoped, will embrace the cultural values expressed by the performance, if only momentarily (cf. MacAloon 1984:10–13; Turner 1984:22–23). What the outsider will or can take with him or her to the outside world after passage through the third stage is another question. At the very least, there has been a complete suspension of the boundaries between ethnic communities during the liminal stage.

Other Sociomusical Settings, Other Cultural Boundaries

The ritualized stage for chamber music in the home is not the only setting for the performance of Western art music as ethnic music in Israel. Several social and musical settings associated with other genres of music also serve to reinforce cultural boundaries and represent historical meanings. These settings, in turn, lead to increased permeability of the community's ethnic boundaries, hence playing a role in the ongoing processes of history. The chamber-music ritual itself occupies one extreme in its relation to these boundaries, namely by taking place within the boundaries, suspending them during moments of liminality, and eventually serving as a marker for the replacement of the boundaries.

Several other settings acquire dual functions by straddling the community boundaries. Many concerts in such settings are completely public, lacking specific ethnic identification yet bearing discernible traces of Central European influences. Some concerts, for example those in which Wagner or Richard Strauss are performed, rely on covert ritualization and therefore require more care in the solicitation of attendance, often utilizing invitations or moving to a stage technically outside of Israeli society. Such care in transposing the stage to a non-Israeli setting often attends concerts of German art song. In some instances, public performance of Lieder concerts is possible because of special qualifications that defer ethnic connotations, for example by drawing attention to several groups of songs with texts by the German-Jewish poet, Heinrich Heine. When deferral of this nature is either not possible or not desirable, Lieder concerts are often staged at the *Erlöserkirche,* the German Protestant church in the Old City of Jerusalem. Potential ethnic tension is therefore diffused by removing the concert to a setting that is neutral in several important ways, yet still not completely dissociated from German culture. The Central European community takes considerable care never to impose its cultural boundaries.

The ethnic boundaries of Western art music in Israel also allow for the emergence of necessary codes of public and ritual behavior. In a neighborhood such as Reḥavia in Jerusalem, with a very dense population living largely in apartment houses, considerable latitude defines those hours of the day when practicing a musical instrument is permissible. In other neighborhoods tolerance of a neighbor's practicing may be considerably less, limiting piano practice very often to the morning and early evening. The ritualized performance of chamber music is itself inseparable from several codes of behavior, ranging from the activities of the core group to the determination of proper moments for entrance and exit from the home hosting a performance. Just as the ritual preserves the community's values, so must the community consciously protect those social patterns that preserve the ritual and its position in society.

Ethnomusicology as the Study of Music History

If the ritualization of performance and the constant shifting of cultural boundaries reveal chamber music to be just one central activity within the complex of social values determining the musical culture of the Yekkes, they further suggest that the persistence of this musical culture depends on the centrality of a common history and its meaning for the community. The resulting historical meaning is therefore a dynamic balance between the standardization of a distinct musical repertory and the symbolic role it has acquired. Neither text nor context alone yields this historical meaning to chamber music; their interaction does. Music history for the German-Jewish community has not depended so much on hagiographic homage to great composers and an inviolable absoluteness in the chamber-music repertory, as on the perception of the community and the constant reformulation of perception through performance.

Implicit in this essay (and, perhaps, at times baldly explicit) is a belief that the history of Western art music—in toto, as a conglomerate of styles, genres, and social contexts—lends itself to ethnomusicological approaches. Indeed, it is only through ethnomusicological approaches that one sees not a single, monolithic music history, but a multitude of music histories. Against this backdrop of many music histories it is nonetheless possible to identify that of the Yekkes, and, therefore, I would like to add just a few words about the Yekkes and their musical culture, and about their modern music history at this point in time. Some readers, especially those accustomed to discussions of ethnicity, will be curious about the ethnic group itself: what is the present state of the Yekkes, and what does the future hold for them and their music history? In short, most Yekkes are rather elderly, and it will not be too many years before there will be no identifiable group known as Yekkes. Similarly, the ritualization of chamber music at the center of their musical culture will likely shift to other genres that redefine cultural boundaries in new ways.

But this essay is not really about an ethnic group. Nor is it about the music per se of that group. I am here concerned with the music history resulting from the response of a group with a shared value system to a musical repertory that articulated those values. Such groups have long populated the history of Western music, as well as non-Western, folk, or tribal musics. Sometimes we call them ethnic groups or communities, sometimes national cultures, and sometimes we label by coupling place with abstraction, for example in "Viennese classicism." All these acts of labeling suggest the process of standing outside a group and looking in to see what sort of music is to be found. Suppose the group is really the product of its musical activities and the cultural values bound to them? What if excessive concern with the musical text deflects one from seeing the formation of diverse groups and music histories? What if one looked at the Yekkes, with their devotion to chamber music, as just another justification for the conditions of absolute music?

Ethnomusicology maintains as its focus the particularity of musical expression and performance. Such particularity, in the best of ethnomusicological approaches, does not simply privilege the group and its repertory; rather, it searches out the dynamic, performative links between these components in the music culture. That these approaches can interpret the use of instrumental works from the Western repertory as ethnic music, the function of chamber music as ritual, and the dynamic of music history as a constant renegotiation of the cultural values attached to absolute music bespeaks far more than an occasional insight from the application of ethnomusicological approaches to Western art music. It may be that the truly diverse and complex levels of meaning in music history can only be explored fully when viewing music and history from the abundant perspectives that ethnomusicology not only tolerates, but encourages.

NOTES

1. The meanings offered to explain the origins of the term Yekke vary, though they generally trace the etymology to the Yiddish or German word for a short coat, i.e., a jacket. Thus, some claim that German Jews were notable for their early abandonment of the caftan for the short jacket of the gentile; others, imputing to the term Middle Eastern origins, note that German Jews persisted in wearing formal woolen jackets even in the heat of Israeli summers. Reinforcing the contemporary use of the term is a genre of ethnic joke poking fun at the punctual, hardworking, and rather inflexible nature of the German-speaking Jew. Technically speaking, only German Jews are Yekkes, but in common parlance the term often applies to German-speaking Jews from Central Europe in general.

2. This was the case in Mannheim, where patronage of the several larger ensembles, notably the city's chamber orchestra, the *Stamitz-Gemeinde*, was officially assumed by the Jewish community during the Weimar period (cf. Herrmann 1954; Watzinger 1984; Bohlman 1985–86).

3. There is considerable precedence for the inclusion of art song among the genres of chamber music (e.g., Adorno 1976:85). Most significant, the social sphere of Lieder is private and its intellectual underpinnings richly influenced by nineteenth-century enchantment with Bildung.

4. Fredrik Barth refers to this complex of different ethnic or group meanings as "multiplex relations," which develop from the increased number of choices available within a modern urban society and from the continued propensity to make a limited number of specific choices (1978:168). Chamber music, with its extensive malleability for yielding diverse performative styles, has an almost ideal potential for multiplex relations.

Epilogue: Paradigms and Stories

Daniel M. Neuman

> The role for history in the human sciences as a whole should be to investigate and clarify the relationship between our knowledge and the sources of its formation.
>
> —Lawrence Scaff, *History of the Human Sciences*

In a soon-to-be-published history and ethnography of that tribe of academic transcribers now known as ethnomusicologists, Ter Ellingson plots out in remarkable detail how this tribe's cultural presuppositions have fundamentally affected its own history of perceptions of and about music (Ellingson, ms.). Lawrence Scaff's mandate in the epigraph to this epilogue is brilliantly executed by Ellingson in clarifying the relationship between ethnomusicological knowledge, the sources of its formation, and the process of this formation as mediated by the struggle to find the most appropriate ways to represent music through transcription.

The coincidence of Ellingson's work with other recent and forthcoming publications (Christensen 1988; Nettl and Bohlman 1991) and with this collection of essays on *Ethnomusicology and Modern Music History* is not mere coincidence. On the contrary, the current interest in ethnomusicology, history, and how we have come to know what we know is itself, I would aver, a historical event of no little moment. It announces a shift from questions of what ethnomusicological problems and methods ought to be, unhindered by the cultural and historical setting of these questions, to questions of how ethnomusicological problems and methods have come to be the way they are, with a critical stance regarding the field's cultural and historical setting.[1]

One can say that ethnomusicologists are no longer a people without history or perhaps more accurately without historical consciousness.

In this sense ethnomusicologists have joined with their informants-turned-consultants, whose own historical consciousness is also the subject of several essays in this collection.

These essays, in fact, reveal that differences between the makers of music history (informants) and the chroniclers of music history (in our case ethnomusicologists) might well be nonexistent, or at any rate only a construct. In recounting the dialogue of Egyptian musicians desiring modernity and German musicologists urging authenticity, Jihad Racy's essay, for example, encapsulates the themes of indigenous/exogenous antipodes and historical consciousness in ethnomusicology. Racy concludes with what I take to be the fundamental problem of any historical effort: "we may wonder about the distinctive nature of our own historical paradigms and about the manner in which we apply our present ideologies in worldwide scholarly encounters."

Wondering about historical paradigms, it seems to me that the loci that history occupies in these essays assume at least three distinct orientations: in this sense we can posit three different historical paradigms.

The first paradigm I will call *reflexive music history,* by which I mean simply the history of music history. The authors of such histories are also, in an extended sense, its subjects. In the essays of Racy and Shiloah, crosscultural musicology itself is the subject of history.

The second paradigm is *interpretive music history.* This is what is conventionally thought of as music history in which music culture itself is the subject of history and the history is externally constructed and conducted. History is written to make a point and present an argument. The argument can be either generated indigenously (to validate musical authenticity, for example, as in the essays by Capwell and Slawek) or exogenously (regarding musical culture change, adaptation or stability, for example, as in the essays by Waterman, Myers, Qureshi, Witmer, Turino, and Levine).

The third paradigm can be termed *immanent music history.* In a number of the articles, most notably Seeger's, but also those by Coplan, Babiracki, and Bohlman, music "writes" or in some manner represents history: a history not so much of music itself as of its creators or consumers. History here is the subject of music: music is the medium—the crucible in which time and its memories are collected, reconstituted, and preserved—and history, its message.

These paradigms are meant to be suggestive, not absolute. Some of the essays can indeed be found to incorporate aspects of more than one paradigm. Nevertheless it is helpful to note the critically different set of relationships between the three constitutive elements of these essays: music history, community, and author. In the reflexive mode, the essays are about the history of musicological debates: the community is musicologists and the authors, their descendants. In the interpretive mode, the essays are about modern music history: the community is the "other," and the authors are outsiders. In the immanent mode, the essays are about music constructing history: the ethnic group is the "other," and the authors are co-authors.

The first paradigm speaks to the fact that surely an aspect of ethnomusicology and modern music history is that ethnomusicology itself is very much part of modern music history. The emergence of ethnomusicology as a distinct field of scholarly research in the United States is a distinctly post-World War II phenomenon. The particular shapes it has assumed in the United States during the four decades since the war is due to a number of factors: its institutionalization in music departments; the institutionalization of research support and the greatly expanded global possibilities for ethnomusicological fieldwork due to the emergence of formerly colonial, now independent, nations; but perhaps most significantly, the peculiarly hybrid pedigree of its practitioners in anthropology and musicology.

It used to be the case that anthropology and ethnomusicology were largely ahistorical when not actively antihistorical. This was due in part to the legacy of the document as the icon of historical research, and in societies where documents were scarce or nonexistent, history and indigenous historical consciousness were deemed to be limited or impossible because of their scarcity or absence. Instead of history, anthropologists and ethnomusicologists found social and cultural change, and the concepts of acculturation, syncretism, revitalization, hybridization, modernization, and Westernization were all forwarded as candidates designed to address the problem of change.

Starting in the 1960s, however, but particularly during the last decade or so, the ethnography, that icon of anthropological and ethnomusicological research, has come under close scrutiny. There is now a considerable literature of a reflexive and critical sort, examining how, through the process of conducting fieldwork and writing ethnographies, particular kinds of accounts of other people's customs get conveyed.[2] This examination has raised a fundamental question: through whose voice and through what mode of authority is an ethnography created? Whereas linguistics had provided the model for theoretical concerns in anthropology into the 1960s, it is no accident that much of the recent thinking surrounding the ethnographic question derives from literary criticism: ethnography is, after all, a story. A study of how ethnography was influenced by "conventional wisdom" stories provides a useful view of how anthropological perceptions have dramatically changed during the last half century. "In the 1930s and

1940s the dominant story constructed about Native American culture change saw the present as disorganized, the past as glorious and the future as assimilation. Now, however, we have a new narrative: the present is viewed as a resistance movement, the past as exploitation, and the future as ethnic resurgence" (Bruner 1986:139).

This change of dominant story illustrates the classic predicament of all interpretive accounts: of interpretation conducted by interpreters, themselves prisoners of their own historical time and place. But such awareness, itself a relatively new rediscovery in anthropology and ethnomusicology, must take care not to yield to the temptation that the awareness is itself the solution to the problem it poses.

The variety of cultural environments encompassed in this collection exemplifies the actuality of the modern world, as it does the field of ethnomusicology and also the distinguished scholarship of Bruno Nettl, who, as teacher to most of the authors, stimulated these diverse approaches and inspired all of the essayists with his openness to the historical issues in ethnomusicology. Similarly, the variety of paradigmatic viewpoints I discussed above, the ways in which history is anchored and utilized, manifests the continually inquiring intellect and absence of theoretical dogmatism that has been the hallmark of Nettl as fieldworker, scholar, writer, and teacher. Put another way, he has encouraged us all in the varieties of storytelling we have engaged.

One of the ironies of ethnomusicology is that, although its field is global, it has largely avoided Western art music in its compass. Central to Nettl's inclusive conception of ethnomusicology, however, is that it concern all the world's music, including the Western classical tradition to which he has recently turned his attention.[3] Philip Bohlman develops this possibility by treating Western chamber music as the music of the contemporary ethnic group known as Yekkes (culturally related, by the way, to ancestors who were the champions of purity and ethnic authenticity in Egypt during the 1930s). The fact that the repertory of Central European Jews is coeval in historical time with the group's own history (never containing works "preceding the inception of enlightened liberalism or subsequent to the forced collapse of European Jewish society in the twentieth century") and that the music itself was a mode of joining its own history with that of the "Western tradition of civilization," illustrates the ability of even "absolute" music to assume shape and meaning for an ethnic community. For Bohlman, the ethnomusicological perspective on Western art music allows us to understand the "dynamic of music history as a constant renegotiation of the cultural values attached to [in this case] absolute music." This study also speaks to a musical repertory that was part of the musical education of many ethnomusicologists, thus making it very much part of the story ethnomusicologists tell about themselves. In this sense also it obeys the immanent historical paradigm outlined earlier.

If these are examples of stories we tell about ourselves as ethnomusicologists, how very different are they from the stories the Suyá tell about themselves, incorporating other peoples' music as the vehicle for their own history? Applied ethnomusicologists, the Suyá perform exogenous songs to reproduce the pattern of their own history, a history of, in Seeger's words, "incorporating into the life of the collectivity the otherness of the others"—a motto for the Society for Ethnomusicology?

Although its extent and acknowledgement may be distinctive to the Suyá, adopting the music of others is, of course, not unique to them. What used generally to be called acculturation[4] is to a certain extent characteristic of each musical culture discussed in this volume. What emerges in most of these essays is the widespread interaction of different (but not indigenously conceived as alien) musical cultures, suggesting it is hard now to discover a musical culture that has not had extensive exchange with other cultures. This is true at varying levels in all the cases in this collection, with the possible exception of Robert Witmer's study. Indeed, it is a measure of what occasions surprise in ethnomusicological discourse today that the stability Witmer discovers, of a Blackfoot song over a sixty-year period, is interpreted as problematic. A generation or so ago it would have been—in a world of static, self-sufficient cultural wholes—the taken-for-granted case.

These essays do suggest that the ethnomusicological story is also changing. Here I refer to both change itself and the interpretation of those societies undergoing it. As early as 1975 Steve Blum drew our attention to the need for a historical consciousness in ethnomusicology (Blum 1975). We could, borrowing from Bruner, say that the story that ethnomusicologists formerly told about what is called "world" music often went as follows: the musical past of a culture was authentic; its present, already under attack, needed to be preserved and not polluted by foreign, and particularly Western, musical influences, in order to avoid the musical homogenization, the musical grey-out so many feared for the future.

In fact, however, as I have already argued, the stories we tell ourselves, in narrative mode, stance, and voice are far from unified. I think this is because ethnomusicology itself emerged only after World War II as a field with a distinct community of scholars. As a consequence, it is perhaps too soon for a unified doctrine—a dominant tale—to have emerged. But it may very well be the case, as Bohlman has elsewhere argued (1991), that the very heterogeneity of tales, what he characterizes as its constant challenging of canons, is the hallmark of ethnomusicology.

But as with paradigmatic types of history, there are patterns of storytelling to be discerned. Ethnomusicology, perched between the humanities and social sciences, as Waterman puts it, is a field that was born to a blurring of genres, to use Geertz's felicitous phrase. But an ethnomusicologist's sensibilities must be at the least partly formed by the culture(s) he or she engages and the academic training undergone. I would argue, accordingly, that the kind of story the ethnomusicologist tells will depend very much on where fieldwork is conducted and which discipline (anthropology or musicology) is the ancestral disciplinary home for a given scholar.[5] If the stories we formulate about change and history are correlated with where we do our work, our stories as histories become very much bound up with and are themselves refractions of the cultural histories of the societies in which we work.[6]

Allow me to illustrate with the two essays concerned with sub-Saharan African societies. Closely following Bruner's description for North America—what Clifford (1988:14) calls "the great narrative of entropy and loss"—it may be as pertinent that both authors in this volume are anthropologists as it is that they are Africanists. For Coplan and Waterman, the past is focused on the pervasive reality of colonial exploitation; the present on reaffirmation, resistance, and persistence; the future is uncertain but focused on the reinvention or reconstitution of musical tradition. (Although one notes that even the term "tradition" has its special valence, as both Coplan and Waterman point out.)

Coplan, seemingly ambiguous about the stand he should take with respect to the inevitability of change in music traditions—the "preservationist" element—appears to find comfort in its invention. Since the notion of "timeless, changeless values of African traditional life" has been used "as an instrument of . . . oppression, [this has] led to the emergence of forms of accommodation and resistance." But he rejects even the search for invention, looking instead for African traditions as "organic, living expressions of collective experience in aesthetic form." He finds such expressions in the "songs of the inveterate travelers," a new genre created to "express the particular social experience of migrant laborers." Apartheid cannot destroy the traditions of Black South Africans, for they live in new traditional genres of self-expression.[7]

Waterman, in considering the relationship between "continuity and change" (itself a somewhat classic expression for his otherwise modernist tone), urges us in his explicitly theoretical essay to take "practice theory" as the guiding formulation for the study of music history. Cultural continuity, rather than being thought of as stasis, is recursive. Practice "feeds back onto structure," which is transformed when "actors are confronted with contradictions." Through this Hegelian scrim, Waterman finds "that the most convincing accounts of the historical development of particular styles are concerned with musical practice as it is conditioned by, and in turn helps to shape, emergent patterns of social interaction and cultural order."

The adoption of talking drums symbolizing a pan-Yoruba identity signals the first change in the before-and-after story of *jùjú* history. Modern jùjú is "simultaneously rooted in Yoruba tradition and oriented toward the world socioeconomic system." Technology is also important, enabling the restructuring of jùjú ensembles. As new varieties of jùjú style emerge, jùjú music plays "a crucial role in the invention of modern pan-Yoruba tradition, the construction of the past with an eye toward an uncertain future."

If we contrast the African cases with that other classic area of colonialist exploitation, India, the story turns out, however, to be quite different, even though both an anthropologist (Qureshi) and musicologists (Babiracki, Capwell, Myers, and Slawek) are represented. It is noteworthy that although the legacy of colonialism and the independence movement is still very much a part of South Asian consciousness,[8] there seems to be hardly any mention of it in writings—either Indian or non-Indian—on South Asian music cultures.[9] This is so, perhaps, because of the particular importance that Indians themselves attach to their own music history, the cultural autonomy they believe it has maintained, and the manner in which it serves even today as a form of cultural strategy and commitment.

The Indian story tells of an ever-present continuity in which authority and authenticity need to be constantly negotiated and reaffirmed against a background, actually often a battlefield, of an indigenous chronicle of music history. (This indigenous chronicle, incidentally, speaks of a glorious golden age past, a diluted present, and a future inevitably gone worse.) It is perhaps no accident then, that the stories ethnomusicologists tell concern histories of musical and social pedigrees. Qureshi, for example, describes Sufi ritual repertory made functionally stable in order to "legitimize local shrine authority through the authenticity of the repertory of words and music. . . . Its prime purpose is to validate the presence of the saint or his representative by showing the authenticity and historical continuity of the songs."[10]

Similarly, Capwell begins his essay by stressing that "the significance of history is its ability to establish and recount the origin, acquisition, and transmission of authority." He exemplifies this by demonstrating how the Visnupur gharānā chooses to remember its origins and construct its own history in the process of an indigenous determination of authenticity.[11] Slawek is in a situation of assisting the establishment (and concomitant authority) of the history he describes, by substantiating a stylistic school that others might claim is still in the process of being formed. The authority and authenticity documented in Slawek's essay is augmented by the very fact of his documentation. This essay raises explicitly the difficult question of the dual roles of researcher as disciple and scholar in the determination of voice and authority.

Babiracki and Myers deal with Indian communities outside the classical and devotional mainstream but nevertheless related to it. The musical "revitalization" of the Hindus of Trinidad that Myers details, with all of its very special musical diversity and seemingly rapid change, also manifests the broad outline of the parent Indian story as well, with its concern for authenticity, authority, and persistence. And in the kaleidoscope of Indian music made available in Felicity, Myers reproduces the multiplicity of refractions increasingly found in sojourns of global musics of which Indian film music is a prime example. Even the relatively remote "tribal" Muṇḍa exhibit the concern for authenticity, in this case what is authentically Muṇḍa. Muṇḍa strategies approximate the situation of the Suyá and also the Yekkes, in that the Muṇḍa *karam* repertory utilizes "the songs of outsiders to reaffirm Muṇḍāri values of communality and equality and [to] establish a cultural boundary. . . . The karam is typically Muṇḍāri, a means of controlling the foreign by adopting it, transforming it, and absorbing it into the 'inside' Muṇḍāri world."

Latin America has a somewhat different legacy and structure of oppression from those of Africa and India, expressed very explicity in Turino's account, in which he tracks the migration of musical instruments, ideas, and innovations from the highlands of Peru to its cities and then back again in a reconfigured prestige nexus. He also develops and highlights a point considered in some of the other essays: the origins of innovations and their persistence or abandonment are a function of who is doing what to whom.[12]

North America is the ancestral homeland for ethnomusicology, and it probably is no accident that the two North American cases share a focus on music repertory and its analysis as the primary object of study. In a sense, Levine's essay is the most classical of music histories in that she is the only one writing about musical practices no longer existing. She relies on artifacts—aural and written—as her sources in reconstructing a musical repertory. The disappearance of the tradition accords with the classical anthropological and ethnomusicological formulation of the disappearing Native American. Witmer, in documenting extraordinary persistence and stability, is the mirror image of this tale. The connectedness of stability and extinction only appears paradoxical, but they are actually aspects of the same conception:

Native Americans were perceived as nonchanging, therefore not capable of adaptation, and therefore inevitably to be assimilated and to disappear. Set against classical notions of Native American societies' static culture and disappearence, it is worth noting that the themes of these North American essays themselves represent a remarkable continuity of ethnomusicological thinking regarding Native American musical traditions.

If we have isolated some patterns of storytelling as correlative of place and disciplinary origin, what is missing in these stories is equally suggestive. Hardly to be found in these essays are many of the classic issues in the ethnomusicological study of history and culture change: differences between history and culture; differences between variation and change; the grey-out of world music; measures of change; the impact of technological change; the status of theoretical concepts such as syncretism, Westernization, or modernization. Although the absence of these issues is perhaps a function of sample size, more likely it manifests the shift in ethnomusicological attention to change and history as natural and expected process rather than the aberrant interlocution of unnatural forces acting on unsuspecting ahistorical societies.

More generally, this collection of essays represents a rethinking of the whole spectrum of concepts of music, including its study in history. What these essays have in common—whether in the reflexive, interpretive, or immanent mode—is the conception that history is less important for the telling of it as such, than for the meanings that can be construed for its participants. Significant not only in the redefinitions and expansion of history's loci, but also in their partaking of its flow, these essays exhibit an increased awareness of the ethnomusicologist's own role and accountability in the making of history. Although this shift may augur confusion about the appropriate relation of subject and object, it is also a sign of the possibilities of its reconstitution on a radically different plane. This I believe is warranted for the growth of knowledge and understanding, and for the stories ethnomusicology has yet to tell.

NOTES

1. This recent interest was the subject of a conference ("Ideas, Issues and Personalities in the History of Ethnomusicology") organized by Bruno Nettl and held at the University of Illinois at Urbana-Champaign on April 14–17, 1988. More recent is the special issue of the *Yearbook for Traditional Music* celebrating the fortieth anniversary of the ICTM, in which a number of articles concern the history of ethnomusicology (Christensen 1988).

2. The problem has recently been given a most magisterial treatment by James Clifford in *The Predicament of Culture* (1988).

3. Examples are a paper delivered at the 1985 SEM conference in Vancouver and his plenary lecture at the 1989 meeting of the ICTM, a recent essay, "Mozart and the Ethnomusicological Study of Western Culture" (Nettl 1989b).

4. I mean it in the loose sense of two different cultures in contact, but not necessarily alien from one another. Acculturation—defined as "modifications within cultures resulting from contact with alien lifeways" (Bee 1974:96 and passim) had its particular career in anthropology because of the peculiarities of anthropology in North America. Kartomi (1981) explores the various meanings of terms associated with change and presents a useful critique of the notion of acculturation.

5. The idea of ethnography characterized by major themes and related to cultural area is explored in great detail by Pratt (1986).

6. It is also sometimes the case that there are distinct subcultures of ethnomusicologists—defined by their area interests, whose intercommunication defines the terms of discourse and its objects, i.e., to create the shape of the narrative. I think this is the case for at least those involved with research in sub-Saharan Africa and South Asia.

7. Clifford twice mentions that "anthropology still awaits its Conrad" (1988:96, 113). Neither he nor Coplan refers to a possible anthropological Conrad in Hoyt Alverson, whose *Mind in the Heart of Darkness* (1978) prefigured the issue of colonialist co-optation and specifically challenged the alleged internalization of the dominant society's worldview on the part of migrant laborers in South Africa.

8. Such consciousness exists in the concrete structures of the English Raj, the capital, the railways, etc., as well as the remembered recent history and the continuing flow of articles (and obituaries) of hundreds of individuals prominent in the Independence movement.

9. Only in the latter part of the nineteenth century was there any concern for the fact that the British had little interest in and typically only contempt for Indian music.

10. Of course Qureshi wants to make a methodological point about the usefulness of such repertories in reconstructing historical musical influences vis-à-vis the classical tradition.

11. And it should be pointed out that this writer has apparently also contributed to the historicity of the origin myth, for which, as Capwell demonstrates, little actual evidence exists.

12. It is unfortunate that we do not have East Asia at all represented in this collection (which may itself be a datum worth thinking about) but it is the case that the high profile of Western classical music in these societies is certainly no longer mourned (if it ever was). Western colonialism and the Westernization of its indigenous traditions have not been issues. The story told here I suspect is not of grey-out but of compartmentalization, indigenous and Western traditions living side by side, as the societies in toto are suspected of doing.

List of References

Abraham, Otto and Erich M. von Hornbostel

1909–10 "Vorschläge für die Transkription exotischer Melodien." *Sammelbände der Internationalen Musikgesellschaft* 11:1–25.

Abrahams, Ruth

1985 "The Life and Art of Uday Shankar." Ph.D. dissertation, New York University.

Adler-Rudel, S.

1974 *Jüdische Selbsthilfe unter dem Naziregime 1933–1939: Im Spiegel der Reichsvertretung der Juden in Deutschland.* Tübingen: J. C. B. Mohr (Paul Siebeck).

Adorno, Theodor W.

1976 *Introduction to the Sociology of Music.* Translated E. B. Ashton. New York: Seabury. First published 1962.

Agawu, V. Kofi

1991 "On the Nature of African Ethnomusicological Discourse." In Katherine A. Bergeron and Philip V. Bohlman, eds., *Disciplining Music: Musicology and Its Canons.* Chicago: The University of Chicago Press.

Aig-Imoukhuede, Frank

1975 "Contemporary Culture." In A. B. Aderibigbe, ed., *Lagos: The Development of an African City.* Lagos: Longman Nigeria, pp. 197–226.

Alaja-Browne, Afolabi

1985 "Jùjú Music: A Study of Its Social History and Style." Ph.D. dissertation, University of Pittsburgh.

Ālāuddina Khāṁ

1981 *āmār kathā.* Transcribed Subhomay Ghosh. Reprint of 1968 edition in *ratnasāgar granthamālā* series. Calcutta: Ananda. (Bengali)

Āl-e Ahmad, Jalāl
1962 *Gharbzadegi*. Tehran: n.p. (Farsi)
Allen, Warren Dwight
1962 *Philosophies of Music History: A Study of General Histories of Music, 1600–1960*. New York: Dover. First published 1939.
Alverson, Hoyt
1978 *Mind in the Heart of Darkness*. New Haven: Yale University Press.
Amir Khan
1966 "The Tarana Style of Singing." In Roger Ashton, ed., *Music East and West*. Bombay: Bhatkal Books International, pp. 22–23.
Amir Khusrau
1974 *Kulliat-e-Ghazaliat-e-Khusrau*. Ed. Iqbal Salahuddin. Lahore: Packages Limited, 4 vols. (Farsi)
Arguedas, José Maria
1985 *Indios, mestizos y senores*. Lima: Editorial Horizonte.
Arian, Émile [Imil 'Aryan]
1924 "Preuve irréfutable de la division de l'échelle musicale orientale en 24 quarts de tons." *Bulletin de l'Institut d'Égypte* 6:159–67.
Aziz Ahmad
1963 "The Sufi and the Sultan in Pre-Mughal Muslim India." *Der Islam* 38:142–53.
1969 *An Intellectual History of Islam in India*. Edinburgh: Edinburgh University Press. (Islamic Surveys, 7)
Badhwar, Inderjit
1987 "Hari Prasad Chaurasiya: The Magic of His Flute." *India Today*, February 28, pp. 64–75.
Barber, Karin
1987 "Popular Arts in Africa." *African Studies Review* 30/3:1–78.
Barth, Fredrik
1969 Ed., *Ethnic Groups and Boundaries: The Social Organization of Culture Difference*. Boston: Little, Brown.
1978 "Scale and Network in Urban Western Society." In Fredrik Barth, ed., *Scale and Social Organization*. Oslo: Universitetsforlaget, pp. 163–83.
Bartók, Béla
1931 "Mi a népzene." *Új Idők* 37/20:626-27. English translation ("What is Folk Music?") in Suchoff 1976:5–8.
1933 "Zum Kongress für arabischen Musik—Cairo 1932." *Zeitschrift für Vergleichende Musikwissenschaft* 1/2: 46–48. English translation ("At the Congress for Arab Music—Cairo, 1932") in Suchoff 1976:38–39.
1943 "Diversity of Material Yielded up in European Melting Pot." *Musical America*, January, 1943. Reprinted as "Folk Song Research in Eastern Europe" in Suchoff 1976:33–42.

Bateson, Gregory
1958 *Naven.* 2d ed. Cambridge: Cambridge University Press. First published 1936.

Bayard, Samuel P.
1954 "Two Representative Tune Families of British Tradition." *Midwest Folklore* 4:13–34.

Becker, Judith
1980 *Traditional Music in Modern Java: Gamelan in a Changing Society.* Honolulu: The University Press of Hawaii.

Bee, Robert
1974 *Patterns and Processes.* New York: Macmillan.

Begg, Mirza Wahiduddin
1960 *The Holy Biography of Hazrat Khwaja Muinuddin Hasan Chishti, the Holy Saint of Ajmer.* Ajmer: M. W. Begg.

Behar, Cem
1987 "Charles Fonton." *Yuzyilda Turk Muzici, Pan Yayincilik* 18. (Turkish)

Beidelman, T. O.
1986 *Moral Imagination in Kaguru Modes of Thought.* Bloomington: Indiana University Press.

Beisele, Megan
1986 "How Hunter-Gatherers' Stories 'Make Sense': Semantics and Adaptation." *Cultural Anthropology* 1/2:157–70.

Belyayev, Viktor M.
1962 *Ocherki po istorii muziki narodov SSSR,* Vol. 1. [Essays on the History of the Music of the Soviet Peoples]. Moscow: Gosudarstvennoye Muzikal'noiy Izdatel'stvo. Translated Mark and Greta Slobin, *Central Asian Music.* Middletown, CT: Wesleyan University Press, 1975.
1965 "Folk Music and the History of Music." *Studia Musicologica* 7:19–23.

Bemba, Sylvain
1985 *50 ans de musique du Congo-Zaïre.* Paris: Présence Africaine.

Berque, Jacques
1972 *Egypt: Imperialism and Revolution.* Translated Jean Stewart. London: Faber and Faber. First published 1967.

Bhaduri, M. B.
1942 "Hindu Influence on Munda Songs." In J. P. Mills et al., eds., *Essays in Anthropology Presented to Rai Bahadur Sarat Chandra Roy.* Lucknow: Maxwell, pp. 256–60.

Bhatkhande, Vishnu Narayan
1951–57 *Hindustani Sangit Paddhati.* Hathras: Sangit Karyalay, 4 vols. (Hindi)

Bhattacharya, Jotin
1979 *Ustad Allauddin Khan and His Music.* Ahmedabad: B. S. Shah Prakashan.

Biernacka, Maria et al.
1981 Eds., *Etnografia Polski.* Vol. 2. Wrocław: Zaklad Narodowy im. Ossolińskich, and Polska Akademia Nauk.

Bin Dhurayl, 'Adnān
1969 *al-Mūsīqá fī Sūriyyah*. Damascus: Maṭābiʿ Alif Baʾ. (Arabic)
Bissoondialsingh, Smt. Tara
1976 "Indian Music in Trinidad." *Jyoti* 9/1–5.
Blacking, John
1977 "Some Problems of Theory and Method in the Study of Musical Change." *Yearbook of the International Folk Music Council* 9:1–26.
Blainville, Charles-Henri
1767 *Histoire générale, critique et philologique de la musique*. Paris: Pissot.
Blum, Stephen
1975 "Towards a Social History of Musicological Technique." *Ethnomusicology* 19:207–31.
1985 "Rousseau's Concept of *Sistême musical* and the Comparative Study of Tonalities in Nineteenth-Century France." *Journal of the American Musicological Society* 38:349–61.
Boas, Franz
1916 *Tsimshian Mythology*. Washington, D.C.: Government Printing Office. (Bureau of American Ethnology, Annual Report, 31)
Bohlman, Philip V.
1984 "Central European Jews in Israel: The Reurbanization of Musical Life in an Immigrant Culture." *Yearbook for Traditional Music* 16:67–83.
1985–86 "The Resurgence of Jewish Musical Life in an Urban German Community: Mannheim on the Eve of World War II." *Musica Judaica* 7/1:34–53.
1989 *"The Land Where Two Streams Flow": Music in the German-Jewish Community of Israel*. Urbana: University of Illinois Press.
1991 "Ethnomusicology's Challenge to the Canon, the Canon's Challenge to Ethnomusicology." Paper read at annual meeting, American Musicological Society, New Orleans. Revised version in Katherine A. Bergeron and Philip V. Bohlman, eds., *Disciplining Music: Musicology and Its Canons*. Chicago: The University of Chicago Press.
Bojko, V. H. and V. K. Borysenko
1980 "Spivvidnoshenni͡a tradycijnoho i novoho v suchasnomu vesilli." *Narodna Tvorchist' ta Etnohrafii͡a* 6:32–37.
Bose, N. K.
1941 "The Hindu Method of Tribal Absorption." *Science and Culture* 7:188–94.
Bourdieu, Pierre
1977 *Outline of a Theory of Practice*. Translated Richard Nice. Cambridge: Cambridge University Press. First published 1972.
Brahaspati, Kailashchandra Deva
1976 *Dhrupad aur Uskā Vikās*. Patna: Bihar-Rashtrabhasha Parishad.
Brăiloiu, Constantin
1949 "Le folklore musical." In *Musica aeterna*. Zurich: Metz, pp. 277–332. Reprinted in Brăiloiu, *Problèmes d'ethnomusicologie*. Geneva: Minkoff, 1973, pp. 63–118.

Bremer, Cora
1907 *The Chata Indians of Pearl River: An Outline of Their Customs and Beliefs*. New Orleans: Picayune Job Print.
Brhaspati, Acharya
1966 *Sangit Chintamani*. Hathras: Sangit Karyalay.
1969 "Muslim Influence on Venkatamakhi and His School." *Sangit Natak* 13:5–27.
Brown, Robert
1988 "T. Ranganathan (1925–87)." *Ethnomusicology* 32:275–78.
Bruner, Edward M.
1986 "Ethnography as Narrative." In Victor W. Turner and Edward M. Bruner, eds., *The Anthropology of Experience*. Urbana: University of Illinois Press, pp. 139–55.
Burke, Kenneth
1961 *Attitudes Toward History*. 2d rev. ed. Boston: Beacon Press. First published 1937.
Burszta, Józef
1980 "Kultura wsi okresu miedzywojennego." In Stefan Inglot, ed., *Historia chłopów polskich*. Vol. 3. Warsaw: Ludowa Spółdzielnia Wydawnicza, pp. 441–97.
Bushnell, David I., Jr.
1909 *The Choctaw of Bayou Lacomb, St. Tammany Parish, Louisiana*. Washington, D.C.: Government Printing Office. (Bureau of American Ethnology, Bulletin, 48)
Bystroń, Jan Stanislaw
1960 *Dzieje obyczajów w dawnej Polsce. Wiek XVI-XVII*. Vol. 2. Warsaw: Państwowy Instytut Wydawniczy.
Capwell, Charles
1986 "Musical Life in Nineteenth-Century Calcutta as a Component in the History of a Secondary Urban Center." *Asian Music* 18/1:139–63.
Carlile, James
1859 Ed., *Journal of a Voyage with Coolie Emigrants from Calcutta to Trinidad. By Captain and Mrs. Swinton, Late of the Ship 'Salsette'.* London: Alfred W. Bennett.
Cavanagh, Beverley
1985 "Algonkian Indian Hymnody: Conflicts in Valuation as Determinants of a Tradition." Paper presented at the 29th annual meeting of the Society for Ethnomusicology, Vancouver, Canada.
Chapman, Anne
1972 *Selk'Nam Chants of Tierra del Fuego*. New York: Folkways Records. Record album with notes, FE 4176.
1978 *Selk'Nam Chants of Tierra del Fuego, Argentina,* vol. 2. New York: Folkways Records. Record album with notes, FE 4179.
Chaube, Sushil Kumar
1977 *Saṅgīt ke Gharānō kī Carcā*. Lucknow: Uttar Pradesh Hindi Granth Academy.

Chaudhury, Vimalakant Roy

1975 *Bharatiya Sangeet Kosh.* New Delhi: Bharatiya Jnanpith.

Chepeliev, V. I. and O. H. Myroniuk

1979 "Propahanda muzychnoho mystetstva sil's'kymy kul'turno-osvitnimy zakladamy Ukrainy v 20-30-kh rokakh." *Narodna Tvorchist'ta Etnohrafiia* 5:30–36.

Christensen, Dieter

1988 Ed., *Yearbook for Traditional Music* 20. Special issue on the history of ethnomusicology and the 40-year development of the International Council for Traditional Music.

Clément, Catherine

1979 *L'opéra: ou, la défaite des femmes.* Paris: B. Grasset. English translation by Betsy Wing, *Opera, or, The Undoing of Women.* Minneapolis: University of Minnesota Press, 1988.

Clifford, James

1988 *The Predicament of Culture: Twentieth-Century Ethnography, Literature, and Art.* Cambridge, MA: Harvard University Press.

Collins, John

1976 "Ghanaian Highlife." *African Arts* 10/1:62–68.

Collins, John and Paul Richards

1982 "Popular Music in West Africa: Suggestions for an Interpretive Framework." In David Horn and Philip Tagg, eds., *Popular Music Perspectives.* Göteborg and Exeter: International Association for the Study of Popular Music, pp. 111–41.

Colvin, Thomas A.

1978 *Cane and Palmetto Basketry of the Choctaw of St. Tammany Parish, Lacombe, Louisiana,* ed. Melba Elfer Colvin. Mandeville, LA: Daybreak Publishing Company.

Comaroff, John L. and Jean Comaroff

1987 "The Madman and the Migrant: Work and Labor in the Historical Consciousness of a South African People." *American Ethnologist* 14/2:191–209.

Coplan, David B.

1985 *In Township Tonight! South Africa's Black City Music and Theatre.* London and New York: Longman.

1986 "Ideology and Tradition in South African Black Popular Theatre." *Journal of American Folklore* 99:151–75.

1987 "Eloquent Knowledge: Lesotho Migrants' Songs and the Anthropology of Experience." *American Ethnologist* 14/3:413–33.

Crawford, James M.

1978 *The Mobilian Trade Language.* Knoxville: The University of Tennessee Press.

Dąbrowska, Grażyna

1981 "Taniec ludowy." In Biernacka et al. 1981:285–326.

Dahlhaus, Carl

1977 "Historisches Bewußtsein und Ethnologie." *Die Musikforschung* 30:144–48.

1978 *Die Idee der absoluten Musik.* Kassel: Bärenreiter.

Dargah Quli Khan

1982 *Muraqqa-e-Delhi.* Ed. and translated Nur-ul Hasan Ansari. Delhi: Delhi University, Urdu Department. (Farsi, with Urdu translation)

Das, B. L.

1980 *Census of India 1971. Series 4, Bihar. Part V-A, Special Tables for Scheduled Castes and Scheduled Tribes.* Delhi: Manager of Publications.

Davies, Norman

1984 *God's Playground: A History of Poland.* Vol. 2. New York: Columbia University Press.

Densmore, Frances

1943 *A Search for Songs Among the Chitimacha Indians in Louisiana.* Washington, D.C.: Government Printing Office. (Bureau of American Ethnology, Bulletin, 133)

De Vale, Sue Carole

1986 "Fewkes, Walter Jesse." In H. Wiley Hitchcock and Stanley Sadie, eds., *The New Grove Dictionary of American Music.* New York: Macmillan, 2:115.

Doroshenko, Volodymyr

1959 *Prosvita, ïi zasnuvanni͡a i praci͡a.* Philadelphia: Moloda Prosvita im. Mytr. A. Sheptyts'koho.

Dournon, Geneviève

1980 *Inde: musique tribale du Bastar.* Paris: Le Chant du Monde. Record album with notes, LDX 74736.

Drechsel, Emanuel J.

1979 "Mobilian Jargon: Linguistic, Sociocultural, and Historical Aspects of an American Indian *Lingua Franca.*" Ph.D. dissertation, University of Wisconsin-Madison.

Drechsel, Emanuel J. and T. Haunani Makuakāne-Drechsel

1982 "An Ethnohistory of 19th Century Louisiana Indians." Unpublished manuscript prepared for the National Park Service.

Dupont-Ferrier, Gustave

1925 *Du Collège de Clermont au Lycée Louis le Grand (1563–1920). La vie quotidien d'un collège parisien pendant plus de trois cent cinquante ans.* Vol. 3. Paris: E. de Boccard.

During, Jean

1984 *La musique iranienne: tradition et évolution.* Paris: Éditions Recherche sur les Civilisations. (Bibliothèque iranienne, 29)

Eaton, Richard S.

1978 *The Sufis of Bijapur.* Princeton: Princeton University Press.

Ekwueme, Laz E. N.

1975 "African Musicological Investigation in a Culture Conscious Era." *African Music* 5/4:4–5.

Ellingson, Ter

ms. *The Discovery of Music: Transcription and the Search for Ethnomusicological Paradigms.*

Ellis, Catherine J.
1984 "Time Consciousness of Aboriginal Performers." In *Problems and Solutions: Occasional Essays in Musicology Presented to Alice M. Moyle*, ed. J. C. Kassler and J. Stubington. Sydney: Hale & Iremonger, pp. 149–85.
1985 *Aboriginal Music, Education for Living: Cross-cultural Experiences from South Australia*. St. Lucia, Queensland: University of Queensland Press.

Elschek, Oskár
1985 "Štýlové vrstvy a štýlové typy slovenskej l'udovej nástrojovej hudby." *Musicologia Slovaca* 10:7–46.

Elsner, Jürgen
1973 *Der Begriff des Maqām in Ägypten in Neuerer Zeit*. Leipzig: VEB Deutscher Verlag für Musik. (Beiträge zur musikwissenschaftlichen Forschung in der DDR, 5)

Elwin, Verrier
1939 *The Baiga*. London: John Murray.

Erlmann, Veit
1987 "African Popular Music in Durban, 1913–1939." Unpublished manuscript.

Fang Kun
1981 "A Discussion on Chinese National Musical Traditions." Translated Keith Pratt. *Asian Music* 12/2:3–11.

Farrer, Claire R.
1980 "Singing for Life: The Mescalero Apache Girls' Puberty Ceremony." In Charlotte J. Frisbie, ed., *Southwestern Indian Ritual Drama*. Albuquerque: University of New Mexico Press, pp. 125–59.

Feld, Steven
1984 "Sound Structure as Social Structure." *Ethnomusicology* 28:383–410.
1987 "Dialogic Editing: Interpreting How Kaluli Read Sound and Sentiment." *Cultural Anthropology* 2:190–210.

Fétis, François-Joseph
1874 *Biographie universelle des musiciens*. Vol. 3. Paris: Firmin, Didot.

Fuchs, Stephen
1973 *The Aboriginal Tribes of India*. New York: St. Martin's Press.

Garg, Lakshmi N.
1978 *Hamare Sangeet Ratna*. Hathras: Sangeet Karyalaya.

Gatschet, Albert S. and John R. Swanton
1932 *A Dictionary of the Atakapa Language Accompanied by Text Material*. Washington, D.C.: Government Printing Office. (Bureau of American Ethnology, Bulletin, 108)

Geertz, Clifford
1968 *Islam Observed*. Chicago: The University of Chicago Press.

Gennep, Arnold van
1960 *The Rites of Passage*. Translated Monika B. Vizedom and Gabri-

elle L. Caffee. Chicago: The University of Chicago Press. First published 1909.

al-Ghazali, Abu Hamid

1979 *Al Ghazali on Islamic Guidance.* Translated Muhammad Abul Qasem. Mangi (Malaysia): Universiti Kebangsaan.

Ghosh, Pradip Kumar

1982 "How Habu Dutta Influenced Acharya Allauddin." In Sisirkona Dhar Chowdhury, ed., *Special Issue on Acharya Alauddin Khan Saheb, Journal of The Department of Instrumental Music* (Rabindra Bharati University) 2:70–76.

Ghurye, G. S.

1943 *The Aborigines—"So-called"—and Their Future.* Poona: Gokhale Institute of Politics and Economics.

Giddens, Anthony

1981 "Agency, Institution, and Time-Space Analysis." In K. Knorr-Cetina and A. Cicourel, eds., *Advances in Social Theory and Methodology: Toward an Integration of Micro- and Macro-Sociologies.* Boston: Routledge and Kegan Paul, pp. 161–74.

1984 *The Constitution of Society.* Berkeley: University of California Press.

1987 *Social Theory and Modern Sociology.* Stanford: Stanford University Press.

Gilman, Benjamin I.

1909 "The Science of Exotic Music." *Science* 30:532–35.

Goffman, Erving

1959 *The Presentation of the Self in Everyday Life.* New York: Doubleday.

Gosvami, O.

1957 *The Story of Indian Music.* Bombay: Asia Publishing House.

Gramophone Company of India

n.d. *Ustad Ali Akbar Khan and Pandit Ravi Shankar with Ustad Alla Rakha at San Francisco.* The Gramophone Company of India. Record album no. ECSD 41516.

n.d. *Great Master, Great Music: Acharya Allauddin Khan.* The Gramophone Company of India. Record album no. ECLP 2757.

Gramsci, Antonio

1971 *Selections from the Prison Notebooks of Antonio Gramsci.* New York: International Publishers

Gregor, Thomas

1977 *Mehinaku. The Drama of Everyday Life in a Brazilian Indian Village.* Chicago: The University of Chicago Press.

Gregory, Hiram F.

1977 "Jena Band of Louisiana Choctaw." *American Indian Journal* 3/2:2–11.

Guma, S. M.

1967 *The Form, Content, and Technique of Traditional Literature in Southern Sotho.* Pretoria: van Schaik.

Gushee, Lawrence
1981 "Lester Young's 'Shoeshine Boy'." In Daniel Heartz and Bonnie Wade, eds., *Report of the Twelth Congress Berkeley 1977*. International Musicological Society. Kassel: Bärenreiter, pp. 151–69.

Haas, Mary
1950 *Tunica Texts*. Berkeley: University of California Press.
1953 *Tunica Dictionary*. Berkeley: University of California Press. (University of California Publications in Linguistics)

Habib, Mohammad
1950 "Chishti Mystics Records of the Sultanate Period." *Medieval India Quarterly*, 1–42.

Haidar Rizvi, S. N.
1941 "Music in Muslim India." *Islamic Culture* 15:331–40.

al-Ḥalaqah
1964 *Al-Ḥalaqah al-Thāniyah li Baḥth al-Mūsīqá al-ʿArabiyyah*. Cairo: al-Majlis al-Aʿlá li Riʿāyat al-Fūnūn wa al-Ādāb wa al-ʿUlūm al-ʿIjtimāʿiyyah.

Hampton, Barbara L.
1980 "A Revised Analytical Approach to Musical Processes in Urban Africa." *African Urban Studies* 6:1–16.
1983 "Toward a Theory of Transformation in African Music." In Pearl T. Robinson and Elliott P. Skinner, eds., *Transformation and Resiliency in Africa, as Seen by Afro-American Scholars*. Washington, D.C.: Howard University Press, pp. 211–29.

Hansen, Kathryn
1987 "Nikhil Banerjee (1931–1986): A Personal Tribute." *Bansuri* 4:2–7.

Harasymczuk, Roman Wlodzimierz
1939 *Tańce huculskie*. Lwów: Nakładem Towarzystwa Ludoznawczego.

Hardy, Peter
1958 "Islam in Medieval India." In William Theodore de Bary, ed., *Sources of Indian Tradition*. New York: Columbia University Press, pp. 367–528.

Harms, Robert W.
1983 "The Wars of August: Diagonal Narrative in African History." *American Historical Review* 88:809–34.

Harrison, Frank
1973 Ed., *Time, Place and Music: An Anthology of Ethnomusicological Observation c. 1550 to c. 1800*. Amsterdam: Frits Knuf. (Source Materials and Studies in Ethnomusicology, 1)

Hebdige, Dick
1985 *Subculture: The Meaning of Style*. London: Methuen.

el-Hefni, Mahmoud
1956 *Aegyptische Musik von Einst bis Heute*. Cairo: Das Home Komitee für Musik.

Herndon, Marcia
1974 "Analysis: The Herding of Sacred Cows?" *Ethnomusicology* 18:219–62.

Herrmann, Wilhelm
1954 *Musizieren um des Musizierens Willen: 125 Jahre Mannheimer Liebhaber-Orchester.* Mannheim: Kessler.

Hertzberg, Hazel W.
1971 *The Search for an American Indian Identity: Modern Pan-Indian Movements.* Syracuse: Syracuse University Press.

Hill, Jonathan D.
1988 "Introduction: Myth and History." In Jonathan D. Hill, ed., *Rethinking History and Myth: Indigenous South American Perspectives on the Past.* Urbana: University of Illinois Press, pp. 1–19.

Himka, John-Paul
1979 "Priests and Peasants: The Greek Catholic Pastor and the Ukrainian National Movement in Austria, 1867–1900." *Canadian Slavonic Review* 21/1:1–14.
1984 "The Greek Catholic Church and Nation-Building, 1772–1918." *Harvard Ukrainian Studies* 8:426–52.

Hnatiuk, Volodymyr
1905 *Kolomyjky.* Vol. 1. L'viv: Naukova Tovarystvo im. Shevchenka. (Etnografichnyj Zbirnik, 17)

Hobsbawm, Eric and Terence Ranger
1983 Eds., *The Invention of Tradition.* Cambridge: Cambridge University Press.

Hoffmann, Rev. John with Rev. Arthur van Emelene and Jesuit Missionaries
1950 *Encyclopaedia Mundarica.* Patna: Government Printing Office.

Hornbostel, Erich Moritz von
1905 "Die Probleme der vergleichenden Musikwissenschaft." *Zeitschrift der Internationalen Musikgesellschaft* 7:85–97; reprinted with English translation in Klaus P. Wachsmann, Hans-Peter Reinecke, and Dieter Christensen, eds., *Hornbostel Opera Omnia.* Vol. 1. The Hague: Martinus Nijhoff, 1975, pp. 247–70.
1913 "Melodie und Skala." *Jahrbuch der Musikbibliothek Peters* 20:11–23.
1933 "Zum Kongress für arabische Musik-Kairo 1932." *Zeitschrift für Vergleichende Musikwissenschaft* 1:16–17.

Howard, James H.
1955 "The Pan-Indian Culture of Oklahoma." *The Scientific Monthly* 81/5:215–20.
1983 "Pan-Indianism in Native American Music and Dance." *Ethnomusicology* 27:71–82.

Howard, James H. and Victoria Lindsay Levine
1990 *Choctaw Music and Dance.* Norman: The University of Oklahoma Press.

Hrysha, Onys'ko
1899 "Vesil'la u Hadi͡ats'komu poviti, u Poltavshchyni." *Materyi͡aly Ukrains'ko-Rus'koi Etnol'ogii* 1:111–55.

Hughes, Arnold and Ronald Cohen
1979 "An Emerging Nigerian Working-Class: The Lagos Experience." In P. Gutkind, R. Cohen, and J. Copans, eds., *African Labour History*. London: Sage Publications, pp. 31–55.
al-Hujwīrī, ʿAli ibn Uthman
1970 *The "Kashf al-Mahjūb," the Oldest Persian Treatise on Sufism by al-Hujwīrī*. Translated R. A. Nicholson. London: Luzac. First published 1911. (Gibb Memorial Series, 17)
Husaini, Syed Shah Khusro
1970 "Bund Samāʿ (or Closed Audition)." *Islamic Culture* 44:177–85.
Hymes, Dell
1981 "Breakthrough into Performance." In D. Hymes, *"In vain I tried to tell you": Essays in Native American Ethnopoetics*. Philadelphia: University of Pennsylvania Press, pp. 79–141.
Idris Khan, Hakim Muhammad
1973 *Risala-e-Samaʿ aur Naghmat-e-Samaʿ*. Bareilly: Maktaba Ala Hazrat Saudagaran. (Farsi, Urdu)
Imam Hakim Mohammed Karam
1925 *Ma'dan-ul-Mausiqi*. Lucknow: Hindustani Press. (Urdu)
1959 "Melody through the Centuries." Chapter 1 of *Ma'dan-ul-Mausiqi*. Translated Govind Vidyarthi, *Sangit Natak Akademi Bulletin* 11/12:13–26, 30.
Inden, Ronald B.
1976 *Marriage and Rank in Bengali Culture*. Berkeley: University of California Press.
Iqtirāḥ
1935 "Iqtirāḥ Ḥawla Idhā'at Isṭiwānāt al-Mu'tamar." *al-Mūsīqá* 10:38–39.
Joyner, Charles
1975 "A Model for the Analysis of Folklore Performance in Historical Context." *Journal of American Folklore* 88:254–65.
Kaden, Christian
1984 *Musiksoziologie*. Berlin: Verlag Neue Musik.
Kartomi, Margaret J.
1981 "The Processes and Results of Musical Culture Contact: A Discussion of Terminology and Concepts." *Ethnomusicology* 25:227–49.
Kaufmann, Walter
1968 *The Ragas of North India*. Bloomington: Indiana University Press.
Keil, Charles
1966–67 "Field Research Notes on Yoruba Popular Music in Ibadan and Lagos, Nigeria." Unpublished manuscript.
1985 "People's Music Comparatively: Style and Stereotype, Class and Hegemony." *Dialectical Anthropology* 10:119–30.
al-Khūlī, Samḥah
1974 "al-Duktūr Maḥmūd Ahmad al-Ḥifnī: Dhikrayāt wa Khawāṭir." *al-Majallah al-Mūsīqiyyah* 1 (January):8–9. (Arabic)

Kieniewicz, Stefan

1969 *The Emancipation of the Polish Peasantry*. Chicago: The University of Chicago Press.

Kiesewetter, Raphael Georg

1842 *Die Musik der Araber*. Leipzig: Breitkopf & Härtel.

Kingsbury, Henry

1988 *Music, Talent, and Performance: A Conservatory Cultural System*. Philadelphia: Temple University Press.

KMMʿA

1933 *Kitāb Muʾtamar al-Mūsīqá al-ʿArabiyyah*. Cairo: al-Maṭbaʿah al-Amīriyyah bil-Qāhirah. (Arabic)

Kniffen, Fred B., Hiram F. Gregory, and George A. Stokes

1987 *The Historic Indian Tribes of Louisiana from 1542 to the Present*. Baton Rouge: Louisiana State University Press.

Knight, Roderic

1983 *Tribal Music of India: The Muria and Maria Gonds of Madhya Pradesh*. New York: Folkways Records. (Ethnic Folkways Library, record album with notes, FE 4028)

Kolberg, Oskar

1964a *Łęczyckie*. Kraków: Polskie Wydawnictwo Muzyczne. (Dzieła wszystkie, 22). First published 1889.

1964b *Chełmskie*. Kraków: Polskie Wydawnictwo Myzyczne. (Dzieła wszystkie, 33). First published 1890.

1964c *Przemyskie*. Kraków: Polskie Wydawnictwo Myzyczne. (Dzieła wszystkie, 35). First published 1891.

Kolenda, Pauline

1978 *Caste in Contemporary India: Beyond Organic Solidarity*. Menlo Park, CA: Benjamin Cummings.

Kolessa, Filaret

1910a *Melodii͡a ukrains'kykh narodnikh dum*. Vol. 1. L'viv: Naukova Tovarystvo im. Shevchenka. (Materyi͡aly Ukrains'ko-Rus'koi Etnol'ogii, 13)

1910b "Pohli͡ad na teperishnyj stan pisennoi tvorchosty ukrains'koho narodu." In *Pershyj Ukrains'kyj Pros'vitno-Ekonomichnyj Kongres, Protokoly i Referaty*. L'viv: Tovarystvo Pros'vita, pp. 226–38.

1913 *Melodii͡a ukrains'kykh narodnikh dum*. Vol. 2. L'viv: Naukova Tovarystvo im. Shevchenka. (Materyi͡aly Ukrains'ko-Rus'koi Etnol'ogii, 14)

Kopernicki, I.

1964 "Przedmowa." In Kolberg 1964c:i–xx. First published 1891.

Kotula, Franciszek

1979 *Muzykanty*. Warsaw: Ludowa Spółdzielnia Wydawnicza.

Krawchenko, Bohdan

1985 *Social Change and National Consciousness in Twentieth Century Ukraine*. Edmonton: Canadian Institute of Ukrainian Studies, University of Alberta.

Kryni͡akevych, Ivan

1910 "Narodni biblioteky." In *Pershyj Ukrains'kyj Pros'vitno-Ekono-*

michnyj Kongres, Protokoly i Referaty. L'viv: Tovarystvo Pros'vita, pp. 201–208.

Kṣetramohana Śarmmā [Gosvāmi]
1879 *saṅgītasāra.* 2d ed. Calcutta. (Bengali)

Kumar, Kuldeep
1984 "Ajmad Challenges Ravi Shankar to 'Jugal-bandi'." *Sunday Observer,* September 23–29, pp. 1–2.

Kvitka, Klyment
1924 *Professional'ni narodni pevtsi i muzikanty na Ukrayni: prohrama dlya doslidu yikh diyal'nosti ta nobutu.* Kiev: Ukrains'koi Akademii Nauk.

La Guerre, John
1974 Ed., *Calcutta to Caroni: The East Indians of Trinidad.* Port of Spain, Trinidad: Longman Caribbean.

Lachmann, Robert
1929 *Musik des Orients.* Breslau: Jedermanns Bücherei.
1935 "Musiksysteme und Musikauffassung." *Zeitschrift für Vergleichende Musikwissenschaft* 3:1–23.

Lachmann, Robert and Mahmud el-Hefny
1931 *Ja'qūb Ishāk al-Kindī Risālā fī Hubr Tā'līf al-Alhān.* Leipzig: F. Kistner & C. F. W. Siegel. (Arabic text with German translation)

Landgarten, Ira
1979 "Ravi Shankar: Genius of the Sitar." *Frets,* November, pp. 28–34.
1987 " 'First My Music Then Everything Else': An Interview with Nikhil Banerjee." *Bansuri* 4:8–26.

Lane, Edward
1973 *An Account of the Manners and Customs of the Modern Egyptians.* 5th ed. New York: Dover. First published 1860 (1st edition 1836).

Larlham, Peter
1985 *Black Theatre, Dance, and Ritual in South Africa.* Ann Arbor: U.M.I. Press.

Lawrence, Bruce B.
1983 "The Early Chishti Approach to Samaʿ." *Journal of the American Academy of Religion: Thematic Studies* 50/1:93–109.

Lee, Dorothy Sara
1979 *Native North American Music and Oral Data: A Catalogue of Sound Recordings, 1893–1976.* Bloomington: Indiana University Press.

Leisiö, Timo
1983 "Surface and Deep Structure in Music—An Expedition into Finnish Music Culture." *Suomen Antropologi,* 1983, no. 4:198–208.

Leppert, Richard and Susan McClary
1987 Eds., *Music and Society: The Politics of Composition, Performance and Reception.* Cambridge: Cambridge University Press.

Lestrade, G. P.
1937 "Traditional Literature." In Isaac Schapera, ed., *The Bantu-*

Speaking Tribes of South Africa. London: Routledge and Kegan Paul.

Levine, Victoria Lindsay
1990 "Choctaw Indian Musical Cultures in the Twentieth Century." Ph.D. dissertation, University of Illinois at Urbana-Champaign.

Lévi-Strauss, Claude
1969 *The Raw and the Cooked. Introduction to a Science of Mythology*. Translated John and Doreen Weightman. New York: Harper and Row. First published 1964.

Linette, Boguslaw
1978 "Folklor muzyczny w tradycjach Grodziska Dolnego w rzeszowskiego." In Zbigniew Jasiewicz, ed., *Tradycja i przemiana: Studia nad dziejami i wspolczesną kulturą ludową*. Poznań: Wydawnictwo Naukowe Uniwersytetu im. Adama Mieckiewicza, pp. 175–86.

Lloyd, Peter C.
1974 *Power and Independence: Urban Africans' Perceptions of Social Inequality*. London: Routledge and Kegan Paul.

Low, John
1982 "A History of Kenya Guitar Music: 1945–1980." *African Music* 6/2:17–36.

Lowenthal, David
1972 *West Indian Societies*. Oxford: Oxford University Press.

Lynch, Jeremiah
1890 *Egyptian Sketches*. London: Edward Arnold.

Lytvynova-Barosh, P.
1900 "Vesil'ni obri͡ady izvychai u seli zemliantsi Hlukhivs'koho pov. u chernykhivshchyni." *Materyi͡aly Ukrains'ko-Rus'koi Etnol'o͡gii* 3:70–173.

MacAloon, John J.
1984 "Introduction: Cultural Performances, Culture Theory." In J. J. MacAloon, ed., *Rite, Drama, Festival, Spectacle: Rehearsals toward a Theory of Cultural Performance*. Philadelphia: Institute for the Study of Human Issues, pp. 1–15.

Maceda, José
1979 "A Search for an Old and a New Music in Southeast Asia." *Acta Musicologica* 51:160–68.

Mackay, Ian
1964 *Broadcasting in Nigeria*. Ibadan: Ibadan University Press.

Malcher, José M. Gama (organizador)
1961 *Mapa Etnografico do Brasil*. Rio de Janeiro: Departamento de Imprensa Nacional.

Man, E. G.
1983 *Sonthalia and the Sonthals*. Delhi: Mittal Publications. First published 1857.

Mansī, Aḥmad Abū al-Khiḍr
1965 *al-Aghānī wa al-Mūsīqá al-Sharqiyyah: bayna al-Qadīm wa al-Jadīd*. Cairo: Dār al-ʿArab Li-al-Bustānī.

Marcus, George E. and Michael M. J. Fischer
1986 *Anthropology as Cultural Critique.* Chicago: The University of Chicago Press.

Marx, Karl
1963 *The 18th Brumaire of Louis Bonaparte.* New York: New World Paperbacks. First published 1869.

Mathur, K. S.
1972 "Tribe in India: A Problem of Identification and Integration." In K. Suresh Singh, ed., *Tribal Situation in India: Proceedings of a Seminar.* Simla: Indian Institute of Advanced Study, pp. 457–61.

Merriam, Alan P.
1955 "The Use of Music in the Study of a Problem of Acculturation." *American Anthropologist* 57:28–34.
1963 "The Purposes of Ethnomusicology: An Anthropological View." *Ethnomusicology* 7:206–13.
1964 *The Anthropology of Music.* Evanston: Northwestern University Press.
1967 *Ethnomusicology of the Flathead Indians.* Chicago: Aldine. (Viking Fund Publications in Anthropology, 44)

Michaud, Joseph
1856 Ed., *Biographie universelle ancienne et moderne.* 2d ed. Vol. 14. Paris: Mme. C. Desplaces.

Miller, Philip L.
1969 "Phonograph and Recorded Music." In Willi Apel, ed., *Harvard Dictionary of Music.* 2d ed. Cambridge, MA: Harvard University Press, pp. 665–68.

Miłosz, Czesław
1968 *Native Realm: A Search for Self-Definition.* Translated Catherine S. Leach. New York: Doubleday. First published 1958.

Mirza, Muhammad Wahid
1974 *The Life and Works of Amir Khusrau.* Delhi: Idarah-i-Adabiyat-i-Delli.

Mitra, S. C.
1921 "On the Karma Dharma Festival of Northern Bihar and Its Munda Analogues." *Journal of the Department of Letters* (University of Calcutta) 4:281–304.

Morton, Sarah E.
1916 Ed., *John Morton of Trinidad. Pioneer Missionary of the Presbyterian Church in Canada to the East Indians in the British West Indies. Journals, Letters and Papers.* Toronto: Westminster Company.

Mosse, George L.
1985 *German Jews beyond Judaism.* Bloomington: Indiana University Press, and Cincinnati: Hebrew Union College Press.

Mukhopādhyāya, Dilīpakumāra
1980 *viṣṇupura gharāṇā.* Reprint of 1963 edition [?]. Calcutta: Book-land. (Bengali)

Myers, Helen

1984 "Felicity, Trinidad: The Musical Portrait of a Hindu Village." Ph.D. dissertation, University of Edinburgh.

Naghmat

n.d. *Naghmat-e-Samā*ᶜ. n.p. (Farsi and Urdu)

Naipaul, V. S.

1961 *A House for Mr. Biswas*. London: Andre Deutsch.

1968 *An Area of Darkness*. Harmondsworth, Middlesex: Penguin Books.

1977 *India: A Wounded Civilization*. New York: Alfred A. Knopf.

Narkiewicz, Olga A.

1976 *The Green Flag: Polish Populist Politics 1867–1970*. Totowa, N.J.: Rowman and Littlefield.

Neitzel, Stuart

n.d. Unpublished field notes and letter to Frank Speck. American Philosophical Society Library, Philadelphia.

Nettl, Bruno

1954 *North American Indian Musical Styles*. Philadelphia: American Folklore Society. (Memoirs of the American Folklore Society, 45)

1978a "Some Aspects of the History of World Music in the Twentieth Century: Questions, Problems, and Concepts." *Ethnomusicology* 22:123–36.

1978b *An Historical Album of Blackfoot Indian Music*. New York: Folkways Records and Service Corp. Record album with notes, FES 34001.

1983 *The Study of Ethnomusicology: Twenty-nine Issues and Concepts*. Urbana: University of Illinois Press.

1984a "Western Musical Values and the Character of Ethnomusicology." *The World of Music* 24/1:29–41.

1984b "In Honor of Our Principal Teachers." *Ethnomusicology* 28:173–85.

1985 *The Western Impact on World Music: Change, Adaptation, and Survival*. New York: Schirmer Books.

1989a *Blackfoot Musical Thought: Comparative Perspectives*. Kent, Ohio: Kent State University Press.

1989b "Mozart and the Ethnomusicological Study of Western Music." *Yearbook for Traditional Music* 21:1–16.

Nettl, Bruno and Philip V. Bohlman

1991 Eds., *Comparative Musicology and Anthropology of Music: Essays on the History of Ethnomusicology*. Chicago: The University of Chicago Press.

Neubauer, Eckhard

1985 "Der Essai sur la musique orientale von Charles Fonton (Textteil)." *Zeitschrift für Geschichte der Arabisch-Islamischen Wissenschaften* 2:277–324.

1986 "Der Essai sur la musique orientale von Charles Fonton (Einleitung und Indices)." *Zeitschrift für Geschichte der Arabisch-Islamischen Wissenschaften* 3:335–76.

Neuman, Daniel M.

1976 "Toward an Ethnomusicology of Culture Change in Asia." *Asian Music* 7/2:1–5.

1978 "*Gharanas:* The Rise of Musical 'Houses' in Delhi and Neighboring Cities." In B. Nettl, ed., *Eight Urban Musical Cultures.* Urbana: University of Illinois Press, pp. 186–222.

1980 *The Life of Music in North India: The Organization of an Artistic Tradition.* Detroit: Wayne State University Press.

1984 "The Ecology of Indian Music in North America." *Bansuri* 1:9–15.

Nisbet, Robert A.

1969 *Social Change and History: Aspects of the Western Theory of Development.* New York: Oxford University Press.

Nizami, Khaliq Ahmad

1957 "Some Aspects of Khanqah Life in Medieval India." *Studia Islamica* 8:51–70.

1958 *Tarikh-e-Mashaikh-e Chisht.* Delhi. (Urdu)

1974 *Some Aspects of Religion and Politics in India during the Thirteenth Century.* 2d ed. Delhi: Idara-e-Adabiyat-e-Delli.

Nizami, Kwaja Hasan Sani, Dehlavi

1973 *Tazkara-e-Khusravi.* New Delhi: Kwaja Aulad Kitabghar. (Farsi, Urdu)

Nketia, J. H. Kwabena

1981 "The Juncture of the Social and the Musical: The Methodology of Cultural Analysis." *The World of Music* 23/2:22–35.

Noll, William

1986 "Peasant Music Ensembles in Poland: A Culture History." Ph.D. dissertation, University of Washington.

Northup, Solomon

1968 *Twelve Years a Slave,* Ed. Sue Eakin and Joseph Logsdon. Baton Rouge: Louisiana State University Press. First published 1853.

Östör, Ákos

1984 *Culture and Power: Legend, Ritual, Bazaar and Rebellion in a Bengali Society.* New Delhi: Sage Publications.

Owens, Naomi

1969 "Two North Indian Musical Gharanas." M.A. Thesis, University of Chicago, Department of Anthropology.

Parmar, Shyam

1977 "Utilising Folk Music in Mass Media." *Sangeet Natak* 46:22–31.

Parmasad, K. V.

1973 "By the Light of a Deya." In David Lowenthal and Lambros Comitas, eds., *The Aftermath of Sovereignty: West Indian Perspectives.* Garden City, NY: Anchor Books.

Parry, C. Hubert H.

1899 *The Evolution of the Art of Music.* New York: D. Appleton.

Peel, J. D. Y.
1984 "Making History: The Past in the Ijesha Present." *Man* n.s. 19:111–32.

Peña, Manuel
1985 "From *Ranchero* to *Jaitón:* Ethnicity and Class in a Texas-Mexican Music (Two Styles in the Form of a Pair)." *Ethnomusicology* 29:29–55.

Peterson, John H., Jr.
1975 "Louisiana Choctaw Life at the End of the Nineteenth Century." In Charles Hudson, ed., *Four Centuries of Southern Indians.* Athens: University of Georgia Press, pp. 101–13.

Poladian, Sirvart
1972 "Komitas Vardapet and His Contribution to Ethnomusicology." *Ethnomusicology* 16:82–97.

Powers, Harold S.
1979 "Classical Music, Cultural Roots, and Colonial Rule: An Indic Musicologist Looks at the Muslim World." *Asian Music* 12/1:5–39.
1980 "India, Subcontinent of, I. The Region, Its Music and Music History." In Stanley Sadie, ed., *The New Grove Dictionary of Music and Musicians.* London: Macmillan, 9:69–91

Powers, William K.
1980 "Oglala Song Terminology." In *Selected Reports in Ethnomusicology* 3/2:23–41.

Pratt, Mary Louise
1986 "Fieldwork in Common Places." In James Clifford and George E. Marcus, eds., *Writing Culture: The Poetics and Politics of Ethnography.* Berkeley: University of California Press, pp. 27–50.

Pratt, Waldo Selden
1907 *The History of Music: A Handbook and Guide for Students.* New York: G. Schirmer.

Qureshi, Regula Burckhardt
1986 *Sufi Music of India and Pakistan: Sound, Context and Meaning in Qawwali.* Cambridge: Cambridge University Press. (Cambridge Studies in Ethnomusicology)

Racy, Ali Jihad
1981 "Music in Contemporary Cairo: A Comparative Overview." *Asian Music* 13/1:4–26.
1983 "Music in Nineteenth-Century Egypt: An Historical Sketch." *Selected Reports in Ethnomusicology* 4:157–79.

Ramaya, Narsaloo
1974 "How 'Bala Joban' Changed the Song in Our Hearts." *Trinidad Guardian,* January 22, p. 4.

Ranger, Terence O.
1975 *Dance and Society in Eastern Africa, 1890–1970.* London: Heinemann.

1983 "The Invention of Tradition in Colonial Africa." In Hobsbawm and Ranger 1983:211–62.

Rāycaudhurī, Bimalākānta

1984 *bhāratīya saṅgītakoṣa.* 2d printing, with revised and enlarged list of *gharānās* by Jayantakumar Mukhopadhyay. Calcutta: Imdadkhani School of Sitar. (Bengali)

Recueil

1934 *Recueil des Travaux du Congrès de Musique Arabe.* Cairo: Imprimerie nationale, Boulac.

Redfield, Robert and Milton Singer

1962 "The Cultural Role of Cities." In Margaret Park Redfield, ed., *Human Nature and the Study of Society: The Papers of Robert Redfield.* Chicago: The University of Chicago Press, 1:326–50. First published 1954.

Rhodes, Willard

1958 "A Study of Musical Diffusion Based on the Wandering of the Opening Peyote Melody." *Journal of the International Folk Music Council* 10:42–49.

Ringer, Alexander L.

1965 "On the Question of Exoticism in 19th Century Music." *Studia Musicologica* 7:115–23.

Rizq, Qisṭandī

1936 *al-Mūsīqá al-Sharqiyyah wa al-Ghinā' al-ʿArabī.* Cairo: al-Maṭbaʿah al-ʿAṣriyyah.

Roberts, John Storm

1972 *Black Music of Two Worlds.* New York: Praeger.

Robertson, Carol E.

1976 "*Tayil* as Category and Communication among the Argentine Mapuche: A Methodological Suggestion." *Yearbook of the International Folk Music Council* 8:35–52.

1979 " 'Pulling the Ancestors': Performance Practice and Praxis in Mapuche Ordering." *Ethnomusicology* 23:395–416.

1987 "Power and Gender in the Musical Experiences of Women." In E. Koskoff, ed., *Women and Music in Cross-cultural Perspective.* Westport, CT: Greenwood Press, pp. 225–44.

Rockwell, John

1981 "Ravi Shankar Brings His Sitar to the Philharmonic." *New York Times,* April 19.

Rothschild, Joseph

1974 *East Central Europe Between the Two World Wars.* Seattle: University of Washington Press. (A History of East Central Europe, 9)

Rouanet, Jules

1922 "La musique arabe et la magie." *Encyclopédie de la Musique et Dictionnaire du Conservatoire.* Paris: Librairie Delagrave, Part I, 5:2676–812.

Roy, Sarat Chandra
1912 *The Mundas and Their Country.* Calcutta: Kuntaline Press.
1915 *The Oraon of Chota Nagpur: Their History, Economic Life, and Social Organization.* Ranchi: City Bar Library.

Royce, Anya Peterson
1982 *Ethnic Identity: Strategies of Diversity.* Bloomington: Indiana University Press.

Roychoudhury, M. L.
1957 "Music in Islam." *Journal of the Asiatic Society of Bengal* 13, part 2:43–102.

Russell, R. V. and Hira Lal
1975 *The Tribes and Castes of the Central Provinces of India.* Vol. 3. Delhi: Cosmos. First published 1916.

Ryś, Józef
1972 *Wesele łąckie.* Rzeszów: Muzeum Okregowe w Rzeszowie.

Sachchidananda
1979 *The Changing Munda.* New Delhi: Concept Publishing Co.

Sachs, Curt
1932 "Kongress der Arabischen Musik zu Kairo 1932." *Zeitschrift für Musikwissenschaft* 14:448–49.
1933 "Zum Kongress für Arabischen Musik-Kairo 1932: Die Marokkaner." *Zeitschrift für Vergleichende Musikwissenschaft* 1:17–18.
1965 *The Wellsprings of Music.* Ed. Jaap Kunst. New York: McGraw-Hill.

Sadie, Stanley
1984 Ed., *The New Grove Dictionary of Musical Instruments.* London: Macmillan, 3 vols.

Sahlins, Marshall
1981 *Historical Metaphors and Mythical Realities: Structure in the Early History of the Sandwich Islands Kingdom.* Ann Arbor: University of Michigan Press.
1985 *Islands of History.* Chicago: The University of Chicago Press.

Said, Edward
1978 *Orientalism.* New York: Random House.

Salomon, Frank L.
1981 "Killing the Yumbo: A Ritual Drama of Northern Quito." In Norman E. Whitten, Jr., ed., *Cultural Transformations and Ethnicity in Modern Equador.* Urbana: University of Illinois Press.

Salvador-Daniel, Francesco
1915 *The Music and Musical Instruments of the Arab.* Ed. H. G. Farmer. London: William Reeves.

Sanders, Irwin T.
1958 "The Peasantries of Eastern Europe." In Irwin T. Sanders, ed., *Collectivization of Agriculture in Eastern Europe.* Lexington: University of Kentucky Press, pp. 24–48.

Sarmadee, Shahab
1975 "Musical Genius of Amir Khusrau." In *Amir Khusrau Memorial*

Volume. New Delhi: Government of India, Publications Division, pp. 33–62.

Sarna, Ks. Władysława

1896 "Obrzędy weselne w Jaszczwi." *Lud* 2:236–51.

Scaff, Lawrence A.

1988 "Culture, Philosophy and Politics: The Formation of the Sociocultural Sciences in German." *History of the Human Sciences* 1:221–43.

Schaedel, Richard P.

1979 "From Homogenization to Heterogenization in Lima, Peru." *Urban Anthropology* 8:399–420.

Schaeffner, André

1936 *Origine des instruments de musique. Introduction ethnologique à l'histoire de la musique instrumentale*. Paris: Payot.

Schafer, R. Murray

1980 *The Tuning of the World: Toward a Theory of Soundscape Design*. Philadelphia: University of Pennsylvania Press.

Scheub, Harold

1975 *The Xhosa Ntsomi*. Oxford: Clarendon Press.

1984 "A Review of African Oral Traditions and Literature." ACLS/SSRC Overview Paper, presented to the African Studies Association, annual meeting, Los Angeles, October 25–28.

Schupman, Edwin, Jr.

1984 "Current Musical Practices of the Creek Indians as Examined through the Green Corn Ceremonies of the Tulsa Cedar River and Fish Pond Stomp Grounds." M.A. thesis, Miami University, Oxford, Ohio.

Schwartzman, Stephen

1988 "The Panara of the Xingu National Park." Ph.D. dissertation, University of Chicago.

Seeger, Anthony

1981 *Nature and Society in Central Brazil: The Suyá Indians of Mato Grosso*. Cambridge, MA: Harvard University Press.

1987 *Why Suyá Sing: A Musical Anthropology of an Amazonian People*. Cambridge, Eng.: Cambridge University Press. (Cambridge Studies in Ethnomusicology)

ms. "Thieves, Myths and History." Paper to appear in a volume commemorating Karl von den Steinen's visit to the Xingu in 1884, ed. Vera Penteado Coelho. São Paulo: University of São Paulo Press.

Seeger, Anthony and Louise S. Spear

1987 Eds., *Early Field Recordings. A Catalogue of Cylinder Collections at the Indiana University Archives of Traditional Music*. Bloomington: Indiana University Press.

Seeger, Charles

1939a "Systematic and Historical Orientations in Musicology." *Acta Musicologica* 11:121–28.

1939b "Grass Roots for American Composers." *Modern Music* 16:143–49.
1951 "Systematic Musicology: Viewpoints, Orientations and Methods." *Journal of the American Musicological Society* 4:240–48.
1953 "Folk Music in the Schools of a Highly Industrialized Society." *Journal of the International Folk Music Council* 5:40–44. Reprinted in Seeger 1977:330–34.
1977 *Studies in Musicology, 1935–1975.* Berkeley: University of California Press.

Shankar, Ravi
n.d. *Ravi Shankar: Raga Parameshwari.* Capitol Records. Record album no. SP-10561.
1968 *My Music, My Life.* New York: Simon and Schuster.
1982 *Ravi Shankar/Zubin Mehta, Shankar: Raga-Mala (Sitar Concerto No. 2).* Angel Records. Record album no. DS-37935.
1986 *Pandit Ravi Shankar.* Paris: OCORA. Compact disk, Ocora C 558674.

Shelemay, Kay Kaufman
1978 "A Quarter-century in the Life of a Falasha Prayer." *Yearbook of the International Folk Music Council* 10:83–108.

Shepherd, John
1982 "A Theoretical Model for the Sociomusicological Analysis of Popular Musics." *Popular Music* 2:145–78.

Sherzer, Joel F.
1977 "Kuna *Ikala:* Literature in San Blas." In Richard Bauman, ed., *Verbal Art as Performance.* Rowley, MA: Newbury House, pp. 133–50.

Shubravs'ka, M. M. and A. I. Ivanyts'kyj
1982 *Vesil'ni pisni.* Kiev: Naukova Dumka.

Sibley, John
1852 "Historical Sketches of the Several Indian Tribes in Louisiana, South of the Arkansas River, and Between the Mississippi and River Grand." Annals of Congress; 9th Congress, 2nd Session, 1806–1807.

Sijzi, Amir Hasan 'Ala
1884 Comp., *Fawa'id-ul-Fu'ad: Conversations of Shaikh Nizamuddin Auliya.* Lucknow: Nawal Kishore Press.

Singh, Kumar Suresh
1966 *Dust Storm and the Hanging Mist.* Calcutta: K. L. Mukhopadhyaya.

Sinha, Surajit
1959 "Tribal Cultures of Peninsular India as a Dimension of Little Tradition Study of Indian Civilization: A Preliminary Statement," in Milton Singer, ed., *Traditional India: Structure and Change,* Bibliographic and Special Series, vol. 10 (Philadelphia: The American Folklore Society), pp. 298–312.
1962 "State Formation and Rajput Myth in Tribal Central India." *Man in India* 42/1:35–80.

1966 "Vaisnava Influence on a Tribal Culture." In Milton Singer, ed., *Krishna: Myths, Rites, and Attitudes*. Honolulu: East-West Press, pp. 64–89.

Sinha, Surajit, Jyoti Sen, and Sudhir Panchbai

1969 "The Concept of Diku Among the Tribes of Chotanagpur." *Man in India* 49/2:121–38.

Skocpol, Theda

1984 Ed., *Vision and Method in Historical Sociology*. Cambridge: Cambridge University Press.

Skvarko, Zakhar

1910 "Pros'vitna organizatsyi͡a chytalen' i filij 'Pros'vityi." In *Pershyj Ukrainsk'kyj Pros'vitno-Ekonomichnyj Kongres, Protokoly i Referaty*. L'viv: Tovarystvo Pros'vita, pp. 173–84.

Slawek, Stephen M.

1987 *Sitār Technique in Nibaddh Forms*. New Delhi: Motilal Banarsidass.

Slobin, Mark

1982 Ed., *Old Jewish Folk Music: The Collections and Writings of Moshe Beregovski*. Philadelphia: University of Pennsylvania Press. (Publications of the American Folklore Society, n.s., 6)

1986 "A Fresh Look at Beregovski's Folk Music Research." *Ethnomusicology* 30:253–60.

Slomka, Jan

1941 *From Serfdom to Self-Government: Memoirs of a Polish Village Mayor*. Translated by William John Rose. London: Minerva Publishing. First published in 1912.

Speck, Frank G. and Leonard Broom

1983 *Cherokee Dance and Drama*. Norman: The University of Oklahoma Press. First published 1951.

Srivastava, Ram P.

1966 "Tribe-Caste Mobility in India and The Case of the Kumaon Bhotias." In Christoph von Fürer-Haimendorf, F. Thurston, and K. Rangachari, eds., *Caste and Kin in Nepal, India, and Ceylon*. Bombay: Asia Publishing House.

Steegmuller, Francis

1979 Ed., *Flaubert in Egypt*. Chicago: Academy Chicago.

Steiner, George

1971 *In Bluebeard's Castle: Some Notes toward the Redefinition of Culture*. New Haven: Yale University Press.

Stęszewski, Jan

1981 "Muzyka ludowa." In Biernacka 1981:245–84.

Strunk, Oliver

1950 Comp., *Source Readings in Music History*. New York: Norton.

Suchoff, Benjamin

1976 Ed., *Béla Bartók Essays*. New York: St. Martin's Press.

Sugar, Peter F.

1969 "External and Domestic Roots of Eastern European Nationalism." In Peter F. Sugar and Ivo J. Lederer, eds., *Nationalism in*

Eastern Europe. Seattle: University of Washington Press, pp. 3–54.

Supičić, Ivo
1987 "Sociology of Music and Ethnomusicology." *The World of Music* 29/1:34–40.

Sürelsan, Ismail Baha
1972 Ed., "Rauf Yekta Bey'in '1932 Kahire Sark Musikîsi Kongresi' ne dâir notlari. . ." *Musikî ve Nota* 3/29:4–6.

Swanton, John R.
1910? Unpublished field notes, archived in the Smithsonian Institution.
1928 "Religious Beliefs and Medical Practices of the Creek Indians." *42nd Annual Report of the Bureau of American Ethnology, 1924–1925*, pp. 473–672.
1930 Unpublished letters to Caroline Dormon, folder 1359, Dormon Collection, Archives Division, Watson Library, Northwestern State University of Louisiana.
1931 *Source Material for the Social and Ceremonial Life of the Choctaw Indians*. Washington, D.C.: Government Printing Office. (Bureau of American Ethnology, Bulletin, 103)
1946 *Indians of the Southeastern United States*. Washington, D.C.: Government Printing Office. (Bureau of American Ethnology, Bulletin, 137)

Taussig, Michael
1987 *Shamanism, Colonialism, and the Wild Man: A Study in Terror and Healing*. Chicago: The University of Chicago Press.

Thompson, Robert Farris
1974 *African Art in Motion*. Berkeley: University of California Press.
1983 *Flash of the Spirit*. New York: Random House.

Treitler, Leo
1989 *Music and the Historical Imagination*. Cambridge, MA.: Harvard University Press.

Turino, Thomas
1987 "Power Relations, Identity and Musical Choice: Music in a Peruvian Altiplano Village and Among its Migrants in the Metropolis." Ph.D. dissertation, University of Texas at Austin.
1988 "The Music of Andean Migrants in Lima, Peru: Demographics, Social Power, and Style." *Latin American Music Review* 9:127–50.
1989 "The Coherence of Social Style and Musical Creation among the Aymara in Southern Peru." *Ethnomusicology* 33:1–30.

Turner, H. W.
1967 *African Independent Church*. Oxford: Oxford University Press.

Turner, Victor
1969 *The Ritual Process: Structure and Anti-Structure*. Chicago: Aldine.
1974 *Dramas, Fields, and Metaphors: Symbolic Action in Human Society*. Ithaca: Cornell University Press.

1984 "Liminality and the Performative Genres." In John J. MacAloon, ed., *Rite, Drama, Festival, Spectacle: Rehearsals toward a Theory of Cultural Performance.* Philadelphia: Institute for the Study of Human Issues, pp. 19–41.

Ulin, Robert

1984 *Understanding Cultures.* Austin: University of Texas Press.

Vail, Leroy and Landeg White

1978 "Plantation Protest: The History of a Mozambican Song." *Journal of Southern African Studies* 5/1:1–25.

1983 "Forms of Resistance: Songs and Perceptions of Power in Colonial Mozambique." *American Historical Review* 88:883–919.

Vansina, Jan

1965 *Oral Tradition.* Translated H. M. Wright. Chicago: Aldine. First published 1961.

1985 *Oral Tradition as History.* Madison: University of Wisconsin Press.

Vennum, Thomas

1980 "A History of Ojibwa Song Form." *Selected Reports in Ethnomusicology* 3/2:43–75.

Vidyarthi, D. N.

n.d. Ed., *Filmindia: The Fabulous Star Magazine* (Port of Spain).

Vilca, Dante

1982 "La Asociación Juvenil Puno." *Tarea* 6:61–64

Villoteau, Guillaume-André

1823 "Description historique, technique et littéraire, des instruments de musique des orientaux." In *Description de l'Égypte.* 2d ed. Vol. 13. Paris: C. L. F. Panckoucke, pp. 221–568.

1826 *De l'état actuel de l'art musical en Égypte, ou relation historique et descriptive des recherches et observations faites sur la musique en ce pays.* In *Description de l'Égypte.* 2d ed. Vol. 14. Paris: C. L. F. Panckoucke.

Virottam, Balmukund

1972 *The Nagbanshis and the Cheros.* New Delhi: Munshiram Manoharlal.

Wade, Bonnie C.

1978 "Indian Classical Music in North America: Cultural Give and Take." *Contributions to Asian Studies* 12:29–39.

1980 "India, Subcontinent of, VI. Folk Music." In Stanley Sadie, ed., *The New Grove Dictionary of Music and Musicians.* London: Macmillan, 9:147–58.

1984 *Khyāl: Creativity within North India's Classical Music Tradition.* Cambridge: Cambridge University Press. (Cambridge Studies in Ethnomusicology)

Wade, Bonnie C. and Ann M. Pescatello

1977 "Music 'Patronage' in Indic Culture: The *Jajmani* Model." In *Essays for a Humanist. An Offering to Klaus Wachsmann.* New York: The Town House Press, pp. 277–336.

Wallace, Anthony
1956 "Revitalization Movements." *American Anthropologist* 58:264–79.

Wallaschek, Richard
1893 *Primitive Music.* London: Longmans, Green.

Warner, Charles Dudley
1887 *My Winter on the Nile.* Boston: Houghton, Mifflin.

Wallis, Roger and Krister Malm
1984 *Big Sounds from Small Peoples: The Music Industry in Small Countries.* New York: Pendragon Press.

Waterman, Richard A.
1952 "African Influences on American Negro Music." In Sol Tax, ed., *Acculturation in the Americas.* Chicago: The University of Chicago Press, pp. 227–44.
1963 "On Flogging a Dead Horse: Lessons Learned from the Africanisms Controversy." *Ethnomusicology* 7:83–87.

Watzinger, Karl Otto
1984 *Geschichte der Juden in Mannheim 1650–1945.* Stuttgart: W. Kohlhammer.

Weber, Max
1921 *Die rationalen und soziologischen Grundlagen der Musik.* Munich: Drei Masken Verlag.

White, Landeg
1982 "Power and the Praise Poem." *Journal of Southern African Studies* 9/1:8–32.

Wilbert, Johannes and Karin Simoneau
1978 *Folk Literature of the Gê Indians.* Vol. 1. Los Angeles: UCLA Latin American Center Publications.
1984 *Folk Literature of the Gê Indians.* Vol. 2. Los Angeles: UCLA Latin American Center Publications.

Williams, Raymond
1977 *Marxism and Literature.* Oxford: Oxford University Press.

Wiora, Walter
1965 *The Four Ages of Music.* Translated M. D. Herter Norton. New York: W. W. Norton. First published 1961.

Witmer, Robert
1982 *The Musical Life of the Blood Indians.* Ottawa: National Museums of Canada. (Mercury Series, Canadian Ethnology Service, Paper 86)

Wolf, Eric R.
1956 "Aspects of Group Relations in a Complex Society: Mexico." *American Anthropologist* 58:1065–78.
1982 *Europe and the People without History.* Berkeley: University of California Press.

Wolf, Johannes
1932 "Die Tagung über arabische Musikreform in Kairo." *Deutsche Tonkünstler-Zeitung* 30/1:121–22.

Zakhariivo, I.
1910 "Orhanizatsyi͡a tovarys'koho zhyti͡a seli͡an." In *Pershyj Ukrain-s'kyj Pros'vitno-Ekonomichnyj Kongres, Protokoly i Referaty*. L'viv: Tovarystvo Pros'vita, pp. 212–20.

Zāyid, Maḥmūd
1973 *Min Aḥmad ʿUrābī ilá Jamāl ʿAbd al-Nāṣir*. Beirut: al-Dār al-Muttaḥidah li-al-Nashr. (Arabic)

Zide, Norman H. and Ram Dayal Munda
1970 "Structural Influence of Bengali Vaisnava Songs on Traditional Mundari Songs." *Journal of Social Research* 13/1:36–48.

Contributors

Carol Babiracki teaches ethnomusicology at Brown University and is completing her dissertation on "Musical and Cultural Interaction in Tribal India: The Karam Repertory of the Muṇḍas of Choṭanāgpur" under the supervision of Bruno Nettl. Her other research interests include classical, folk, and tribal musics in South Asia; folk and ethnic music in North America; dance ethnography; and musical interaction and change.

Stephen Blum, Professor of Music at the City University of New York Graduate School and Associate Editor of *The Universe of Music: A History,* was Bruno Nettl's first doctoral candidate in musicology at the University of Illinois. Studies based on his dissertation, "Musics in Contact: The Cultivation of Oral Repertoires in Meshed, Iran," appeared in *Eight Urban Musical Cultures,* ed. B. Nettl (University of Illinois Press, 1978) and elsewhere. He is currently completing a monograph on European and American ideas of tonality and a study of counterpoint in American shape-note hymnody.

Philip V. Bohlman is Assistant Professor of Music at the University of Chicago and author of *The Study of Folk Music in the Modern World* (1988) and *"The Land Where Two Streams Flow": Music in the German-Jewish Community of Israel,* published by the University of Illinois Press (1989). He is Co-General Editor with Bruno Nettl of the monograph series, "Chicago Studies in Ethnomusicology," and is co-editor with Bruno Nettl of *Comparative Musicology and Anthropology of Music: Essays on the History of Ethnomusicology* (1991).

Charles Capwell is Associate Professor of Music and Chair of the Musicology Division at the University of Illinois at Urbana-Champaign. He has served as editor of the journal, *Ethnomusicology,* and has written *The Music of the Bauls of Bengal* (1986). He is currently investigating the roles played by Sourindro Mohun Tagore, a nineteenth-century Bengali musical scholar, in the histories of musicology and of colonial relations in India.

David B. Coplan is Associate Professor of Anthropology at the State University of New York College at Old Westbury. He completed his Ph.D. at Indiana

University under the supervision of the late Alan P. Merriam. He contributed an essay on Ghanaian highlife to *Eight Urban Musical Cultures* (University of Illinois Press, 1978), edited by Bruno Nettl, and he has published a book, *In Township Tonight! South Africa's Black City Music and Theatre* (1985). In 1988–89, Dr. Coplan continued his field research on the oral poetry of Sotho mine workers.

Victoria Lindsay Levine, Assistant Professor of Music and Southwest Studies at The Colorado College, completed her dissertation on "Choctaw Indian Musical Cultures in the Twentieth Century" at the University of Illinois under the guidance of Bruno Nettl. She specializes in American Indian musical cultures and is particularly interested in revitalization movements. She is currently engaged in research on Spanish folk musics of southern Colorado and northern New Mexico.

Helen Myers is Assistant Professor of Music at Trinity College and chief ethnomusicologist for *The New Grove Dictionary of Music and Musicians.* She has edited *The Grove/Norton Handbook of Ethnomusicology,* and she edited the revised edition of Bruno Nettl's *Folk Music in the United States* (1976). Her current work on "The Bhojpuri Song Atlas" involves field research in India, the West Indies, and Fiji.

Daniel M. Neuman is Professor and Director of the School of Music, University of Washington. He was Bruno Nettl's first doctoral candidate in anthropology at the University of Illinois. He has published *The Life of Music in North India: The Organization of an Artistic Tradition* (1980; repr. 1990) and has written on the social role of the gharānā in North Indian music in *Eight Urban Musical Cultures,* ed. B. Nettl (University of Illinois Press, 1978). He is currently working on a musical atlas of western Rajasthan.

William Noll , a research associate at the Harvard Ukrainian Research Institute, holds a Ph.D. in ethnomusicology from the University of Washington. A specialist in the folk musics of Eastern Europe, he has taught at Wesleyan University, Dartmouth College, and other institutions. He has done extensive fieldwork in Poland and the Ukraine, most recently under a grant from IREX. His research interests include the transformation of peasant societies into modern nation states.

Regula Burckhardt Qureshi teaches on the faculty of music at the University of Alberta. An anthropologist and an accomplished cellist, she has published *Sufi Music of India and Pakistan: Sound, Context and Meaning in Qawwali* (1986). She is currently completing a historical and sociomusical study of bowed string playing in South Asia.

Ali Jihad Racy is Professor in the Department of Ethnomusicology and Systematic Musicology at the University of California, Los Angeles, where he directs the Near East Ensemble. Born in Lebanon, he received his B.A. from the American University of Beirut and completed his doctoral studies at the University of Illinois with Bruno Nettl. Among the recordings of his performances and compositions is *Taqāsim—The Art of Improvisation in Arabic Music.*

Anthony Seeger is Director of the Folkways Recording Project at the Smithsonian Institution. He holds a Ph.D. in anthropology from the University of Chicago and has taught at the National Museum of Natural History in Brazil and at Indiana University. His principal research concerns have been music of the Amazonian peoples and musical anthropology, and his book, *Why Suyá Sing: A Musical Anthropology of an Amazonian People* (1987), received the Otto Kinkeldey Prize of the American Musicological Society.

Amnon Shiloah is Professor of Musicology at the Hebrew University where he recently completed a term as Provost of the Rothberg School for Overseas Studies. Among his many books are *The Theory of Music in Arabic Writings (c. 900-1900)* (1979) and a translation and commentary on the *Kitāb kamāl adab al-ghinā'* of al-Hassan (1972). The recordings he has edited include *Beduin Music of Southern Sinai* and *The Musical Heritage of Iraqi Jews.*

Stephen M. Slawek, Associate Professor of Music at the University of Texas at Austin, is the author of *Sitār Technique in Nibaddh Forms* (1987). His University of Illinois dissertation, "Kirtan: A Study of the Sonic Manifestations of the Divine in the Popular Hindu Culture of Banaras," was supervised by Bruno Nettl. His main research interests include the instrumental music of North India, the modernization of Hindustani music, and Hindu devotional song. An accomplished sitarist, Dr. Slawek is a student of Ravi Shankar and of the late Lalmani Misra.

Thomas Turino is Assistant Professor of Music at the University of Illinois at Urbana-Champaign. His dissertation, "Power Relations, Identity and Musical Choice: Music in a Peruvian Altiplano Village and among Its Migrants in the Metropolis" (University of Texas), was based on over three years of field research in Peru. His writings have appeared in *Ethnomusicology* and *Latin American Music Review.*

Christopher A. Waterman is Assistant Professor of Music and Adjunct Professor of Anthropology at the University of Washington. He completed his Ph.D. in anthropology at the University of Illinois, under the supervision of Bruno Nettl. He has published the book *Jùjú: A Social History and Ethnography of an African Popular Music* (1990). His interests include sub-Saharan African performance traditions and aesthetics; popular music; economics of music; African-American musics; and the intellectual history of ethnomusicology and anthropology.

Robert Witmer is Associate Professor of Music at York University, Toronto, where he is Director of the Graduate Programme in Ethnomusicology. He undertook graduate studies in ethnomusicology at the University of Illinois under the supervision of Bruno Nettl. He has published *The Musical Life of the Blood Indians* (1982) and is preparing a multi-volume computer-generated *Pedal Steel Guitar Chord Dictionary.*

Index

Aboriginal peoples, 9, 45
Abrahams, Ruth, 164
Absolute music, 255, 259–61, 266–67, 271
Academy of Oriental Music (Cairo), 69–71, 82
Accordion, 41, 107, 148
Acculturation: process of cultural change, 41, 232, 240–41, 242, 270, 272, 277n.4
Adanson, Jean-Baptiste, 188
Adesh, H. S., 238–39
Adorno, Theodor, 255
Aesthetics, 12, 37, 39, 44, 46–47, 61, 63–64, 76, 124, 128, 130, 134, 136, 231
Africa, 19, 35–67, 82, 273–74
Àgídìgbo, 62–63
Agogo, 63
Agra gharānā, 179n.5
Ahmad, Bahauddin, 119n.5
Ahmad, Hayat, 119n.3
Ahmad, Inam, 119n.3
Ahmad, Mahmud, 119n.3
Ahmad, Meraj, 112, 119n.3
Akhaṛa, 16, 211, 213, 215–16, 228n.7
Akinsanya, Adeolu, 62
Alabama (Native American people), 15, 191–93, 197, 202–3, 205n.4
Alaja-Browne, Afolabi, 55
"Āl-an-Nabī" (Sufi song), 117–18
Ālāp, 168, 171–72, 175, 177
Alberta, 243–44, 250
Aleppo, 183
Algeria, 72, 85
Algonkian, 23
ʿAlī, Muhammad, 69, 81
Ali Akbar College of Music, 166
All India Radio, 173
Allauddīn gharānā, 10, 96. See also *Gharānā*
All-India Music Conferences, 120n.13
Alverson, Hoyt, 277n.7
Amancaes: folklore festival of, 128
Amaro, 54
American Museum of Natural History, 244
Amplification, 62, 64
"Ān roz" (Sufi song), 118
Analysis of music, 74, 243, 251
Ancestors, 6, 8, 130, 137, 179n.4, 209, 231, 271
Anganāi, 216, 217–18
Anthropology, 6, 28, 38, 46, 49, 270–71, 273–75, 277nn.4, 7
Anti-Semitism, 261
Apache, Mescalero, 5
Apartheid, 38, 47
Arab music, 68–91, 181
Araba, Julius O., 59
Arabia, 82
Aranda, 9
Arawaks, 231
Archives, 86, 251
Argentina, 5
Armenia: musical culture of, 3
Art music, 19, 84, 105, 146–47. *See also* Classical music
Artisans, 209–11, 224–25, 226
Aryavarta (historical area of Indian civilization), 10, 95–96, 100–101
"Ashk rez" (Sufi song), 116–17
Aṣíkò, 58, 62
Asociación Juvenil Puno (AJP), 132–34, 136–37, 138n.3
Assimilation: process of cultural change, 131, 193, 204n.3, 207, 212, 225, 271, 276
Atakapa, 194

Audiences, 42, 54, 60, 66, 114, 128, 146, 167, 172, 178, 255, 263
Auliya, Nizamuddin, 11, 104–5, 111, 115–16, 120n.9. *See also* Nizamuddin Auliya Shrine
"Auliyā tere dāman" (Sufi song), 117
Australia, 9
Austria, 145, 151, 157, 257, 261
Authenticity, 10, 15, 37, 72, 85, 87, 104, 108–9, 110–11, 114–16, 162, 176, 178, 240–41, 255, 269, 274–75
Authority: of a musical tradition, 10, 95, 101, 110; within a musical tradition, 9–10, 26, 42, 274–75; social, 9–10, 40, 108, 114, 209, 270, 274; spiritual, 11, 109–10
Avoyel, 193
Ayarachi, 121–22
Aymara, 11–12, 122–30, 134–35

Babajide, Ojo, 55
Babiracki, Carol, 12, 14–16, 267, 274–75
Bach, J. S., 260
Bachche (Sufi musicians), 104, 106, 111–12, 116, 119n.3
"Back-and-Forth Dance" (Louisiana pantribal repertory), 200
Badejo, E. O., 65
Baghdad, 91n.10
Bahar, Cem, 182
Bakare, Ayinde, 14, 16, 55, 59, 61–64, 66
Balasaraswati, 166
Balogun, C. A., 64
Banaras baj, 97
Banaras gharānā, 102. See also *Gharānā*
Banaras Hindu University, 178n.1
Bandits, 97
Bandleaders, 14, 61, 63–65
Bandyopadhyay (musician family in Visnupur gharānā), 99
Bandyopadhyay, Romescandra, 100
Banerjee, Nikhil, 167, 171, 174
Bangladesh, 95
Banjo, 54, 58, 62
Banjo, Tunji, 55
Bantu, 39, 44
Barth, Fredrik, 256, 267n.4
Bartók, Béla, 9, 71–73, 85, 91n.3
Basant ritual, 11, 115–16
Basketry, 190–91, 193, 203, 208, 221, 228n.5
Basotho, 39, 43, 46–47. *See also* Sotho
Basy, 144, 148
Beatles, 166
Becker, Judith, 19
Beethoven, Ludwig van, 260–61
Beg, ʿAli. *See* Bobovsky, Albert
Beguine, 148
Beidelman, Thomas, 40
Beirut, 71
Benjamin, Walter, 52
Bengal, 10, 13, 95–102, 165, 168–69, 176, 209–10, 221, 227n.1, 235
Bengali. *See* Bengal
Beregovski, Moshe, 1
Berlin, 14, 69
Berlin, Hochschule für Musik, 71
Berlin, University of, 69
Berlin school of comparative musicology, 68
Bey, Masud Jamil, 71, 77
Bey, Rauf Yekta, 71, 73, 90n.1, 91n.7
Bey, Tanburi Jamil, 71
Bhajan, 235, 238
Bhaktī, 107, 172
Bhatkande, V. N., 176, 179n.4
Bhattacarya, Ramsankar, 100–101
Bher, 209
Bielorussia, 157n.1
Bihar, 208–9, 213, 221, 223, 227, 227n.1, 235
Bildung, 256, 261, 267n.3
Bilingualism, 237
Biloxi (Native American people), 192–93, 205n.4
Bīn, 168, 171–72
Bīnkār. See *Bīn*
Bīnkār ālāp: explanation of, 171–72
Bir Hambir, 97–98
Bizanti, Colonel, 71
Black Consciousness Movement, 39
Black Plume, Bob, 244, 249–50
Blackfoot, 17, 242–53, 272
Blacking, John, 52
Blainville, Charles-Henri, 186
Blakeley, Thomas, 37
Blood. *See* Blackfoot
Blum, Stephen, 52, 272
Boas, Franz, 47
Boatman, Charlie, 197, 198n, 201, 204n.2
Bobovsky, Albert, 181, 189n
Bohlman, Philip, 17, 269, 271–72
Bolivia, 123
Bombos, 121
Boogie-woogie, 148
Borrowing, 29, 80, 83, 211–13, 223, 225–27
Botswana, 37
Boundaries: cultural, 10, 226, 256–58, 260, 264–65, 275; ethnic, 37, 142, 256–58, 162; regional, 140
Bradri. *See* Lineages
Brahaspati, Kailashchandra Deva, 179n.4

Brahmin, 97, 101, 117, 164, 169, 210, 221, 238
Brahms, Johannes, 260
Brass bands, 125–26
Brazil, 5, 23–34, 54, 55, 58, 63
Brhaspati, Acharya, 113
Brokerage, 50, 54. *See also* Brokers, cultural
Brokers, cultural, 13–17, 59, 66, 211, 222
Broussard, Clementine, 202
Brown, Robert, 166
Bruner, Edward, 272–73
Bulgaria, 145
Bull, Chief, 244, 250, 252n.2
Busk Ceremony. *See* Green-Corn Ceremony

Caddo, 193
Cairo, 8–9, 68–91, 183
Caitanya, 98
Cajas, 121
Cajun, 204
Cakraborty, Gadadhar, 99
Calcutta, 96–97, 168–69, 238
Calderón, Augusto, 125–26
Calderón, Lucho, 128–29
Calderón, Natalio, 13, 16, 124–28, 130
Calypso, 232, 236, 240
Cantemir, Demetrius, 181, 188, 189n.2
Cantoni, F., 70, 77
Capacity: factor in historicity, 112
Capitalism, industrial, 4
Captives, 26, 28–31
Capwell, Charles, 10, 13, 269, 274, 277n.11
Caribs, 231
Carra de Vaux, Baron, 71, 77–79, 84
Cassette tapes, 24, 26, 33, 238, 250
Caste, 101, 119n.8, 168, 207–28, 236, 238; interaction with tribal peoples in India, 207–28
Cavanagh, Beverley, 23
Caxton-Martins, Isola, 54–55
Ceremonies, 5, 16, 23, 26–27, 29–30, 32, 64, 194–97. *See also* Funerals; Ritual; Weddings
Chakravarty, Ramdas, 166
Chamber music, 17; as ethnic music in Israel, 254–67, 271
Change: concepts of, 7, 20, 50–52, 208, 242, 270
Chant form, 201–2
Chełm, 143
Cherokee, 196
Chickasaw, 202
Chiriguanos, 121–22
Chishti (lineage of Sufis), 104, 106, 116, 120n.14
Chishti, Khwaja Muinuddin, 104, 109. *See also* Chishti
Chitimacha, 194
Chīz, 113
Choctaw, 15, 190–93, 195–96, 200–203, 204n.3, 205n.4
Choirs, village, 13, 150–53
Choṭanāgpur, 14–15, 207–28
Chottin, Alexis, 71–72
Christianity: as determinant of cultural history, 36, 38–39, 45, 58–61, 64; influence on traditional music, 195, 206n.6
Ciṭiḍ, 216, 217–18, 220, 228n.9
Clarinet, 148, 154, 169
Class, social, 37, 60, 101, 121, 131–34
Classical music: Hindustani, 14–15, 105, 108, 112–13, 118–19, 120n.11, 161–80, 222, 238; Western, 15, 17, 35, 65, 75, 163, 178, 242, 254–67, 271, 277n.12
Clifford, James, 273, 277n.2
Clubs, 131–34, 145, 150–53
Codes, 8, 40–42, 52
Collangettes, Father Xavier Maurice, 71, 74, 84
Collins, John, 53
Colombia, Putumayo Intendency of, 5
Colonialism, 37, 49, 53, 59–60, 66, 81, 270, 273–74, 277nn.7, 12
Columbia University, 177
Comanches, 192
Comaroff, Jean, 37
Comaroff, John, 37
Communities: musical, 1, 5, 60, 103, 119, 169, 270; of scholars, 272; social, 10, 13, 15, 17, 23, 27–28, 31–33, 39, 56, 59, 104, 106, 109, 123–26, 128, 135, 150, 155, 194, 204, 207, 209, 226–27, 249, 255–64, 266, 267n.2, 269–71
Comparative musicology, 4, 7, 9, 18, 68, 72, 80, 83–90, 91n.3
Competence, 124
Competition, 41, 55, 65, 148, 170–71
Concerto, 163, 176–78, 260
Congress of Arab Music, 8–9, 14–15, 68–91
Congress of Tovarystvo Prosvita, 13, 151
Conima, 121–30, 134, 135–37, 137nn.1, 2, 138nn.3, 4
Conimeño. *See* Conima
Consciousness: historical, 268–77; national, 139–58

Consensus, 11–12, 123, 136
Constantinople, 181–83
Contact: class, 2, 19; cultural, 2, 19, 28, 52; ethnic, 2, 24, 27–28
Converts, 61, 211
Coplan, David, 6, 16, 53, 269, 273, 277n.7
Copland, Aaron, 177
Coptic church music, 72
Courts: ʿAbbasid, 82; Mughal, 10, 95–96, 99, 102, 105–6, 209, 217; Muslim, 105, 111; Ottoman, 188; Sotho, 43
Coushatta, 15, 191–92, 202–4
Crawford, James, 190
Creek, 196, 202–3
Creoles, 232, 237
Cuba, 54, 62–63
Curing, 26, 191, 193
Cymbaly, 144, 148
Czechoslovakia, 145, 157n.4, 262

Daf, 109–10
Dagar (family of dhrupad singers), 99
Dahlhaus, Carl, 4–5
Dance, 5–6, 9, 15–16, 39, 47, 63–64, 121–22, 128–29, 147, 149, 153–55, 164–65, 193–204, 207, 210–16, 222–27, 228n.9, 232. *See also* National dances
al-Darwīsh, Shaykh ʿAlī, 74
Davies, Akamo, 54
"Daybreak Dance" (Louisiana pantribal repertory), 201–2
Delhi, 11, 96, 106, 111, 116, 119n.3, 209, 220, 233
Demons, 42–44. *See also* Spirits
Density referent, 58
Depression (Great), 49, 60, 203
Devi, Annapurna, 170–71
Dhārma, 225
Dhikr, 72. See also *Zikr*
Ḍholak, 107, 109, 215
Dhrupad, 97–98, 100, 168–69, 172, 175
Diaphony, 213
Diaspora: African, 52
Dichotomies, 7, 52, 83. *See also* Dualisms
Diffusion, 131
al-Dik Ahmad Amin, 74, 77
Diku, 12, 209–11, 213, 220–21, 222–27
al-Dīn, Safī, 74, 188
Disk jockeys, 65
Diviners, 43–44
Diwali festival, 234–35
Dixon, Joseph, 244, 249–50, 253n.6
Dormon, Caroline, 203
"Double-Head Dance" (Louisiana pantribal repertory), 199–200, 202, 206nn.7, 8
Drama, musical, 39, 228n.9
Dreaming: Aboriginal concept of, 9–10
Drumming, 63, 107, 109, 113–15, 172, 200, 212–15, 222, 228n.7, 235
"Drunk Dance." *See* "Midnight Dance"
Dualisms, 8–9, 81–82. *See also* Dichotomies
Ḍulki, 215–16, 226n.7
Dumang, 215, 228n.7
Dumy (Ukrainian historical epic), 142
Dupont-Ferrier, Gustave, 183
Durang, 212

Eagle Plume, Willie, 244, 249–50
East Germany, 157n.4
East Indian music, 231–41
Eastern music. *See* Oriental music
Ebute Metta (area of Lagos), 55
Ecuador: ritual dance-drama in, 6
Egalitarian relations. *See* Equality
Ege, Akanbi, 14, 61, 66
Egypt, 68–91, 271
Ekiti, 65
Electronic music, 173
Elites, 5, 14, 55, 59–61, 64, 66, 117, 123, 125, 132, 146
Ellingson, Ter, 268
Emblems: of identity, 122, 125, 130, 136–37, 210
Emic: approach to cultural analysis, 182, 188, 250, 252
England, 71, 187
Epics, 226, 228n.9. See also *Dumy; Ramayan*
Equality, 12, 124, 126, 211–12, 220, 226, 258, 275
d'Erlanger, Baron Rodolphe, 69–70, 74
Essai sur la musique orientale comparée à la musique européene, 181–89
Esugbayi, Ladipo, 55
Ethnic music, 254–67
Ethnographers, musical, 18, 142, 146
Ethnography, 40, 47, 144, 270, 277n.5
Ethnology, 18, 36
Evolution, 70, 73, 75, 82–86, 90
Exchange: cultural, 17, 19, 28, 139, 237, 272. *See also* Musical approximation
Expansion, European, 4, 18–19. *See also* Colonialism
Exploitation, 12, 37, 125, 271, 273–74
Extemporization. *See* Improvisation

Factions, 123–24, 130
Fariduddin, 115
Farmer, Henry George, 71, 75, 77–78, 84
Farsi, 107, 110, 114–17
Fāṣil, 73
Fatḥī, Moḥammad, 9, 77, 78–80
Fees. *See* Payments to musicians
Felicity (Trinidad), 16–17, 231–41, 275
Festivals, 16, 100, 115, 124, 128–29, 212–13, 222–27, 235
Fétis, François-Joseph, 181
Fewkes, Jesse Walter, 252n.1
Fiddle, 144, 148, 204
Fieldwork, 87, 91n.3, 151–52, 161, 242, 252, 270
Fiestas. *See* Festivals
Film music. *See* Indian film music
Fischer, Michael, 40
Fitelberg, Grzegorz, 146
Flathead, 23, 33
Flaubert, Gustave, 82
Flute, bamboo, 170
Folk music, 9, 73, 84–85, 87–88, 108, 168, 176, 222, 235, 243, 255, 266
Folklore, 7, 18, 36, 42, 46–47, 128, 131
Folsom-Dickerson, Mr., 198n, 204n.2
Fonton, Charles, 15–16, 181–89
Fourah Bay, 54
Fox-Strangways, A. H., 88
Fox-trot, 148
France, 71, 183–84, 187
de Freneuse, le Cerf de la Viéville, Seigneur, 184
Function, social, 8
Funerals, 64, 155, 209

Galicia, 12, 145–46, 149–52, 154–55, 157n.8, 158
Gandā bandhan, 162. See also *Nādā bandh*
Ganges River, 95, 233
Gat, 172
Gazal. See Ghazal
Gê (language family), 24, 30, 32–33
Geertz, Clifford, 273
Gennep, Arnold van, 264
Genre: cultural, 6, 40, 44, 47, 53, 273; musical, 6, 19, 26–27, 41–42, 45, 58, 73, 85, 88, 106, 108, 110, 128, 142–43, 148, 168, 176, 208, 211, 227, 255, 258, 260, 262, 266; of self-expression, 273
George, Lamidi, 54
Germany, 91, 157n.4, 187, 257, 259, 261, 265
Gesudaraz, 120n.14
Gharānā, 10–11, 14, 95–103, 120n.12, 170–71, 175; definition of, 170–71, 173–75
Ghāsis, 209–11, 221–22, 226, 227
Ghazal, 115, 168, 239
Ghazipur, 164
Ghosh, Jnan Prakash, 166
Ghosh, Pannalal, 170
Giddens, Anthony, 46
Gillis, Frank, 253n.6
Glasgow University, 71
Glass, Philip, 163
Goethe, Johann Wolfgang von, 17
Gòmbé, 62
Good taste (*bon goût*): as a measure of musical value, 181–89
Gore, Nasiruddin Khan, 111–13
Goswami, Krishnamohan, 99
Goswami, Ksetromohan, 13, 99
Gramsci, Antonio, 123
Great Britain, 71
"Great Sitar Explosion," 166
Great Tradition (of Indian culture), 95–96, 102n.1, 146
Greco, José-Luis, 177
Green-Corn Ceremony, 194–96, 205–6n.6
Gregory, Hiram, 205n.4
Grey-out, musical, 241, 272, 276, 277n.12
Guimet Museum, 71
Guitar, 54, 62–64, 132
Guitar-banjo, 55, 58
Gurū, 14, 161–62, 165, 171, 174–75, 211
Gushee, Lawrence, 249

Haas, Mary, 191, 194–95, 204n.2
Hába, Alois, 71, 77
Habsburg Empire. *See* Austria
Ḥadīs, 109
Haifa, 257
al-Hajjāj, Muḥammad, 75
Hamburg University, 71
Hampton, Barbara, 19
Handclapping, 107, 109
Hansen, Kathryn, 167
Harmonium, 107. *See also* Accordion
Harmony, 12–13, 58–59, 64, 85, 127–29, 131, 134, 137n.2, 148, 152, 166. *See also* Diaphony; Polyphony
Harms, Robert, 46
Harrison, Frank, 182
Hauskonzert, 17, 262–64
Havan sacrifice, 238
Hawaii, 29
Hebrew University, 257, 263
Hegel, Georg Wilhelm Friedrich, 7, 273
Hegemony, 37, 104, 123, 136–37, 215, 255
Heine, Heinrich, 265
Heinitz, Wilhelm, 71
Herbalists, 43, 191
Hermeneutic, 46, 50
Herndon, Marcia, 52
Herskovits, Melville, 52, 232

Hertzberg, Hazel, 194
Hickmann, Hans, 88
al-Ḥifnī, Maḥmūd Aḥmad, 14, 68–70, 74, 78, 80, 87–89
Highlife: term designating West African popular music, 65
Hindemith, Paul, 71, 77, 80
Hindi, 107, 115
Hinduization: process of cultural change, 222, 227, 228n.8
Hindustani music, 14–15, 95–120, 161–80, 186. *See also* Classical music: Hindustani; North India
Historical consciousness, 1, 6, 11, 104
Historicity, 47, 103, 106, 111–12, 116
Histories of music, general, 4
Historiography, 84, 89, 103–4, 108, 208
Hobsbawm, Eric, 37
Hodjia, 188
Hoffmann, John, 212, 225
Holi festival, 235
Holidays, 147–48, 152, 155
Hornbostel, Erich M. von, 71–72, 77, 80, 84–85, 89, 245
Horned-Owl Dance. *See* Stickball Game/Night Dance
Horo, 12, 209–10, 226
Horticulture, 29–30
Howard, James, 197
Human rights, 3, 38
Humanities, 50, 273
Hungary, 145
Hutsulka (Ukrainian dance genre), 154
Hyderabad (Deccan), 106, 111
Hymns: Christian, 23, 45, 57–59, 61, 63; Sufi, 115

Ibadan, 55, 59, 61, 65
Ideal types, 18–19
Identity: cultural, 6, 11–12, 14, 16, 39, 60–61, 63, 66, 86, 123, 130, 136–37, 138n.4, 142, 207, 226–27; ethnic, 14, 32, 141, 165; national, 12–14, 122, 140, 145, 146, 165; peasant, 122, 141–42
Ideologies, 14, 37, 39–40, 53, 67, 68, 81, 86, 90, 107–9, 121–23, 130, 132–36, 146–47, 254–55
Illinois, University of, at Urbana-Champaign, 276n.1
ʿilm-e-safīnā, 107, 110
ʿilm-e-sīnā, 107, 110
Imam, Hakim Muhammad Karam, 112, 114
Improvisation, 6, 41–45, 58, 113, 177
Inden, Ronald, 101–2
India, 12, 16–17, 95–102, 207–28, 231–41, 274–75. *See also* North India
Indian film music, 63, 163, 173, 235, 238, 275
Indianization: process of musical change, 240–41
Indigenismo (ideological movement in Peru), 121, 125–27, 130, 132–37
Indigenista. See *Indigenismo*
Innovation, 14, 16, 33, 49, 63, 105, 112, 122, 125, 128–30, 135–36, 137n.2, 162, 170–71, 173, 176, 224, 275
Institutions: 3, 12, 16, 19, 38, 66, 88, 145, 270; cultural, 46, 105, 145, 151, 155–56, 257; musical, 139–58; regional, 10, 12, 16; state, 3, 12, 16, 35, 38, 150, 158n.10
Institutionalization: of ethnomusicology, 270; process of musical change, 155–56
Insurrections, 100, 106
Intellectuals, 12, 125, 145–46, 149–50, 261, 263–64
Interaction, 52, 54, 124. *See also* Transaction, social
Interpretation, 2, 4, 12–13, 23–24, 40, 45–46, 49–52, 66, 87, 90, 130, 163, 179n.3, 212, 243, 255, 271
Intonation, 74, 77, 245. *See also* Tuning
Invasions, 95, 208–9, 211, 221
Invention of tradition, 6, 36–38, 63, 129, 273
Īqāʿāt, 71
Iran, 19
Iraq, 71–72, 91n.9
ʿĪsá, Muḥammad Ḥilmī, 69–70
Isale Eko (quarter in Lagos), 55
Islam: as determinant of cultural history, 103–20
Israel, 254–67
Israel Museum, 257
Israel Philharmonic Orchestra, 257
Israeli, Central European (ethnic community of), 17, 254–67
Italy, 71, 183, 187
Izmir, 183

Jadur (Muṇḍāri song type), 214
Jause, 263
Java, 19
Jerusalem, 17, 257, 265
Jerusalem Theatre, 257
Jhalawar, 164
Jibowu, Esumbo, 55
Johannesburg (South Africa), 38–39
Johnson, "Snake," 55
Journals, musical, 14, 88
Judaism: as determinant of cultural history, 36
Jüdischer Kulturbund, 259
Jùjú: derivation of term, 58–59; musical style and repertory in Nigeria, 6–7, 14, 46, 49–67, 274

Kabra, Brij Bhushan, 170
Kaman, 188
Kāmil, Muṣṭafá, 83
Kanchan, 239–41
Karachi, 106, 116
Karah, 215
Karam, 16, 212–13, 215–16, 222–27, 228n.14, 275
Karma, 225, 235
Karma, Brahmchari, 235
Kartomi, Margaret, 19–20, 277n.4
Kemençe, 76, 91n.5
Khan, Ahmad Ali, 168–69
Khan, Ali Akbar, 10, 96, 166–67, 170–73, 178n.1
Khan, Allauddin, 10–11, 14, 96–97, 165, 168–70, 173–76, 179nn.3, 5; teachers of, 169
Khan, Amir, 174
Khan, Amjad Ali, 167
Khan, Ashish, 170
Khan, Bahadur, 99–102, 171
Khan, Behere Wahid, 179n.5
Khan, Bilas, 99
Khan, Dargah Quli, 111
Khan, Enayat, 179n.3
Khan, Faiyaz, 179n.5
Khan, Hafiz Ali, 179n.3
Khan, Hamid Ali, 168, 179n.4
Khan, Imdad, 11, 174, 179n.3
Khan, Iqbal Husain, 119n.4
Khan, Tanras, 111–12
Khan, Vilayat, 167, 174, 179n.3
Khan, Wazir, 97, 165, 168–69, 179nn.3, 4
Khan, Yusuf Ali, 179n.5
Khayāl, 105, 113, 168–69, 172
Khod, 212
Kholm. *See* Chelm
Khusrau, Amir, 11, 105–6, 108, 111–12, 115–17, 119
Kiepja, Lola, 1
Kiesewetter, Raphael Georg, 181
Kimberley (South Africa), 41
Kinder (Louisiana), 191–97, 200–201, 203
al-Kindī, 69
King, Abdulrafiu Babatunde (Tunde), 54–57, 59–60, 64–65
King Fu'ād, 68–70
King Moshoeshoe II, 43
Kinship, 27, 31, 211, 213, 220–21. *See also* Specialists, hereditary
Kirana gharānā, 179n.5
Kirtan, 235
Kitāb Mu'tamar al-Mūsīqá al-ʿArabiyyah (Book of the Congress of Arab Music), 68–91
KMMʿA. See *Kitāb Mu'tamar al-Mūsīqá al-ʿArabiyyah*
Knowledge, configuration of, 49, 51, 104, 112, 173–74, 268
Kolberg, Oskar, 141–44, 157n.6
Kolessa, Filaret, 13, 149, 151–52
Kolomyjka (Ukrainian dance genre), 142–43, 154–55
Komitas Vardapet, 2–3
Kónkómbà, 62
Kozak (Ukrainian dance genre), 154
Kraków, 146, 157n.8
Krishna, 98, 223, 224–25
Krusbass, 58
Kurdish music, 2–3
Kūṛukh language, 207

Labelu, Alabi, 55
Labor: indentured, 231–33, 237; migratory, 38–39, 41, 47, 66, 273; wage, 54, 60
Lachmann, Robert, 69, 71–72, 77–78, 80, 85
Lafiaji (neighborhood in Lagos), 55
Lagos, 54–56, 58–62, 64–66
La Guerre, John, 236
Landlords, 123, 210, 216–17, 220–21
Lane, Edward, 80
Langley, Arzelie, 16, 190–206
Langley, Jackson, 194, 205n.5
Law, 37, 220–21, 256
Leadership, 64, 129–30, 136, 176, 220–21
Learning, social, 52, 140
Lebanon, 71, 77
Legitimacy, 9–10, 15, 32, 100, 110, 114, 122, 125, 135, 175, 178, 274
Lemberg. *See* L'viv
Lesotho, 41. *See also* Sotho
Lestrade, G. P., 44
Levine, Victoria Lindsay, 14–15, 269, 275
Lévi-Strauss, Claude, 30
Liberalism, 17, 261, 271
Libraries, 145, 150, 153
Lieder, 262, 265, 267n.3
Lifela, 6, 41–47, 273
Likheleke, 6, 41
Likhojane, Makeka, 43, 47
Likoata, 6, 41
Lima, 121–22, 125, 128, 130–35, 137n, 138n.3
Lineages, 6, 10–11, 61, 98, 101–2, 106, 108, 111–12, 119n.3, 170, 220–21
Lingua franca: use of, 197, 207
Linguistics, 270
Listeners, 53, 59, 109–10, 112. *See also* Audiences
Literacy, 45, 145, 147, 150
Lithoko, 41–42, 44
Lithuania, 157n.4
Little Traditions (of Indian culture), 96, 102n.1, 146
Livingston (Texas), 191, 193, 203–4

Local histories, 4–5, 87
London, 164
Louisiana, 15, 190–94, 197, 199–204
Louisiana Pantribal Dance Inventory, 196
Louisiana Pantribal Dance Songs (Claude Medford Collection), 198
Lowenthal, David, 292
Lucknow, 96, 112, 120n.15
Lullabies, 26
Lully, Jean-Baptiste, 184, 186
L'viv, 13, 149–53, 156n
L'vov. *See* L'viv
Lwów. *See* L'viv
Lynch, Jeremiah, 82
Lyric Theatre of Madrid, 71
Lysenko, Mykola, 149

Madras, 166
Magic, 43, 59, 65, 82
Mahler, Gustav, 260
Maihar gharānā, 10–11, 14–15, 162–63, 167–69, 171–74, 176, 178n.1. See also *Gharānā*
Malm, Krister, 19
"Man kunto Maulā" (Sufi song), 113, 115
Māndar, 215–16
Mangae initiation songs, 45
Mannheim, 267n.2
Mapuche, 5
Maqāmāt, 71, 74, 117
Marcus, George, 40
Marginalized groups, 14, 210, 222
Markers, 137, 265
Marksville (Louisiana), 191, 193–96, 199–200, 202–3, 204n.2, 205nn.5, 6
Marx, Karl, 28–29, 49, 51
Mazur rhythm (in Polish folk music), 142–43, 155
Meanings, 11, 40, 46–47, 52, 67, 78–79, 90, 105, 122–23, 254–55, 259–60, 266–67, 276
Medford, Claude, 190–92, 195, 197, 198n, 199–200, 202, 204n.1
Mediator: between musical traditions, 161–80. *See also* Brokers, cultural
Mehta, Zubin, 176
Mekoa le maele, 6, 42
Memory, 40, 107, 112, 119, 250–51, 269
Mendelssohn, Felix, 260
Mendicants, 15, 211
Mendoza, V., 125–26, 128
Merriam, Alan, 23, 33, 36, 52
Mestizos, 11–13, 121–38
Metaphor, 43, 50, 56, 66, 119, 257
Meters: of poetry, 108, 114
Michaud, Joseph, 181
"Midnight Dance" (Louisiana pantribal repertory), 200–201
Migration, 6, 24–25, 28, 30, 54–55, 61, 121–22, 131, 192–93, 208, 232, 257, 275
Minorities, 155. *See also* Marginalized groups
Miskal, 188
Misra, Lalmani, 166, 178n.1
Missionaries, 23, 38, 45, 238–39
Mississippi River, 192, 203
Mobilian trade language, 192, 197, 200
Models, 19, 51–52, 86–87, 135, 208, 222, 240
Modernity: as status acquired by traditional music, 161–80, 254
Modernization: as cultural policy, 8; as process of cultural change, 13, 168; as process of musical change, 63, 84, 86, 88, 90, 114, 270, 276
Mojela, Leotholi, 42
Mokorotlo, 42
Montana, 243, 250, 252n.2
Morocco, 72
Morton, John, 233
Motivation: factor in historicity, 112
Motiyaburuj, 96
Movement patterns, 64, 84, 213
Movements: musical, 130–31; national, 83, 120n.13, 140, 145, 150, 164, 274, 277n.8. *See also* Black Consciousness Movement; *Indigenismo;* Prosvita; Young Poland
Movies, 147. *See also* Indian film music
Mozambique, 45
Mozart, Wolfgang Amadeus, 261
Mridangam, 166
Mukhopadhyay, Dilipkumar, 100, 102
Muṇḍa, 12, 15–16, 207–28, 275
Muṇḍāri language, 207–28
Museum of Musical Instruments (University of Berlin), 71
Music Academy of Prague, 71
Music as culture, 161
Music history, modern: as area of ethnomusicological research, 1–5, 17–20, 67–68, 83–84, 86–87, 208, 241, 254, 265–77
Music in context, 50, 66
Musical approximation, 211–12, 215–16, 226
Musical composition, 2, 9, 70–71, 73–74, 77, 98, 163, 166, 173, 176–78

Musical culture, 12, 18, 127, 136, 143, 163, 165–66, 168, 182, 203, 210, 212, 217, 266–67, 269, 272
Musical drama, 39
Musical forms, 27, 52–53, 58, 63, 72–73, 105, 172, 188, 197, 199–203, 216, 223–24, 236
Musical idioms, 104, 107, 152
Musical knowledge: reproduction of, 1, 7–11, 16, 53, 104–5, 110, 112, 162, 169, 174–75
Musical life, 1, 7, 151, 204, 258–59
Musical practices, 2, 8, 13, 52, 67, 130, 139–40, 143–45, 147–49, 151, 161
Musical resources, 53, 60, 66
Musical styles, 2, 11, 16, 49, 53, 65–67, 68, 116–18, 122, 128–31, 133–37, 170–73, 196–203
Musical systems, 18, 87, 188
Musical tradition, 8, 35–48
Musicology, general, 2, 20
al-Mūsīqá (musical journal), 14, 88, 91n.9
Muskhogean, 197
Myers, Helen, 16–17, 269, 274–75
Myth, 2, 6–8, 23, 29–31, 33, 277n.11. *See also* Structure: mythic

Nādā bandh, 99. See also *Gandā bandham*
Nāgaṛa, 215–16, 228n.4
Naḥḥās, Najīb, 77–78
Naipul, V. S., 234–35, 240
Names: reproduction of, 2, 8–9
Natchez (Native American people), 193, 202
National Conservatory of Paris, 71
National dances, 36, 153–54
National Indian Foundation (Brazil), 31
National Library (Berlin), 71
National music, 15, 80, 155, 183–84, 187, 261
National Music Academy of Lebanon, 71
Nationalism: in music, 139–58, 154, 261. *See also* Consciousness: national
Nation-states: formation of, 12, 37, 53, 146, 270
Native American Church, 23
Nawbah, 72
Nazis, 259
Neitzel, Stuart, 191, 194–96, 200, 205–6n.6, 206nn.7–10
Nettl, Bruno, 5, 19–20, 23, 49, 161, 242–43, 251, 252n.2, 253n.8, 271, 276n.1
Networks, 126, 139, 155, 158n.11
Neubauer, Eckhard, 182
Neuman, Daniel, 10–11, 96–99, 166, 179n.3
New Orleans, 192
New York City, 176
New York Philharmonic Orchestra, 176
Ney, 188
Ngugi wa Thiong'O, 37
Nigeria, 49–67
Nigerian Broadcasting Service, 65
Nigerian Civil War, 62
"Night Love Song" (Blackfoot song), 243–44, 246–50, 252
"Night Serenade Song" (Blackfoot song), 244, 246–48, 250, 252
Nightengale, Tunde, 64
Nisbet, Robert, 50
Niyazi, Manzur, 119n.5
Nizamuddin Auliya Shrine, 104, 106, 111, 115–16, 119n.2
Noll, William, 12–13
Non-Western music, 8, 17, 35, 84, 182, 252n.1, 255, 266
Norms, 11–12, 44, 52, 63–64, 109, 113–14, 116, 140, 141, 150, 176, 184–85, 187, 250
North Africa, 71
North India, 10, 15, 96, 161, 163, 166–70, 175–76, 238
North Piegan, 251
Northup, Solomon, 205n.4
Northwestern State University of Louisiana, 198n
Notation of music, 3, 13, 19, 83, 99, 154, 156, 176–77, 181–82, 188, 189nn.1, 2. *See also* Transcription of music
Nyzhankivskyj, Ostap, 149

Ofo. *See* Picote, Alice
Ojibwa, 243
Oklahoma, 193, 197
Olowogbowo (quarter in Lagos), 54
Opera, 89, 183–84
Oral history, 103–4, 119, 122, 128
Oral tradition, 7, 11, 17–19, 36, 40–41, 44–47, 103–20, 176, 190, 208, 252
Oriental music, 73, 78, 80, 82–83, 182–83, 186–88. *See also* Non-Western music
Oriental Music Festival, Durham, 9, 15
Orientalism: scholars furthering, 9, 81–82, 86, 89, 181, 183
Orientalists. *See* Orientalism
òrìsà worship, 61

Ottoman Empire, 2–3, 82, 157n.7, 182
Outsiders, 11–12, 27, 29, 31, 33–34, 123, 207, 209, 220–21, 226–27, 258, 270, 275. *See also* Strangers
Owens, Naomi, 98–100

Pakhāvaj, 169, 172, 175
Pakistan, 10, 106, 108, 116
Palestine, British Mandate of, 257
Palm-wine music, 54–56
Pandit, Kedar, 235
Pandit, Suruj, 235
Panditji, 100–102
Panpipe, 11–13, 121–38. See also *Miskal*
Pantribal: musical practices, 15, 190–206
Paradigms, historical, 86, 90, 268–77; forms of, 269–72; stylistic, 49, 58, 63–65
Paris, 165–66, 178
Parmasad, K. V., 236
Passamaquoddy, 252n.1
Pathak, Rameshsvar, 179
Patronage, 15, 49, 54, 57–59, 63–65, 97, 107, 110–12, 120n.9, 211, 213, 216–17, 220–22, 255
Pavia, University of, 71
Pavlova, Anna, 164
Payments to musicians, 55, 60, 64, 106
Peasant music. *See* Folk music; Village music
Pennsylvania, University of, 166
People without history, 4, 268
Peremyshchyna (region in the Ukraine). *See* Przemyskie
Peremyshl'. *See* Przemyśl
Performance, musical, 23, 33, 47, 49, 51–53, 66, 80, 107
Peru, 11–13, 121–38, 275
Peyote song, 243
Philologists, 84, 86
Phonogram Archive (University of Berlin), 71
Piano, 75–79, 91nn.6, 10, 261–62, 265
Picote, Alice, 193, 205n.5
Pierite, Joseph, 194–95, 199, 206n.7
Pilgrims, 98, 100
Pinkillus, 124, 128, 131, 135–36, 138n.4
Pitjantjatjara, 9–10
Pitus, 124, 128, 135–36, 138n.4
Plains Indians, 23, 33, 245, 250–51
Plantations, 45, 231
Plato, 186
Pluralism, 87, 168, 236, 258
Podniprovia͡, 152
Poland, 3, 12, 14–15, 139–58
Policies of states, 8, 40, 68–70, 88, 147, 150
Politics: as determinant of music history, 121–38
Polskie Towarzystwo Ludoznewcze, 157n.4
Polymusicality, 23, 26
Polyphony, 77, 83, 213
Popo, Sundar, 239, 241
Popular music, 19, 35–36, 49, 53, 62, 64–65, 91n.7, 108, 235, 242
Power: musical, 9–10; of groups, 9, 11, 27, 32–34, 36–37, 46, 121–23, 135–37
Powers, Harold, 166
Powwow, 197, 204
Practice theory: as approach to ethnomusicological analysis, 49–67, 273
Praise-singing, 56–57, 61, 63. See also *Lithoko; Mokorotlo*
Prejudice, 5, 123, 131, 133, 185–86
Preservation of music, 11, 36, 80, 115, 272
Prestige, 40, 42, 102, 121, 129, 133, 179n.4, 275
Production: cultural, 46, 50; economic, 33, 38–39, 49, 65
Progress, 39, 75, 77, 83, 85–86, 90
Prostitution, 222, 228n.13
Prosvita, 13, 149–55
Protest songs, 26
Proxemics, 64. *See also* Movement patterns
Przemyskie (region of Poland), 139–41, 143–45, 147–49, 152, 154–55, 156n, 157nn.3, 8
Przemyśl, 139–40, 153, 158n.8
Publicity, 65
Puno, 121–38
Purnananda, Swami, 238–39

Qānūn, 75
Q'ara, 11–12, 123
Qaul, 115–18
Qawwal. See Qawwali
Qawwali, 11, 104, 106–8, 110–17, 119n.1
Qhantati Ururi, 124, 126–31, 134–37
Quantz, Johann Joachim, 184–85
al-Qubbānjī, Muḥammad, 72
Quechua, 122
Queen Victoria, 38
Qur'anic chant, 57
Qureshi, Regula Burckhardt, 10–11, 269, 274, 277n.10

Rabaga, 215, 228n.7
"Rabbit Dance" (Louisiana pantribal repertory), 200–201
Racism, 59–60
Racy, Ali Jihad, 8–9, 13, 269

Radcliffe-Brown, A. R., 38
Radha, 98, 223, 224–25
Radio, 55, 61, 63, 73, 88, 135, 147–49, 234, 238
Radio Association of Istanbul, 71
Rāg. *See* Raga
Raga, 111–14, 116–18, 120n.11, 162, 168, 175–78, 179–80n.6, 222, 238
Rāga-Mālā (Concerto No. 2 for sitar and orchestra by Ravi Shankar), 176–78
Raghunath II, 98–100
Rajasthan, 164, 221
Rakha, Alla, 120n.12
Ramayan, 234
Rampur gharānā, 97, 168–69, 172–73, 175
Ranchi, 208, 213, 217, 227n
Ranganathan, Tanjore, 166
Ranger, Terence, 37
Rationalization, 18, 83
Ravi Shankar Institute for Music and Performing Arts in Benares, 174–75
Rebellions, 100, 106
Recordings, 55, 59–60, 63–65, 70–73, 77, 88, 90–91n.2, 91n.9, 113, 128, 131, 147–49, 162, 174–75, 190, 204n.2, 238–40, 242–51
Redfield, Robert, 102n.1
Reform, 68–69, 84, 86–88, 123
Reggae, 235
Regionalism, 140, 146
Regionalization: process of musical change, 144
Reḥavia, 17, 257, 265
Rehearsal, 13, 126, 129, 177
Reinterpretation: as process of musical change, 52–53
Repertories, musical, 7, 11, 16, 30–31, 72, 85, 104, 107, 110–11, 115–16, 118–19, 134, 144, 147–48, 153, 155, 162, 172, 190–91, 196–98, 210, 213–16, 222–27, 232, 235–37, 240–41, 242–43, 259–62, 271, 274–75
Reproduction, social, 26, 33–34, 52
Resistance, 12, 38, 40, 271, 273
Revitalization: process of musical change, 63, 135, 232, 237, 240–41, 242, 270, 275
Revolution, 29
Reymond, Władysław, 146
Rhodes, Willard, 243
Richards, Paul, 53
Riḍā, Musṭafá, 70
Ringer, Alexander, 181
Rio Lindo Orchestra, 62
Rites of passage, 27, 30, 33, 64, 264
Ritual, 11, 17, 26–27, 44, 104, 106–9, 114–16, 144, 194–95, 209–10, 212, 223–25, 233, 236, 255, 258, 262–64, 267, 274
Ritualization: process of musical change, 162–65
Roberts, Helen, 88
Roberts, John Storm, 52
Robertson, Carol E., 5
Romania, 145
Rouanet, Jules, 82
Roy, Sarat Chandra, 212, 220, 225
Royal Academy of Arab Music, 88
Royal Opera (Cairo), 70
Royalties. *See* Payments to musicians
Royce, Anya Peterson, 256
Rubin Academy of Music, 257, 263
Rumba, 148
Russell, John, 232
Russia, 145, 152, 157nn.2, 4, 5. *See also* Soviet Union

Sabra, Wadīʿ, 71, 77
Ṣabri, ʿAbd al-Fattāḥ, 91n.7
Sachchidananda, 225
Sachs, Curt, 69, 71, 76–78, 80, 85, 90, 91n.8
Sādāni language, 207, 224
Sādāns (nontribal peoples in Choṭanāgpur), 209–14, 216–17, 220–26, 228n.8
Sahai, Sharda, 166
Sahlins, Marshall, 28–29, 51
Śahnāi, 209
Sai Baba movement, 239
St. Joseph University (Beirut), 71
Saints, 104, 109–11, 114–16, 274
Sāl, Durjan, 220, 221–22
Salazar, Adolfo, 71
Salvador-Daniel, Francesco, 82
Samāʿ, 11, 17, 106–10, 112, 114–16, 119, 120n.14
Sámbà, 54, 58, 63
Sandhya (Vedic daily prayer), 238
Sangitguru (Hindustani "Music Master"), 100
Sanskrit, 98, 235, 238
Sapara, Oguntola, 55
Sarangi, 107
Sarasvati, 168
Saro, 54
Sarod, 167, 169–70
Śāstriya saṅgīt, 221. *See also* Classical music: Hindustani
Saxophone, 148, 154
Scaff, Lawrence, 268
Scales, musical, 70–71, 74–75, 77–78, 83,

91n.5, 122, 143, 145, 155, 182, 188, 197, 216, 224
Schaeffner, André, 18
Scheub, Harold, 36, 44
Schoenberg, Arnold, 260–61
Scholarship, musical, 1–3, 12–13, 16–20, 53, 69, 87–89, 98–99, 166, 268–76
Schools, 63, 66, 73–75, 80–81, 135, 150, 155
Schumann, Robert, 260
Schünemann, Georg, 71
Schwartzmann, Stephen, 32
Seeger, Anthony, 5, 10, 17, 269, 272
Seeger, Charles, 7
Sefela. *See* Lifela
Ṣẹ̀kẹ̀rẹ̀, 54–55, 58, 62–63
Seniya gharānā (gharānā stemming from Tansen's heritage), 97
Serfdom, 141
Sesotho, 6, 42, 44–45. *See also* Sotho
Shah, Muhammad, 111–12
Shah, Ragunath Sahadev, 221–22
Shah, Wajid Ali, 96, 112
Shamans, 5, 224
Shankar, Ravi, 10–11, 14–16, 96, 161–80
Shankar, Shubhendra, 170
Shankar, Uday, 164–66, 169
Shankar Hara Chauduri, Shyam, 164–65
Sheikhs, 110, 115–16
Shepherd, John, 67
Shevchenko, Taras, 152
Shiloah, Amnon, 14–15, 269
Shrines, 11, 104, 106, 110–11, 114–16, 120nn.14, 15, 274
Sibley, John, 192
Sierra Leone, 54–55, 58
Signs, 28. *See also* Emblems; Markers; Symbols
Sikumorenos, 121–22, 132–34, 136. See also *Sikuris*
Sikuris, 121–22, 124–25, 128, 130–37, 138n.4. See also *Sikumorenos*
Singer, Milton, 102n.1
Singh, Kumar Suresh, 215
Singh, Misri, 168
Śiṣya, 161–62, 174
Sitar, 107, 119, 163, 166, 169, 176–77, 238
Slavery, 36, 232
Slawek, Stephen, 10–11, 14–15, 269, 274–75
Smithsonian Institution, 197, 198n, 204n.2
Soca, 240
Social Darwinism, 81
Social sciences, 50, 52, 89, 146, 273
Society for Ethnomusicology, 272
Sociology, 18
Sohar, 234–35
Somers, Geoff, 243
Song: as distinguished from speech, 26–28, 32, 45, 58, 61, 63; as history, 28–34
Sotho, 6, 38, 41, 47
South Africa, 35–48, 54, 273, 277n.7
South India, 161, 166, 173, 176, 179–80n.6, 238
South Piegan, 251
Southeastern Native American peoples: musical traditions of, 190–206
Soviet Union, 12, 149, 152, 157n.7, 158n.11, 163. *See also* Russia
Soweto, 38
Spain, 71
Specialists, hereditary, 10–11, 101–2, 104–6, 110
Speck, Frank, 195
Spirits, 8, 23, 33, 42–44, 223–25
Srivastava, Ram, 211
Stage presentation, 128–29, 131–32, 146–47, 150–54, 165, 210, 214, 216
Steinen, Karl von den, 24, 31
Steiner, George, 255
Stereotypes, 49, 185
Stickball Game/Night Dance, 194–96
Stomp Dance songs. *See* "Double-Head Dance"
Stories: reproduction of, 8–9, 270–74
Strangers, 10, 12, 17, 23, 29, 31–32. *See also* Outsiders
Strauss, Richard, 265
Stravinsky, Igor, 33
Structure: counterpoised with anti-structure, 264; of creativity, 40; musical, 7–8, 23, 32–33, 47, 50, 53, 224; mythic, 6, 29; of performance, 53; social, 44, 51–52, 109, 273
Sufis: musical traditions of, 10–11, 103–20, 274; religious practices of, 11, 17
Sultan Ahmet III, 188, 189n.2
Sultan Mehmed IV, 189n.1
Supičić, Ivo, 18
Surbahār, 170
Surinam, 237
Suyá, 5, 8, 10, 12, 16–17, 23–34, 272, 275
Swanton, John, 191, 194–97, 203, 205n.5
Switzerland, 91n.6
Symbols, 12, 36, 39–40, 42, 45–46, 50, 53, 56, 60–61, 64–66, 121, 125–26, 130, 139, 154–56, 167, 178, 195, 211,

237, 254, 261, 266, 274. *See also* Emblems; Markers
Syncretism: as process of musical change, 52, 105, 136, 270, 276
Syria, 71–72
Szymanowski, Karol, 146

Tabla, 97, 102, 119, 120n.12, 166, 169, 175, 238
Tagore, Jotindro Mohun, 99
Tagore, Sourindro Mohun, 99
Tal. See Tāla
Tāla, 111–14, 117, 172–73, 175, 212, 214–16, 222, 224, 238
Ta'līf, 71
Talking drum, 61, 63
Tambourine, 54–55, 63
Tanbur, 76, 91n.5, 182, 189n.2
Tango, 148
Tansen, 97, 100, 102, 168, 179n.4
Tarāna, 108–9, 118, 120n.16
Tarkas, 124, 131, 135–36, 138n.4
Taste, musical, 15, 27, 60, 112, 236, 238. *See also* Good taste
Tayil, 5
Teague, Fred, 177
Techniques: of musicians, 52–53, 60
Technology, 67, 250, 274, 276
Tel Aviv, 257
Tel Aviv Museum, 257
Tempo, 59, 63, 148, 172, 177, 200, 224
Tewari, Laksmi Ganesh, 166
Texas, 191–93, 205n.4
Texts of songs, 23, 26–27, 32–33, 41–46, 56–57, 63, 91n.7, 98, 106–7, 109, 118, 197, 213, 216, 221–25, 235–36. *See also* Vocables
Textures, musical, 63–64
Theater, 66, 99, 168
Third World, 53
Thompson, Charlie, 204n.2
Thompson, Robert Farris, 52
Ṭhumrī, 118, 168, 175–76, 178, 239
Tieck, Ludwig, 255
Timbre, 63, 83, 136, 138n.4
Time, cosmological, 6
Timing, 8, 213–14
Titicaca, Lake, 123
Tone-system, 18, 26, 245. *See also* Scales, musical
Tovarystvo Prosvita (Society for Enlightenment). *See* Prosvita
Townships: as administrative units in South Africa, 39
Traders, 209–10
Tradition, meaning of, 35–48. *See also* Invention of tradition
Traditional music: as concept, 6, 17, 35, 47, 170. *See also* Musical tradition
Transaction, social, 50, 67
Transcription of music, 13, 16–17, 50, 70, 143, 151–52, 157n.4, 188, 242–47, 268. *See also* Notation of music
Transmission, 10, 17–19, 83, 107, 112, 235, 243–52, 274. *See also* Musical knowledge
Treatises on music, 13, 15, 69–71, 75–76, 78, 99, 102n.1, 181–89
Tribal histories, 5, 23–34, 190–228
Tribe-caste interaction. *See* Caste
Trinidad, 231–41, 275
Trombone, 148
Tropa, 127–29
Trumpet, 148
Tunica, 191, 193, 202–3, 205n.5, 206n.8
Tuning, 71, 76–78, 91n.10. *See also* Voicing
Tunisia, 72, 91n.9
Turino, Thomas, 11–13, 269, 275
Turkey, 3, 71, 85, 91n.9
Turkish music, 2, 14–15, 115, 117, 181–89
Turner, Victor, 264

ʿūd, 75
Ukelele-banjo, 62
Ukraine, 12–15, 139–58
Umm Kulthūm, 84, 89
United States, 7, 28, 270
Urban music: as concept in Poland, 139–58
Urbanization: process of social change, 40–41, 257
Urdu, 107
Usul, 188

Vail, Leroy, 45
Vaiśnavas, 211–13, 222–23, 224–25
Values: artistic, 8, 40, 185; musical, 12–13, 17, 23, 49, 66, 129, 136–37, 163; sociocultural, 17, 27–28, 40, 44, 46–47, 50, 51–53, 61, 66–67, 124, 126, 129, 136, 208, 212, 224, 254, 261, 264, 266–67, 271
Van Leer Institute, 257
Vansina, Jan, 119
Velasco, Juan, 132
Vennum, Thomas, 243
Vibrato, 58, 85
Vichitra vīṇā, 170
Vienna, University of, 71
Vietnam War, 27
Vilca, Dante, 134
Village music: as concept in Poland, 139–58

Villoteau, Guillaume-André, 181
Violin, 76, 85, 169–70. *See also* Fiddle
Violoncello, 76
Visnu, 98. *See also* Vaiśnavas
Visnupur gharānā, 10, 13, 95–102, 274. See also *Gharānā*
Viswanathan, Tanjore, 166
Vocables, 199–202, 244–245
Vocal production, 58, 64, 84, 202, 239
Vocal quartets, 54
Voicing: of panpipes, 127–28, 130

Wade, Bonnie, 163, 179n.2
Wagner, Richard, 260–61, 265
Wallis, Roger, 19
Wanamaker Historical Expedition II, 249
"War Dance" (Louisiana pantribal repertory), 203
Warner, Charles Dudley, 82
Warsi, Aziz Ahmad Khan, 119n.4
Wasiuzzman, 119n.3
Water drum, 199
Waterman, Christopher, 6–8, 13, 16, 46, 269, 273–74
Waterman, Richard, 52, 136
Weddings, 64, 144, 148–49, 154, 209, 216
Wellesz, Egon, 71, 80
Wesleyan University, 166
West Africa (cultural region), 54, 58, 62–63
West Bengal, 95
West Indian music, 231–41
West Indies, University of, 236
Western art music: as ethnic identity, 254–67. *See also* Classical music: Western
Westernization: process of musical change, 63, 83, 85–86, 240–41, 270, 276, 277n.12
White, Landeg, 41, 45–46
Wind bands, 154–55
Wiora, Walter, 254
Witmer, Robert, 17, 253n.8, 269, 272, 275
Wolf, Johannes, 71
Women: ceremonies of, 30; preferences of, 112; roles of, 137n.1, 222; songs of, 30, 32, 45, 137n.1, 216, 224–25, 234–35
World history, 4, 68, 82–84, 87, 254
World War I, 27, 58, 145, 147, 152, 155, 164, 232
World War II, 14, 49, 55, 61, 63–64, 155, 156n.2, 203, 237, 270, 272
Wyspiański, Stanislaw, 146

Xingu River, 24, 30–32

"Yār-e-man be-ā, be-ā" (Sufi song), 120n.16
Yekkes: as designation of German Jew, 254–67, 271, 275
Yoruba, 6, 14, 46, 49–67, 274
Youchigant, Sesostrie, 204n.2, 206n.10
Young Poland, 146
Yugoslavia, 145

Zafar, Bahadur Shah, 111
Zaghlūl, Saʿd, 83
Zaïre, 37
Zakhariivo, I., 151
Zampieri, Gusto, 71
Zampoñas, 125
Zikr, 108–9, 118. See also *Dhikr*